MW01423511

TWO-TIMING MODERNITY

Homosocial Narrative in
Modern Japanese Fiction

Harvard East Asian Monographs 352

TWO-TIMING MODERNITY

Homosocial Narrative in Modern Japanese Fiction

J. Keith Vincent

Published by the Harvard University Asia Center
and distributed by Harvard University Press
Cambridge (Massachusetts) and London, 2012

© 2012 by The President and Fellows of Harvard College

Printed in the United States of America

The Harvard University Asia Center publishes a monograph series and, in coordination with the Fairbank Center for Chinese Studies, the Korea Institute, the Reischauer Institute of Japanese Studies, and other faculties and institutes, administers research projects designed to further scholarly understanding of China, Japan, Vietnam, Korea, and other Asian countries. The Center also sponsors projects addressing multidisciplinary and regional issues in Asia.

Library of Congress Cataloging-in-Publication Data

Two-timing modernity : homosocial narrative in modern Japanese fiction / J. Keith Vincent.
    p. cm. -- (Harvard East Asian monographs ; 352)
Includes index.
    ISBN 978-0-674-06712-7 (hardcover : acid-free paper) 1. Japanese fiction--20th century--History and criticism. 2. Homosexuality in literature. 3. Male friendship in literature. I. Vincent, Keith, 1968–
PL721.H59V96 2012
895.6'344093538--dc23

2012019145

Index by the author

∞ Printed on acid-free paper

Last figure below indicates year of this printing

22 21 20 19 18 17 16 15 14 13 12 12

For my mother,

Carol Christine Vincent

(1944–2001)

Acknowledgments

It took me a long time to understand that the most important step in actually finishing a book like this one is letting go enough to allow other people to help you with it. Once I finally did let go, I felt incredibly privileged and grateful to have so many smart friends and colleagues willing to read and comment on my work.

Will Waters, Erin Murphy, and Carrie Preston gave me helpful comments on the Introduction and Chapter 1 and in the process helped me to see that what I had written was actually starting to resemble a book. Thanks to them and to Mimi Long and Matthew Fraleigh, who came through with careful and helpful critiques of the Ōgai chapters. I am also grateful to the members of the Modern/Contemporary Japan Workshop at the Reischauer Institute of Japanese Studies at Harvard University for reading the Ōgai chapter in its earliest form and providing a forum in which to discuss the overall book project. Kirsten Cather and her graduate students at the University of Texas at Austin read an early version of the Sōseki chapters and provided me not only with an enthusiastic critique but also with the first outside confirmation that I was onto something interesting. Thanks to Alan Tansman, Bruce Baird, and Sari Kawana for inviting me to present versions of the Sōseki chapters at UC Berkeley, UMass Amherst, and UMass Boston, and thanks to their students for their lively feedback. I was honored and grateful at a later stage to have Reiko Abe Auestad give me her comments on the Introduction and the Sōseki chapters. Thank you also to Kimura Saeko and Naitō Mariko for arranging to have an earlier version published in Japanese. Alan Tansman patiently read and critiqued multiple versions of the Hamao chapter in its earlier incarnation as a chapter in his edited volume, *The Culture of Japanese Fascism*. Thanks to Steve

Kotz for his generous comments on the latest version. Sam Perry, Gina Cogan, Suzanne O'Brien, and Kirsten Cather gave me great ideas and moral support as I struggled with the Mishima chapter. Thanks also to Tomi Suzuki for identifying herself as the anonymous reader of the manuscript when it was with a different press and encouraging me to keep working on it. My former student Kristin Sivak's incisive editing and always smiling face was an absolute godsend during the final stages of writing this book. I am extremely grateful to Tomiko Yoda and Ann Sherif, who identified themselves to me as the readers for Harvard University Asia Center and gave me excellent advice. I was also incredibly lucky to have the help of Marc Dones at the revision stage. Thank you, Marc, for telling me when I was not making sense, for holding my hand through the last stages of the process, and for helping me to remember why it all mattered. William Hammell at the Harvard University Asia Center has been an exemplary editor and I thank him for taking on the manuscript and shepherding it through the publication process with such skill and grace.

I have always been able to count on Nina Cornyetz to read my writing with just the right mixture of criticism and support. Thank you Nina, both for reading every word of this manuscript multiple times, and for your friendship, generosity, and sheer intellectual energy over these last two decades. I have been lucky enough to know Sarah Frederick for even more than two decades and feel immeasurably grateful to have ended up as her colleague at Boston University and the happy recipient of her support and encouragement. I really don't know how to thank Eugenio Menegon, who knew I needed a writing coach and spontaneously took the job on himself. Without his colorful highlighting on every page, his gentle prodding and unwavering support, this book would simply never have seen the light of day. Thanks to Peter Schwartz, my office neighbor, for always being available to chat and to Cathy Yeh for helping me hunt down that reference to "sidelocks like the wings of a cicada" and somehow managing to keep the pressure on me without making me feel pressured. I can't believe how fortunate I am to have colleagues like these as well as Wiebke Denecke, Abigail Gillman, Gisela Hoecherl-Alden, Margaret Litvin, Roberta Micallef, Katherine O'Connor, Bob Richardson, and Sunil Sharma. Thanks to all of you for showing me what a fully functional and unfailingly collegial academic department looks like. And finally, thanks to Will Waters for creating such a supportive atmosphere as chair and being such a model of grace and collegiality. This book was also enabled in many ways by the invaluable intellectual community of the Boston University Faculty Group on Gender and Sexuality Studies, especially Gina Cogan, Catie Connell, Anna Henchman, Jennifer Knust, Marie McDonough, Erin Murphy, Carrie Preston, Deborah Swedberg, Zsuzsanna Varhelyi, and Karen Warkentin.

I also want to thank my professors at Columbia, Paul Anderer, Carol Gluck, Donald Keene, Haruo Shirane, and Henry Smith, for their support and encouragement over the years. Thanks to Janet Poole, my former colleague at New York University, for so many thrilling conversations and book recommendations, many of which found their way in one way or another into this book. Thanks to Maggie Childs, my first professor of Japanese literature, who taught me by fierce example that it was possible to be an "out" academic, even in Kansas during the late 1980s. Thanks to Douglas Crimp and to Henry Abelove for their friendship, their steadfast support, and for showing me what good writing can do in the world. Thanks also to Heather Ayares, Anna and Mark Elliott, Phil Harper and Thom Freedman, Chris Hill, Stefan Knust, Dawn Lawson, Hiromi Miyagi-Lusthaus, Yoshiharu Muto, Miri Nakamura, Tim Screech, and Christophe Thouny for their friendship and support at various stages of this process. And thanks to my teachers at Bikram Yoga Boston, under whose calm and expert guidance many a knot came unraveled.

The initial research for this book was conducted while I was a Robert and Lisa Sainsbury Postdoctoral Fellow in Japanese Arts and Cultures at the University of London's School of Oriental and African Studies in 2001–2002. I am very grateful for this support and thrilled that there is now finally a book to show for it.

I could not have written this book without the support of my family. Thanks to my aunt Sherrill Nilson, for all those hours on the phone when we were both struggling to write and who finished her book just before mine. Thanks to my father Jim and my sisters Abbie and B.J., whose love has been the bedrock of my existence. And finally, thanks to my partner Anthony Lee, who has made my life so much more beautiful in so many ways.

Contents

	Introduction: Remembering the Homosocial Continuum	1
1	Toward a Definition of Homosocial Narrative	24
2	Between the First and the Third Person in Mori Ōgai's *The Wild Goose*	43
3	The Uncut Gem: Stereoscopic Homosociality in *The Wild Goose*	63
4	Sensei's Bloody Legacy: Sōseki's *Kokoro* in the Male Homosocial Imagination	86
5	*Kokoro* and the Primal Scene of Modern Japanese Homosociality	120
6	Gothic Homosociality in *The Devil's Disciple*	152
7	The Still Birth of Gay Identity in Mishima Yukio's *Confessions of a Mask*	175
	Epilogue	199

Reference Matter

Works Cited	215
Index	227

TWO-TIMING MODERNITY

Homosocial Narrative in
Modern Japanese Fiction

INTRODUCTION

Remembering the Homosocial Continuum

I Have Known You So Well:
"Two-Timing" the Queer Past

In a passage from one of the lesser-known novels of Kawabata Yasunari, the male narrator makes an unabashed declaration of love: "I adored your fingers, your hands, your arms, your chest, your cheeks, your eyelids, your tongue, your teeth, and your legs. I was in love with you. And I think you were in love with me as well."[1] In the Japanese edition of Kawabata's collected works, the first sentence forms one vertical line in which each successive body part is represented by a single Chinese character, creating a plunging visual analogue for this long caress from fingers to eyelids to legs. Readers familiar with Kawabata's work might not be surprised by such frank eroticism from one of modern Japan's most canonical novelists, but they might well raise an eyebrow upon learning that the "you" the narrator is addressing is not a woman or a girl but the boy to whom the novel, titled *The Boy* [*Shōnen*], seems to refer.[2] The novel's narrator, whose name is Miyamoto, explains that these lines are quoted from a long love

---

1. Kawabata, *Shōnen*, 161. Even out of context, the narrator is marked clearly as male in Japanese because he uses the male pronoun *boku*.

2. The word *shōnen* could be plural as well as singular and could, in some instances, refer to boys and girls, as it seems to in Tanizaki Jun'ichirō's short story by the same title, which Anthony Chambers has translated as "The Children." Barbara Hartley, in an article about what she calls "ambivalent desire" in Kawabata's *Shōnen*, has chosen not to translate the title, perhaps in order to retain this ambiguity. In this book, however, I will refer to the text as *The Boy* to emphasize its remarkable focus on one boy's love for another.

letter he wrote thirty years earlier to this boy, whose name was Kiyono. He even went so far as to submit it first to his Japanese teacher as an essay so that it could be proofread. His teacher read the letter and corrected it without any comment on its content. Miyamoto then sent the letter to Kiyono, but only after removing six of its thirty pages, among which these lines were included. These pages, he explains, he was too embarrassed to send, and Kiyono has long since died of tuberculosis. Hence they never reached their intended addressee.

I begin with this remarkable passage because it encapsulates so well what I call in this book the "two-timing" quality of stories of love between men in the first half of Japan's twentieth century. While Kawabata's text itself is frank and open in its expression of same-sex desire, it has survived, in a sense, only because its author was afraid to send it to the person for whom it was meant. Miyamoto's love for Kiyono comes to life here only in retrospect, sparking across the gap between the second decade of the twentieth century, when it could not be communicated directly, and the late 1940s when it could be included in a novel—a fragment of a relationship long past, its object dead and buried. At the same time, even in the earlier moment, the letter was already in the past tense. It was also, already, a piece of *writing*, an essay submitted in class, as much as an act of confession. Miyamoto was afraid to show it in its entirety to Kiyono, but not afraid to show it to his teacher, who seems to have been less than scandalized when asked to check this love letter from one schoolboy to another for style and grammar.[3] If the teacher became its first reader in this way, the letter also reaches different readers at a series of later moments. Thus while Kiyono never read its most passionate lines, and the relationship between the two boys, the narrator assures us, never went beyond an ardent but innocent longing, thirty years later the text was still there to feature in this novel.

Understanding and appreciating what texts like this one convey about the history of love between men in Japan requires a sensitivity to forms of belatedness and between-ness enabled by literary narratives that I have only begun to describe here. It also requires a keen awareness that the forward movement of time has not always brought unambiguous progress and liberation with regard to sexuality. On the contrary, for at least the first

---

3. The older narrator seems aghast at the lack of "common sense" of his younger self. "I have forgotten how many points the teacher gave me for it but I don't have any recollection of being scolded for the content. I imagine him with a pained smile on his face. The First High School [Ichikō] was a liberal place, but submitting such an essay showed a lack of common sense on my part" (Kawabata, *Shōnen*, 166).

half of the twentieth century in Japan it was the past and not the future that beckoned with the most imaginative possibilities for men who loved other men.

Until the late nineteenth century, Japan could boast of an elaborate cultural tradition surrounding the love and desire that men felt for other men. It figured in the cultural imagination as a familiar literary trope, as a legitimate and widely accepted practice, and as a nexus of cultural value. In this patriarchal but not yet heteronormative world, moreover, relations between men in general could be mapped on an increasingly uneasy but still navigable topography in which "men-loving-men" and "men-promoting-the-interests-of-men" coexisted and colluded in relative harmony. By the first years of the twentieth century, however, as exclusive and compulsory heterosexuality became associated with an enlightened modernity, love between men was increasingly branded as either "feudal" or immature. The resulting rupture of what Eve Kosofsky Sedgwick has famously theorized as the "male homosocial continuum"[4] thus constituted one of the most significant markers of Japan's entrance into modernity. And yet just as Japanese modernity often seemed haunted by stubborn remnants of the premodern past, the nation's newly heteronormative culture was unable and perhaps unwilling to expunge completely the recent memory of a male homosocial past now read as perverse.[5]

---

4. These phrases are drawn from Sedgwick, *Between Men*. The homosocial continuum "connects "men-loving-men" on the one hand with "men-promoting-the-interests-of-men" on the other. In many premodern patriarchal societies, such as that of ancient Greece and premodern Japan, this continuum was "quite seamless." As Sedgwick writes of ancient Greece, "It [was] as if in our terms, there were no perceived discontinuity between the male bonds of the Continental Baths and the male bonds at the Bohemian Grove or in the board room or Senate cloakroom (4)." With the onset of modernity, however, the visibility of the continuum is "radically disrupted," giving rise to a more or less strictly policed "homosocial divide" running between the newly constructed categories of "heterosexual" and "homosexual." Sedgwick was the first to "draw the 'homosocial' back into the orbit of 'desire,' of the potentially erotic" (1) in order to render visible the radical disruption of the homosocial continuum in modern Western culture. While Sedgwick's book deals with British literature, her insights have also been foundational in thinking about homosocial desire in Japan. *Between Men* and Sedgwick's second book *Epistemology of the Closet* were published in Japanese in 2000 and 1999 (i.e., in reverse order) and are widely cited in Japanese literary scholarship. For the phrases quoted above, see Sedgwick, *Between Men*, 3. In Japanese see Sedgwick, *Kurozetto no ninshikiron* and *Otokodōshi no kizuna*.

5. My study builds on recent scholarship in English and Japanese on the literary, historical, and medical discourses surrounding male-male sexuality in premodern and

This book discusses works by Japanese male authors for whom the modern divide between male homosexuality and heterosexuality was shadowed by the male homosocial continuum that prevailed in the Edo (1600–1868) and early Meiji (1868–1912) periods. All of these writers retained some cultural memory of a past in which love between men was still imaginable, but none were free from the pull of modernizing and developmental narratives that installed heterosexual object choice as a natural and normative telos. The result was a double tendency to *preserve* male homoeroticism in the past as something precious and worthy of remembrance while also working to *quarantine* it there as something that had no further claim on the present.[6] But compromised as it may have been as a result of its positioning on the backward end of a narrative of progress, love between men could still persist in the amber of memory. The device that held it there is what this book calls the "homosocial narrative."

The texts that I have chosen to discuss here are thus literally "two-timing" narratives in the sense that they stage tensions between two forms of temporality at once: the forward-looking time of modernization and normative development, and the "perverse" time of nostalgia, recursion, and repetition. If they struggle, in other words, to encompass both a straight future and a queer past, they are also "two-timing" in the colloquial sense of being "unfaithful" to more contemporary, identity-based understandings of love between men: they are not "gay" texts. Desire here is never understood simply as an emanation of identity or a response to the intrinsic appeal of its object, but as the result of mediation through a variety of third terms. This means not only that that these texts are not gay in any unified way, but that they are not "homosocial" in any uniform way either. If male homosociality can indeed be understood as a continuum, it is one that encompasses many points between the poles of overt homoeroticism and what is sometimes called "male bonding," between loving intimacy between men and defensive alliances against women. At various points, this book will

---

modern Japan. Gregory Pflugfelder, Furukawa Makoto, Jim Reichert, Mark McLelland, Kuroiwa Yūichi, Ubukata Tomoko, Fujimori Kiyoshi, Miyazaki Kasumi, and Ōta Tsubasa have documented the emergence of heteronormative thought and behavior in Japan, the eclipse of premodern sexual cultures and practices, and the production of diverse forms of "perversion" both as objects of pathologizing scrutiny and as new forms of sexual subjectivity.

6. Kuroiwa Yūichi has recently analyzed this "quarantining" of homosexuality in the past in Hori Tatsuo's 1932 novella "Moyuru hoo" (translated into English under the French title "Les joues en feu"). See Kuroiwa, "Hori Tatsuo 'Moyuru hoo' no dansei dōseiai hyōshō," 38.

speak of the consequences for both men and women of a variety of forms of male homosociality, including what I will call "stereoscopic homosociality," "patriarchal homosociality," "Oedipal homosociality," "gothic homosociality," "insomniac homosociality," and even "gay homosociality." Indeed, one of the primary goals of this book is to begin to pluralize and taxonomize the understanding of male homosociality as a spectrum of different ways in which desire between men can and has been mediated. This includes, of course, mediation through women as in the classic homosocial triangle, but also through other men, through literary tropes, hero-worship, national community, and various sexual ideologies and identities.

In *Two-Timing Modernity* I have assumed that not only the content of narratives but also the way they are structured, how they are narrated and by whom, and the ways in which they order events can instantiate, reinforce, and deconstruct sexual identities and subjectivities. I have also tried to show how the disturbances effected by sexuality work both to propel and to disrupt teleological narratives. Rather than focusing on individual representations of male-male sexuality and contextualizing them within "larger" historical narratives, I have tried to show how narrative itself is inherently "perverse," looping back on itself even when it appears to be headed unerringly towards a satisfying closure. In Peter Brooks' formulation, narrative "perverts time."[7] Taking narrative seriously, therefore, means rethinking historicist models of "transition" from one regime of sexual normality into another. As what Leo Bersani has called a "sickness of *uncompleted narratives*,"[8] the "perversion" that is men's love for other men has been imagined at various points along the historical trajectories of modernization and maturation as that which ought to have been outgrown and abandoned and yet continues to haunt the present.

Both developmentalist accounts of sexuality and models of historical "rupture" often miss the multiplicity and malleability of the trope of men loving men. Thus the full import of any of its iterations can only begin to be understood within the context of specific narratives. This specificity makes literary close reading an ideal and even crucial method for a project like this one. By focusing on what is going on *within* each text rather than on the sweep of history that connects them, one can attend to the ways in which sexuality and subjectivity are negotiated and reconfigured with each retelling. Of course this reconfiguration proceeds within certain historical constraints. The chapters in this book proceed in chronological order and

---

7. Brooks, "Freud's Masterplot," 111.
8. Bersani, *The Freudian Body*, 32.

each text is placed loosely within its historical context. But literary texts do not exist only or even chiefly in the historical moments when they are written, published, or translated. For this reason, I have focused extensively not only on the novels in their own historical contexts but also on their reception and translation over time.

Writing Across the Rupture: Between-ness as Category

An astonishing number of Japan's best known twentieth-century male writers wrote openly about love between men. In some cases they wrote of their own experiences, although it was typically their fictional alter egos and narrators who did the reporting. Whether veiled by fiction or not, however, the relative nonchalance with which these texts treated the subject makes for a striking contrast with the fear and loathing that tended to accompany the notion of men in love in their American and European counterparts.[9] I have already mentioned Kawabata's *The Boy*, which includes this disarmingly straightforward sentence: "My diary entries from September 18, 1915 to January 22, 1917 contain the record of a homosexual affair."[10] Tanizaki Jun'ichirō wrote a novel in 1917 that dealt with a love affair between two schoolboys, as did, during the 1920s and 30s, Edogawa Ranpo, Satomi Ton, Hori Tatsuo, Uno Kōji, Mushanokōji Saneatsu, Origuchi Shinobu, and many others.[11] Although in some cases these writers employed pathologizing terminology when referring to same-sex love—often taken from newly imported sexological discourse—the relationships and the objects of the narrators' affections are for the most part described in nothing short of loving detail, as in the passage discussed earlier from *The Boy* in which Kawabata's narrator hovers so delightedly

---

9. It hardly seems necessary to cite examples of cases in which "the love which dare not speak its name" was repressed and excluded from European literature, but E. M. Forster's refusal to publish his novel *Maurice* (a love story between two men with a happy ending) until after his death in 1970 comes to mind as a particularly poignant example. On the idea that Forster gave up writing novels altogether because he had come to chafe at the heteronormative constraints of novelistic narrative itself, see Matz, "'You Must Join My Dead.'" See also Moffat's excellent new biography of Forster (*A Great Unrecorded History*).

10. Kawabata, *Shōnen*, 156.

11. Tanizaki's novel (*Nyonin shinsei*), along with those by Mushanokōji (*Chiisaki sekai*) and Satomi Ton (*Kimi to watakushi to*), have recently been reprinted along with several other similar texts in Furukawa, *Ansorojī bungei sakuhin ni egakareta dōseiai*. See also Hori, "Moyuru hoo" (translated into English as "Les joues en feu"); Uno, "Futari no Aoki Aisaburō," and Origuchi, "Kuchibue."

over the various parts of his beloved's body. In many cases, the naïve purity and romantic intensity of the same-sex love affair being recounted is compared favorably to the narrator's later career as a heteronormative adult. These literary depictions of youthful male same-sex experiences, fondly remembered and rarely a source of shame or revulsion, have struck many readers living in the more homophobic decades that followed as surprisingly frank and even positive accounts of non-normative sexuality.

Such texts were written in surprising numbers, but their openness about male-male homoeroticism was, of course, hardly universal in twentieth-century Japanese fiction. Much better known and also more common among canonical texts are works located toward the opposite end of Sedgwick's male homosocial continuum. In these narratives, relations between men are still the focus but there is little or no overt homoeroticism. Instead, the male-male relations take the form of love triangles in which two men compete over a single woman. Although the woman at the apex of the triangle is the ostensible object of desire for the men at its base, it is the rivalrous relationship she mediates between them that takes center stage. Not only that, but the men's very desire for the woman is often initiated and always intensified by the currents of jealousy and identification that flow between the men. The "bonds of rivalry" that result are often, like those that Sedgwick described in a similar narrative tradition in British literature, "equally powerful and in many senses equivalent" to heterosexual love.[12] Homosocial narratives like this are so common that virtually the entire edifice of modern literature in Japan could be said to rest on a foundation in the shape of the homosocial triangle comprising two male rivals and a woman. Beginning with Japan's first modern novel, Futabatei Shimei's *Ukigumo* (1886), and continuing through Mori Ōgai's *The Wild Goose* (*Gan*; 1911–1913), Natsume Sōseki's *Kokoro* (1914), and Mushanokōji's *Friendship* (*Yūjō*; 1919), the list of texts featuring such triangles is effectively synonymous with the modern Japanese canon.

Of course, the open protestations of male-male love in texts like Kawabata's *The Boy* tend to strike readers in the twenty-first century as utterly and categorically distinct from the homosocial rivalries described in novels like *Ukigumo* or *Kokoro*. In the one case, libidinal desire between men is directly expressed and focused immediately on its object, and in the other it can at best be inferred retrospectively as a disavowed motive force behind a structure of triangulation and mediation. While the overtly homoerotic texts seem to offer an alternative to entrenched norms of sex and gender,

---

12. Sedgwick, *Between Men*, 21.

the obliquely homosocial works not only repress the possibility of love between men but also tend to reduce women to nothing more than the mediators of that desire. Finally, while the former texts constitute a minoritized and, until recently, relatively little-known side current of the Japanese novel, the latter flow straight through the heart of its mainstream.

Not surprisingly, different scholars have been drawn to these homoerotic and homosocial texts for different reasons. In recent years, scholars with an interest in gender and queer theory have begun to construct a kind of literary genealogy focusing on those representations of non-normative forms of sexuality and gender found on the homoerotic end of the homosocial continuum. Takahara Eiri, for example, has argued that the figure of the beautiful boy [*bishōnen*] as represented in works like *The Boy* or Origuchi Shinobu's "The Whistle" ["Kuchibue"] (1914) can be read not only as a rejection of heteronormative gender roles but also of the phallocentrism of modern subjectivity itself.[13] Writing in English, Barbara Hartley also finds something subversive in *The Boy*, and praises its author for his ability to "subtly yet comprehensively resist hegemonic interpretations of gender and sexuality."[14] Jeffrey Angles provides the most comprehensive picture yet of a "queer literary subculture" in prewar Japan in which he finds the origins of a "new, modern Japanese aesthetic of love between boys."[15]

On the other hand, beginning in the 1980s, feminist scholars of Japanese literature have critiqued the relentlessly male homosocial focus of so many works of modern Japanese fiction. Some of the best work in this vein has been done on the male homosocial dynamics in the novels of the canonical author Natsume Sōseki by scholars including Komashaku Kimi, Nakayama Kazuko, Iida Yūko, Morimoto Takako, Sasaki Hideaki, and, most recently Pak Yuha.[16] The title of Iida Yūko's brilliant 1998 book

---

13. See Takahara, *Muku no chikara*. "Subjectivity" here is not meant in a psychoanalytic sense, but more in the sense of the ostensibly autonomous modern self—the *shutaisei* of the *kindai jiga*.

14. Hartley, "The Ambivalent Object of Desire," 125.

15. Angles focuses on Murayama Kaita, Edogawa Ranpo, Hamao Shirō, and Inagaki Taruho (*Writing the Love of Boys*, 24). Kuroiwa Yūichi and Ōta Tsubasa have also done excellent work on the shifting representation of male-male sexuality in early twentieth-century Japanese fiction. See Kuroiwa, "'Danshoku' to 'hentaiseiyoku no aida'; "Kuroiwa, "'Homosexuel' no dōnyū to sono hen'yō"; Kuroiwa, "Hori Tatsuo 'Moyuru hoo' no dansei dōseiai hyōshō"; Ōta, "Origuchi Shinobu 'Kuchibue' shiron"; Ōta, "*Kaijin* ni okeru nanshoku-teki yōso"; Ōta, "Mori Ōgai *Seinen* ron."

16. The following is a selection of feminist readings of the relations between men in Sōseki's novel *The Wayfarer* [*Kōjin*], which is, even among Sōseki's works, particularly tightly focused on male homosociality and what Gayle Rubin calls "the traffic in

Karera no monogatari: Nihon kindai bungaku to jendā succinctly summarizes the centrality of male homosocial desire to much of modern Japanese literature. Translated into English the main title means *Their Stories*, but the word "their" in Japanese implies masculinity more strongly than its English counterpart.[17] A better translation, then, together with the subtitle, might be *All About the Boys: Modern Japanese Literature and Gender*.

Given what seem to be such clear differences between these two bodies of texts, and the two streams of scholarship that treat them, it is tempting to subscribe to the neat division they imply between the homoerotic and the homosocial. For one thing, such a division establishes a sort of division of labor, according to which queer critics celebrate non-normative homoerotic texts and feminists criticize the homosocial ones. If these two endeavors are understood as somehow complementary, this division of labor might work in the interest of a sort of alliance between feminists and queer critics. While the feminist work clarifies the common enemy (homosocial androcentrism) and shows what was wrong with a past that was both misogynist and homosocial, the queer critics mine a different past in order to imagine what a hopefully less sexist and homophobic future might look like.[18]

The problem with such a division of labor, however, is that the tendency to see these "queer" and "homosocial" texts as belonging to different categories best analyzed and critiqued with separate methodologies may have more to do with an anachronistic insistence on the homo/hetero binary than with anything inherent in the texts themselves. Even more problematically, the division itself is informed by a particular understanding of sexuality as something that is either "in the closet" (in the "homosocial" texts) and therefore in need of liberation or "out" (in the "homoerotic" ones) and therefore subversive and good. I would ask, instead, how modern readers might approach these texts as windows into a world of homosocial relations that far exceeds contemporary assumptions about gay/straight relations. Only by doing so does it become possible to account for the fact that many of the very same (male) authors wrote homo-

---

women." See Komashaku, "Towards an Absolute State"; Morimoto, "*Kōjin*-ron"; Sasaki, "Otoko no kizuna"; Iida, *Karera no monogatari*. See also Pak, *Nashonaru aidentiti to jendā*.

17. "Karera no," like "their" in English can be used to refer to both genders, but unlike "their," it is formed by the addition of a plural suffix to the masculine pronoun "he" [*kare*] thus making it harder to overlook the default masculinity of this theoretically sexually indifferent pronoun.

18. For an important critique of a tendency toward a similar "division of labor" in the early days of queer theory in the United States, see Martin, "Extraordinary Homosexuals and the Fear of Being Ordinary" and Butler, "Against Proper Objects."

erotic *and* homosocial texts, often without alluding to much (or any) contradiction between the two.

I will argue that if these two groups of texts appear to belong to two separate genealogies, this impression has less to do with actual differences between them than with the intervening rupture of the homosocial continuum both in Japan and on a global level. Looking back on the past from this side of the rupture, a text like Kawabata's *The Boy*, for example, seems to belong to an entirely different category from his more famous novel *The Dancing Girl of Izu* [*Izu no odoriko*] simply because the former describes a boy's love for another boy and the latter describes a boy's desire for a girl. One text "contests hegemonic gender norms," whereas the other is more typical of Kawabata's tendency to objectify women as aesthetic objects. The subsequent schism in the homosocial continuum, which suggests that boys are supposed to desire either boys or girls, but never both, has made it harder to grasp the fact that *The Boy* and *The Dancing Girl of Izu* are actually not only by the same author, but were originally part of the same text.[19] Thus Barbara Hartley's praise for the author of *The Boy* as a gender radical, cited earlier, had to be qualified by her recognition that what she calls his "scopophilic texts" (such as *The Dancing Girl of Izu* and, most notoriously "The House of Sleeping Beauties" ["Nemureru bijo"]) "entrench a questionable view of women."[20]

Rather than reading texts like *The Boy* and *The Dancing Girl of Izu* separately as the work of a queer, gender-bending Kawabata on the one hand and a misogynist Kawabata on the other, this book tries not only to read

---

19. This divide has been both confirmed and perpetuated by the history of the texts' publication. Both were originally written in 1923 as parts of a continuous piece titled *Memories of Yugashima* [*Yugashima de no omoide*]; the sections that constituted *The Dancing Girl of Izu* were published in 1926, but *The Boy* had to wait until 1948–1949. In English, this situation has been exacerbated even further as a result of the politics of translation. *The Dancing Girl of Izu* remains one of Kawabata's best known works, with a partial translation by Edward Seidensticker appearing in *The Atlantic Monthly* already in January 1955, but *The Boy* has never been translated into English and so might as well not exist for the Anglophone reader. And yet when Kawabata wrote them in 1923 they formed parts of a single whole—at least to the extent that any text by the modernist Kawabata can be considered "whole." As long as the logic of the homo/hetero divide continues to treat these two texts separately, however, readers are left with two irreconcilable views of Kawabata.

20. Hartley, "The Ambivalent Object of Desire," 125. "The House of Sleeping Beauties" is about a house of prostitution in which old men pay simply to gaze upon young girls as they sleep in drugged oblivion. See Kawabata, *The House of the Sleeping Beauties and Other Stories*.

them alongside each other but also to question the categories that would separate them in the first place. This will require a synthesis of queer and feminist approaches capable of recognizing a remarkable feature of the modern Japanese literary scene—that despite what long-established linear narratives of repression followed by liberation would suggest, not only did homoerotic and homosocial texts coexist alongside each other in the same historical eras, in many cases the two impulses are embedded within the very same texts. As the late William Sibley wrote, "In works by Sōseki (as well as others one can think of) the homoerotic often coexists with the homosocial in a fashion that the codification of Sedgwick's thesis by queer studies would not allow for."[21] Sōseki's *Kokoro*, for example (discussed in Chapters 4 and 5), epitomizes for one critic the misogynist male homosocial traffic in women,[22] while for another it is nothing short of *homo marudashi*, "full-on homo."[23]

How, then, did it come to pass that the continuum Sedgwick and others have worked so hard to show has become obscured? What does it mean when Sibley gestures towards the "codification of Sedgwick's thesis by queer studies" as a possible culprit? It is hard to know precisely, but I think he was most likely referring to a common (and distinctly "un-queer") tendency to reduce Sedgwick's theory of homosocial desire to a kind of unveiling of a latent or disavowed homosexuality beneath the homosocial bonds of male friendship or rivalry, or, as the *New York Times* obituary of Sedgwick put it, "teasing out the hidden socio-sexual subplots in writers like Charles Dickens and Henry James."[24] Such a characterization of Sedgwick's work is ironic given that it relies, uncritically, on precisely the tropes of visibility and knowability that she put so much work into deconstructing in *Between Men* (1985) and *The Epistemology of the Closet* (1990). The notion of "teasing out," or unveiling a hidden "socio sexual subplot," smacks of what Michel Foucault called the "repressive hypothesis," which falsely posits that sexuality is a prediscursive "thing" that is either "in" or "out," "hidden" or "known."[25] Unfortunately, to the extent that most people, academics included, have any awareness at all of the work of queer theorists, that aware-

---

21. Sibley, review of Reichert, *In the Company of Men*, 332.

22. See Iida, "*Kokoro*-teki sankakkei no saiseisan."

23. The phrase, which is meant humorously and not homophobically, is from Hashimoto, *Hasu to katana*, 230.

24. Grimes, "Eve Kosofsky Sedgwick, a Pioneer of Gay Studies and a Literary Theorist, Dies at 58."

25. For Foucault's critique of the "repressive hypothesis," see *The History of Sexuality*, 15–49.

ness tends to center on this image of the more or less paranoid critic, obsessed with same-sex sexual identity, "ferreting out" the signs and symptoms of same-sex desire from literature's closet.[26] Or as some of my students have (perhaps understandably) asked me when we have discussed the workings of the homosocial triangle, "So does this mean that these characters are *actually gay*?" To the extent that this sort of either/or logic underpins the understanding of (homo)sexuality it would indeed be surprising to find the homoerotic coexisting with the homosocial, insofar as, according to this model, the former is understood to be inherently non-normative and immediate and the latter is normative and mediated. Once the cat is out of the bag, so to speak, how can it simultaneously remain inside?

The question is reflective of the extraordinary knowingness that surrounds the question of sexual orientation both in the contemporary United States and in Japan.[27] It suggests that if one could only pinpoint the exact fixity of a person's sexuality—or as another student memorably phrased it, "Was Sensei in *Kokoro* actually gay for K?"— the work of reading would be done and the questions raised by the text about gender and desire somehow resolved. The problem with such an approach, and the reason I will not adopt it in this book, is that it reduces gender and sexuality in literature to a matter of content—and reading itself to a mere act of decoding—rather than recognizing how all three are forms of relation mediated and constructed through narrative acts. Sedgwick herself was always very clear that her work was not about sorting out who was and was not gay. "It will become clear, in the course of my argument," she wrote on page 2 of *Between Men*, "that my hypothesis of the unbrokenness of this continuum is not a *genetic* one—I do not mean to discuss genital homosexual desire as 'at the root of' other forms of male homosociality—but rather a strategy for making generalizations about, and marking historical differences in, the *structure* of men's relations with other men."[28]

One danger of overlooking this crucial point—namely, that homosexual desire itself is not at the root of male homosociality—is that it can lay the blame for the structural violence of homosocial patriarchy at the feet of an essentialized (male) homosexual desire located within individual bodies. One typical and instructive example of such a reading by a Japanese feminist scholar is Nakayama Kazuko's otherwise compelling reading of Sōseki's

---

26. The term "ferreting out," a particularly off-putting image for the rodent-like snake-hunting that supposedly defines the queer critic, is also taken from the *Times* obituary.

27. On "knowingness," see 159, n. 15.

28. Sedgwick, *Between Men*, 2 (emphasis in original).

1907 novel *And Then* [*Sorekara*], about a love triangle between its protagonist Daisuke, his friend Hiraoka, and Hiraoka's wife Michiyo. In this article, originally published in 1991 before any of Sedgwick's work had appeared in Japanese, Nakayama characterizes the bond between Daisuke and his rival Hiraoka as a "homosexual relation" [*homosekushuaru na kankei*] that Daisuke must first leave behind if he is ever to know Michiyo on her own terms and escape from the bonds between men that structure the Meiji patriarchy.[29] Although Nakayama is right to point to what Sedgwick would call the homosocial mediation through Hiraoka of Daisuke's desire for Michiyo, her invocation of a "homosexual relation" between the two men reduces what is a structure of desire (that is to say the framework of desire in which these actors are embedded) to an essentialized (if not pathologized) quality that is located and rooted in the bodies of those actors. In a later, revised version of the essay that appeared in 2003, Nakayama adds the term "homosocial desire" [*homosōsharu na yokubō*] to the essay's title and, clearly—if only partly— under the influence of Sedgwick, points out that the issue is not "simply about homosexuality." Even in this revised version, however, Nakayama's fundamental argument, which conflates homosocial patriarchy with male homosexuality, has not shifted significantly. Here she simply adds the term "latent" [*senzai-teki*] to the "homosexual relations" that she identified earlier between Daisuke and his rival. This has the unfortunate—and distinctly un-Sedgwickian—consequence of making men's desire for other men seem like the primary stumbling block preventing genuine mutuality between men and women. Moreover, in Nakayama's reading, homosexual desire between men is associated with a (premodern) homosocial patriarchy while authentically heterosexual desire, which she calls "real love" [*honrai no ren'ai*], is imbued with a radical modernity. This move not only invokes a temporal, or modernizationist hierarchy that, this book will argue, has long been used to make love between men unimaginable in Japan unless it is somehow relegated to the past, it also associates love between men with the oppression of women.[30] A more genuinely Sedgwickian reading, by contrast, would ac-

---

29. Nakayama, "*Sorekara*: Natsume Sōseki 'shizen no mukashi' to wa nani ka."

30. See Nakayama, "*Sorekara*: 'shizen no mukashi' to homosōsharu na yokubō," 84. I do not single out Nakayama to suggest that her reading is exceptional or even particularly egregious, but that it is representative. In its failure or lack of interest in distinguishing between homosexuality and homosociality Nakayama's work is quite typical of most writing on male homosociality in Japanese literature. For another example of this kind of reading, which tends to conflate male homosexuality with the "family system" (*ie seido*) and (perhaps) inadvertently privileges heterosexual romance, see Morimoto, "*Kōjin*-ron."

count for the structural bases of gender oppression and the mediation of desire, homosocial and otherwise, without needing to posit either a "latent" homosexuality as the culprit or an idealized heterosexual couple as the cure.

There are at least two immediate advantages, both of them crucial to the readings in this book, to conceiving of desire as a structure rather than as a more or less freely flowing current of (identity-affirming) libido: first, it avoids pitting individuals against each other, specifically gay men against women, in the struggle against forms of oppression that are systemic and structural; second, it allows alternatives to narratives of liberation that cannot help assuming essentialized identities, as in the "coming out" narrative, which posits an intrinsic gay or lesbian self waiting to be liberated. Not only was this narrative simply unheard of for most of the twentieth century in Japan, but reading the past on these terms makes it impossible to appreciate the dynamics of the homosocial continuum and to understand how individuals of all genders were affected by it.

In the place, then, of the teleological narrative of desire and its liberation that is inevitably implied by "the codified version of Sedgwick's thesis," this book proposes a narratology of homosocial desire inspired by the ethic of close reading that Sedgwick's actual work exemplified.[31] It sees what happens in literary texts as a negotiation of subjectivity staged through a series of encounters between readers, translators, characters, and authors positioned at different times and in different affective relations to each other. It argues that the figure of male-male sexuality in all its variants was neither antithetical to nor synonymous with Japan's homosocial modernity, but rather an always tenuous and contested back-formation of modern narratives of development, both on the individual and the national level. Like the "gay child" who is only recognized as such in retrospect, this book argues that what might be called Japan's "gay past" has to be understood as a cultural category that comes into existence through the desirous recursivity

---

31. In addition to Sedgwick, Jesse Matz's work on narratology and sexuality has also been enormously helpful to me in thinking through the relationship between narrative, narratology, and sexuality. In an essay on Forster's *Maurice*, for example, Matz shows how Forster understood novelistic narrative and temporality to be fundamentally heteronormative (i.e., driven by the "marriage plot"). It was this *narratological* insight that made it possible for him to create an alternative in *Maurice*: "For the same reason that there cannot be, for Forster, gay narrative, there must be gay narratology, for it is the narratological view that discovers narrative's conventionality" ("Maurice in Time," 207).

of narrative, indelibly "queering" along the way the understanding of developmental narratives of maturation and modernization.[32]

Most crucially, this book thinks of desire as arising not from within the depths of a splendid isolation or the embrace of an idealized lover, but from a structural positioning in relation to others. What was so remarkable about the above-cited passage from Kawabata's *The Boy* was not solely that the desire it described existed "in between" two different historical eras and was differently enacted in the minds of different readers and narratees, but the way in which it foregrounded these modes of deferral and between-ness, which in fact characterize all human desire.

The Mediation of Desire

It may be useful here to turn back to the Edo and early Meiji periods to contextualize the modern "homosocial narrative" in relation to the larger history of the way desire has been mediated in Japanese literature. My use of the notion of the "mediation of desire" is indebted to the work of René Girard, whose classic work *Deceit, Desire, and the Novel* was also a key theoretical source for Sedgwick's *Between Men*. As I hope will become clear in the following pages, Girard's work, despite its unfortunate blindness to what Sedgwick called "gender asymmetry," is still extremely useful for the purposes of queer critique as a way of linking historical shifts in the techniques of literary narration to the different conceptions of what Girard was the first to term "triangular desire."[33]

Sometime around the turn of the twentieth century in Japan, a major shift occurred in the way sexuality figured in fictional narratives. For centuries leading up to that moment, sex was a topic that could be and often was named in more or less explicit terms, and portrayed thematically by narrators who shared with their readers an interest in the subject that ranged from the prurient to the censorious (and just as often combined the two). Narrators in the popular Edo genres of *ukiyozōshi*, *sharebon*, and *kibyōshi*, for example, gleefully retailed the well-worn themes of male-female love in the pleasure quarters, just as they treated their readers to elaborate literary feasts on the subject of *shudō*, or "the way of boys." In the works of writers

---

32. Katherine Stockton's writes of the "gay child" that "the Freudian concept of latency doesn't quite fit, though it looks like it fits, ghostly gay children. . . . Since they are 'gay children' only after childhood, they never 'are' what they latently 'were'" (*The Queer Child*, 15).

33. For more on this discussion, see "Gender Asymmetry and Erotic Triangles," the first chapter of Sedgwick, *Between Men*.

from Ihara Saikaku in the seventeenth century, to Santō Kyōden and Koikawa Harumachi in the eighteenth, and Narushima Ryūhoku in the late nineteenth, narrators tended to be gendered male and to serve quite openly as the "mediators" of the desire of their presumptively male readers. These narrators instructed their readers in what it was desirable to desire, taught them how not to make fools of themselves in the pleasure quarters, and shaped their understanding of love and sex as practices tempered by a judicious balance of urbanity [*iki*] and genuine feeling [*ninjō*]. The result was that the reading experience itself constituted a kind of male-homosocial triangle of desire.[34]

If this desire was both homosocial and triangular, however, it was also *externally mediated*, in the sense developed by Girard. Although all desire is arguably mediated in one way or another, Girard uses the term "external mediation" to describe cases where the presence of the mediator is both openly avowed and in some way distanced from the subject. Girard's model for external mediation is Don Quixote's relation to his mediator, the chivalric hero Amadis de Gaul. As Girard writes, Quixote "proclaims aloud the true nature of his desire. He worships his model openly and declares himself his disciple."[35] In cases of external mediation the subject's open admiration for and identification with the mediator is so strong that there is no question of rivalry: Amadis was too exalted and grand a figure for Quixote ever to feel that he was in competition with him. The combination of the mediator's distance and the subject's avowed admiration of him means that the mediator "sheds a diffuse light over a vast surface" and no single object ever dominates. If one object escapes him, moreover, the subject moves on easily to the next one—hence Don Quixote's remarkable (and amusing) ability to dust himself off and sally forth again and again after the most humiliating episodes. Girard sees external mediation as resulting both in the picaresque (or paratactic) flow of the narrative itself and in Quixote's unshakeable faith in his fellow man. "In Cervantes," Girard writes in an earlier passage, "the mediator is enthroned in an inaccessible heaven and transmits to his faithful follower a little of his serenity."[36]

---

34. For examples of such texts, see Shirane, ed. *Early Modern Japanese Literature*, especially Saikaku's *Life of a Sensuous Man* [*Kōshoku ichidai otoko*], Harumachi's *Mr. Glitter 'n' Gold's Dream of Splendor* [*Kin-kin sensei eiga no yume*], and Kyōden's *Grilled and Basted Edo-Born Playboy* [*Edo umare uwaki no kabayaki*]. See also Matthew Fraleigh's superb translation of Narushima Ryūhoku's *New Chronicles of Yanagibashi* [*Ryūkyō shinshi*].

35. Girard, *Deceit, Desire, and the Novel*, 10

36. Ibid., 8.

In similar fashion, the desire of characters in Edo-period fiction, whether it was directed towards a woman or a boy, was often modeled on that of amorous literary heroes, whether Heian heartthrobs such as Ariwara no Narihira or Prince Genji, or more recent lovers of love such as Saikaku's Yonosuke in *Life of a Sensuous Man* [*Kōshoku ichidai otoko*]. In Saikaku's text, the hero Yonosuke is imitating Prince Niou from the *Tale of Genji* already at the age of seven.[37] And in Santō Kyōden's classic eighteenth-century work, *Grilled and Basted Edo-Born Playboy* [*Edo umare uwaki no kabayaki*], the hero Enjirō is comically obsessed with imitating famous playboys of the past. If Don Quixote read too many chivalric romances, Enjirō has read too many tales of love in the pleasure quarters. He cooks up one outrageously imitative scheme after another to boost his reputation as a great lover, culminating in an elaborate but botched love suicide, the pinnacle of true love.[38] But if Enjirō's excessively slavish imitation of his models was meant to provoke laughter, the idea that one learned to love by imitating other men was never in question. The narrators in works of this sort served openly as the external mediators of their (male) readers' desire. At the same time, the external mediation of desire was apparent in the way the characters tended to move, again like Don Quixote, across a vast, exterior landscape rather than focusing inward on the dramas of the individual psyche. In these narratives, moreover, people actually had sex.

Over the course of the Meiji period, by contrast, as the novel was elevated from a commercialized entertainment to a "civilized" genre charged with the conveyance of truth, the amorous hero as model and the narrator as mediator began to disappear from view just as the narrator's affective and libidinal involvement in the sexual content of the stories he told—so exuberantly apparent in Edo fiction—began to be invested, more obliquely now, in the act of narration itself. One result of this shift was that in modern Japanese fiction, actual sex was largely replaced by interminable talking about, or, more often around, it. As sex thus became increasingly a matter for discourse rather than action, the triangle of desire that obtained between the narrator, his reader, and their subject matter began to resemble the Girardian triangle of internal mediation.

---

37. Shirane, *Early Modern Japanese Literature*, 49.
38. For a full translation that also retains all of the original illustrations, see Kern, *Manga from the Floating World*.

In internal mediation, the mediator is someone very similar to the subject and inhabiting the same world. Because the subject of internally mediated desire lives in close proximity to his mediator and by definition wants the same thing as he does, they inevitably become rivals. When the mediator becomes the rival in this way, the last thing the subject wants is to admit his debt to the mediator. As Girard writes, "the romantic *vaniteux* does not want to be anyone's disciple. He convinces himself that he is thoroughly *original*."[39] So rather than openly admitting his desire to imitate the mediator as Don Quixote did with Amadis or Yonosuke with Prince Niou, the subject of internal mediation convinces himself that his desire is intrinsic and based on the attractions of the object alone. In the Japanese context, the shift to internal mediation reflects the disappearance of the obtrusive and opinionated narrator of Edo fiction and his replacement either by a silent omniscience or a figural or character narrator. In the modernizing Meiji novel, the premodern narrator's characteristic direct address to the reader gave way to narrators who seemed to be speaking to no one in particular about sex that was not happening at all.[40] In these texts, the object of desire (now—not coincidentally—more often a woman than a boy) begins to appear to have her own intrinsic charms that suffice to motivate the desire of the protagonist, and of the readers as well.

A good example of such a text using third-person narration is Tayama Katai's *The Quilt* [*Futon*] (1906), in which the protagonist Tokio yearns silently and desperately for the young female aspiring writer who has come to live with him and his wife, while putting on an outward show of indifference. If Katai's narrator was still mediating the desire of his readers, he was no longer doing so openly in the manner of the Edo narrator, but relying covertly on the reader's (ostensibly natural) ability to identify with and imitate his (heterosexual) desire. Katai's third-person narration helped make it possible to imagine Tokio's desire as an uncontrollable natural attraction to an intrinsically attractive object: the very logic of heteronormativity.[41]

---

39. Girard, *Deceit, Desire, and the Novel*, 15.

40. For a reading of the political consequences of this shift in Futabatei's *Ukigumo*, see Kamei, "The Disappearance of the Non-Person Narrator."

41. Of course Tokio's desire *is* in fact mediated—not through any of his male friends but through his obsession with European literature. He constantly compares himself to Johannes Vockerat, the protagonist of Gerhart Hauptmann's *Lonely People* [*Einsame Menschen*], who is similarly attracted to a beautiful young girl student. One might even argue that it is mediated by the ideal of modern heterosexuality itself as represented in European novels like Hauptmann's. See Tayama, *The Quilt and Other Stories*.

In this new form of narration, heterosexual desire itself was thus naturalized. At the same time, and as a result of the disavowal of mediation, the narrative seemed to *tell itself*. If what was known as "naturalism" in Japanese literature was almost always about heterosexual desire, this was not unrelated to the fact that it tended also to employ "heterodiegetic" narrative strategies in which the narrator does not exist in the world of the story, thus downplaying the narrator's own participation in the mediation of desire.

This book focuses on writers who wrote against the heteronormative and heterodiegetic tendencies of naturalism. Their narrators are, without exception, "homodiegetic," meaning that they exist within the story world. Homodiegetic narration posits a narrating subject who looks back on his or her own past, often having reached an ostensibly more advanced stage of development as a result of the experiences being narrated. The result is a sort of triple vision whereby the reader is aware not only of two subjective perspectives in the text, that of the narrator at the moment of narration and that of his or her former self within the time of the story, but also of the implied author who has orchestrated this confrontation between present and past—in some cases, to very different narrative ends. This complex perspective is particularly well matched to the types of disavowal and self-ignorance typical of modern homosocial subjectivity. At the same time, it makes it possible to narrate sexual development and maturation while still maintaining the potential of an ironic or critical viewpoint vis-à-vis ideologies of progress.

The homosocial narrators examined in this book tend to tell stories not directly about their own desire or that of a lone protagonist (as Katai did with his protagonist in *The Quilt*) but about the desires of other men, often a best friend, a brother, or a roommate with whom they find themselves in a rivalrous relationship over a woman. This serves to highlight the mediated quality of their individual desires. They also tend to present themselves not as always already heterosexual but as having "grown up" into heteronormative subjects, often between the end of the story and the moment of narration. In all of these ways, the texts under discussion do not simply engage male-male sexuality as a theme (indeed sometimes it never appears explicitly at all), but they do so by employing narratological strategies that both highlight and problematize how the continuum of male homosocial relations in fact continued to mediate and structure their male characters' desire. This was true even, and perhaps especially, when the object of that desire was a woman.

At the same time, by limiting the perspective to that which can be known by a single person, homodiegetic narration highlights the ever-growing gulf between individuals that was the hallmark not just of modernity, but of male homosocial modernity in particular. In the place of what Masao Miyoshi has described as the paradoxically collective nature of the naturalist I-novel,[42] these texts show men in utter isolation from each other as a result of the ongoing rupture of the homosocial continuum.

In Chapter 1 I discuss several examples of homosocial narrative while providing a more detailed and contextualized account of the way in which love between men was relegated to the past in modernizing Japan. In Mori Ōgai's *The Wild Goose* (1911–1913), the subject of Chapters 2 and 3, the unnamed narrator tells of his friend Okada, an attractive, ambitious young man, and Otama, an equally beautiful young woman who dreams of Okada rescuing her from her life as a moneylender's mistress. The romance that seems in the offing never materializes, however, and the telling of the tale itself becomes the narrator's way of engaging a homosocial rivalry with Okada over Otama. The narrator's shifts from homo- to heterodiegetic narration and back again over the course of the novel reflect its shifting allegiances to a male homosocial mentality that excludes women altogether on the one hand and a more modern form capable of extraordinary insight into a fully fleshed out female mind (that of Otama), but that remains the product of an intensified and largely disavowed erotic rivalry between the two men.

In Sōseki's *Kokoro* (1914), which I discuss in Chapters 4 and 5, the novel's first narrator looks back on his admiration for an older male friend "Sensei" with the implication that it was a homosexual "stage" that he has since outgrown. *Kokoro* itself has had a powerful afterlife in Japan and I have devoted Chapter 4 exclusively to a reading of the novel's reception and two different translations as a way of gauging the state of the male homosocial continuum in Japan from the time it was written until today.

---

42. As I discuss in Chapter 7, the "I-novel" is something of a misnomer, since most examples of the genre are actually written in the third person. Miyoshi offers the following useful definition: "the orthodoxy of Japanese fiction is 'I-fiction' that records the life of the author. And yet, paradoxically, it is not egocentric. Quite unlike the autobiographical novel (whether in first or third person) such as *David Copperfield*, *The House of the Dead*, or *Sons and Lovers* that fashions a critically selected persona, the *shishōsetsu* is a form of documentary chronology that supposedly exemplifies the normative life of a member of the collective. The writer can be eccentric, but in his or her difference, the reader merely sees the limits of homogeneity. Supposedly, I-fiction is always honest and factual, and it rejects fictionality and mediation. Thus is cannot come to a true end, for instance, until the author comes to the end of his life" (*Off Center*, 48).

In Chapter 5, I turn to my own reading of Sōseki's novel, to show how the text reveals in subtle ways the homosocial rivalry that both animates and undermines the first narrator's claim to have moved beyond his youthful homoeroticism. The chapter closes with a reading of the story that Sensei relates in a letter to the younger narrator of his own past relationship with his friend K as the "primal scene" of the modern Japanese male homosocial imaginary—a traumatic memory in which heterosexual love registers, in a horrific zero-sum game, as a betrayal of the world of men.

In Chapter 6 I discuss Hamao Shirō's 1929 short novel *The Devil's Disciple* ["Akuma no deshi"]. Hamao's novella could be said to continue the work done by *The Wild Goose* and *Kokoro* in anatomizing the origins of heteronormativity in modern Japan from its sources in a melancholic relation to a homosocial past. *The Devil's Disciple* takes the form of a letter written by its protagonist Shimaura to his former (male) lover Tsuchida, who abandoned him years earlier. Despite his claim to have "moved on" to loving the opposite sex, the letter makes it clear that he is still suffering from Tsuchida's rejection and that his relations with women are in fact elaborate attempts to work through his unresolved attachment to his ex-lover. But because male-male sexuality has become increasingly pathologized since the time he and Tsuchida broke up, Shimaura finds himself without a culturally legitimate script through which to mourn his loss. As a result, he has come to think of his former lover as a "devil." The letter itself, I argue, is his attempt to create such a script and to find a way to mediate his heartbreak over Tsuchida.

It is worth noting here that next to the towering canonicity of Ōgai's *The Wild Goose* and Sōseki's *Kokoro*, *The Devil's Disciple* is a minor work by a minor writer.[43] Very few critics have written about it until recently, which means that I have far fewer interlocutors in this chapter. This lack of critical attention is due no doubt both to the relatively "lowbrow" genre of detective

---

43. I might never have run across Hamao's text had it not been listed in a 1993 guide to "aesthetic novels and gay literature," one of the more useful works to emerge from the so-called gay boom of the early 1990s. The presence of Hamao's story in the guide helped rescue it from obscurity, but it did so by minoritizing it in a very particular way. Most of the listed works were relatively obscure, which is, of course, why such a guide was necessary, although it must be said that it also includes an article on Sōseki's *Kokoro*. I note also that the expertise to compile the guide came not from gay men knowledgeable about their "own" history—in other words, not from readers motivated by "identity"—but from a group of women writers and *yaoi* aficionados with a passionate interest in male homosexuality. The short article about *The Devil's Disciple* was written by Egami Saeko, who went on to a successful career as a writer of *yaoi* fiction (Kakinuma, *Tanbi shōsetsu*, 160).

fiction to which it belongs, and to the fact that it deals much more explicitly with male-male sexuality than does either *Kokoro* or *The Wild Goose*. One reason I include it here is to highlight the interrelation of these two factors. If by 1929 love between men in Japan was well on its way to being relegated to the margins and placed outside of continuity with "normal" masculinity, this made it perfectly suited as subject matter for a genre like the detective novel, fascinated as the latter was with the abnormal and the marginal. If *The Devil's Disciple* is a minor work in a less prestigious genre, then, this is at least partly due to the minoritization of male-male sexuality itself as a result of the widening of Japan's homosocial divide. For this reason I have found it all the more important, given this book's project of rethinking and remembering the homosocial continuum, to discuss a minoritized text like *The Devil's Disciple* alongside these other major works of the Japanese homosocial canon.

In Hamao's short novel, the narrator is fixated on another man from his past; in contrast, Mishima Yukio's 1949 novel *Confessions of a Mask* [*Kamen no kokuhaku*], the subject of Chapter 7, depicts how the narrator's desire for other men threatens to undermine the very distinction between past and present. Instead of looking back on his past as either a developmental stage or a melancholic wound, Mishima's narrator asserts the non-narratable facticity of his desire. In so doing, *Confessions* collapses the doubled temporality of its own first-person narration and rejects the developmental arc of homosocial narrative. This does not, however, signal the beginning of "gay identity," but rather the impossibility of any notion of identity in the absence of mediating structures and cultural scripts. Situated uncomfortably between the end of homosocial narrative and what one critic called "the dawn of modernity in homosexual literature,"[44] *Confessions* marks, I argue, the "stillbirth" of modern gay identity in an atemporal zone of shame.

I hope that drawing connections between such otherwise disparate texts will go some way toward both "queering the canon" and "canonizing the queer." In doing so, my intention has been to examine as large a swath as possible of the homosocial spectrum, while allowing for (and perhaps encouraging) the possibility of overlap. My point is to emphasize the kind of reading that can be done *in between* the categories of the homosocial and the homoerotic and emphatically not just to "draw attention to the homoerotic

---

44. Atogami, "Saisho no dōseiai bungaku," 73.

element."[45] Such a strategy can only play into the either/or logic that underpins the homosocial divide.

It would also mean buying into the romantic narrative of progress that sees something like "modern gay identity" as a sort of cure for a patriarchal and misogynist homosociality because it allows for the direct expression of desire rather than its triangulation. When critics whose thought is shaped by that narrative look back on the past, they tend to sort texts according to whether and to what extent they contributed to or impeded that progress, without ever questioning the assumption that they themselves live in a more enlightened time. I try to resist this tendency and instead point out that desire itself is not simply "there" waiting to be liberated (never simply in or out of the closet) but intersubjectively produced and mediated in myriad ways, as people tell each other stories.

---

45. Grimes, "Eve Kosofsky Sedgwick, a Pioneer of Gay Studies and a Literary Theorist, Dies at 58."

ONE

Toward a Definition of Homosocial Narrative

Love in the Past Tense

In this book I chart the shape of the homosocial continuum in twentieth-century Japan first by focusing on what I call the "two-timing" quality of Japanese sexual modernity itself and second by showing how this quality was enacted in and enabled by the mediation of literary narrative. First, by Japan's "two-timing modernity" I refer to the way in which male-male sexuality was both relegated to and simultaneously preserved within the past, both on the level of national history and on the level of the individual. Thus, while it was true that by the early twentieth century in Japan the influences of European sexology and "enlightened" modernization had colluded to pathologize and condemn male-male sexuality, it was also true that its full disqualification was prevented by the persistent and relatively recent memory of a cultural tradition of male-male love, celebrated in literature and in full collusion with the premodern patriarchy. As Gregory Pflugfelder, Paul Schalow, Jim Reichert, and others have extensively documented, up until the late nineteenth century male-male sexuality, known by the indigenous terms *nanshoku* [male love] or *shudō* [the way of boys] was a common literary trope and even an idealized aesthetic practice or "way" comparable to other "ways," such as the way of the samurai, tea ceremony, or flower arrangement.[1] Although this tradition faded with the coming of modernity, it remained within recent memory as a resource and refuge for many writers.

---

1. *Nanshoku* was a common theme in Edo-period literature. Paul Schalow has estimated that in the popular vernacular genre or *kanazōshi*, 10 to 15 percent of 200 titles published between 1600 and 1680 dealt with the topic "exclusively or in large part" ("The Invention of a Literary Tradition of Male Love," 3).

One moving (and sometimes hilarious) example of this can be found in a collection of at least 123 letters exchanged during the early 1930s between the eccentric folklorist and naturalist Minakata Kumagusu (1867–1941) and his much younger admirer Iwata Jun'ichi (1900–1945). Iwata wrote to the elder scholar to ask for his help in researching the tradition of male love in Japan, and Minakata obliged with letter after letter brimming with recondite erudition on the subject culled from premodern Japanese sources and interspersed with materials from China, ancient Greece, and other more exotic locales. The tone of Minakata's letters is one of intense nostalgia and frustration with the vulgar state to which what he calls Japan's "pure way of men" [*jō no nandō*] had been reduced in the modern world of sexology and journalistic sensationalism. At one point he mourns the fact that "today, in the absence of any contemporary models, it would be extremely difficult for you or anybody else, I think, to write fiction about homosexual love [*nanshoku shōsetsu*] which could convey even so much as a pale reflection of the Pure Way of Men."[2] And yet Minakata does his best to convey something of it privately in these letters, partly by relating the story of his own love as a youth in the early Meiji period for a pair of beautiful brothers. The letters themselves also read like an elaborate courtship of their young addressee through the mediation of Minakata's arcane knowledge of a lost queer past. Minakata, whose other great love was the study of slime molds, signals his passion for the material and for Iwata when he notes at one point in a letter that runs to 38 pages in the printed edition that "in the course of writing this letter, I have let spoil three containers of fungus samples."[3]

If male-male sexuality could survive ensconced in history, it also had a place in the past of the individual, in the period of adolescence.[4] Kawabata's *The Boy*, discussed in the Introduction, is worth revisiting as a prime example of this. Although the letters and diaries that the narrator claims comprise the bulk of *The Boy* were mostly written in 1923, the novel was serialized from 1948–1949, when Kawabata was assembling the first edition of his collected works on the occasion of his fiftieth birthday. The narrator of *The Boy*, who is also publishing his collected works, frames the diaries from this later historical moment, by which point the love affair with his class-

---

2. I quote from William Sibley's excellent if partial translation of this exchange. See Minakata and Iwata, "Morning Fog," 151. For the Japanese original, see Hasegawa and Tsukikawa, *Minakata Kumagusu nanshoku dangi*, 47.

3. Minakata and Iwata, "Morning Fog," 161; Hasegawa and Tsukikawa, *Nanshoku dangi*, 77.

4. G. Stanley Hall's *Adolescence* (1904), which originated the term, was published in Japanese in 1910 as *Seinenki no kenkyū* (Tokyo: Dōbunkan).

mate Kiyono is already more than thirty years in the past and Kiyono himself long dead. Recalling the nature of his youthful sexuality from this later moment, he writes:

> There were no women around when I was growing up, which may account for the pathological aspect to my sexuality [*sei-teki ni byō-teki na tokoro*] that had me indulging in licentious fantasies from a young age. Perhaps this was why I felt a desire for beautiful boys that was more monstrous than most people's [*hito-nami ijō ni kikai na yokubō*]. When I was taking entrance exams, I was still more tempted by boys than by girls, and here I am now turning that sort of desire [*sōshita jōyoku*] into material for a novel."[5]

There are strong echoes here of the sexological discourses that by this point had begun to classify forms of desire according to whether they were "normal" or "abnormal," "wholesome" or "pathological." At the same time, the phrase "more monstrous *than most people's*" suggests that, for this narrator at least, his attraction to other boys, while it might have been extreme in degree, was not sufficient to separate him qualitatively from the rest of the human race. "Most people," the sentence suggests, could be expected to experience desires that were at least a little monstrous, at least when they were young. The phrase "I was still more tempted by boys," moreover, echoes the widely held notion that same-sex attractions belonged to a distinct developmental stage that would (and should) eventually be outgrown, even if in this narrator's case it seems to have lasted a little longer than usual.[6]

Although the passage is clearly colored by the pathologizing impetus of sexology and paints same-sex desire as a transient stage, it ends with the narrator's recognition that "that sort of desire" can still serve as material for a novel. It need not, in other words, be erased or hidden from history altogether. This is perhaps why, aside from a few passages like this one, the narrator who creates this novel by compiling and commenting upon his old diaries is strikingly unashamed of his past and makes few attempts to explain or justify it. For the most part, he lets the documents speak for themselves, treating them with the respect of a museum curator, as records of something long gone that deserves careful preservation. In the context

---

5. Kawabata, *Shōnen*, 64.

6. Jeffrey Angles writes, "Late adolescence . . . was the time when the distinction between homosociality and homoeroticism was driven home. In the minds of many, graduation from school meant that students should also leave behind the adolescent appreciation of boys and enter the 'adult' realm of cross-sex desire and family. Late adolescence represented a transition when the male-male desire of youth was generally expected to give way to love between a man and a woman. The two forms of desire might spill over into one another during youth, but as youth gave way to adulthood, society typically expected the two to diverge" (*Writing the Love of Boys*, 34).

of immediate postwar Japan, as he sits in a bombed-out Tokyo, he looks back nostalgically and with extraordinary candor on his youthful same-sex affair with Kiyono as if it were a precious remnant of a long-lost Japan. The intimate moments he shares with Kiyono are described in moving and loving detail, as in the following passage:

> Just before the morning wake-up bell, I rose to relieve myself. It was bitterly cold. When I returned to my bed, I took Kiyono's warm arm, embracing his breast and the nape of his neck. Kiyono, in turn, placed his head over mine and powerfully embraced me, as if in a dream. As we lay with our faces together, I covered his eyelids and brow with my dry lips. I felt rather sorry for him, since my body was so cold. Kiyono occasionally spontaneously opened his eyes as he embraced me. I looked fixedly at his closed eyelids. He seemed to be thinking of nothing in particular. We lay like this for half an hour or so. I wanted nothing else. I wanted Kiyono, also, to want nothing else.[7]

I mentioned in the introduction that *The Boy*, according to its narrator, was originally part of a manuscript entitled *Memories of Yugashima* which also included the text of Kawabata's more famous novel *The Dancing Girl of Izu*. The latter work, which described its narrator's fascination with a fourteen-year-old girl member of a group of outcast performers, was published in 1926, but Kawabata did not publish *The Boy* until 1948. One factor that might explain this later date is what Mark McLelland has described as the "loosening of traditional sex and gender ideologies" in the immediate postwar period.[8] In other words, even though the homoerotic affair described in the text takes place during the Taishō period (1912–1926), one might imagine that it was only in the more liberated atmosphere of the postwar era that Kawabata felt enabled to publish a text about same-sex desire. Hartley has described this characteristic of *The Boy* as "a double or laminated structure by means of which the differing extra-textual settings [of the two moments of the text's production and publication] are nuanced against each other."[9] For Hartley, the "laminated structure" of the text has more to do with its ability to critique both prewar and postwar "authorities" that would enforce "hegemonic" understandings of gender and sexuality. I agree with both McLelland and Hartley's readings of the relationship between the text itself and the two extratextual historical moments that it might be seen to critique or resist. At the same time, however, I would note that *The Boy* owes its ability to narrate same-sex desire to its

---

7. Kawabata, *Shōnen*, 156. The translation of the passage above is taken from Hartley, "The Ambivalent Object of Desire," 127.

8. Cited in Hartley, "The Ambivalent Object of Desire," 135.

9. Ibid., 124.

status as a "two-timing" text on the intratextual level as well. This is clear in comparison to the relatively straightforward, and also "straight," narrative of *The Dancing Girl of Izu*. In that text, the narrator meets a group of traveling entertainers on a trip to the Izu peninsula. He decides to follow them on their travels and they seem to adopt him as one of their own extended family. During the trip he experiences a sort of wistful and ultimately unconsummated desire for the girl dancer (a fourteen-year-old virgin), and eventually goes back to Tokyo. As this short summary suggests, while the narrative of *The Dancing Girl of Izu* does not lead to any conclusive closure, it is linear and focused for the most part on the girl as a singular object of desire.[10]

The Boy, on the other hand, is an extremely complex and convoluted text. The voice of the 50-year-old man comes in throughout—commenting, explaining, organizing, reminiscing. The texts are not arranged in chronological order and the narrative does not focus exclusively on the relationship with Kiyono. The first third of the text is a kind of record of the emergence of the narrator's authorial voice. It describes, for example, his habit during the war of reading various classical texts to calm his nerves during the air raids—mostly various versions of the *Tale of Genji*, including Kitamura Kigin's annotated version entitled *Moon on the Lake Commentary* [*Kogetsushō*] from 1673. He describes his fascination with other people who studied the *Genji* in times of war and social unrest—such as Minamoto no Mitsuyuki and Fujiwara no Teika, both of whom compiled edited versions of the tale around the time of the Jōkyū rebellion (1221) near the beginning of the Kamakura period (1192–1333). Then he mentions some poems he himself wrote in the style of the young Shimazaki Tōson (1872–1943), but says his pride would not allow him to transcribe them because they are so derivative. He copies out a section of an essay written in 1914 describing a class trip to Minooyama, which is full of clichéd poetic expressions. Nowhere in these texts, he says, "did I ever write about my own experiences in my own words."[11] There is another essay, however, where he describes a lively visit to the home of a couple of attractive brothers who were friends of his. This text, he explains, has moments in which one can begin to perceive something like his own authorial voice, but it is also interspersed with self-conscious literary mannerisms. For example, when he leaves their home, he writes that he heard the sound of "straw being thrashed far and near, high and low." But the older narrator comments that he can no longer tell if he

---

10. See Kawabata, *The Dancing Girl of Izu and Other Stories*.
11. Kawabata, *Shōnen*, 153–54.

actually heard this or whether it was just a clichéd literary device [*tsukinami no bunshoku ni suginu*]. When he leaves his house to go to visit the brothers, he writes, "I went out the gate" [*mon o izu*] using classical grammar. Here too, the older narrator comments that this was a literary embellishment. He and his grandfather were poor and their house "had no gate, just an encircling evergreen hedge. The boys' house, however, did have an imposing wall and gate."[12] The implication seems to be that as an orphan with no parents or siblings of his own, he has imagined himself living in the livelier home of his friends. In the resulting confusion of going and coming and whose gate is whose, it becomes clear that writing is working to mediate his desire—both for a better home and for the beautiful brothers. When he writes a few lines later that he felt an affectionate longing (*shibo*) for the two boys "as one would have for the opposite sex," he notes that young boys often feel this way for each other and "there was nothing like homosexuality between us" (*shikashi dōseiai to iu yō na koto wa nakatta*).[13]

It is hard to miss the note of disavowal here, but it is also true that Kawabata's text is less concerned with "homosexuality" per se than with "history"—both of the self as author and of the self as a sexual subject. Kawabata's narrator acts both as a historian of his own life and as a novelist who is making it up all over again. I would argue that just as much as or more than the "liberated" atmosphere of postwar Japan, it is this historical and literary stance, along with the disjointed and fragmentary nature of the text, that makes it possible for Kawabata's narrator to write about same-sex desire with such relative openness. His candor may also be enabled by his strong awareness of his own mortality, having lived already far longer than his parents, who passed away when he was only three. "It's probably because I'm getting older," he writes, " but lately I've started to look at people in the context of their whole life, and to pay attention to the flow of history. Perhaps the war has something to do with it as well. I've started to measure the present with a long ruler that goes back to the past and forward to the future."[14]

This new interest in "the flow of history" seems to spark the composition of this text about his love for Kiyono and the other boys. And yet the last line of *The Boy* reads, "Now that I have written this, I have burned *Memories of Yugashima*, my old diaries, and Kiyono's letters." It is a queer historian indeed who burns the records of his own history. But perhaps he does so

---

12. Ibid., 155.
13. Ibid.
14. Ibid., 144.

in order to jettison the literal past and create a literary one. The editors of Kawabata's collected works, working under the assumption—all too common in Japanese literary studies—that the author and his narrator are the same person,[15] dutifully tell us in the notes, "the diaries and manuscript on which this work are based are no longer extant." Not unlike Mori Ōgai's *Vita Sexualis* [*Wita sekusuarisu*], which describes its narrator Kanai throwing his manuscript, also the "record" of his sexual past, into an old trunk with the sound of a thud in the last line of the text, Kawabata's narrator has written his sexual history in order to be able to throw it away—to silence and preserve it at once.[16]

In Kawabata's *The Boy* and in the correspondence between Minakata and Iwata, as in so many other early twentieth-century texts located on the homoerotic end of the homosocial continuum, the expression of love and intimacy between men is enabled by the past tense. One could write a novel about it, as Kawabata's narrator does, but however much this queer past might beckon to those who wanted an alternative to an increasingly straight present, it was only accessible as history, and rarely if ever invoked as a viable model for life in the present, let alone the future. Seth Jacobowitz has noted a similar tendency both to idealize and quarantine youthful same-sex love affairs in his reading of the wildly popular detective novelist Edogawa Ranpo's memoir of his own queer youth, "Confessions of Ranpo" (1927) ["Ranpo uchiakebanashi"]. Jacobowitz writes,

Having witnessed the historical juncture when *nanshoku* gave way to the modern configurations of homosexuality with the violent containments it entailed, Ranpo evinces a tendency for homophobic cover-up that consistently maps onto his professions of homoerotic ardor. His confessions thus consist of a double maneuver that affirms the author's "platonic" love affair with other boys, but just as quickly disavows any sexual misconduct. If Ranpo could imagine homosexuality as a consensual relationship be-

---

15. This assumption was clearly also operative when the editors of the series *Autobiographies of Authors* [*Sakka no jiden*] decided to include a fragment of *The Boy*. By 1994, the "homosexuality" of the narrator/author seems to have been the most salient aspect of the text, as witnessed by the fact that this "fragment" actually opens with the sentence quoted in the Introduction, "My diary entries from September 18, 1915 to January 22, 1917 contain the record of a homosexual affair." See Kawabata, "*Shōnen*-shō," 57. In the full text, this sentence appears ten pages into the work (*Shōnen*, 156).

16. It should be said that Kanai's ostensible motive in writing his text is to give it to his young son when he grows up as a kind of sex education manual. In this sense he finds pedagogical value in his own past. But because Kanai's narrative itself is framed by another, unnamed narrator telling Kanai's story, its straightforward "educational" value is undermined and ironized. See Mori, *Vita Sexualis*, 153; *Ōgai zenshū*, vol. 5, 179.

tween equals unlike the hierarchical pressures of *nanshoku*, it remained a possibility all but foreclosed in his adulthood.[17]

Of course, however "foreclosed" the possibility of intimacy between men might be in the actual present or future, thanks to the "double maneuver" that Jacobowitz describes, narratives like Ranpo's and Kawabata's made it possible to shuttle back and forth between both times in the space of the imagination. As Kawabata's narrator puts it in the passage quoted earlier, "Here I am now, turning that sort of desire into material for a novel." The "I" here has presumably "outgrown" his earlier attraction to boys, but here he is writing about it anyway. This two-timing characteristic of both Kawabata and Ranpo's texts is a key aspect of what this book calls "homosocial narrative."

Homosexuality Is History

It may be useful here to discuss an example of how this rhetoric of two-timing was employed not in a fictional narrative, but in a journalistic article by a well-known prewar authority on sexuality. In an article titled "The Historical View of Homosexuality" ["Dōseiai no rekishikan"] published in the popular magazine *Chūō kōron* in 1935, the psychiatrist and cultural critic Yasuda Tokutarō referenced what was by then a widespread association of male-male sexuality with the past and with adolescence. Yasuda writes,

> *Nanshoku* was once quite common in middle schools and [XXX]. It was particularly rampant in Kyushu and Shikoku, where sword fights over prized boys were a common occurrence. But as modern recreational facilities for men have gradually developed, *nanshoku* persists today only as the remnant of a barbarian feudal age [*yaban na hōken ibutsu*] or as a form of substitute eroticism in adolescence [*shishunki no daiyō erotishizumu*].[18]

In Yasuda's account, the memory of a culture of male homoeroticism still persisted in Japan until well into the twentieth century, but by his day it was dying out thanks to modern "facilities" (presumably involving female prostitution) on the one hand and the "natural" process of human sexual development past adolescence on the other. Whether understood as a superannuated local custom or a spent stage in an individual's psychosexual development, love between men was irrevocably mired in the past.

Despite his prediction of its imminent demise, however, Yasuda's attitude toward male-male love as it existed in the past is quite positive in the

---

17. Jacobowitz, "Translator's Introduction," xxxvi.
18. Yasuda, "Dōseiai no rekishikan," 322. The other location is censored in the original publication. Most likely it was "the military."

rest of the article. He notes with patriotic satisfaction that this "remnant of a barbarian feudal age" represents the traces in Japan of a "grand history of homosexuality the likes of which one would be hard-pressed to find anywhere in the world" [*sekai mare ni miru rippa na dōseiaishi*].[19] This "grand history" was even extraordinary enough to have caught the attention of European scholars. Yasuda notes that he himself learned about the history of the Japanese "way of boys" from the work of the German sexologist and homosexual rights campaigner Magnus Hirschfeld. The history of *nanshoku* and *shudō* might have faded away in Japan itself, but they had entered global circulation as part of a universal "history of homosexuality." Arriving back in Japan after this legitimizing circuit through Western eyes, they took on the sheen of a precious cultural treasure.[20]

Yasuda's article is typical of prewar discourse on sexuality in that it contains multiple competing terms and concepts, each with its own (still unfolding) historicity and ideological charge. It is a good example of the way that native Japanese terms could be strategically combined with newer sexological ones as new sexual identities and histories were being negotiated. In the title of his essay, he subordinates the native terminology of *nanshoku* to the sexological one (*dōseiai* being one Japanese translation for the sexological neologism "homosexuality"). At the same time, however, Yasuda recognizes a certain residual cultural value in the native terms that counter the pathologizing effects of sexology. He mentions, for example, that each of the great warlords who unified Japan in the sixteenth century—Oda Nobunaga, Toyotomi Hideyoshi, and Tokugawa Ieyasu—had a "favorite boy." Did this mean that these "heroes" were "sufferers of sexual perversion" [*hentai seiyoku no byōnin*] he asks, using the language of sexology? Not at all, he responds, in the language of premodern Japan: "They were lovers of boys [*nanshoku-ka*] as well as women [*nyoshoku-ka*], masters of the twain path [of love] [*nidō no tatsujin*]."

Sexology itself, of course, was not uniformly pathologizing and had its more progressive proponents as well, including Hirschfeld himself and, in

---

19. Ibid.

20. Yasuda explains that he and a friend were lucky enough to purchase Hirschfeld's works for next to nothing thanks to runaway inflation in interwar Germany. Since the Nazis burned Hirschfeld's Institute for Sexual Research and all of his books along with it two years previously, Yasuda unexpectedly become the custodian of what is now a rare archive of materials on homosexuality. For a fascinating account of a similarly roundabout discovery of the Japanese queer past via Germany by the writer Edogawa Ranpo, see Angles, "Haunted by the Sexy Samurai," 2008.

Japan, Miyatake Gaikotsu, Tanaka Kōgai, Mori Ōgai, and others.[21] In Yasuda's case, his relatively non-judgmental attitude may be related to the fact that he was one of Japan's earliest readers of the work of Sigmund Freud.[22] In his "Three Essays on Sexuality (1905)," which had been published in Japanese in 1931, Freud had recognized an innate disposition towards bisexuality in all human beings and bravely declared (albeit in a footnote that had been added only in 1915) the "most decided" opposition of psychoanalysis "to any attempt at separating off homosexuals from the rest of mankind as a group of special character."[23] But if Yasuda may have shared Freud's reluctance to minoritize homosexuality (especially as long as it was clothed in native Japanese garb as *nanshoku* or *shudō*), it is clear that he also shared Freud's interest in *historicizing* it. In the "Three Essays," Freud argued that all humans start out in the state of infantile "polymorphous perversion," but that the process of sexual development would ideally pare away the perversions until only genital heterosexuality remained. As for homosexuality, or "inversion," which constituted one of those perversions when it persisted into adulthood, Freud described it as a form of anachronism characterized by "a predominance of archaic constitutions and primitive psychical mechanisms."[24] Rather than condemning homosexuality outright, then, Freud in the "Three Essays" placed it on a developmental timeline that predicted its eventual obsolescence.

Of course Freud's refusal to "separate homosexuals off as a group of special character" went mostly unheard in Europe and the United States, where the rupture of the homosocial continuum gave rise to a strictly policed divide running between the newly constructed categories of "heterosexual" and "homosexual." These categories became so decisive as to introduce a rupture within the male gender itself. Thus in the modern Western heteronormative imagination, male homosexuals were not considered men. These categories became important in twentieth-century Japan as well, but there the cracks in the homosocial continuum became manifest less through the imposition of discrete identity categories than through the temporal mechanism of two-timing. Thus rather than cutting off one

---

21. For an argument against the notion that sexology in modern Japan was an erotophobic European import grafted uncritically onto "a pre-Meiji utopia of permissiveness," see Driscoll, "Seeds and (Nest) Eggs of Empire."

22. Yasuda published a translation of Freud's *Introductory Lectures on Psychoanalysis* in 1926. He read *The Interpretation of Dreams* as a high school student in 1910. See Blowers and Yang, "Freud's Deshi."

23. Freud, "Three Essays on the Theory of Sexuality (1905)."

24. Ibid., 146.

group of men (the homosexuals) from another (the heterosexuals), the male gender in Japan could remain whole so long as the present was cut off from the past and adulthood from the world of the adolescent. Such relegation to the past, whether in Yasuda's essay or Freud's, was perhaps less actively noisome than the phobic violence and moralistic condemnation that faced male homosexuals in many other countries. But it nevertheless could be devastating in the context of modernizing Japan, where progress and futurity themselves were paramount values.[25] So long as male-male sexuality was associated with the "feudal" past, modernization itself became a primary motor of heteronormativity.

This persistent relegation of male homosexuality to the past suggests that simple repression and disavowal, while certainly partly responsible for the increasingly heteronormative culture of modern Japan, do not capture the complete story. In Japanese two-timing homosocial narratives, love between men is not so much repressed as it is contained within the past as an always early chapter in a tale of its own obsolescence through maturation and modernization. In these narratives, moreover, the personal and national pasts tend to be superimposed upon each other such that the achievement of heterosexual "normality" on the part of the protagonist doubles as a kind of modernizing national allegory.[26] In most cases, however, far from unsettling or threatening the normative future of the individual or the nation

---

25. Interestingly enough, while Yasuda insisted that male homosexuality was on the way out, he spent much of the article arguing that *female* homosexuality was very much on the rise. After pointing to the decline of *nanshoku*, he continues, "and yet the society pages of the newspapers these days are overflowing with reports of female homosexuality. One gets the impression that homosexuality today has been monopolized by the women" ("Dōseiai no rekishikan," 322). Here Yasuda refers to the sensationalistic coverage of a recent spate of love suicides carried out by female same-sex couples. He goes on to argue that this new prominence of female homosexuality puts Japan at the cutting edge of modernity and heralds the end of a society structured according to a binary gender model. If the traditional forms of male homosexuality such as *nanshoku* and *shudō* harked back to a world in which the subject of all sex was presumed to be male and the male homosocial continuum was still firmly in place, this "new" and "modern" female homosexuality was a transitional phenomenon on the way towards a genderless society of the future. I find an interesting resonance here with the observation of Susan Gilbert and Sandra Gubar in their founding work of feminist literary criticism *The Madwoman in the Attic*: "The son of many fathers," they write, "today's male writer feels hopelessly belated; the daughter of too few mothers, today's female writer feels that she is helping to create a viable tradition which is at last definitively emerging" (50).

26. On the "national allegory," see Jameson, "Third-World Literature in the Era of Multinational Capitalism."

with a "return of the repressed" or a revelatory "coming out," the homosexual past could be made to function much as "tradition" does in relation to modernity: as an inert and unthreatening heritage ready for preservation in the museum of progress.[27] Like all objects installed in such museums, once there, it took on an abstract and denatured quality. As a piece of the past thus preserved in the interest of the present, Japan's male homosexual past existed nowhere on its own terms. At the same time, like a "two-timing" married man who keeps a male lover on the side, it was usually making someone unhappy.

"The Little Historian"

Nishimura Suimu's little known but intriguing novella *The Little Historian* [*Shō rekishi-ka*] (1907) provides another good example of how this two-timing quality of male-male sexuality in modern Japan both featured in and structured literary narratives. The story opens with its first-person narrator Mitsuya, a teacher of Japanese history, relating how his wife once accused him of having an affair with one of his pupils, a stunningly beautiful boy and a star history student named Kasai Sumio.[28] Mitsuya asserts his innocence, but the text gives us any number of reasons to doubt him. Thus outfitted with an unreliable first-person narrator, *The Little Historian* qualifies as an early example of psychological fiction and produces sophisticated ironic effects. It also participates in the construction of a modern notion of homosexuality as an unspeakable and yet defining aspect of individual subjectivity.

But what marks this text as belonging to this particular moment in the history of sexuality and novelistic narrative in Japan is its striking juxtaposition of two very different understandings of male-male sexuality that are often thought of as being historically distinct. First, there is the narrator's understanding. Surprisingly "modern" in his perplexity over his own

---

27. As Gregory Pflugfelder has written of Meiji-period attempts to "preserve" knowledge of the *nanshoku* tradition, "one of their effects was to 'museumify' male-male erotic traditions by ensconcing them in the recesses of history, where they could be studied but no longer lived" (*Cartographies of Desire*, 206).

28. Given the ages and social positions of the narrator and his student, twenty-first-century readers might be inclined to focus more on the potential for sexual harassment in this situation than on the same-sex eroticism per se. But the predominance of age-stratified relations in the history of male-male sexuality in Japan was such that this "pedophilic" aspect of the text would have been unremarkable to its first readers. The anxiety in the text itself also centers on Sumio's gender and not his age or his student status.

sexuality, he is very much "in the closet" about his own desire and refers to the accusation made against him as something that cannot be spoken [*ohanashi ni mo naranu koto*]. But there is another character in the text for whom love between men is far from being unable to speak its name. This is Teshigahara, a fellow teacher at Mitsuya's school. It is Teshigahara who has revealed to Mitsuya's wife the alleged affair with Sumio. Teshigahara is a native of the former domain of Satsuma on the island of Kyushu, an area well known in Meiji Japan for the storied tradition of male-male love among its samurai. As a Satsuma man, Teshigahara has simply assumed that the narrator's fondness for the boy has an erotic component and taken it upon himself to share this information with Mitsuya's wife.

So while the narrator may be locked in his own private closet, being unable not only to express but even to know his own desire, the presence of his colleague from Satsuma makes clear that the Tokyo they both inhabit is not entirely a historically uniform space. To Teshigahara, it is obvious and ordinary that a man might fall in love with a boy. But when Teshigahara insists that Mitsuya's love for Sumio is there on the surface for anyone to see, Mitsuya experiences it as an x-ray of his very soul. "He fixed his eyes on me," he states, "and stared straight into my face as if he were trying to unlock the secret of my heart" [*me o suete, mune no uchi made miyaburou to suru mono no gotoku, waga kao o jitto mitsumeta*].²⁹ Thus the "truth" about male-male sexuality alternates in this text between an externalized and culturally intelligible phenomenon and an interiorized and inscrutable secret locked up within the heart of the unreliable narrator—giving the reader a sense of having one foot in premodern Japan, where love between men was simply part of the landscape of possible relations, and the other in a paranoid modernity in which homosexuality could be a secret even to the subject himself.

The Little Historian shows how conflicting understandings of male-male sexuality could coexist and overlap in ways that belie any simple notion of historical transition from a permissive premodernity to a repressive modernity. At the same time, and even more importantly, it shows how sexuality itself was coming to be understood in narrative terms. In response to Teshigahara's knowing assumption that the narrator's feelings for the boy belong to a recognizable cultural tradition with a name, the narrator insists that these feelings cannot simply be named [*ohanashi ni mo naranu*], but rather constitute a story, or rather, a *history*. "It's like this," he says, "This is the *history* of it" [*kōiu rekishi ga arunda*].³⁰ The narrative that follows does not so

---

29. Nishimura, "Shō rekishi-ka," 8.
30. Ibid.

much disprove Teshigahara's assumption but lends depth and meaning to the narrator's feelings for the boy, and, by hinting at the narrator's own imperfect self-knowledge, endows him with a complex interiority. It would be a very different story if Mitsuya had responded to Teshigahara by simply acknowledging that he was involved in a relationship with Sumio that fit the pattern of, for example, the *nanshoku* tradition practiced by Satsuma samurai, or of *shudō*, the "way of youths" that developed as a practice of sexual connoisseurship among Edo sophisticates. At least as they were represented in literature, the highly conventionalized characteristics of these traditions left little room for the exploration of the subjective interiority of their practitioners. Indeed, it is the narrator's *lack* of access to these traditions that lends him his complex interiority and makes his "sexuality" something that requires narrative exposition. By thus converting sexuality from a thing to be named into a history to be recounted, *The Little Historian* does the work of homosocial narrative. It does this through the mediation of "history" itself: Mitsuya, after all, is a teacher of history and Sumio is the teacher's pet.

Sōseki and Mediated Desire

If the two-timing coexistence of a queer past with an increasingly heteronormative present and the conversion of sexuality into narrative are two defining aspects of the homosocial narrative, a third is its explicit attention to the homosocial mediation of desire. A writer like Natsume Sōseki was particularly savvy about this. In his later works especially, he explored the dilemmas of first-person narrators caught in structures of desire that preceded and exceeded their individual subjectivities. The hapless Sunaga Ichizō, in Sōseki's 1911 novel *To the Spring Equinox and Beyond* [*Higan-sugi made*], for example, finds himself caught in a homosocial triangle, and feels all the pulsions of jealousy and desire that result, while still being almost uncannily aware of their structural causation. He finds himself wanting to triumph over his rival—even having daydreams of murdering him—but he is also aware of this desire not as an intrinsic part of himself but as a sort of involuntary vertigo: "the sort of nervous reaction which makes one who looks down from a high tower feel, along with the sensation of awe, that he can't help but jump."[31] If the jealousy he feels toward his rival thus has an external and structural origin, so is the love he is supposed to feel toward the woman in the triangle, his cousin Chiyoko. Sensing this very well herself in one climactic moment, Chiyoko asks him a question that reveals her own

---

31. Natsume, *To the Spring Equinox and Beyond*, 254; *Sōseki zenshū* (henceforth *SZ*), vol. 7, 276.

exasperated insight into the male homosocial mediation of desire: "Only why is it that you neither love me nor think of taking me for your wife . . . and yet . . . Why are you jealous?"[32]

The unfortunate result of these events in *Spring Equinox* is what Sōseki describes in a similar situation in another novel as a "clash of centerless interests never capable of developing into either harmony or discord."[33] The novelist's solution to this dilemma, however, is neither to have Sunaga awaken to an actual love for Chiyoko, nor to dwell on the possible "homosexual" connection that ties him to the rival, but actually to remove himself from the structure of the triangle altogether. "The triangular relationship involving Chiyoko and Takagi and me developed no further after that. As the weakest of the three, I escaped from the whirlpool halfway, as though I knew beforehand the ultimate working of fate, and so my story must be quite disappointing to a listener."[34] Sunaga's recognition that by dropping out of the homosocial triangle he has also made his story less interesting suggests the centrality of the triangle to the production of *narrative enjoyment itself*. At another point, Sōseki even has Sunaga suggest that some element of homosocial rivalry may be synonymous with the novel genre. After realizing that he has been indulging in fantasies of killing his rival, Sunaga says, "The moment I discovered my sentiments were turning into a novel, I became astonished and returned to Tokyo."[35]

Sunaga accomplishes his escape from the whirlpool, as do many of Sōseki's characters, by literally removing himself spatially from the situation, first by returning to Tokyo and later by taking a trip into the country during which he imagines himself at a temporal remove as well—back in the Edo past.[36] Once he is out of the tight confines of the homosocial triangle, he can allow his desire to be mediated by a wider range of objects without dwelling on any one too obsessively. In Girardian terms this could be described as a shift from internal to external mediation as I discussed in the

---

32. Ibid., 279–80; *SZ*, vol. 7, 305–6.

33. Natsume, *The Wayfarer*, 72; *SZ*, vol. 8, 70.

34. Natsume, *To the Spring Equinox and Beyond*, 252; *SZ*, vol. 7, 274.

35. Ochiai and Goldstein have "a kind of novel," which I have changed to "a novel." Sōseki's Japanese reads *boku no kibun ga shōsetsu ni narikaketa setsuna ni* (ibid., 254; *SZ*, vol. 7, 276).

36. Sunaga writes to his uncle Matsumoto about a couple of old women he meets on his travels, while visiting a male friend. "My friend looked back at me and laughed. 'Quite a rustic scene isn't it?' he said. I laughed too. Not only did I laugh, but I felt as much at home as if I had been born a century ago. I want to take that feeling back to Tokyo with me as a souvenir" (ibid., 306; *SZ*, vol. 7, 337).

Introduction. After describing to his uncle an amusing scene he has witnessed between a man and two geisha rowing around on a boat, Sunaga writes,

> Dwelling on these trifles as though they were rarities will likely as not earn your mocking smile over my whimsical curiosity. But take this as proof that I've improved, thanks to my trip. For the first time, I'm learning how to make a companion of the free air. Doesn't my not hating to write in detail about such trivia indicate that I can after all observe without thinking? To look without thought is now the best remedy for me.[37]

Of course it is not always possible to extricate oneself from, much less to choose, the forces that structure our desire. In the context of Meiji-period patriarchal society, this was particularly difficult for women, whose lack of mobility Sōseki had one of his women characters describe as making her feel "no better than a potted plant."[38] But as this description itself shows, Sōseki's awareness of desire as a *matter of location* rather than an innate motor of individual identity made it possible for him to write novels that were highly critical of the structures of male homosociality without resorting to romantic notions of the liberation of individual desire or the lure of "true love."

Mashed Sweet Potatoes and Sweetened Chestnuts

A close reading of one final text may help both to round out the picture of how homosocial narratives portray the mediation of desire and to prepare the way for the discussion of Ōgai's *The Wild Goose* in Chapter 2. The passage in question is a scene from Ōgai's 1909 novel *Vita Sexualis*, which preceded *The Wild Goose* by two years. The scene is remarkable for the way it evokes the narrator's desire for a woman not by showing it directly or from the inside but by choreographing its emergence in an intersubjective, and indeed homosocial space.

The narrator of *Vita Sexualis*, whose name is Kanai, has almost nothing to do with women for most of the novel. As a teenager he prefers hanging out with two male friends, one of whom is a professed aficionado of male-male love, and the other of whom follows a policy of scrupulously repressing *all* of his sexual urges. The narrator identifies with both of them and looks down on his other fellow students who have succumbed to the love of women, which he considers a sign of weakness and compromised masculinity. In this scene, however, Kanai is suddenly "awakened" to the ex-

---

37. Ibid., 312; *SZ*, vol. 7, 342–43.
38. Natsume, *The Wayfarer*, 237; *SZ*, vol. 8, 342–43.

istence of women and hence, the narration suggests, to something like his "own" sexuality.

The scene is a common one in Meiji literature by men. It describes a traumatic moment of entry into a modern heterosocial world, where the desire for a woman is equated with a betrayal among men. The result is a sudden separation from what might be called the "homosocial fold" and an awareness of one's separateness from others. This separation is also figured as a kind of birth of interiority that comes at the expense of an unthinking male homosocial communion.[39] The setting is a party attended by (male) students and professors at which a number of geisha are also in attendance. The narrator thinks that a certain geisha is offering him a cup of sake and reaches out to take it, but she spurns him haughtily and gives it instead to one of the professors who is actually sitting with his back turned to her. The narrator's "awakening" thus happens not because he suddenly beholds a beautiful woman but because he is humiliated by one in a group of other men. This is how Ōgai's narrator describes the moment of his "awakening": "From that very moment I felt as if I were completely awake. I felt, for example, as if I were looking at violent waves after I had been flung on the seashore from inside a swirling maelstrom. All the members of the party were mirrored in my eyes with perfect objectivity."[40]

Sundered into an "objective" interiority, the narrator then begins to consolidate something like his own sexuality. But he does so, fascinatingly, in a highly "homosocial" fashion: in relation to another man. This other man is Kojima, the beautiful and sexually repressed friend I mentioned earlier, whose name means "little island" and who represents what the text presents as an outmoded form of homosocial masculinity that is completely indifferent to women. Kojima, unlike the narrator, is lucky enough to attract the attentions of a geisha, but he is not capable of appreciating them. The following passage is long, but worth citing in its entirety.

Sitting two or three persons away to the left of me was Kojima. He seemed absentminded. He didn't look much different from the state I had been in before my awakening. A geisha was sitting in front of him. The balance of her well-knit body was perfectly ordered, and her face was equally beautiful. If she had made the borders of her eyes more conspicuous, she would have appeared more like the Vesa seen in Western painting. From the moment she had come in to distribute our small dining trays, she had attracted my attention. My ears were so poised I even heard her fellow-geisha [*sic*]

---

39. Recall how Sunaga described his escape from the torsions of the homosocial triangle in the passage cited earlier as the recovery of the ability to "observe without thinking."

40. Mori, *Vita Sexualis*, 117; *Ōgai zenshū*, vol. 5, 153.

call her Koiku. She was making several attempts to engage Kojima in conversation. As for Kojima, he was replying quite reluctantly. Even without trying to listen, I could hear their exchange:

"What is it, my dear, you like best?"

"Mashed sweet potatoes with sweetened chestnuts tastes delicious to me."

His was a serious response. Wasn't that an odd reply from a handsome, rather imposing twenty-three-year-old youth? Certainly among the graduating students at the thank-you party that evening, not one could rival him. Having become this strangely cool-headed, I felt awkward and ridiculous.

"Oh you do?"

Koiku's gentle voice trailed behind her as she got up from where she had been kneeling. I was watching the development of this affair with a certain amount of interest. After a while she brought in a fairly large porcelain bowl and put it in front of Kojima. It contained mashed sweet potatoes with sweetened chestnuts.

Kojima kept eating these until the end of the party. Sitting directly in front of him, Koiku watched each single piece disappear behind Kojima's beautiful lips.

I left the party early without telling Kojima, hoping, for Koiku's sake, he would eat as much of that mixture as possible and as slowly as possible.

From what I heard later, Koiku was the most beautiful geisha in Shitaya. And yet all Kojima did was eat the *kinton* which this beautiful geisha had carried in for him. Now Koiku is the wife of a famous politician belonging to a certain political party.[41]

In this scene we see the emergence of a new kind of homosocial subjectivity in the mind of the narrator. Unlike his beautiful friend Kojima, who is impervious to the charms of the beautiful woman in front of him, the narrator is all too aware of her alluring presence. But rather than pursuing her himself or feeling jealous of his friend, he just watches, allowing his own desire to hover somewhere between his friend's "beautiful lips" and what he imagines as the woman's desire. If he himself has a complex, interiorized "sexuality," it is produced in this interstitial space between a woman whose desire is immediate and externalized for all to see and a beautiful boy who "seemed absentminded." The scene speaks volumes about the sexual landscape of modern Japan in the homosocial imagination. A voluptuous woman tries in vain to coerce a reluctant male into desire, all under the watchful eyes of another, vicarious bystander who imagines himself as the man who might satisfy her—but who never does.

Whose sexuality is this? Can it be located "inside" the narrator or any of these characters individually? What function is served by the attribution of

---

41. Mori, *Vita Sexualis*, 117–19; *Ōgai zenshū*, vol. 5, 154–55.

mindlessness to the boy Kojima and of such obvious intentionality and desire to the geisha Koiku? Is this about them at all, or about the narrator, who "wishes for Koiku's sake that he would eat as much of that mixture as possible and as slowly as possible?"

One could argue, perhaps, that the narrator is secretly gay and that what really turns him on is the sight of his friend's "beautiful lips." But it seems to me that that would be an unnecessarily internalizing understanding of this scene. The sexuality being enacted here cannot be localized within a single interiorized consciousness. It is distributed among all three minds in the scene, and that of the reader as well.

As it turns out, this scene is like a miniature version, or perhaps the germ, of Ōgai's *The Wild Goose,* which he would go on to serialize in 1911. There, too, the narrator watches desirously as a handsome but hopelessly homosocial friend misses the opportunity to have a relationship with a beautiful woman who wishes he would just make a move. This narrator also chooses to tell the story of this relationship that does not happen rather than to enter into competition over a woman with his friend. The result is a quintessential homosocial narrative in which none of the characters get what they want and men and women remain walled off from each other in utterly separate narrative worlds. Unlike his counterpart in *Vita Sexualis*, however, the narrator of *The Wild Goose* writes in order to repair this rift between men and women, creating a new form of homosocial narrative whose purpose is to leave the homosocial past behind.

TWO

Between the First and the Third Person in Mori Ōgai's The Wild Goose

"He was a beautiful man"

The third paragraph of *The Wild Goose* gives the following first-person description of a man named Okada:

> If I were to explain what kind of man he was, I would have to begin by saying that he was both approachable and imposing. In other words, he was a beautiful man. Not one of those pale-faced and willowy types, but ruddy and well built. I have hardly ever seen another man with a face like his. The only person who came close was Kawakami Bizan, whom I got to know much later when he was a young man. The writer Kawakami, that is, the one who finally met such a tragic end. When he was young he looked a little like Okada. Then again, Okada was on the crew team so he far surpassed Kawakami when it came to his physical build.[1]

Who is speaking here? Is it a woman or a man? This level of interest in the physical charms of a man, in a heteronormative world, tends to signify femaleness, and there is nothing in this paragraph that necessarily contradicts that possibility, especially as long as the reader encounters the text in

---

1. Mori, *The Wild Goose*, 4; *Ōgai zenshū*, vol. 8, 491–92. *The Wild Goose* was serialized in *Subaru*, a journal founded and edited by Ōgai himself. It appeared in monthly installments from September to December 1911, from February to July 1912, in September 1912, and then again in March and May 1913. It was published as a complete book by Momiyama shoten in May 1915. It has been translated twice into English, first by Kingo Ochiai and Sanford Goldstein, and most recently by Burton Watson. (I cite Watson's translation throughout, with some modifications.)

English. The reader of Ōgai's Japanese, on the other hand, is unlikely to make this assumption since the narrator uses the first-person pronoun *boku*, which is marked as male and thus helps to clear up the ambiguity. Or does it? Apprized of this fact about the gender of the narrator, how might the English reader's attitude change? What might the reader do, for example, with the hint of desire that seems to hover over the text?

I open with this example of a slight gender indeterminacy in the English translation of Ōgai's text as a way to begin thinking about an important set of questions. Namely, how does the reader know about the gender and sexuality of literary narrators and characters? Can identities and desires be said to "belong" to narrators and characters? Or are they equally the artefacts of language and of narrative structure? In what ways are gender and sexuality enacted by narrative?[2] What can the mediation of subjectivity through narrative tell us about male homosocial desire? I will get to all of these questions in turn, but for now I want to move a little bit more slowly through this description of Okada.

Once the reader is made aware that the narrator is not a woman, why not read this as the beginning of a love story between two men? The reader in Japanese may well have gotten there already thanks to the male pronoun *boku*, and readers familiar with the association discussed in Chapter 1 between male-male love and the Japanese past might have felt their "gaydar" kicking in even at the novel's opening sentence: "This is an old story [*furui hanashi de aru*]." A gay, or gay-friendly, reader's interest might be further piqued upon learning that the story takes place specifically in the early Meiji period (1880 to be exact), a time when *nanshoku* was still a viable topic for literature.

The kind of interest that this narrator shows in the physical appearance of another man is also likely to catch the attention of readers on this side of the homosocial divide. Not only does the narrator notice Okada's looks,

---

2. I am using the word "enacted" here in reference to the notion of "enactment" recently developed in cognitive psychology and literary theory, which has been extremely helpful as a way of thinking through Ōgai's experiments in narrative, particularly his problematization of the distinction between first and third person in *The Wild Goose*. Enactment theory contests the Cartesian division of mind and world to argue that "cognition is not the representation of a pregiven world by a pregiven mind but is rather the enactment of a world and a mind on the basis of a history of the variety of actions that a being in the world performs" (Varela, Thompson, and Rosch, *The Embodied Mind*, 9). For an excellent discussion that uses the cognitive theory of "enactment" to critique the literary commonplace that modernist literature was characterized by an "inward turn" towards the psyche and away from "the world," see Herman, "Re-Minding Modernism."

but his comparison of Okada with the good-looking writer Kawakami Bizan indicates that he is in the habit of making these sorts of observations: he is a man who looks at other men. His description of Okada as simultaneously "approachable" [*tejika*] and "imposing" [*kiwadatta*], moreover, makes the latter into a quintessential object of desire—close enough to reach out and touch and yet forever looming on the horizon and always just out of reach.

And yet there is something ominous in this description as well. That these simultaneously attracting and intimidating qualities are presented as synonymous with Okada's good looks ("In other words, he was a beautiful man") serves as an apt gloss on the combined pleasures and perils of male homosocial desire in an increasingly heteronormative context. These pleasures and perils are adumbrated again by the elegiac affection tinged with the ambivalent and uneasy feeling that accompanies the mention of the "tragic end" of Okada's look-alike Kawakami.[3] Here, at the opening of *The Wild Goose*, then, hints of rivalry mix freely with a relatively unselfconscious homoeroticism in a way that reveals something about the state of the male homosocial continuum when Ōgai was writing. The vagaries of that continuum are matched here by a parallel tension on the narratological level, raising the question: to what extent can the reader understand what boku says simply as information "about Okada" and to what extent do his words express how he feels about Okada? Another way of saying this is to ask where boku's narration falls on the continuum between first and third person.

Not only is Okada extremely good looking, *boku* tells us, he also has a winning personality that renders the landlady at the boarding house (where he is *boku*'s neighbor) like putty in his hands. Okada works hard at his studies (he and the narrator are both medical students at the newly founded Tokyo Imperial University) but not so hard as to be off-putting. He is eminently reliable and keeps such a regular schedule that other boarders set their watches by his when they miss the noon gun. After explaining all of this, the narrator gives a turn-by-turn description of the precise routes of Okada's nightly walks around the neighborhood. Some readers might assume that the narrator is just acting like a narrator by providing all of this information; others might begin to wonder how he knows all of this. Two interpretations suggest themselves: either the two men are very close indeed, or *boku* is given to stalking.

---

3. Kawakami was a novelist associated with the literary circle Ken'yūsha who committed suicide in 1908, partly out of despair over his inability to adapt to the trend toward literary naturalism.

Of course, while many twenty-first-century gay or gay-friendly readers might be tempted to assume that the narrator is attracted to Okada, for other readers none of these clues are definitive and the narrator's interest in his fellow boarder could seem perfectly normal—just a friend talking about a friend, or, indeed, a narrator describing his protagonist. The historians among them might observe that this is, after all, a canonical modern Japanese novel, and although it may be *set* in 1880, Ōgai wrote it in 1911, by which time the culture of *nanshoku* was rapidly fading from the collective memory. The Foucauldians among them might go on to argue that such a gay reading is anachronistic, that it projects a current notion of "sexual orientation" into a text and a time when it did not yet exist.

But then again the hopeful gay readers and their friends could easily counter that the homoerotic (if not precisely the "gay") reading of the novel's opening chapter would actually have been *more* plausible for its original readers in 1911. *Nanshoku* might have been fading from the foreground by that point, but it was still a much fresher memory then than it is for the present-day reader. As evidence, they could cite Ōgai's own most recent novels, both of which dealt quite explicitly with love between men. Not only was *nanshoku* present as a theme in *Vita Sexualis* (1909), the novel I discussed briefly in the previous chapter, but at least one critic has recently argued that it was the only form of sexual desire to be represented positively in its narrator's otherwise quite erotophobic account, suggesting that the narrator himself (which is to say Ōgai's "alter-ego") is himself a "latent" *nanshoku-ka*.[4] This narrator provides a detailed and much discussed account of the culture of *nanshoku* among students just a little younger than *boku* and Okada, and set just a few years earlier. In the student culture the narrator describes, students fashioned themselves as belonging either to the "soft faction" [*nanpa*], which preferred women, or the "hard" [*kōha*], which favored other men. Contrary to what a twenty-first-century reader used to the equation of male homosexuality with effeminacy might expect, the girl-chasing "soft faction" was considered effeminate, decadent, and

---

4. Ubukata Tomoko refers to the narrator's "latent desire for nanshoku" [*naizai suru nanshoku e no yokubō*]. The notion of *nanshoku* being "latent" is a striking example of the two-timing quality of Japanese sexual modernity: it combines the notion of sexuality as based in outward behavior (the traditional understanding of *nanshoku*) with a more modern understanding of sexuality as based in some underlying identity. The ambiguity here has interesting resonances with the ambiguity between third and first person narration in *The Wild Goose*, which problematizes a similar tension between the "subjective" and the "objective," "inside" and "out" (Ubukata, "*Wita sekusuaris* nanshoku no mondai-kei," 153. For a similar argument, see Komori, "Hyōshō toshite no nanshoku."

overly concerned with appearance, while adherents of the "hard faction" affected a kind of hypermasculinity.⁵ The gay-friendly reader of *The Wild Goose* could point to echoes of this typology in the passage quoted earlier in which *boku* specifies that Okada was not the "pale-faced and willowy type" (terms that recall the dandified stereotype of the woman-loving *nanpa*) but "ruddy and well built," a description that puts him very much in the *kōha* camp. In a later passage, the narration refers to Okada as a "red-cheeked beautiful boy" [*kōgan no bishōnen*], another phrase strongly associated with the *nanshoku* tradition.⁶

Not only was Ōgai conversant with the modified *nanshoku* tradition as practiced by early Meiji students, but as a medical doctor and the translator of Richard von Krafft-Ebing's pioneering work *Psychopathia Sexualis*, he was also at the cutting edge of the modern science of sex.⁷ He was one of the first Japanese to use the Japanese neologism for "sexual desire" in his writing—as early as 1896—and was also familiar with the newly minted concept of homosexuality and not shy about referencing it in his works.⁸ His novel *The Youth* [*Seinen*] (1910), written immediately prior to *The Wild Goose*, contains the following remarkable passage in which a young man named Ōmura—who also happens to be described as "ruddy-faced and well built" [*kesshoku no ii, ganjō na*]⁹—wonders to himself about the nature of his feelings for Jun'ichi, the novel's eponymous "youth":

---

5. For more on the *kōha/nanpa* pairing, see "Nanshoku and Naturalism in Mori Ōgai's *Vita Sexualis*," in Reichert, *In the Company of Men*. See also Pflugfelder, *Cartographies of Desire*, 214–15.

6. I say "narration" here rather than "narrator" because, as I discuss later, there is some ambiguity as to whose perspective is being enacted. On the homoerotic associations of the term *bishōnen* at this time and in Ōgai's work in particular, see Ōta, "Mori Ōgai *Seinen* ron," 256–58. *Boku*'s description of Okada also has a lot in common with what Jim Reichert calls the "unaffected masculinity" of Dairoku in Kōda Rohan's novel *Hige otoko*. Reichert argues convincingly that Dairoku represents an updated Meiji version of the medieval warrior ideal associated with *nanshoku*. He also has a "crimson face" (*In the Company of Men*, 159).

7. The title of *Vita Sexualis* is itself, of course, an allusion to Krafft-Ebing's work, which included hundreds of case histories of various kinds of sexual perversion. Ōgai's translation was published as *Seiyoku zassetsu*, and came out in 1902–1903. See Mori and Kawamura, *Seiyoku zassetsu*.

8. Ōgai used the term "sexual desire" [*seiyoku*] in an essay on literary naturalism. See Ubukata, "*Wita sekusuaris* nanshoku no mondai-kei," 143.

9. Mori, *Youth and Other Stories*, 409 (translation modified); *Ōgai zenshū*, vol. 6, 317.

Each time Ōmura saw Jun'ichi laugh, he thought how charming this man's eyes were. At such times, the thought of same-sex love [*dōsei no ai*] would pop into his head. There is a dark, bottomless region in the heart of human beings. Normally he enjoyed the company of men older than himself, but since he met this young man he had abruptly stopped socializing with anyone else and came only to Jun'ichi's place. Normally he hated conversations that felt like lectures and certainly did not seek out people to speak to in that fashion, but this young man made him talk on and on. As far as he knew he was not [a] *homosexuel* [*homosexuel de wa nai tsumori da ga*], but the thought occurred to him [*chotto atama ni ukanda*] that even with normal people the seeds of such things can lie submerged somewhere in their hearts.[10]

While Ōmura seems to believe that he is not a *homosexuel,* and he and Jun'ichi do not become lovers, his willingness to entertain the possibility is remarkable. His ability to do so clearly has to do with his access to a cultural memory of the age-stratified *nanshoku* model of male-male love, with its relatively positive and pedagogical associations, echoes of which are evident in the fact that Ōmura's friendship with Jun'ichi is mediated by their mutual love of ideas and their study of the French language.[11] At the same time, this passage employs the language of a newer, sexological notion of homosexuality as an innate form of desire that can lie submerged in one's heart. In his relatively matter-of-fact introspection on the nature of his own desire, Ōmura seems to be anticipating the famous footnote Freud added in 1915 to his "Three Essays on the Theory of Sexuality" in which he pointed out that psychoanalysis "has found that all human beings are capable of making a homosexual object choice and have in fact made one in their unconscious." Although the publication of *The Youth* predates the 1915 footnote, Ōgai had in fact read Freud's "Three Essays" in 1907 or 1908.[12] As Kuroiwa Yūichi has argued, moreover, the Freudian, or "sexological" model is rendered in a relatively positive light here—its pathologizing tendency lessened in Ōmura's mind by his use of the term *dōsei no ai,* or "same-sex love" the most "spiritual" sounding of the various terms then circulating as translations of "homosexuality." Kuroiwa also notes the curious fact

---

10. Mori, *Youth and Other Stories*, 486; *Ōgai zenshū*, vol. 6, 429–30. I have slightly modified the translation from Ono and Goldstein's translation of *The Youth* in Mori, *Youth and Other Stories* to reflect my interpretation. They translate *dōsei no ai*, for example, as "homosexuality," which loses the emphasis that that Japanese expression places on "love" [*ai*].

11. Although the mediation of desire is usually thought of as being effected through human mediators, it can also work externally through ideas, abstract concepts, etc. The mediation of Omura and Jun'ichi's relationship through their study of French is a good example of external mediation enabling a relatively unpanicked intimacy between men.

12. See Driscoll, "Seeds and (Nest) Eggs of Empire," 201; for the footnote itself, see Freud, "Three Essays on the Theory of Sexuality (1905)," 145.

that the word *homosexuel* appears in French (the language he shares with Jun'ichi) rather than German (the language of Freud and Krafft-Ebing's sexology).[13] All of this would suggest that in *The Youth*, as much as in *Vita Sexualis*, Ōgai was not only willing to write about male-male love, but to do so in a relatively destigmatized fashion. For a reader just coming off these earlier novels, then, a homoerotic reading of the opening of *The Wild Goose*, published just a year after *The Youth*, would have been quite easy indeed.

But then the reader turns the page, and the impression that *The Wild Goose* is a novel about love between men does not last past the first chapter. Chapter 2 finds Okada encountering a mysterious and beautiful woman living in a secluded house on the route of his daily walks, and with her introduction, the machinery of heteronormative narrative churns into motion: Who is this beauty? Will she marry Okada? Or will she perhaps prefer the narrator?

Of course most readers today are sufficiently conversant in the conventions of heteronormative reading not to have been fooled in the first place by the narrator's interest in Okada. They would have known that a female love interest was bound to appear and that these were just the preliminaries, the setting of the stage for the *real* story.[14] Those familiar with late Meiji fiction would have been helped along in this assumption by the fact that not a few novels from this period begin with a scene between men that borders on the homoerotic. Early in Sōseki's *To the Spring Equinox and Beyond*, which was serialized in 1911, two men soak in a public bath, and one of them comments on the other's impressive physique:

Keitarō was already having the bathman scrub his back when Morimoto finally got out of the water and exposed his body in its entirety, so red that steam was rising from it. Doing so, he had a look on his face as if to say, "Boy that feels good!" and just as Keitarō noticed that he had plopped himself down Indian style on top of the drain, he started to praise Keitarō's body, saying, "That's quite a physique you have."

"This is nothing compared to how it used to be."[15]

---

13. Other translations included *dōsei seiyoku*, and *dōsei shikijō*, both of which put the emphasis on sexual desire over "love." See Kuroiwa, "'Homosexuel' no dōnyū to sono hen'yō."

14. As Keiko McDonald puts it, "He appears to be setting a stage, assigning roles to actors" ("The Wild Geese Revisited," 212).

15. Natsume, *Higan sugi made*, in *SZ*, vol. 7, 6 (translation mine). The editors of Sōseki's collected works chose the page depicting this scene from the original manuscript as a frontispiece for the volume. Interestingly enough, one can see from the revisions in Soseki's hand that he was very carefully modulating the level of intimacy in this scene of male homosocial "skinship"—specifically by filtering Morimoto's actions through

Sōseki's novel *Kokoro* famously begins with a scene on the beach in which, as I discuss in Chapter 5, its narrator seems almost to be "cruising" the man whom he will come to know as Sensei.[16] Sōseki's *The Wayfarer* [*Kōjin*] also begins with the story of two male friends and shares the same basic structure of the other two novels, which taken together form his so-called late trilogy. That structure might be summarized as: first narrate male-male friendship, then move on to relations with women.[17] The same pattern emerges in Ōgai's *Vita Sexualis* and *The Youth*. In both cases, the male-male experiences are found toward the beginning of the novels and precede more serious and in-depth explorations of relations with women. As I discussed in Chapter 1, this association of male-male relations with superficial youth and with the past was all pervasive at this time and would have been reinforced for Ōgai by his recent reading of Freud's "Three Essays on Sexuality," in which "inversion" is associated with infantile sexuality, with the "primitive" and "archaic dispositions."

But what distinguishes *The Wild Goose* from these earlier novels (and brings it closer to Sōseki's) is that, while the topos of male-male love is implied in Okada's "ruddy cheeks" and the narrator's eroticized gaze, it is never spoken of directly. It is soon eclipsed, moreover, by the appearance of a beautiful woman named Otama, the kept mistress of a local moneylender. Otama's appearance immediately reconfigures what looked like a homoerotic connection between Okada and *boku* as a case of homosocial rivalry over a woman. This "conversion" of the homoerotic into the homosocial is, as noted earlier, a well-worn narrative trajectory in late Meiji fiction. I want to focus here, however, on the way in which, as the "romantic" story between Okada and Otama comes to occupy the story's explicit content, both the homosocial rivalry and the homoerotic connection between Okada and *boku* retreat to the level of discourse—into the act of telling it-

---

Keitarō's consciousness. For a slightly different English translation that largely misses these subtleties, see Natsume, *To the Spring Equinox and Beyond*, 11.

16. On the predominance of scenes like this in novels from this period—which often tend to happen in the "liminal" space of the seaside, see Sezaki, "Umibe no homososhiariti."

17. The first chapter of *The Wayfarer* is called "Friend" [*tomodachi*] and centers on the narrator's relationship to his friend Misawa, with whom he finds himself in a sort of love triangle. But, like all of the novels in the late trilogy, the "serious" portions come later, as the narrator's older brother is driven insane by his doubts of whether his wife loves him or not.

self. To put it more succinctly, the homosocial content is enacted by the narrative form.

A few more details about the plot are revealing. In *boku*'s telling, Otama is quite smitten with Okada and harbors a romantic fantasy that he might rescue her from her life as a moneylender's mistress, but Okada turns out to be wedded to the male romance of worldly "success and advancement" [*risshin shusse*] which renders him all but oblivious to Otama's longing glances. In the end he leaves to study in Germany before anything can happen between the two of them.[18] At the end of the novel, *boku*, for his part, reveals that he somehow got to know Otama after Okada's departure, but he denies ever having been involved with her romantically. In other words this is not only *not* a "gay" novel, it does not deliver on the straight marriage plot, either. In the place of both the male-male romance that hopeful gay readers and their friends might have wanted and the cross-class heterosexual romance that the narrator has primed the reader to anticipate, there is instead a vivid novelistic account of the gaping chasm that separated both the classes and the sexes in the early Meiji period. *The Wild Goose* is thus a novel that refuses, quite relentlessly, to satisfy the identifying reader's desire to see the characters get what they want. Desire here is quintessentially homosocial; it is always mediated through a third term and never fulfilled.

But *The Wild Goose* is not just a narrative about homosociality. It is also a narrative enactment of homosocial desire. *Boku* as narrator mediates his homosocial desire through the very telling of his tale, rendering the subjectivity of both Okada and Otama into objects of his own consciousness, all in the service of his homosocial rivalry with Okada. In this sense, *The Wild Goose* qualifies an exemplary homosocial narrative. It is also, of course, an exemplary novel insofar as it calls into question the very possibility of a discrete separation between subject and object, and between one mind and another. It does this, I argue, by employing a peculiar blend of first- and third-person narration that serves as a formal, *narrative* analogue of the state of the homosocial continuum circa 1911.

Otama Wakes Up

It may be useful here to discuss a brief example of the way that Otama's female subjectivity is mediated through *boku*'s male homosocial one. The

---

18. Masao Miyoshi made the fascinating observation that departure for study abroad often provided closure in Meiji novels the way marriage did in Victorian novels, a fact that speaks volumes about the dominance of male homosocial relations over the heterosexual couple at this time (*Accomplices of Silence*, 53).

example has to do with the reference to Okada I mentioned earlier as a "red-cheeked beautiful boy." This expression actually occurs in a passage later in the novel when the narration has shifted from *boku*'s first-person perspective into a heterodiegetic mode. This shift is what makes it possible in the novel to know what is going on in the minds not just of *boku*, but of all sorts of characters, including Otama, from whose mind this description of Okada seems to emerge. The reference to Okada occurs in Chapter 16, when the narrative uses free-indirect discourse to depict Otama's thoughts as she picks Okada out of a stream of students she is in the habit of observing as they pass by the house where she is being kept as the mistress of Suezō the moneylender. Not long before the moment when she sees Okada, the narration catalogues the different "types" of students passing by in a way that is strikingly reminiscent of the typology discussed earlier from Ōgai's *Vita Sexualis*: "Those with pale, delicately molded features failed to elicit a positive response because of their shallow, conceited manner. Others appeared to be too rough to appeal to a woman's eye, though some among these were perhaps excellent scholars. Whatever the type, Otama, without really meaning to, would each day watch them pass by her window."[19]

The students with "pale, delicately molded features" sound a lot like the womanizing *nanpa* described in *Vita Sexualis*, and Otama is perhaps well advised to stay away from them given their playboy-like character and their "vanity." The other "rough" ones sound like the boy-loving *kōha*—obviously not right for a woman, though perhaps excellent scholars. This distinction evokes William Sibley's characterization of the *kōha*, who were known not only for their hypermasculinity mentioned earlier, but also for their "interest in Chinese classics and German philosophy alike."[20] Otama's view of these students, then, resonates quite strongly with the typology described in *Vita Sexualis*. At the same time, however, she is very different from the narrator of that work. Although still very much caught within the patriarchal "traffic in women," she is also a budding modern woman for whom none of these men are viable partners. Our narrator, for his part, thanks to his dual insight into Meiji student culture *and* into Otama's mind, knows this as well. As Otama watches the students, the reader senses not just her perspective, as a woman, on this culture of male students, but also the narrator's own. Thus whereas the earlier novel portrays this student culture from an exclusively male perspective, in *The Wild Goose* this depiction is mediated by a perspective that is simultaneously male *and* female. As such, it is "homosocial" in a very different way from Ōgai's narrator in *Vita Sexualis*.

---

19. Mori, *The Wild Goose*, 98; *Ōgai zenshū*, vol. 8, 555.
20. Sibley, review of Reichert, *In the Company of Men*, 328.

As it happens, this is a crucial scene in the book. Right after this description of Otama mindlessly observing the students in all their typecast predictability, the passage continues: "And then one day she became aware of something that startled her, something that seemed to have sprouted in her mind. Engendered in the realm below the threshold of consciousness, it suddenly burst upon her in the form of crowded imaginings that filled her with alarm."[21]

This awareness is nothing less than the emergence of Otama as a subject endowed with consciousness and interiority, a sort of female version of the moment when Kanai was sundered into subjectivity in *Vita Sexualis*. In the paragraphs that follow, the narration describes how Otama has been transformed from a passive "commodity" traded between men (having been essentially sold by her father to the moneylender Suezō) into a "split subject" capable of strategically pleasing both Suezō and her father on the outside while keeping her "true self" on the inside: "From then on she began quietly scrutinizing her own words and actions. When Suezō came, she no longer met him with her former unreserve, but set about consciously to welcome and entertain him, putting to one side for the moment her true self. And this self laughed in ridicule at both Suezō and his plaything, Otama."[22]

This awakening to subjectivity on the part of a female character is unprecedented in Ōgai's work and largely unheard of in male writers at the time. It is reminiscent in some ways of the work of Higuchi Ichiyō (1872–1896), of whom Ōgai had been a great supporter during her short life.[23] It may also have something to do with timing, in that the publication of *The Wild Goose* coincided almost exactly with the birth of modern feminism in Japan. Ōgai's work began serialization in September 1911, the very same month in which the first issue of Japan's earliest feminist journal *Seitō* [The Blue Stockings], founded by Hiratsuka Raichō (1886–1971) and others, was published, which no doubt spurred Ōgai's awareness of issues of female autonomy and subjectivity. Henrik Ibsen's *A Doll's House*, which depicts a similar awakening to Otama's, was staged for the first time in Japan on September 22 at Tokyo's Bungei kyōkai, and Ōgai would produce his own translation of Ibsen's play two years later.[24]

---

21. Mori, *The Wild Goose*, 98; *Ōgai zenshū*, vol. 8, 555–56.

22. Ibid., 98; *Ōgai zenshū*, vol. 8, 556.

23. For an excellent discussion of the emergence of female subjectivity in Ichiyō's novella "Child's Play" ["Takekurabe"], see "Subjection in the Yoshiwara" in Van Compernolle, *The Uses of Memory*, 139–80.

24. On the historical context of *The Wild Goose* in relation to feminism, see Hattori, "*Gan* seiritsu no shakai-teki sokumen ni kansuru ichi kōsatsu."

However, if Nora's awakening involved leaving her husband and family behind, Otama's is about trading one man for another. Otama's sudden onset of subjectivity occurs when she sees Okada for the first time and invests him with all of her newly awakened hopes for a better future. If she has awakened as a new kind of woman, this is entirely dependent on her perception of him as a new kind of man—one who precisely does not fit into the *kōha/nanpa* typology. This is the way she describes him, at a moment in which the text suggests runs parallel to the earlier moment when "something sprouted in her mind":

> It was at this time that Otama got to know the face of Okada. At first he seemed to her like just another of the many students passing by her window. But then she noticed that despite his imposing features as a red-cheeked beautiful boy [*kōgan no bishōnen*], he did not seem vain or affected and she began to think of him as a person of very appealing character. After that, whenever she looked out the window, she found herself waiting and wondering when that boy would pass by.[25]

In this account, Okada seems paradoxically to combine the good looks of the *nanpa* playboy with the studious respectability of the *kōha*. In this way, in Otama's fantasy, Okada is not a "type" of man at all—but a modern (heterosexual) individual—one who might be capable of actually seeing and appreciating the true self that she has just discovered in freeing her mind, if not yet her body, from the constraints of the patriarchal system. In the space of this brief paragraph, Otama has been transformed from a woman who watches the parade of students "without really meaning to" into one who actively desires one of them, in whom she sees the reflection of her true self.

And yet, even as all of these things occur in Otama's mind—in narratological terms it is "focalized" through Otama—the words themselves are always still coming from *boku*. The word "imposing" [*kiwadatte rippa na*], for example, is exactly the same word *boku* used to describe Okada's good looks. An even more striking echo of *boku*'s earlier discourse is the use of the term "red-cheeked beautiful boy," which has, as previously mentioned, strong associations with the *nanshoku* tradition. As such, it appears not to "belong" to Otama's female perspective alone, but also to be reflecting a male perspective—perhaps the narrator's evaluation of Okada.[26] Given that the narrator, although not explicitly present, does claim authorship of the entire text at the end of the novel, whose mind, exactly, is represented here?

---

25. Mori, *Gan*, in *Ōgai zenshū*, vol. 8, 557 (translation mine).

26. Of course, the term can also be hers—which might make Otama Japan's very earliest *yaoi* aficionado! For a definition of *yaoi*, see page 116, note 89

More importantly: whose desire is this? If this passage suggests the awakening in Otama's mind of a sort of feminist consciousness, moreover, how does that relate to the male narrator and to the passing into oblivion of the *nanshoku* tradition?

Many Voices, One Mouth: Narrator or Character?

I will come back to the question of Otama's subjectivity in the following chapter, but first I want to think a little more about the slippery quality of *boku*'s narration and what it has to do with his desire for and homosocial rivalry with Okada. This tension between desire and rivalry may help to account for one of the most puzzling aspects of the narration in *The Wild Goose*: the inability of *boku* to decide whether he is a first-person character or a third-person narrator. In the opening scene, *boku* describes himself in the world of the story together with Okada, but just a few pages into the novel, *boku* disappears and the narration begins to free itself of the limits of first-person perspective to move unimpeded across time and space, and into the *minds* of Okada, Otama, her elderly father, the duplicitous moneylender Suezō, and even Suezō's unfortunate wife Otsune. But in Chapter 18, *boku* suddenly returns as a character and towards the end of the novel he explicitly claims authorship of the entire text,[27] which raises the question not only of how he has come to know all that he knows but what this knowledge says about him as a character. In the final chapter, he offers the following explanation for the first question:

> Half of the story derives from the period when I was on close terms with Okada. The other half comes from a time long after Okada's departure, when quite by chance I became acquainted with Otama and heard her description of what occurred. Just as two images combine in a stereoscope to form a single picture, so the events I observed earlier and those that were described to me later have been fitted together to make this story of mine.[28]

According to this explanation, then, it must have been Otama herself who told the narrator enough of her own life and the people in it for him to reconstruct the thoughts of Suezō, Otsune, and her father, not to mention Otama's maid Ume and the various gossipy housewives who feature in the text. As many critics have noted, however, this rather strains credulity

---

27. In the last chapter, he refers explicitly to the novel as "his" story, first when he notes that "this was not the end of the affair, but the rest of the happenings lie outside the scope of *my* story of *The Wild Goose*" (Mori, *The Wild Goose*, 165; *Ōgai zenshū*, vol. 8, 603); emphasis mine.

28. Ibid., 166; *Ōgai zenshū*, vol. 8, 603.

given that not even Otama could possibly have known all of these things. Thus despite his claim to have woven his story together from these two human sources, it would appear that *boku* is exercising the transcendent powers of a heterodiegetic narrator. But how can the reader understand that he makes this claim regardless of its implausibility? What does it mean that he seems to want to explain away his omniscience? Is he a narrator or a character?

Critics have struggled for years to explain this peculiarity in the narrative of *The Wild Goose*. For those in the "modernizationist" camp, who saw the Japanese novel in terms of a more or less successful importation and adaptation of techniques developed in the West, the answer was simply that Ōgai lacked the technical skill to create the kind of consistent narrative point of view (supposedly) required by a modern novel. Here, for example, is Masao Miyoshi's description of the problem:

> The narrative structure of *The Wild Goose* is a bit awkward, a frequent problem with Japanese novels. The narrator, Okada's friend, begins by reminiscing on past events, but soon disappears from the tale, almost making it a third-person story. He returns in Chapter 18 when it becomes increasingly clumsy to present events which the narrator cannot have been in a position to know.[29]

Not only is Ōgai's technique "awkward" and "clumsy," then, but Miyoshi claims that this is a problem shared by other Japanese novelists as well. As Atsuko Sakaki points out, modernizationist critics like the "early" Miyoshi took this "inconsistency" of narrative viewpoint in *The Wild Goose* as evidence "that Ōgai's fiction—if not the whole of modern Japanese fiction of that period—is structurally deficient and underdeveloped."[30]

More recent critics, including Sakaki, have given Ōgai more credit. They note that he was perfectly capable of writing from a consistent narrative viewpoint—it was he, after all, who produced the very first piece of Japanese fiction with a consistent first-person perspective, already two decades earlier in his debut novella "The Dancing Girl" ["Maihime"]—but that he chose not to in *The Wild Goose* because he wanted to experiment with and foreground the ways in which the choice of narrative perspective and voice

---

29. Miyoshi, *Accomplices of Silence*, 48.

30. Sakaki, "Thinking Beauty, Unseeing Scholar," 140. I say the early Miyoshi here because in his later work Miyoshi became one of the most eloquent critics of modernizationist theory, especially in his work *Off Center*.

affects the story being told.[31] As Dennis Washburn writes, "The ambivalent quality of the narrative voice in *The Wild Goose* represents a crucial step in the development of Ōgai's concept of fiction: it makes central the difficulties created by the influence the narrative voice—even a detached, supposedly objective voice—asserts on the story."[32] Stephen Snyder has linked this problem to the question of sexuality, noting that what appears to be an uncertainty as to how to deal with the question of the narrator's involvement in the story world is at the same time an "uncertainty about how to deal with (that is, in this case, how to write) his own sexual desire."[33] Sakaki has argued further that the shift from first to third person should be read in terms of the homosocial rivalry between the narrator and Okada over Otama. If he confines himself to the role of bystander rather than rival in the potential love affair between Okada and Otama, *boku* is still able to triumph over Okada not only by reporting the fact that he and Otama never get together, but by demonstrating that, as omniscient narrator, he knows Otama better than Okada ever did or could.[34]

Sakaki is certainly right to say that Okada and *boku* are involved in a homosocial rivalry. But whereas Sakaki claims that *The Wild Goose* "actively suggests rivalry and even betrayal between the two central male characters,"[35] I read the rivalry as, if not entirely disavowed, at least disguised and displaced for much of the text. Not only does the narrator of *The Wild Goose* avoid open competition with Okada for Otama, the rivalry between the two men has been transmuted and absorbed within the very form of the narrative itself. As Sakaki herself suggests, the narrator's victory in discourse is only possible thanks to his withdrawal from the diegesis. Thus the homosocial rivalry in *The Wild Goose* has been sublimated into, or become embodied by, the narrative form. While in earlier texts such as Ōgai's *The Youth*

---

31. For a superb reading of "The Dancing Girl" that situates its narrative technique in the larger study of modern subjectivity, see Yoda, "First-Person Narration and Citizen-Subject."

32. Washburn, *The Dilemma of the Modern in Japanese Fiction*, 189.

33. Snyder writes, "Ōgai has drawn a subtle comparison between the sexual ambivalence of the narrator (and hero) and the rhetorical one with which he has structured his text" (*Fictions of Desire*, 30, 32).

34. Sakaki writes: "At the expense of his autonomy as a character, *boku* gains the authority with which he controls the narrative" ("Thinking Beauty, Unseeing Scholar," 157).

35. In a wonderful turn of phrase in the same passage, Sakaki argues that *The Wild Goose* has a "sarcastic view of male homosociality" (ibid, 142), particularly in comparison to a work like Sōseki's *Kokoro*, which, as I discuss in Chapters 4 and 5, treats it with a sort of elegiac reverence.

or even "The Dancing Girl" the homosocial bond was a theme—something one could talk or write *about*—in *The Wild Goose* it has become part of the *way* in which one talks. It has migrated from content to form. In this kind of "formal" homosociality, which bears similarities to what I discussed as "internally mediated" desire in Chapter 1, male rivalry tends to be less apparent. In internally mediated homosocial narratives, moreover, while the narrative's interest in women may appear more genuine or "spontaneous," it is all the more insidiously the product of triangular desire between men.

In *The Wild Goose*, the first-person narrative flirts with male homoerotic desire while the third-person narrative provides a powerful glimpse of female subjectivity. By weaving these two components together into the stereoscopic vision of the novel as a whole, the narrator enacts a new and powerful kind of homosocial subjectivity. In order to understand how exactly this homosocial subjectivity is enacted by the narrative strategy of *The Wild Goose*, it helps to recall that, unlike the "gay" or "straight" readings that I caricatured at the beginning of this chapter, both of which rely on the assumption of an underlying sexual desire (be it homo or hetero) that is somehow "inside" the characters, sexuality as it is expressed in literary texts is better thought of as a product of certain narrative strategies. For that matter, sexuality is not necessarily locatable "in" the readers either, despite what my earlier caricatures of the gay and heteronormative readers might have suggested. Although a "gay identity" or a "homophobic disposition" might indeed influence the way a reader reads a text, the text itself is also part of the equation and can enact a sexuality in the experience of reading that may have little to do with the reader's actual sexuality—whatever that might be.

One way of thinking about this is to consider that the tendency, or ability, of readers to overlook what might (given all of the evidence I discussed earlier) seem obvious signs of homosexual desire in the opening chapter of *The Wild Goose* can be understood not just as a sign of the reader's obstinate heteronormativity or homophobia, but also in narratological terms. On the most basic level, it may reflect an unspoken assumption that narrators who speak with authority are heterosexual and male. Of course one could certainly argue that this assumption is itself heteronormative, misogynistic, and perhaps even homophobic. But what if the reader approaches the naturalization of the narrator's interest in Okada as a *structural artefact* of his role as narrator? In other words, to the extent that it is possible to think of the narrator as a narrator rather than as a character, the reader may be willing to bracket the question of whether he might be attracted to Okada. Bracketing, in this sense, is not necessarily the same thing as "repressing" or "disavowing."

By "naturalization" I mean that process by which readers suspend their skepticism about a narrator's statements that seem implausible or awkward (that is, unnatural) because the information they gain in doing so is either necessary for their understanding, or provides a sufficient bonus of pleasure to their enjoyment of the narrative. A simple example of this phenomenon in a different context is the way readers tend to accept what James Phelan, in his study of character narrators, calls "redundant telling"—the common phenomenon whereby a narrator tells a narratee in the world of the story something he or she already knows because it is necessary for the *reader* to know it. Redundant telling happens especially often with character narrators because, being both characters and narrators, they are charged with what Phelan calls "disclosure functions" and "narrator functions," where the former "refer to communication along the track from the narrator to the authorial audience" and the latter to "communication along the track from narrator to narratee [within the story world]." In Robert Browning's poem, "My Last Duchess," the line "The Count *your master's* known munificence" contains a succinct example. As Phelan explains, "The Duke knows that the envoy knows that the Count is his master, and so this reminder seems uncharacteristically gratuitous in the Duke's carefully calculated speech."[36] It is not the envoy but the reader (the "authorial audience") who needs to be informed of this fact. So even if it is a little unnatural for the envoy to say it to the Duke, the reader is willing to overlook the awkwardness of the statement, and the slight contradiction it presents in terms of the Duke's characterization (as a man of careful calculation), in exchange for the information it provides.[37]

Significantly, Meiji novels are rife with redundant telling much more flagrant than this example, which may reflect the fact that the proper, or default understanding of the relationship between narrator functions and disclosure functions was far from settled at the time. One of many examples of this would be the long speeches in Kōda Rohan's "Five-Storied Pagoda" (1891) in which characters seem to be either addressing a narratee in dialogue (and therefore engaging on a subjective level with others) or talking

---

36. Phelan, *Living to Tell about It*, 2.

37. Phelan notes that many readers have objected to him that the phrase "your master" here is not in fact redundant, but explicable "naturalistically" in terms of the Duke's characterization: the Duke mentions the envoy's status not in order to inform the reader about it but in order to remind the envoy of his subordinate position and thus assert his own power. While this may also be true, Phelan reads the objection itself as evidence of the power of readers' desire to "preserve the mimetic component of the story by finding a plausible, naturalistic rationale for the narration" (ibid., 25).

to themselves (and therefore in possession of a precocious sort of interiority) but are actually simply telling the *readers* what they need to know.[38] This can also seem quite "awkward" and "clumsy" to readers today.

If in redundant telling the reader is willing to sacrifice mimeticism in exchange for information, however, late Meiji readers of *The Wild Goose* may similarly have assumed that the narrator mentions Okada's good looks not because *boku* as a character is himself attracted to Okada but because it is information necessary to their understanding and/or enjoyment of the story. Of course this is made significantly easier in a heteronormative context where it can be assumed *a priori* that Okada's good looks are not relevant to *boku's* desire as a character. The more heteronormative the context, in other words, the more likely it is that we will read *boku's* observation of Okada's good looks as an exercise of the disclosure function, that is, a communication of information to the reader in his role as narrator. In this sense, the heteronormative context itself might be said not only to "promote" *boku* to the status of narrator rather than character but also to mandate a stricter distinction between the two.

In less heteronormative contexts, however, there is not as much need to distinguish these two roles in such explicit fashion, at least when the character narrator is male and the topic is beautiful boys. In Kōda Rohan's "The Bearded Samurai" ["Hige otoko"] (1896), for example, the protagonist Dairoku has a long monologue of redundant telling in which he serves both as narrator and character in describing the young Kōtarō, a boy whose life he spared on the battlefield upon beholding his beautiful face, which, "flushed and moist from excitement, was as pure and fair as a glistening white jewel. His tightly pulled petals of lips were flaming red, his soft eyebrows blue-black, and his rage-widened eyes shimmering with gentle dew. A beautiful young boy, too delicate to be handled by rough hands."[39] Thanks to the fact that this story was written slightly earlier than *The Wild Goose* and set in the sixteenth century, when the homosocial continuum was as intact as it ever would be, there is nothing awkward about the ambiguity here between the first and the third person: the text proceeds on the assumption that *anyone* would have found Kōtarō beautiful and sexually attractive.[40]

---

38. See especially the opening monologue by Okichi (Kōda, *Pagoda, Skull, and Samurai*, 22–23).

39. Ibid, 243. For the Japanese text, see Kōda, *Hige otoko*, 380–81.

40. As Jim Reichert has discussed, this scene is also strongly mediated by an even more distant past, namely the famous moment in the *Tales of the Heike* when Kumagai kills the beautiful Atsumori on the battlefield, "which became a source for numerous *nanshoku* texts." By evoking such a well known and prestigious moment from the past,

In *The Wild Goose*, however, such ambiguity has become more problematic. To the extent that the reader assumes that Okada's good looks are important to *boku* as narrator rather than to *boku* as a character they must portend the arrival of someone within the story world to whom they *will* be relevant. In a heteronormative context, that would have to be a woman. Thus the reader skilled in heteronormative reading would assume that Chapter 1, with its male-male focus, can only be preparatory and that a female love interest must be waiting somewhere in the wings.[41] If, by contrast, Okada's good looks are considered important to *boku* as a character, this would suggest that a "gay" romance was indeed in the offing.

While an identity-based "gay" reading might anticipate (in this case in vain) that the narrator would play a major role in the narrative as a result of his attraction to Okada, *boku*'s transformation into a narrator and designation of Okada (somewhat reluctantly) as "the hero of this story" makes readers anticipate a heterosexual romance.[42] In this context, readers will be prepared to look *through* the narrator to the main attraction—the heterosexual coupling that the text seems to promise for the future, or rather that heteronormative reading makes it appear to promise.

In the case of *The Wild Goose*, however, *boku is still both a character and a narrator*. As I have shown, the novel switches from first-person "homodiegetic" narration, in which *boku* exists in the story world, to third-person "heterodiegetic" narration, in which *boku* disappears and the focus zeroes in on the heterosexual romance, and then back again at the end. This oscillation between the homo and the hetero, I contend, far from being a sign of Ōgai's technical ineptitude, is both a brilliant formal enactment of the novel's resistance to *any* notion of identity-based desire and an index of the state of the homosocial continuum at the time he was writing.

It is not just the ambiguity surrounding the status of *boku* as narrator or character, but also the question of whether he is a minor or a major character upon which a reader's interpretation will turn. Phelan points out that readers are more tolerant of disclosure functions "usurping" narrator functions when the narrator is not the protagonist. One example cited by Phelan

---

the scene is elevated and Kōtarō imbued with an "aura of tragic beauty" (*In the Company of Men*, 153).

41. I emphasize that a reader skilled in "heteronormative reading" is not necessarily the same thing as a heteronormative or homophobic reader.

42. At the beginning of Chapter 4, *boku* refers to the narrative as, "This story of which I must make Okada the hero" [*Okada o shujinkō ni shinakute wa naranu kono monogatari*]. Watson elides this and translates it as, "my story, which centers on Okada" (Mori, *The Wild Goose*, 16; *Ōgai zenshū*, vol. 8, 499).

is the reader's willingness to accept the character narrator Nick Carraway's promotion to omniscience in Fitzgerald's *The Great Gatsby* when he narrates the scene in Michaelis's garage after Myrtle Wilson is run down. Because Gatsby, not Nick, is the focus of interest, the reader is willing to overlook the contradiction posed by the fact that Nick cannot possibly know what happened since he was not present at the scene. The reader's desire for more information relevant to Gatsby trumps the concern for mimeticism. In a similar way, *boku*'s ostensibly minor status in "the story called *The Wild Goose*" helps make it possible to read *boku*'s description of Okada's precise route on his walks, for example, without asking too many questions about how he obtained this information and without inferring that his possession of this information says something about him (again—that he is in love with or has been stalking Okada).

Of course, this is further aided by the minoritization of male-male sexuality in a heteronormative context. In contexts (such as premodern Japan) where male-male sexuality is universalized, any man's comment about another man's good looks will necessarily be open to interpretation as an expression of desire, as was the case in "The Bearded Samurai." Where it is minoritized, on the other hand, such a comment is usually interpreted as referring to someone else's (i.e., a woman's) desire, hence marking the speaker as a narrator. It would only be "relevant" to the speaker in exceptional and clearly marked contexts (namely, in "gay literature"). The fact that *The Wild Goose* was written precisely at the moment when male-male sexuality was in the process of being minoritized in Japan may have something to do with the text's indecision as to whether *boku* is a character or a narrator, and if he is a character, whether his role is a minor or a major one. Thus the changing shape of the homosocial continuum itself helps explain the shift in *The Wild Goose* from first to third person and back again. At the same time, *boku*'s ability to accommodate both perspectives marks him as the subject of a form of homosociality that was new to the modern Japanese novel.

THREE

The Uncut Gem:
Stereoscopic Homosociality in The Wild Goose

What, then, is *The Wild Goose* about? Can the reader ever be certain that *boku* is just the person who presents this story and that his role as a character is a minor one? What if, despite his relative marginalization in the diegesis itself and his disappearance in the novel's middle sections, the reader does take *boku* as *both* narrator and character and interpret the novel as being not primarily about the romance that never happened between Okada and Otama, but all about *boku*? What if this novel were in fact primarily about the development that *boku* has undergone in the three-plus decades that have elapsed since the time when the story took place? This would include his disillusionment with romance in both its male and female versions, his development of the capacity to look beyond class and gender to appreciate and learn about the lives of people like Otama, and his newly acquired understanding and facility with the techniques of the modern novel that make it possible to tell stories like this one. It would also, of course, be the story of his modernizing transition from a homosocial to what might be called a heterosocial way of being in the world.

To read the novel this way is to see it as a variant of a genre that Kenneth Bruffee has defined as the "elegiac romance." As Bruffee describes it, the elegiac romance typically features a male first-person narrator who tells the story of another man whom he admires very much but who has since died.[1]

---

1. *The Wild Goose* includes two clues that suggest that Okada has died since the time of the story, aside from the simple fact that the narrator says nothing about any further developments in their relationship after Okada leaves for Germany. First is *boku*'s com-

Although the narrative appears on the surface to be primarily about this "hero," however, the reader realizes eventually that the true protagonist of the tale is the narrator, who by telling the story of his hero has reached a new level of emotional maturity and freed himself of what Bruffee calls "the dependent state of hero worship." The novel that Bruffee claims illustrates "most simply and clearly" the dynamics of elegiac romance is, interestingly enough, Fitzgerald's *The Great Gatsby*—the same novel that Phelan used to discuss the function of the character narrator as discussed in the previous chapter and also a novel that displays an inconsistency between homo- and heterodiegetic narration not unlike that in *The Wild Goose*.[2] Read as elegiac romance, the focus of *The Great Gatsby* shifts away from Gatsby to Nick, and the reader sees that by the end of the novel, "Nick reveals implicitly a new understanding of himself and his world through a heightened awareness of his earlier identification with Gatsby, through a 'certain shame' he feels for Gatsby, and through a more accepting view of past and present."[3]

According to Bruffee, then, Nick is not a minor character at all. *The Great Gatsby* is actually Nick's story, although in somewhat disguised form. But if, as I also discussed in the last chapter, the reader was able to ignore the inconsistency presented by Nick's sudden omniscience in the scene in Michaelis's garage, Bruffee's thesis would suggest that this was possible only through *misreading* the novel—by seeing Gatsby rather than Nick as its protagonist. Obviously Phelan and Bruffee are writing in very different contexts. One is talking in the abstract about how narrative conventions work and the other is offering a psychoanalytic reading of an entire literary genre.

But something quite fascinating emerges when juxtaposing Phelan and Bruffee in this way that is also relevant to my reading of *The Wild Goose*. In both novels, the unnatural aspect of the narration (the narrator's sudden and unexplained accession to omniscience) is repressed or ignored thanks to the filter of a romantic view of literature that privileges the more heroic-

---

parison of him (in his good looks) to the actor Kawakami Bizan mentioned earlier, which he follows with the pointed observation that Bizan tragically committed suicide. Second is his assertion at the end of the novel that the coincidence that mackerel and miso soup was served at his boarding house the night before Okada's departure for Germany (which led to the narrator being with Okada on his walk when Otama had hoped he would be alone) "kept Okada and Otama apart *for all time.*" Mori, *The Wild Goose*, 4, 165; *Ōgai zenshū*, vol. 8, 602 (emphasis mine).

2. Bruffee, *Elegiac Romance*, 136.
3. Ibid., 141.

seeming figure as the protagonist (with a corresponding de-emphasis on the narrator's role as character). But heeding the lesson of the elegiac romance, which Bruffee also describes as breaking out of "arrested development," yields an understanding that the narrator is in fact the true protagonist, which will in turn bring the narrative's unnaturalness back into view. Faced again not only with this unnatural narrative technique but also with what can only be called the "queerness" of the male homodiegetic narrator's almost homoerotic obsession with the male protagonist, the elegiac romance proposes not to repress these again but to *narrate* them as developmental stages that have since been outgrown. If, in the romantic reading, the naturalization of an otherwise "awkward" and "underdeveloped" narrative strategy depended on sustaining not only the belief in the hero but also the ability to openly admire him (without appearing to desire him), the novelistic elegiac romance simply jettisons these narrative foibles and homoerotic hero-worship into the past. As a result, in the place of heroes openly admired,[4] all that remain are "a certain shame" and "a more accepting view of past and present."

As the term "elegiac romance" suggests, the genre Bruffee describes is a descendant of the romance. But insofar as the genre's purpose has to do with "an effort to dispense with heroes and heroism entirely" as "an atavism representing adherence to outworn values and archaic modes of thought," it is very much a form of the modern realist novel as well.[5] In *The Wild Goose*, the narrator uses precisely this tension between romance and realist novel as means of triumphing (again in the narrative discourse) over Okada, his homosocial rival.

Okada *the* Romancier *and* Boku *the* Novelist

Before entering into this discussion of romance and the realist novel in *The Wild Goose*, let me make clear how I am using these terms. For "romance," I will use the definition offered by the *Routledge Encyclopedia of Narrative Theory*: "a narrative with an episodic plot structured by the protagonist's quest for love and honor within an idealised, imaginative, often mythical setting."[6] The romance tends to be either nostalgic or utopian and thus to focus on the past or the future. It also has a quasi-revolutionary element, in that it can imagine the sudden transformation of current social conditions such as

---

4. This, of course, is related to the notion of the "external mediation" of desire by Don Quixote, as discussed in the Introduction.

5. Bruffee, *Elegiac Romance*, 55.

6. *Routledge Encyclopedia of Narrative Theory*, 506.

the class order. The realist novel, as I will use the term here, deals primarily with contemporary reality and has a depoliticizing tendency that combines acceptance or aestheticization of the everyday with the naturalization of doctrines of progress and development.[7]

Although the lower-class urban setting of *The Wild Goose* is more typical of the realist novel than the romance, the fact that this setting is described from the perspective of the narrator's late Meiji/early Taishō moment also gives it an idealized and nostalgic quality that tends toward romance. The middle sections (Chapters 4–17), in which a heterodiegetic narrator focuses on Otama and her world, are marked both by a novelistic realism suffused with a sense of resignation to a forbiddingly intransigent gender hierarchy and by the romance of (potential) class mobility. The latter is manifested in fantasy as Otama's desire for Okada (whom she imagines might "rescue" her) and in reality by the affordances of early finance capitalism, as exemplified by the meteoric rise of Suezō from errand boy to wealthy moneylender. The two male characters, moreover, seem to belong in different genres. Okada, as a member of the male elite, seems destined to participate in Japan's quest for modernity and thereby embodies a romantic role, but the older narrator's seeming disillusionment with romance and attunement to (female) subjective experience mark him as a figure who better belongs in a realist novel. I should clarify here that from here on I reserve the term "the narrator" for the voice of the older man who looks back from 1911–1913 at his youth and use *boku* to refer to the person he was in 1880—when he was just as much of a romantic as Okada.

This generic hybridity is an important way in which *The Wild Goose* is a two-timing text. The tension between novel and romance is to be found throughout the novel and on various levels, sometimes even that of the sentence or paragraph. Elements of romance are typically parodied or put in scare quotes by the text's novelistic elements. This scare-quote treatment is part of what pushes *The Wild Goose* as a whole further into the novel column and what ensures not only that the novelistic aspects of *The Wild Goose* will dominate in the end, but that the narrator will triumph over Okada as well. As novels since *Don Quixote* have demonstrated, the novel is capable of subsuming the romance within it—and indeed is largely defined by its ability to do so—but the reverse is not the case.

---

7. On the revolutionary aspect of romance, see Jameson, "Magical Narratives"; on the depoliticizing tendencies of the realist novel in the Japanese context, see Ueda, "The Production of Literature and the Effaced Realm of the Political."

Perhaps the most blatant example of *The Wild Goose*'s novelistic containment and parodying of the romantic is the scene where Okada and Otama first speak. Okada is in the habit of taking daily walks around his neighborhood in a way that suggests a parody of the "episodic quest" convention of romance. One day, as he has "sallied forth" on one of these walks, he notices a great commotion in front of Otama's house. Suezō has purchased a pair of linnets for her that she has hung in a cage in her window and a snake has forced its way between the bars. The snake is in the process of devouring one of the birds while the other flaps about in terror on the other side of the cage. Okada "heroically" kills the snake and rescues the remaining bird, to the delight of Otama and a crowd of admiring girls from the sewing school next door to Otama's house. Otama, as a sort of caged bird herself, becomes convinced that Okada has rescued the bird out of love for her. The scene, which evokes St. George and the dragon in miniature, is clearly a parody of romantic conventions. When Okada relates the story to the narrator, he jokingly characterizes it as such in the final lines of Chapter 18.

> "I slew the serpent." Okada turned to face me.
> "And rescued the beautiful lady?"
> "No, I rescued a bird. But it had something to do with a beautiful lady."
> "Sounds interesting. Tell me about it."[8]

The following chapter is given over to "Okada's story," which the narrator retells second hand from Okada, thus endowing it with yet another feature of romance—the oral quality of the narrative itself.[9] The narrator is clearly fascinated by Okada's romantic story, but by framing it within his own (novelistic) narrative, he also manages to appropriate it as a kind of gloss on the kind of person Okada is—namely, someone who lives in a world of romance and is blind to everyday reality, particularly that of the "world of women." This is made clear not only in what the narrator actually says about Okada, but also, and more importantly, in the contrast he sets up between himself as novelist and Okada as a romantic hero whom

---

8. Mori, *The Wild Goose*, 113; *Ōgai zenshū*, vol. 8, 566. I have slightly altered the translation. Watson has "I slew the dragon—I mean the snake," which suggests St. George rather too strongly, and downplays the possibility of another intertext, the story of Li Chi slaying of the *serpent* in Gan Bao's *In Search of the Supernatural* [*Soushenji*] from the fourth century CE. In this well-known Chinese story, the beautiful woman kills the serpent herself and no man is necessary. For the story, see Gan, *In Search of the Supernatural*, 230–31.

9. Chapter 19 begins with the line "This was Okada's story" [*Okada wa konna hanashi o shita*].

he once admired but has since outgrown, as in the elegiac romance. This is apparent already in Chapter 2, when the narrator gives the reader access to Okada's mind.

It is on one of his regular walks around the neighborhood that Okada first encounters Otama just as she has returned from the public bath and is about to enter the secluded house in which Suezō has installed her as his mistress. In subsequent days, he notices her peering at him from her window and wonders whether she has been waiting for him intentionally. Already in this chapter, the narrator starts to exceed the constraints of his first-person perspective by giving us Okada's thoughts as he begins "to feel quite friendly with the woman in the window" and to unconsciously raise his cap in greeting to her when he passes. The following passage is the novel's first description of Otama:

She was wearing a summer kimono of dark blue crepe tied with a sash of black satin and tea-colored facings, the slim fingers of her left hand languidly holding a finely woven bamboo basket containing a wash towel, a box of soap, a bag of rice-bran, and a sponge, and her right hand resting on the lattice door. The figure of the woman as she turned to look at him made no deep impression on Okada, but for a moment the details of her image lingered in his eyes—the hair freshly done up in gingko-leaf style, sidelocks thin as the wings of a cicada, the high-bridged nose, the rather melancholy face that seemed somehow from the forehead to the cheeks a little too flat. But it was no more than a momentary perception, and by the time he had descended to the foot of the slope he had completely forgotten her.[10]

The two modes of description employed in this paragraph represent the competing genres of novel and romance, and provide an early glimpse of the homosocial rivalry between the narrator and Okada that animates the entire narrative. Although the reader might expect first-person narrators to limit themselves to the description of things they have actually witnessed or heard, *boku* here provides a level of detail that would seem to exceed his ability to know, at least based on what the reader knows of his sources so far. The first sentence, which focuses closely on Otama's clothing and the mundane items she carries with her, shows an extraordinary, almost "feminine" sensitivity to detail (how many straight men notice "tea-colored facings"?).[11] Given that he claims in the very next sentence that Otama's

---

10. Mori, *The Wild Goose*, 11–12; *Ōgai zenshū*, vol. 8, 496–97. I have slightly modified Burton Watson's translation, chiefly because he leaves out the list of items in the basket and refers to them simply as "toilet articles." The narrator's careful observation of these mundane articles is, of course, crucial to my point.

11. On the feminization of detail in modern Chinese literature, see Chow, "Modernity and Narration." On a similar phenomenon in French, see Schor, *Reading in Detail*.

figure "made no deep impression" on Okada, these details must be coming from *boku* himself. Someone reading the novel for the second time would know that he met Otama later, so the reader might assume that he has gotten this information from her and combined it with what he heard from Okada to produce the stereoscopic vision he is providing. At this point, however, the source of this information is unclear and seems somehow to emanate from *boku*'s novelistic eye.

The novelistic details that *boku* presents have a prosaic quality that contrasts with the language used to describe Otama in the paragraph's third and fourth sentences. Here Okada apparently does pay some attention ("for a moment the details of her image lingered in his eye"), but what he sees is very different from *boku*'s preceding description. Okada's observations have to do exclusively with Otama's outward appearance and oscillate between Sinified poetic similes ("sidelocks thin as the wings of a cicada"),[12] and somewhat crude evaluations of her body (the too-flat face). Taken together, the two very different modes of description suggest that while the narrator, thanks to his connection with Otama, is possessed of an exquisite sensitivity to the everyday reality of her existence as well as the work it takes to produce herself as an object of the aesthetic and sexual attentions of men (hence his cataloguing of the toilet articles in her basket), Okada sees her as he sees all women—either as the beautiful, ethereal creatures he has read about in Chinese literature, or physical bodies to be evaluated according to shape. What the narrator seems to be saying by offering these contrasting descriptions, then, is that *he* has a more "realistic" view of Otama than Okada does. In literary terms, his attitude toward her is closer to that of a realist novelist and Okada's is typical of romance. Whereas the narrator's novelistic mode claims to be able to see women as they actually are, Okada's romantic vision can see only ideals (or their absence). As the two modes vie with each other in this passage, and in the text as a whole, the homosocial rivalry between the narrator and Okada is translated into a competition between literary genres and descriptive techniques.

---

12. Thanks to my colleague Catherine Yeh for verifying that this expression can be found in Chinese poetry. It appears, for example, in the tale "Scholar Liu Qiqing Drinks Wine and Composes Poetry on the Tower of the Xi River," in which the narrator describes the courtesan Zhou Yuexian using the following couplet: "Her cloud-like hair is lightly combed in the style of cicada wings / Her moth-like eyebrows are cleverly painted to resemble spring mountains" [雲鬢輕梳蟬翼，娥眉巧畫春山]. See Hong, ed., *Qingpingshan tang huaben*, 3. This modern edition is based on copies of the original Ming text that have survived only in Japan and are held in the National Diet Library.

If the narrator presents himself as a realist novelist and Okada as *romancier*, he does so not only to claim that he is better able to "see" Otama, but also to ally himself with the forces of modernization in literature. He does this by stressing the relatively antiquated state of Okada's literary taste and hinting at the greater sophistication that he knows will characterize the literature of the late Meiji period, once the Western novel has been introduced.

It was their shared love for a certain kind of literature, the narrator tells us, that brought him and Okada together in the first place, when *boku* outbid Okada on a copy of the late Ming novel *The Plum in the Golden Vase* [*Jin Ping Mei*] at a secondhand book store near their boarding house. *Boku* agrees to loan the book to Okada, and in the scene discussed earlier where Okada "slays the serpent," the reader learns that he had just been reading this text, which, he suggests, had transported him to a different world and primed him to interpret the scene in romantic terms. "I had just been reading that sort of book, you see," Okada explains, "and I must have had a pretty stupid expression on my face as I walked along."[13] In the following passage, *boku* characterizes his friend Okada's reading habits.

> Okada's visits to secondhand bookstores were prompted by what nowadays would be termed a "taste for literature." But at that time the new style novels and plays had yet to make their appearance. In the field of lyric poetry, the haiku of Masaoka Shiki and the waka of Yosano Tekkan were a thing of the future. People read literary magazines such as *Kagetsu shinshi*, printed on rice paper, or the white pages of *Keirin isshi*, and regarded the sensuous "fragrant trousseau" Chinese-style poems of Mori Kainan and Ue Mukō as the latest word. I remember because I myself was an avid reader of *Kagetsu shinshi*. That was the first magazine to carry a translation of a work of Western fiction. . . . That's the kind of era it was, so Okada's "taste for literature" meant little more than that he read with interest some event of the times that a scholar of Chinese studies had chosen to work up in literary style.[14]

This is one of many moments in the text where the narrator refers to the historical change that has rendered the world of 1880 almost like a foreign country from his perspective in 1911. The word "literature," as he notes here and as many recent scholars have also confirmed, had a completely different meaning in 1880 than it did in 1911.[15] A full discussion of the nature of this transformation is beyond the scope of this chapter, but there are a few developments that are especially relevant here. First is the rise of

---

13. Mori, *The Wild Goose*, 114; *Ōgai zenshū*, vol. 8, 566.
14. Ibid., 7–8; *Ōgai zenshū*, vol. 8, 494.
15. See, for example, Ueda, "The Production of Literature and the Effaced Realm of the Political." For an excellent discussion of a similar transformation in Korean, see Hwang, "The Emergence of Aesthetic Ideology in Modern Korean Literary Criticism."

the realistic modern novel and its ability to capture the vagaries of individual subjectivity, including the technique of first-person figural narration that I discussed in the Introduction and that is being employed in this very passage. Second is the rejection of Chinese models and the promotion of a native literary tradition comparable to that of the modern West. If "romance" in *The Wild Goose* is considered less evolved than the novel, this is partly because it is closely associated in the narrator's mind with Chinese literature. This rejection of Chinese literature as insufficiently modern colludes with the "de-Asianizing" work of critics like Tsubouchi Shōyō who wrote not long after the story of *The Wild Goose* takes place.[16]

Running through both of these components of literary modernization, moreover, is the assumption that the inability of Chinese and "traditional" literature to represent modern subjectivity had to do with the predominantly male homosocial context of its production and consumption. Thus the narrator implies that the idealized romances favored by Okada and his like could accommodate only superficial and "hopelessly romantic" portraits of women. In Chapter 3, the narrator describes Okada's view of women as "beautiful beings, loveable beings, who could be content in any setting whatever, and whose beauty and loveliness it was his duty to guard and protect."[17] This view, he points out, derived from Okada's absorption in the "sentimental" and "fatalistique" works of Ming and Qing literature such as the *Jin Ping Mei*. These two terms, incidentally, are in French in the Japanese text, reinforcing the sense that the narrator is evaluating (and devaluing) this tradition from a Euro- (and novel-)centric perspective.[18]

When the representation of women is not overly idealized in texts like the *Jin Ping Mei*, the narrator suggests, it is pornographic. As the narrator puts it, referring to this famous novel, "Chinese novels, this among them, as a rule run on for ten or twelve pages in a quite ordinary manner, and then, as though fulfilling a promise made to the reader, come up with a decidedly racy passage [*keshikaran koto ga kaite aru*]."[19] As I mentioned earlier, it is a volume of this text that provides the impetus for the narrator's friendship

---

16. See Ueda, "Colonial Ambivalence and the Modern *Shōsetsu*."

17. Mori, *The Wild Goose*, 14; *Ōgai zenshū*, vol. 8, 499.

18. I want to emphasize that these works are not necessarily as "romantic" or superficial as Okada and *boku* seem to think they are. As Atsuko Sakaki has pointed out, for example, Okada selectively interprets the story of the Chinese beauty Xiaoqing, leaving out "her poetic talent and her self-awareness." My point, however, is how the text codes this legend and Chinese literature in general as unmodern. Sakaki, "Thinking Beauty, Unseeing Scholar," 171.

19. Mori, *The Wild Goose*, 114; *Ōgai zenshū*, vol. 8, 566.

with Okada in the first place, when the narrator outbids him for a used copy.[20] This suggests that the narrator was just as smitten with "this sort of literature" as Okada, but he implies strongly that he has outgrown it in the interim.[21] If Okada, then, is characterized by his affection for a type of literature this is not only old fashioned, but also *Chinese* and romantic, the narrator presents himself, from his vantage point decades in the future, as cutting-edge, *Japanese*, and novelistic by comparison. The poets Masaoka Shiki and Yosano Tekkan that he mentions as *not having written yet* at this time were both known for their devotion to the national cause. And Shiki, through his association with Natsume Sōseki, would have an enormous impact on the development of the modern Japanese novel. I would argue, moreover, that running throughout all of these distinctions is a concomitant contrast between Okada's outmoded homosociality and the (older) narrator's modern heterosociality.

The Wild Goose, as discussed, contains elements of romance over which the novelistic elements ultimately dominate, making the novel a good example of the elegiac romance. But whereas Bruffee's analysis of that genre can be said to subscribe relatively unambiguously to a certain ideology of progress (speaking unselfconsciously as it does of "arrested development," and "loosening the grip of the past"), Ōgai's novel does not completely share either Bruffee's optimism about personal growth and historical progress or his disdain for "outworn values and archaic modes of thought." Ōgai's narrator *boku* may indeed be trying to tell such a story of progress. There is little doubt that *his* strategy is to "get over" his hero-worship of (or love for?) Okada and demonstrate how much further he has come in his development. But the novel itself clearly exposes these intentions to the reader's scrutiny. One way in which it does this is by having *boku* offer such an implausible explanation of his superhuman omniscience. However close he might have become with Otama after the fact, it is simply impossible for him to have known all of the things that the novel knows about Otama and her world. If he could not possibly have known all he claims to know about the past, that past must itself be at least partly the product of his imagination in the present. The slight gap this creates between what the novel seems to know and what the narrator could have known makes *The Wild Goose* a two-timing narrative and invites reflection on a meta level about

---

20. For a partial English translation of the novel, see the multivolume *The Plum in the Golden Vase*. Four out of the planned five volumes had been published as of 2012.

21. Ōgai's representation of *boku* and Okada's enthusiasm for Chinese literature has something of the pejorative quality some might stereotypically associate with adolescent male fans of *Dungeons and Dragons* or *World of Warcraft*.

the narrator's attempts to portray the history of the Meiji period as one of unambiguous and unidirectional progress.

It is worth mentioning here that the way Ōgai's narrator converts an ostensible concern for women's "reality" into the grist of a homosocial contest with other men was by no means limited to the prewar period. The narrator's critique of Okada's outmoded romantic vision of women, for example, was repeated in almost the same terms decades later in Masao Miyoshi's influential reading of the novel, although Miyoshi directed his critique at Ōgai himself: "Ōgai knew only a certain kind of relationship with the women in his life. He used to call his second wife (having divorced his first) his 'object [sic] d'art.' He seems to have been unable to engage himself at a close emotional level with women, and his relationships were all carried on as though from a distance."[22] Although this may well have been true of Ōgai, the fact that he not only created a character like Okada and critiqued him through the narrator of *The Wild Goose*, but also critiqued both Okada *and* the narrator by strongly implying that the latter's account was itself motivated by homosocial rivalry, suggests that he was at least self-aware on this count. The irony here is that while each man (Ōgai's narrator and Miyoshi) is so eager to distinguish himself from his counterpart based on his more enlightened treatment of women, the motivation for such assertions of greater understanding of women itself lies in the competition with other men. In the end, it seems, it really is all about the boys.

Third-Person Female

Despite this, however, the most striking difference between an earlier work of Ōgai's such as "The Dancing Girl" and *The Wild Goose* is how each portrays female subjectivity. In the former work, Ōta's beloved Elise is accorded no interiority and appears only as the passive recipient of his charity and subsequently as the victim of his heartlessness. Otama in *The Wild Goose*, by contrast, is a fully "rounded" and fascinating character in her own right. Indeed, the greatest interest of the novel for many readers has been its portrayal of Otama's awakening as a woman with her own desires. The famous scene in which Otama seems to masturbate to the thought of Okada ("surrendering herself to unbridled imaginings") is surely one of the earliest moments in modern Japanese literature in which female sexual desire is so openly recognized.[23] As I discussed earlier, the novel also details the process

---

22. Miyoshi, *Accomplices of Silence*, 49–50.
23. Mori, *The Wild Goose*, 137; *Ōgai zenshū*, vol. 8, 582. When the narration mentions what "the pedagogues say" about the dangers of masturbation in the same passage

by which Otama overcomes her childish naïveté and learns to dissimulate and to manipulate others in order to get what she wants.

At the same time, however, the text is suffused with the tragic sense that Otama will *never* get what she wants because of the immensely limiting constraints of her gender and her class position. If "The Dancing Girl" was about the process by which its elite male protagonist was disciplined into modern (male, homosocial) subjectivity, *The Wild Goose* tells a similar story, but transposed into the feminine register.[24] But whereas in "The Dancing Girl," the male subject encompassed both a "feminine" and a "masculine" self,[25] in *The Wild Goose* these two halves of the subject are projected onto female and masculine characters (namely Otama and Okada) while *boku* remains in a third position quite unlike that of Ōgai's earlier narrator. The two texts thus enact very different forms of homosociality: one that manages to exclude women entirely (by eliding Elise's interiority) while associating the split subject of modernity with masculinity alone; and another that *appropriates* the woman (Otama) as the exemplary modern subject with which a seemingly transcendent (or ambiguously positioned) masculine subject (the narrator) can covertly identify.[26]

It will be helpful here to return then to a discussion of how the text presents the process of Otama's subjective awakening. Raised under the protective guardianship of her adoring father as the "apple of his eye,"[27] Otama is at first in complete accord with her father. She and he are able to speak to each other without hiding anything, and when bad things happen (such as when Otama's first husband turns out to have a wife already) they

---

Stephen Snyder detects a "leering, almost voyeuristic quality (cloaked in moralization).'' But it seems to me that the tone is more sympathetic; I sense less moralizing than irony. See Snyder, *Fictions of Desire*, 29.

24. For this argument about "The Dancing Girl," see Hill, "Mori Ōgai's Resentful Narrator."

25. "I felt as unsure of myself as a young girl. . . . Before I left home I was convinced I was a man of talent. I believed deeply in my own powers of endurance. Yes, but even that was short-lived. I felt quite the hero until the ship left Yokohama, but then I found myself weeping uncontrollably. I thought it strange at the time, but it was my true nature showing through. Perhaps it had been with me from birth; or perhaps it came about because my father died and I was brought up by my mother" (Mori, *Youth and Other Stories*, 11).

26. My reading here is partly inspired by Nancy Armstrong's argument, made in the context of a discussion of the eighteenth-century rise of the British novel, that the modern individual is "first and foremost a woman" (*Desire and Domestic Fiction*, 4).

27. The narrative puns on Otama's name in this expression: *me no tama yori mo taisetsu ni shiteita*.

feel united against the world.[28] But not long after Otama moves into the house Suezō has rented for her, the local fishmonger's wife refuses to sell to her maid Ume, saying "We have no fish for a moneylender's mistress."[29] If the awakening of Otama's subjectivity was completed by her desire for Okada as discussed earlier, it was the shaming force of this incident that initiated the process. One reason to think through this issue of shame is that it is also the mechanism by which, according to the historicist logic of the elegiac romance, "heroes" get left behind. Just as Nick felt shame over his own attitude toward Gatsby, *boku*'s admiration for Okada presumably also succumbs to shame as he "outgrows" their friendship and the homosocial world it comes to signify. But while *boku*'s shame is kept hidden outside the narrative, Otama's is made into a spectacle that redounds to the narrator's benefit.

In her later work, Eve Sedgwick drew on the theories of the psychologist Silvan Tomkins to describe the power of shame in the constitution of the self. Tomkins theorized that by interrupting the circuit of identification with others, shame "floods" the subject with an excruciating awareness of her separateness and isolation. In thus delineating the boundaries between self and other, shame does the work of establishing identity. "By interrupting identification," Sedgwick writes, "shame, too, makes identity."[30] At the same time, however, the "contagiousness" of shame has the effect of *violating* the boundaries between self and other. When one witnesses someone else in an embarrassing or shameful situation, one can feel "flooded" by their shame, even experiencing sympathetically the same physiological effects (for example, blushing on their behalf). In this sense, shame has the power to make people exquisitely aware of both their isolation and their connectedness to others.

The moment when Otama learns from Ume that the fishmonger's wife has refused to sell them fish is a classic instance of this simultaneously individuating and collectivizing effect of shame. This is how the narrator describes it:

As Otama listened, her face turned pale and for some time she remained silent. The heart of the unworldly young woman was overcome by a chaos of emotions; even she herself could not have untangled their jumbled threads. A great weight pressed down

---

28. "In the past, when they had been deceived by the fraudulent police officer, they had been ashamed before the neighbors, but both of them had known in their hearts that the blame lay with him, and they had discussed the whole affair without the slightest reserve" (Mori, *The Wild Goose*, 66; *Ōgai zenshū*, vol. 8, 532).

29. Ibid., 54; *Ōgai zenshū*, vol. 8, 523.

30. Sedgwick, "Shame, Theatricality, Queer Performativity," 36.

on her heart and the blood from throughout her body rushed to it, leaving her white and cold with perspiration. Her first conscious thought, though surely of no real importance, was that after such an incident Ume would no longer be able to remain in this house.[31]

In the throes of an attack of shame, Otama becomes excruciatingly aware of her "self." As Tomkins writes, "In contrast to all other affects, shame is an experience of the self by the self." But despite that, her first conscious thought in this passage is, quite tellingly, about Ume. "Ume would no longer be able to remain in this house." Why should the thought of Ume's shame be the first conscious thought to come to Otama's mind in this situation? The narrative itself (ventriloquizing Otama?) suggests that this is "surely of no real importance" [*kakubetsu jūdai de nai koto*]. One could argue that Otama is simply afraid that Ume will abandon her. But the way the sentence is phrased suggests rather that she has placed herself in Ume's position—that she has involuntarily imagined and sympathized with Ume's shame, which is quite typical of the way shame works. "Shame," Tomkins continues, "is the most reflexive of affects in that the phenomenological distinction between the subject and object of shame is lost."[32] Paradoxically, it is this loss of the subject/object distinction—this *contagion* whereby shame seems indiscriminately to surge into the bloodstream of everyone in the room—that will give rise to Otama's "subjectivity."

Ume is a spunky girl and when she sees how upset Otama is by this news she tries to cheer her up. She announces that she will go buy fish from someone else and "bound[s] off with a clatter." The passage continues: "Otama remained for a while without moving. Then her taut nerves began gradually to relax and tears welled up in her eyes. She pulled a handkerchief from her sleeve to press them back. In her mind there was only a voice that screamed—how humiliating! how humiliating!"[33]

The shame-induced loss of the distinction between subject and object is reinforced here as Otama hears a disembodied voice crying out with shame. The Japanese phrase "*Kuyashii! Kuyashii!*" takes the form of a "subjective" adjective that can only be uttered in the first person. And yet although the shame here clearly "belongs" to Otama, it does not seem to be localized *within* her: the first-person voice seems to emanate from outside. Again, it seems to fill the room with its contagion. As if to emblematize this con-

---

31. Mori, *The Wild Goose*, 54; *Ōgai zenshū*, vol. 8, 523. I have slightly modified Watson's translation.
32. Sedgwick, Frank, and Alexander, *Shame and Its Sisters*, 136.
33. Mori, *The Wild Goose*, 54–55; *Ōgai zenshū*, vol. 8, 523.

founding of borders between discrete individuals, the character used to write *kuyashii* (悔しい) bears a striking resemblance to Ume's name (梅), which shares space on the same page, having been repeated three times in the previous paragraph.

But Ume is not the only character who seems involved in Otama's shame. The narrator is not present in this scene as a character, but his perspective floats over and through it (just as it did in the scene discussed earlier where Otama first saw Okada), and given the contagious nature of shame and the way he has penetrated Otama's consciousness, it would not be surprising if he felt it as well. In Ōgai's Japanese, the English word "chaos" (in the earlier passage) is written in Roman letters, which reminds us that the language here is that of the narrator who, although he has abandoned the first person and is not literally present on the scene, still speaks in the marked language of the educated (male) elite. As the passage itself tells us, Otama would never have been able to formulate such a description of her feelings at this moment. They are still in the realm of pure affect and have yet to be verbalized—let alone in English! If the narrator is no longer *speaking* here, is he not *seeing* Otama in her distress? In a fascinating article, Ōishi Naoki has used Gérard Genette's concept of focalization to argue that *boku* is the narrator throughout *The Wild Goose*, even when it shifts into the third-person.[34] But others have disagreed, arguing that by now *boku* the narrator has vanished, leaving the reader to deal with a purely heterodiegetic narrator. I would argue that it is precisely this ambiguity, which yet another critic has called the "uneasiness" [*modokashisa*] of *The Wild Goose* as a whole,[35] that makes the reader wonder about the narrator's involvement in Otama's shame. If he is the narrative focalizer of this passage, what motivates his narration of it? Is this passage ultimately about her or about him?[36] In order to begin to answer this, I will consider the nature of *boku*'s subjectivity.

---

34. See Ōishi, "Mori Ōgai *Gan* shiron." Genette defines focalization as the answer to the question "*who is the character whose point of view orients the narrative perspective?*" He proposed the notion of focalization to answer "the question *who sees?*" as opposed to "the question *who speaks?*" Among its many advantages, the concept of focalization makes it possible to distinguish between different types of third-person narrative, whereas traditional narratology tends to assume that third-person narrative is always "omniscient." Genette, *Narrative Discourse*, 186.

35. Hosoya, "*Gan* no 'modokashisa.'"

36. There is of course also the shame that *the reader* feels on Otama's behalf and which no doubt produces readerly sympathy and identification with her.

Boku *as Vacuous Vessel*

In a fascinating article on Ōgai's "The Dancing Girl," Tomiko Yoda argues that the split subjectivity of that novella's protagonist is represented linguistically in the text by the contrasting pair of first-person pronouns he employs: *yo* (余) and *ware* (我). Neither pronoun is explicitly gendered,[37] but Yoda points out that while the former tends to be used in the nominative (when it is the subject of a sentence) and reads as masculine, literary, and abstract, the latter appears more often when the self is an object and represents those aspects of the self that are passive and concrete, hence stereotypically "feminine." The narrator's "self-authorizing" subjectivity in "The Dancing Girl," Yoda argues, is produced in the echo between *yo* and *ware*. This split subjectivity belongs to a narrator whose male gender actually derives from its ability to encompass two genders.

In *The Wild Goose*, by contrast, the narrator uses only one first-person masculine pronoun: *boku*. While *yo* suggests an adult,[38] masculine, and literary authority, *boku* is the prototypical pronoun for a *young* elite male [*seinen*]. In *The Wild Goose* it is used by Okada as well as the narrator and their friend Ishihara, another male student who features briefly at the end of the text. But since the narrator has no other name, it is most strongly associated with him.[39] What *boku* has that *yo* and *ware* do not is *the suggestion of the potential for growth*. That *boku* has indeed grown is suggested by the very existence of the text of *The Wild Goose*, which, insofar as it can be read as an elegiac romance—and like many first-person novelistic narratives—is in many ways "the story of how I came to be able to tell this story."[40]

But how exactly does the reader know that boku is capable of growth and that he has in fact grown? The answer has to do with the only other character who exhibits major transformation in the text: Otama. Toward the end of the text, *boku* finally admits what some readers have surely been assuming all along—that he was once jealous of Okada and wished Otama

---

37. Except perhaps *yo*, which is conventionally read as masculine. But since it is a written, classical form and its use mostly predates the imposition of modern essentialist gender categories, the impression of masculinity it gives is more conventional than naturalized and may be a retrospective effect.

38. Actually *yo* may signify less adulthood so much as a subjective position outside of developmental time altogether, a sort of abiding, depersonalized locus of enunciation.

39. As for the other males in the text, Otama's father, who is working class, uses the pronoun *ore*, as does Suezō the moneylender.

40. For a useful discussion how gender affects first-person narration in the nineteenth-century British novel, see Case, "Gender and History in Narrative Theory," 318.

loved him instead. As he watches Okada walk away from Otama on Okada's last evening in Japan, *boku* describes the emotions that he felt:

> I followed along in silence, troubled by a number of conflicting emotions. Dominant among them was the feeling that I would very much like to be in Okada's place. But my conscious mind was loath to admit this fact. I'm not that kind of contemptible fellow! I told myself firmly, and did my best to suppress the thought. Failing in my efforts to do so, I began to fume.
>
> When I say I wished I were in Okada's place, I do not mean I wanted to surrender myself to the woman's enticements. Only I thought how delightful it must be to be loved, as Okada was, by such a beautiful woman. What would I do if I were the object of such ardor? I would want to reserve the liberty to decide that when the occasion arose. But I definitely would not flee the way Okada had. I would meet with the woman and talk. I would not do anything reprehensible, of course, just meet with her and talk. And I would love her as I would a younger sister. I would put all my strength at her disposal. And somehow I would rescue her from her sordid surroundings. My imaginings raced on until they reached this fanciful conclusion.[41]

In this passage, it becomes clear that *boku* himself, more than Okada, adheres to the romantic viewpoint—or at least that he did in 1880. The scene that he conjures for himself here is the continuation of Okada's "serpent slaying" scene. While Okada himself insisted that "that story was over" at the time, *boku* insisted that "there must be something else." *He*, more than Okada, it would seem, has been harboring fantasies of being the romantic hero who would "rescue" Otama. In the later, retrospective moment of narration, however, he seems to have realized the futility of letting his fantasies get so out of hand as to have "reached this fanciful conclusion." But rather than overtly emphasizing his own growth and development, he puts the focus instead on Otama's awakening and subsequent disappointment.

I asked earlier whether the narrator might somehow be subject to or implicated in Otama's shame. Now let me suggest that Otama may in fact represent a part of the narrator—that part of him that experiences shame, desire, and subjectivity. It is his sensitivity to these things, after all, which, if considered as a character, distinguishes him from the rigidly homosocial and "unseeing" Okada.[42] It is also this sensibility that seems to have allowed him to write this novel. His identification with Otama is subtly suggested on the textual level as well by another graphic similarity between characters. Otama, whose name means "jewel," is referred to once in the text by her father as an *aratama* or "uncut gem," the character for which

---

41. Mori, *The Wild Goose*, 149; *Ōgai zenshū*, vol. 8, 591–92.

42. "Unseeing" is Atsuko Sakaki's descriptor for Okada in her chapter on *The Wild Goose* ("Thinking Beauty, Unseeing Scholar").

(撲) could easily be mistaken for *boku* (僕). As the only character to undergo emotional growth *in the novel*, Otama's growth stands in for what the reader can assume to have been *boku*'s growth *outside the novel*. Like an uncut gem, moreover, *boku* is a classic example of the Meiji "youth" or *seinen*, which Yoda describes as a "vacuous vessel of potentiality . . . always ready to absorb what arrives from the future without becoming overly invested in the present that keeps slipping into the past."[43] But whereas the process by which Otama's gem is cut is rendered visible in the text, leaving her possibly unable to transform herself further, *boku*'s transformation is not represented. As the narrator whose story "is not part of this tale," *boku* is able to remain a "vacuous vessel of potentiality," while Otama bears the full shaming force of subjectification and Okada the shame of "outmoded" homosocial values.

Thus the vision combining male and female that the narrator describes as the technique he has used to compose the text yields a new form of homosocial subjectivity as well. If, in "The Dancing Girl," Ōta seems to create his subject position out of thin air in the echo chamber between his masculine and feminine self (*yo* and *ware*), in *The Wild Goose*, the narrator is like the midwife at the natural birth of a new subjectivity that he himself will come to occupy. From this newly established position, he has the advantage not only of hindsight but of selective invisibility as well: unlike Okada, he has changed and grown; and unlike Otama, his shame has been sheltered from prying eyes. As the two halves of heterosexuality come together *under his homosocial auspices*, he shows the reader the painless progress he has made as the novel reveals its stereoscopic vision of homosocial subjectivity.

The Parallax Principle

The text's final irony, of course, is that the heterosexual love story that has tempted us all along is never forthcoming. Just as Otama's shame and her sexual difference have been subsumed in the context of homosocial rivalry as "proof" of the narrator's growth against Okada's "arrested development," desire itself in *The Wild Goose* is always either just shy of its object

---

43. One might argue that Okada, in his obliviousness, is a better representative of the *seinen*, but while he displays a relentless forward-looking orientation, it is *boku*'s simultaneous awareness of the past and his ability to present himself as having moved beyond it, precisely by projecting its constraints onto Okada and Otama, that makes him the perfect "vacuous vessel." It also makes him a great example of a two-timing subjectivity. See Yoda, "First-Person Narration and Citizen-Subject," 295. For more on the category of the *seinen*, see Kimura, *"Seinen" no tanjō*.

or arbitrarily displaced onto something else. The narrator's stereoscopic homosociality thus promotes a heterosexuality without sex.

In Chapter 21, Suezō is out of town and Otama has had her hair done, finally ready to zero in on the target of her desire: "Today Mr. Okada would surely pass by. Often he passed the house twice, so even if she should somehow miss him on his way down the hill, she would certainly meet him as he came back. And today, at whatever cost, she would speak with him without fail, and he would of course stop to listen."[44]

Unfortunately for Otama, though, a series of trivial contingencies interfere with her plans. On that day of all days, the narrator explains, the landlady of his boarding house decides to serve a dish that he cannot abide: mackerel in miso sauce, so he asks Okada to join him for dinner out instead. As a result, when Okada passes by Otama's house, he is not alone, but accompanied by *boku*, and Otama's plans to speak to him are dashed. If the homosocial triangle of two men and a woman sometimes *enables* heterosexual romance, here the homosocial bond is just strong enough to prevent it. This scene, which is the closest *The Wild Goose* comes to closure, is structurally almost identical to the scene in *Vita Sexualis* where the geisha Koiku serves Kojima the bowl of mashed sweet potatoes and chestnuts while the narrator looks on. There, the geisha Koiku, like Otama, watches a man not unlike Okada (beautiful but mindless) while the narrator (less beautiful but full of foreclosed and vicarious desire) looks on. In both texts, desire is mediated through the figure of a beautiful man. And in each case it is the woman whose desire is most dazzlingly on display while the narrator's is hidden in a newly produced interiority. The only difference is that here it is the narrator's presence itself, his status as a *homodiegetic* narrator, as much as the indifference of the male lead, that prevents the romance from happening.

Otama stood in front of the house. Even in ill health she would have been beautiful, but in fact she was young and healthy, and today her usual good looks had been heightened by careful makeup and grooming. To my eyes she seemed to possess a beauty wholly beyond anything I had noted earlier, and her face shone with a kind of radiance. The effect was dazzling.

As though in a trance, Otama fixed her eyes on Okada. He raised his cap in a flustered greeting and then unconsciously quickened his pace.

---

44. Mori, *The Wild Goose*, 144; *Ōgai zenshū*, vol. 8, 588.

With the unreserve of a third party, I turned several times to look back. She watched him for a long time.[45]

If Kojima was "absentminded," Okada is "unconscious" in this scene. But the narrator's mind brims with an intense awareness of Otama's dazzling beauty. His first-person narrative, moreover, has merged with "the unreserved of a third party," thus completing his stereoscopic vision.

But what does the text do with the powerful desire it has produced in the mind of its narrator? After this scene, the two men run into a third student named Ishihara. As they are strolling around a pond, they see a flock of wild geese swimming on its far side. Ishihara, whose name means "stone on a plain," challenges Okada to try and hit one of them with a rock. At first, Okada declines, not wanting to disturb the birds. But when Ishihara says that he will throw a rock himself, Okada, worrying that Ishihara might actually hit one, decides to throw a stone first to scatter them. As it happens, however, the stone that he throws actually hits and kills one of the geese. A little shocked at this unintended violence, the boys decide that they should at least retrieve the goose and eat it.

For a while both of us remained silent. Then Okada, as if talking to himself, said "Some wild geese are just unlucky." Though there was no logical connection, the image of the woman on Muenzaka flashed through my mind.

"All I did was throw in the direction where the geese were," said Okada, this time speaking to me.

"Sure," I said, continuing to think about the woman. "Still," I added after a moment, "I'd like to see how Ishihara goes about retrieving it."

"Sure," Okada agreed as he walked along lost in thought. Probably he was still feeling bad about the wild goose.[46]

If Otama is clearly associated with the goose here in the narrator's mind, the irony of course is that while Okada had only aimed "in the direction" of the goose, he ends up hitting it, while Otama had aimed directly at Okada and missed. Not because of bad aim, one might say, but because of a combination of factors both arbitrary and structural: the bad luck that the boys' landlady happened to have served mackerel in miso sauce on that night of all nights, and the powerful force of the homosocial bonds between the men.

---

45. Mori, *The Wild Goose*, 148; *Ōgai zenshū*, vol. 8, 591. As Atsuko Sakaki has also noted, Watson has Otama watching "us" for a long time, but Ōgai's Japanese suggests that she is looking at Okada alone ("Thinking Beauty," 250*n*26).

46. Mori, *The Wild Goose*, 154; *Ōgai zenshū*, vol. 8, 595. It bears mentioning here that the place name "Muenzaka" is both a real area in Tokyo and a signifier for loneliness. Its literal meaning is something like "Hill of Disconnection."

In these scenes, Ōgai's text shows itself to be as aware as Sōseki's of the belated and structural nature of homosocial desire. Ishihara's plan to retrieve the goose, for example, involves first *waiting* for half an hour for it to get dark and then employing the "parallax principle" to triangulate his coordinates off of two upright lotus stems sticking up in the pond. As the other two boys guide him, calling "left" and "right," the scene starts to read like a slapstick parody of the triangulation of desire with the dead goose serving as object. As they hurry back to the boarding house under cover of night, Ishihara begins talking in a loud voice about the formula for finding the volume of a cone. Later he says that this was to distract the police officer in his box. But insofar as a cone is a triangle spun on one of its points, it works as another arresting image both for the triangulation of desire and the eternal non-convergence of desiring subject with desired object. Although *The Wild Goose* holds out the promise of a heterosocial world in the narrator's future, where men and women might actually come together, this possibility is dramatically foreclosed in this final scene, which has three boys feasting on a goose in a kind of homosocial totem meal, and one woman sadly, even shamefully alone, waiting for a love that would never arrive. The next day Okada leaves to study in Germany.

But perhaps the narrator himself managed later where Okada failed? Perhaps he got together with Otama and this is why he knows so much about her. A reasonable assumption, perhaps, but one that the narrator explicitly rejects in the novel's final paragraph.

> Readers may perhaps ask how I came to know Otama and under what circumstances I heard her recital, but these matters too lie outside my story. I would only add that, needless to say, I am wholly lacking in the kind of qualifications that would fit me for the role of Otama's lover, so readers may spare themselves useless speculation on that point.[47]

If the story the narrator has told is "his" story, it is not because it is about him, but precisely because he figures in it so minimally. He remains on the margins, all the better to determine the narrative's borders, and to shift the focus from himself to Otama and Okada. His seeming humility here over his supposed lack of "qualifications" as Otama's lover is better read as an irony-laden rejection of his own youthful romanticism. It is also a powerful assertion of the superiority of his hard-won novelistic vision over the homosocial romance that kept Okada and Otama from being able truly to perceive each other. And yet the novel that is *The Wild Goose* is not coterminous with what the narrator calls "my story." By exposing the narra-

---

47. Mori, *The Wild Goose*, 166; *Ōgai zenshū*, vol. 8, 603.

tor's ambivalent feelings for both Okada and Otama, while quietly propelling itself forward on the strength of his desire to have left both of them behind, *The Wild Goose* maintains its two-timing stance, simultaneously critical of and nostalgic about Japan's homosocial past.

On Ōgai's Anachronism

One often has the sense, in reading Ōgai's work, that it contains something peculiarly anachronistic—simultaneously ahead of and behind its time. "The Dancing Girl," for example, has come to vie for the title of "first modern novel" because it was among the first to employ consistent first-person narration and "vanishing point" perspective, and yet critics took almost a century to realize this because the story was written in a stiff, neoclassical Japanese that by 1890 was already starting to look old fashioned.[48] Later in his career, just after writing *The Wild Goose*, when other Japanese writers were plunging headlong into European-style modernism, Ōgai famously abandoned fiction altogether to devote himself exclusively to the research and writing of historical biographies, spending the rest of his life "buried in the documentary remains of individuals whom history had left behind."[49] The first of these works, moreover, arose out of an interest in the anachronistic practice of *junshi*, or "following one's lord in death," spurred by General Nogi Maresuke's shocking revival of the long defunct (and proscribed) practice after the death of the Meiji emperor. According to Karatani Kōjin, even Ōgai's theoretical understanding of history was curiously out of joint with that of his age. In a series of debates with Tsubouchi Shōyō in the 1890s, Ōgai took a historicist position informed by the latest European theorists that was virtually unheard of in Japan at the time and seems to have mystified the formalist Shōyō and his contemporaries.[50] But no sooner had historicism taken firm root among Japanese professional historians in the 1910s, than Ōgai summarily abandoned his earlier commitment to linear, developmentalist history. As a result, in his historical biographies he allowed the material facticity of the historical documents

---

48. On the modernity of "The Dancing Girl," see Kamei, "'An Oddball Rich in Dreams'"; and Karatani, *Origins of Modern Japanese Literature*, 49–51. On the story's use of vanishing point perspective, see Maeda, "Berlin 1888."

49. Marcus, *Paragons of the Ordinary*, 2.

50. On Ōgai's debate with Shōyō, see Karatani, *Origins of Modern Japanese Literature*, 146–51.

with which he worked to remain relatively unmolested by the imposition of causal explanations and teleological perspective.⁵¹

The Wild Goose was the last realist novel with a contemporary setting that Ōgai completed. Some critics see a break between it and the historical and biographical works that he turned to subsequently, but I am more persuaded by the arguments for continuity. What Darrell William Davis writes about "The Abe Family" ["Abe ichizoku"], a historical novella written in 1912—between his starting and finishing *The Wild Goose*—strikes me as just as relevant to the latter novel: "The uneasy coexistence and overlapping of ethics deriving from succeeding historical eras finds an inscription in Abe's predicament, caught as he is between succeeding, conflicting regimes."⁵² The succeeding historical regimes I have identified in *The Wild Goose* are two different forms of homosociality, one romantic and the other novelistic. But rather than showing how one neatly supersedes the other, the novel dramatizes the "unrationalized coexistence" of both.⁵³

---

51. As Marvin Marcus writes, "Overall, the *shiden* project is marked by an unmistakable shift toward what can only be termed unvarnished scholarly exposition. The move toward 'pure *kōshō*,' in the words of Okazaki Yoshie, was finally realized in the author's last projects, annalistic compilations of imperial posthumous names and era names that once and for all eliminated any vestige of literary manipulation" (*Paragons of the Ordinary*, 65–66).

52. Davis, "Historical Uses and Misuses," 53.

53. The expression is from Eve Kosofsky Sedgwick's "Axiom 5," which reads, in part, "issues of modern homo/heterosexual definition are structured, not by the supersession of one model and the consequent withering away of another, but instead by the relations enabled by the unrationalized coexistence of different models during the times they do coexist" (*Epistemology of the Closet*, 47).

FOUR

Sensei's Bloody Legacy:
Sōseki's Kokoro *in the Male Homosocial Imagination*

Between Friendship and Love

Early on in Natsume Sōseki's novel *Kokoro*, the novel's young narrator finds himself in a conversation with his older, enigmatic friend Sensei about the dividing line between male friendship and love. They have come to see the blossoms in Ueno Park but have arrived "in a wooded area that had neither blossoms nor crowds" when Sensei proposes that the narrator's interest in him might have something to do with "love." "You came to me because of some lack you sensed, didn't you?" he asks, and the younger man replies:

"That may be so. But that isn't love."
"It's a step on the staircase towards love. You gravitated towards someone of the same sex as the first step toward embracing someone of the opposite sex."
"I think the two things are completely different in nature."
"No, they're the same. I'm just not the kind of person who can satisfy you as a man. Besides, certain things make it impossible for me to be all that you want me to be."[1]

---

1. Translation adapted from Meredith McKinney's 2010 translation of *Kokoro*. In some instances I will cite Edwin McClellan's 1957 translation. All references to *Kokoro* will be cited in one or both translations, with the translator's name and the page number of the passage in the Japanese original from vol. 9 of the *Sōseki zenshū* (abbreviated as *SZ*). For this passage, then, the citation is Natsume, *Kokoro*, 27 (McKinney), 36–37 (*SZ*).

In this scene, two men face each other across the gaping chasm introduced by the ongoing rupture in Japan of the male homosocial continuum. For Sensei, love between men is not categorically distinct from love between men and women but rather a step on the way towards it. For his younger protégé, by contrast, love is heterosexual from start to finish. Sensei, unlike his young friend, seems to remember a time when men looked chiefly to other men not only for companionship and intimacy but even, perhaps, for "love."[2] His mention later in the chapter of a friend whose grave he visits every month in the cemetery at Zōshigaya implies some long-ago personal experience behind his words, and later in the novel, Sensei suggests to his young friend that the differences between them may also be understood historically as a result of the scant decade or so that separates them in age.[3] But whether personal or historical in its origins, Sensei's haunted past stands in stark contrast to the insouciance of the younger man who is both unaware of the story of Sensei and his dead friend and who has grown up in a world where romantic love between men and women has eclipsed the world of men.

In his ability to imagine and remember a less heteronormative past, Sensei is perhaps not unlike Sōseki himself. It is often said about Sōseki that his birth in 1867 meant that he "belonged to the last generation of Japanese who could remember the old Edo culture,"[4] thus giving him something of a critical outsider's perspective on Japanese modernity. But critics have yet to give much consideration to what it meant that his life also straddled the modern homosocial divide.[5] In his memoir *From Within*

---

2. Ōta Tsubasa discusses a similar dynamic between Ōgai's protagonist Jun'ichi in *The Youth* and the slightly older novelist Ōishi. See Ōta, "Mori Ōgai *Seinen* ron."

3. The passage in question actually refers to what Sensei imagines as the younger man's inability to understand his decision to kill himself, but to the extent that his suicide was motivated by his melancholic attachment to another man, it amounts to the same thing. He writes, "Two or three days later I finally decided to kill myself. I would guess that my reasons will be as hard for you to fully grasp as I found General Nogi's reasons to be. If so, it must simply be put down to the different eras we belong to. Or perhaps, after all, our differences spring from the individual natures we were born with. At any rate, I have done my best in these pages to explain to you my own strange nature" (Natsume, *Kokoro*, 232–33 [McKinney]; 246 [McClellan]; 298 [*SZ*]).

4. Natsume, *Theory of Literature and Other Critical Writings*, 3.

5. One notable exception to this lacuna is Reiko Abe Auestad, who notes: "Sōseki belongs to the generation of Meiji intellectuals for whom homosocial/sexual relations were not taboo, and yet who were hesitant to acknowledge the sexual component in homosocial relationships openly. Their nostalgia for the fading image of the patriot (*shishi*) of one generation earlier can be seen as a manifestation of their wish to reimagine and vali-

My Glass Doors [*Garasudo no uchi*], written in 1915, the year after *Kokoro* was serialized in the *Asahi shinbun*, Sōseki reminisced about a story his older brother had told him about his experience in school as the object of other men's attentions.

When my older brother was in school there were still students being sent there by the feudal domains and apparently there were still things going on here and there that would be unimaginable for today's young men [*ima no seinen ni wa sōzō dekinai kifū ga kōnai no sokokoko ni nokotte ita rashii*]. He told me once about getting a love letter from an upperclassman. Apparently this upperclassman was quite a bit older than my brother. Having been brought up in Tokyo where this custom did not exist, he wasn't sure what to do with the letter. He said that after that every time he saw the man in the school bath he felt uncomfortable.[6]

Sōseki's reference here to *kōshinsei* (which I have translated as "students being sent there from the feudal domains") places the events he describes somewhere around 1870, not long before the period that Mori Ōgai wrote about in *Vita Sexualis* and *The Wild Goose* as discussed in the last chapter. His emphasis on both the pastness and the provinciality of these male-male "goings on" is yet another example of what Gregory Pflugfelder has described as the "marginalization" of male-male sexuality "to the Japanese past, the Southwestern periphery, and the world of adolescence."[7] By Sōseki's time this culture had receded even further and male-female love was becoming increasingly normalized. And yet Sōseki remembered the earlier culture and continued to be drawn to the possibility of intimacy between men. As Jim Reichert and Stephen Dodd have both noted, one of Sōseki's first published articles (in 1892) was a somewhat gushing tribute to Walt Whitman's "manly love of comrades."[8] As I have discussed elsewhere, as a young man Sōseki wrote a playful "love letter" to his close friend, the haiku poet Masaoka Shiki.[9] And although not quite as "expert" as Ōgai, Sōseki was also familiar with recent work in sexology, and had copies of both

---

date homosocial/sexual relationships in the pervasive mood of homophobia" (Auestad, *Rereading Sōseki*, 36).

6. "Garasudo no uchi," *SZ*, vol. 12, 607. For a different English translation, see Natsume, *Inside My Glass Doors*, 105–6.

7. Pflugfelder, *Cartographies of Desire*, 203.

8. Dodd, "The Significance of Bodies in Sōseki's *Kokoro*" 479–82; Reichert, *In the Company of Men*, 168. For Sōseki's text, see "Bundan ni okeru byōdō shugi no daihyōsha Uoruto Hoitoman no shi ni tsuite" in *SZ*, vol. 13, 3–20. For a discussion of Whitman in this context, see Herrero-Brasas, "The Love of Comrades."

9. For a discussion and translation of this "love letter," see Vincent, "The Novel and the End of Homosocial Literature."

Havelock Ellis's *A Study of Human Secondary Sexual Character* and *Studies in the Psychology of Sex* in his personal library.[10] In his copy of Charles Letourneau's *The Evolution of Marriage and of the Family*, next to a passage discussing the custom in ancient Crete of abducting beautiful boys from their family homes, he wrote in the margin, "Compare this to Greek and Roman literature and to the customs of feudal Japan."[11]

I should emphasize that my point here in mentioning these sightings of the biographical Sōseki at scenes involving male-male sexuality is not so much to "adduce" them "as extratextual evidence for such undercurrents" in his works, much less to equate Sōseki with the character Sensei in *Kokoro*.[12] But by reminding the reader of these facts I do hope to do some remedial work toward restoring the visibility of a male homosocial continuum that Sōseki experienced but which has been repeatedly and "radically disrupted" in the interim.[13] Like Stephen Dodd, I believe it is crucial to recognize that Sōseki was, like Ōgai, both aware of and perhaps even "open to a wider range of erotic possibilities than has generally been acknowledged."[14] My own approach to this issue in Sōseki is located somewhere in between Dodd's work, which gravitates toward the minoritizing and explicitly homoerotic end of the continuum, and that of psychoanalyst Doi Takeo, who famously supplied a powerfully universalizing and homosocial reading of Sōseki in his classic 1971 work *The Anatomy of Dependence*. After first distinguishing what he called "homosexuality in the narrow sense" [*kyōgi no dōseiai*] from (desexualized) "homosexual emotions" [*dōseiai-teki kanjō*] Doi wrote that he knew of "no literary work that portrays so accurately the nature of homosexual emotions in Japanese society as Natsume Sōseki's *Kokoro*."[15] Although I disagree with Doi's arbitrary division between "homosexuality in the narrow sense" and "homosexual emotions," he was certainly right to note that *Kokoro* has a great deal to say about relations between men in modern Japan. For this reason and because it has been even more influential in the canon of modern Japanese literature than *The Wild Goose*, I have devoted two chapters to *Kokoro* as well. The current chapter

---

10. A complete list of the books in Sōseki's collection can be found in *SZ*, vol. 27. These works by Ellis are listed on p. 93.

11. "Zōsho ni kakikomareta tanpyō zakkan," *SZ*, vol. 27, 190. Letourneau, *The Evolution of Marriage and of the Family*.

12. These phrases are taken from Sibley, review of Reichert, *In the Company of Men*, 331.

13. Sedgwick, *Between Men*, 2.

14. Dodd, "The Significance of Bodies in Sōseki's *Kokoro*," 496

15. Doi, *The Anatomy of Dependence*, 114.

treats the novel's critical reception and two translations into English as a way of gauging the state of the homosocial continuum at various points over the course of the twentieth century and beyond. In Chapter 5 I offer my own reading of the novel as what I call the "primal scene" of modern Japanese homosociality.

Toward Heterosociality

The question of where exactly to locate the relationships described in *Kokoro* between the two extremes of the homosocial continuum remains an open one, all the more so given that Sōseki wrote the novel during a period in which words like gay and lesbian did not exist, and although the term "homosexuality" had been recently translated into Japanese, it possessed nowhere near the ontological heft that it has today. It was also a time, however, when both the understanding and the lived experience of sexual and gender identity were undergoing major transformations that Sōseki registered with extraordinary sensitivity over the course of his short but remarkably varied writing career. The world depicted in his early works such as *I Am a Cat* [*Wagahai wa neko de aru*] (1905), *Botchan* (1906), and *The Poppy* [*Gubijinsō*] (1907), for example, centers almost exclusively around men's relations to other men, with women figuring only as otherworldly temptresses (such as Madonna in *Botchan* or Fujio in *The Poppy*) or beatific mother substitutes (Kiyo in *Botchan*). In later works, such as *The Wayfarer* (1913) and *Light and Darkness* [*Meian*] (1916), by contrast, he increasingly focused on the world of relations between ordinary (bourgeois) men and women.[16] In the increasingly heterosocial world of the late Meiji elite, romantic love between men and women was no longer seen as it once was—as either somehow ridiculous or embarrassing or as a betrayal of other men—even as the androcentric world of early Meiji had come to seem hopelessly old fashioned. *Kokoro* is a novel that dramatizes this shift.

If the chasm that separates Sensei and his young friend (the novel's two narrators) is the same chasm that separates a homosocial past from the heterosocial future, it is of course also true that the two men's lives and experiences overlap. Insofar as the novel gives both narrators a voice

---

16. As Mizumura Minae writes, referring to Sōseki's first newspaper novel *The Poppy* [*Gubijinsō*], "After *Gubijinsō* the possibility of not taking women seriously—of not succumbing to the temptation of sharing the same world with them—was no longer a viable option for him. The works after *Gubijinsō* are not necessarily better, yet, because they place a greater centrality on the world of men and women, they are closer to the novel as we normally conceive it" ("Resisting Woman," 33).

without ultimately adjudicating between them, it can be read simultaneously as Sōseki's melancholic tribute to the male homosocial world of his youth and as a "progressive" critique of that same world for its exclusivity and misogyny.[17] In this sense, *Kokoro* is a quintessentially two-timing text. To read *Kokoro* only in either of these ways, however, is to miss the way its complex narrative structure not only allowed its author to avoid passing a definitive judgment on the different modes of sexuality and sociality it presents in the persons of its two narrators, but also how it enacts a way of thinking about sexuality and subjectivity that was new to twentieth-century Japan. Employing not just one but two first-person narrators to tell its story, *Kokoro* made intimacy among men and men, and between men and women, into a highly subjective and inherently narrative phenomenon—one that could no longer simply be *named* but now had to be *told*. As a matter for narration rather than nomination, the precise *qualia* of the love and intimacy experienced by characters in the novel became fatefully indeterminate, thus leading to still *more* narrative in the form of critical reactions. Critical debate has raged for years over the exact nature of the relationship between Sensei and his dead friend, as well as that between Sensei and his young protégé, between Sensei and his wife, and between Sensei's wife and the younger man. Were the men simply friends? Could they have been lovers? Did Sensei

---

17. Miyazaki Kasumi sees Sōseki's work as exemplifying the same kind of melancholic relation to a homosocial past that I have found there. I was both stunned and pleased to find the following passage, which might as well serve as a summary of my own thesis, in her essay about Sōseki's novel *The Gate* [*Mon*]. "The misfortune of men in the Meiji period was that they had to face actual women who could no longer be like Tanagra statuettes [i.e., pretty objects] while being forever cut off from the community of men to whom they had once belonged. Aside from a few exceptions like Sakai [the protagonist Sōsuke's neighbor in *The Gate*], the love for men and the love for women could not exist simultaneously—just as one cannot get back the time that has already passed. When Meiji Japan set out to become a modern nation it had to make the choice to bury the homosocial continuum in the past and yield absolute dominion over the present to the heterosexual system. The result was that men in the Meiji period were eternally split between the eros of the past and the eros of the present. Such was the misfortune of Japan, where homophobia had not ruptured the connection between homosociality and homosexuality as it had in the West. This rupture between heterosexuality and homosexuality was an inevitable part of modernization but was internalized as a sort of original sin in the minds of individual [men]. Why? Because to love a woman was to betray the community of men and to betray men was to lose the right to belong to that community. Only by breaking the compact with other men and tasting the fruits of the forbidden [by loving women] could the time of the present—that of modern history—begin to flow" ("Erosu no tsumi to norowareta kako," 201).

ever really allow himself to love his wife? Did the younger man make a "cuckold" of Sensei with his mentor's wife? These are just a few of the questions that readers, critics, and translators have asked about *Kokoro* as they have continued to engage in a process that Sōseki and other modern novelists began—that of narrativizing sexuality.

A Quick Plot Summary

Kokoro consists of three sections. In the first two a young man known only as "I" (*watakushi*) tells the story of his friendship with a mysterious older man whom he calls "Sensei." In these sections we learn of the younger narrator's meeting with his older mentor and his insatiable, almost invasive, curiosity about the latter's past. Despite the respectful appellation "Sensei" (teacher) that the young man uses in referring to him, the older man does not work as a teacher or a professor, but lives quietly withdrawn from the world together with his wife Shizu. Sensei and Shizu (whom *watakushi* calls "Okusan," a respectful term for a married woman) have no children—a fact that Sensei enigmatically attributes to "divine punishment."[18] Although the two of them get along well enough, their marriage is without passion. Sensei seems haunted by some memory from his past about which he promises to tell the youth at some point. But for now he keeps it to himself.

The young man seems to have learned the story of Sensei's past over the interval between the end of the story he tells and the moment when he sat down to write it, but in his sections of the novel he does not reveal much to the reader about what he has learned. Instead, he drops hints along the way that serve both to heighten the suspense for the reader and to emphasize the ignorance and immaturity of his younger self.[19] When he is summoned by his family in the countryside to attend to his dying father, he receives a letter from Sensei in which the latter states his intention to commit suicide. The younger man immediately leaves his own father's deathbed to board a train for Tokyo. While on the train he reads the letter from beginning to end. It is this long letter that constitutes the third and final section of *Kokoro*.

---

18. Natsume, *Kokoro*, 18 (McKinney), 17 (McClellan), 24 (*SZ*).
19. In one typical passage toward the beginning of the novel, the narrator says, "I could not know that there had been in Sensei's life a frightening tragedy, inseparable from his love for his wife . . . I shall not speak here of the tragedy in Sensei's life." Ibid., 24–25 (McClellan), 25–26 (McKinney), 34 (*SZ*).

In his letter Sensei tells of how in his youth his parents died and his uncle cheated him out of most of his inheritance. Having lost his faith in his fellow human beings he becomes a boarder in the home of a soldier's widow (whom he calls "Okusan") and her daughter ("Ojōsan," a respectful term for a young lady). Soon, he invites his close friend "K" to come and live in the same house. K is a studious type who has no experience with women and Sensei hopes to "humanize" and "soften" him by exposing him to the company of Okusan and Ojōsan. When K tells Sensei that he has fallen in love with Ojōsan, Sensei is awakened to his own affection for the young woman and, rather than counseling his friend, decides to act in his own interest by preempting him. Without saying anything to K, he asks Okusan for her daughter's hand in marriage. A few days later K commits suicide and Sensei is saddled with a burden of guilt that irrevocably destroys his faith in himself and others. Sensei tells his young friend in the letter that he has decided to kill himself both to atone for his betrayal of K and as a tribute to "the spirit of Meiji" on the occasion of the death of the Meiji Emperor. "I felt as though the spirit of the Meiji era had begun with the Emperor and had ended with him," Sensei writes. "I was overcome with the feeling that I and the others, who had been brought up in that era, were now left behind to live as anachronisms."[20] When General Nogi Maresuke commits suicide together with his wife Shizuko on the day of Meiji's funeral (in penance for having lost the Emperor's banner in the Seinan War 35 years earlier) Sensei cements his resolve to kill himself. He ends his final testament with the request that its young recipient never reveal the secret of his past to his widow. But since the end of Sensei's letter is also the end of the novel, the reader is left without knowing what happened to Sensei's wife and the novel's first narrator. The only way to know is to go back to the novel's first two sections and try to extrapolate from the clues he has left behind.

Father, Son, and Sensei's Ghost: The Paternalistic Homosocial Reading

I begin this section by reminding the reader that the story of Sensei's betrayal of his friend K is told not directly to the reader, but to Sensei's younger friend *watakushi*, with whom he strolled in Ueno Park. In Sensei's letter, the reader is essentially put in the position of reading someone else's mail—of eavesdropping on a communication between two men. When

---

20. Ibid., 245 (McClellan), 231 (McKinney), 297 (*SZ*).

Sensei says to his young confidant, "Among the many millions of Japanese, it is to you alone that I want to tell the story of my past,"[21] some readers, perhaps especially those who are male and Japanese, will feel as if they themselves are being addressed by Sensei. They might even feel a tinge of vicarious pride at having been chosen to hear this precious transmission, which will encourage them further to read his words from what they imagine to be *watakushi*'s position. In exchange for the compliment, as it were, they will evacuate any particular bias or ambivalence that *watakushi* might have as a character, imagining him as a passive and neutral narratee, and later narrator, of Sensei's story.[22]

Another way of putting this is to say that, for readers who tend to identify with Sensei's values and who see his dilemma as a tragic one, the idea that *watakushi* has faithfully transmitted Sensei's story to them will be extremely important, just as it was important for Sensei that *watakushi* be the right narratee for his testament. He explains his choice of *watakushi* "among millions of Japanese" in the next sentence by saying "Because you are sincere. You are serious in your desire to learn lessons from life."[23] The sincerity and fidelity of *watakushi*-as-narratee/narrator functions here as a kind of compensation for the terrible betrayal that is described in Sensei's letter. This was true for Sensei, it seems, who wanted somehow to communicate to his dead friend the abject apology ("I'm sorry. It's all my fault") that he spoke to "the two ladies" after K's death but which "was really meant for K, whom it could no longer reach."[24] By writing his testament, he hopes that these words will reach *watakushi* intact as a sort of proxy for K and thereby somehow expunge the sin of his part in K's death. The price of this belated and compensatory communication, however, is death, figured in *Kokoro* through the metaphor of blood as a conduit of a kind of male homosocial reproduction. Sensei prefaces his account to *watakushi* by saying, "Now, I myself am about to cut open my own heart, and drench your face with my blood. And I shall be satisfied if, when my heart stops beating, a new life lodges in your breast."[25] As many critics have noted, this image resonates powerfully with Sensei's description of K's spurting blood in the scene of his suicide. If in that scene, K's blood had "gushed out in one tre-

---

21. Ibid., *Kokoro*, 123–24 (McKinney), 128 (McClellan), 157 (*SZ*).
22. Other readers, who may feel less in synch with the values expressed in Sōseki's story, will have more trouble forgetting that *watakushi*, as well as Sensei, are both characters and that neither is a neutral narrator. I will get to those other readers later.
23. Natsume, *Kokoro*, 124 (McKinney), 128 (McClellan), 157 (*SZ*).
24. Ibid., 219 (McKinney), 232 (McClellan), 281 (*SZ*).
25. Ibid., 129 (McClellan), 124 (McKinney), 158 (*SZ*).

mendous spurt"²⁶ after he slit his carotid artery only to splatter against the sliding doors, this time Sensei hopes that his own blood will somehow be recuperated and reabsorbed, bringing new life to his younger friend. *This time*, with *this* young man, he might be able to breach "that insurmountable wall" that had gone up between men, with words "spoken beyond my will, directly from my natural being."²⁷

It was just such a compensatory fantasy of belated but sincere communication between men that informed the vast majority of male-authored critical readings of *Kokoro* throughout most of the postwar period, when *Kokoro* first achieved its canonical status.²⁸ In this interpretation of *Kokoro*, which I call the "paternalistic homosocial" reading, Sensei's betrayal of K is elevated into a parable about "loneliness" and the evils of selfishness and individualism in the modern age. The moral of the story according to this reading is Sensei's realization, spoken to an innocent and ingenuous *watakushi*, that "loneliness is the price we have to pay for being born in this modern age, so full of freedom, independence, and our own egotistical selves."²⁹ In this reading, *watakushi* is supposed not only to have learned this lesson from Sensei, but also, in writing his account, to be passing it on to the reader. Insofar as that transmission is enabled only *by death* and *between men*, however, it takes "loneliness" as an inevitable result of modern life and places intimacy between men in the present completely out of reach.

Etō Jun's classic 1970 description of Sensei's hard-won and tragic wisdom is a famous example of the paternalistic homosocial reading that makes clear its collusion with an Emperor-centered national mythology as well:

The Emperor Meiji's death and General Nogi's *junshi* made [Sensei] realize that the spirit of Meiji had not entirely died within him. Now the shadow of the entire value structure of this great era emerged from his tortured past, smiling at him like the ghost

---

26. Ibid., 233 (McClellan), 220 (McKinney), 282 (*SZ*)
27. Ibid., 219 (McKinney), 232 (McClellan), 281 (*SZ*).
28. Satō Izumi points out that in the prewar period, Sōseki was best known as a virtuoso stylist and *Kokoro* was far from his most popular work. He was better known at the time for his earlier works in ornate classical styles like *The Poppy* and *Nowaki* [*Autumn Wind*], neither of which is read much today. *Kokoro*'s canonization (and its inclusion in high-school textbooks) began only during the late 1950s and 1960s, when it was perceived as offering a model of the kind of responsible subjectivity or *shutaisei* that modernizationists felt Japan was lacking. See Satō Izumi, *Kokugo kyōkasho no sengoshi*. Thanks to Tomi Suzuki for this observation and reference.
29. Natsume, *Kokoro*, 30 (McKinney), 30 (McClellan), 30 (*SZ*). The Japanese reads "*jiyū to dokuritsu to onore ni michita gendai*." McKinney has the slightly more neutral: "this age of freedom and independence and the self."

of a loved one. Perhaps the ghost whispered to him: "Come to me." And Sōseki responded, indicating through his novel's protagonist that a part of himself had died with the passing of the Meiji era. Thus Sōseki wrote *Kokoro* to make it clear that he was on the side of the ghost of the traditional, but somehow universal, ethics—the ethics of stoic self-restraint or anti-egoism—even though fully aware that the whole value system of the Meiji era had crumbled long before the Emperor's death, and that a new age was emerging from this chaos—an age in which the unrestrained assertion of the ego would be considered not an act of ugliness but the privilege of younger generations.[30]

Etō's nostalgic reading not only focused primarily on the figure of Sensei but also conflated him with Sōseki himself, whom he assumes is speaking "through his novel's protagonist." For Etō and other conservative critics, the "traditional, but somehow universal" values expressed in Sensei's testament were absolute. For this reason they tended to ignore the obvious mediation of Sensei's story through the younger narrator and focus exclusively on the novel's final section, in which Sensei writes in his own voice. The novel's protagonist, as Etō's description also casually assumes, was Sensei and his young protégé simply the person who faithfully brought us Sensei's story. As Valdo Viglielmo, another proponent of this style of reading, wrote in an introductory essay on the novel for English readers, "That Sensei is the protagonist is never in question."[31] The prominent postwar Sōseki scholar Miyoshi Yukio went so far as to characterize the first narrator as "nothing more than a mouthpiece, a puppet"[32] and even a "selfless recorder" [*mushi no kijitsusha*].[33] This last expression is remarkable in Miyoshi's Japanese text, where the word "selfless" [*mushi* 無私] actually negates the only name that *watakushi* [私] has. The tendency to downplay *watakushi*'s role and to conflate Sensei with Sōseki himself was also shared by Edwin McClellan, whose 1957 translation of *Kokoro* will soon become key to our discussion. In an article published around the same time as the translation, McClellan begins by invoking what seems to be a reflexively New Critical refutation of the conflation of author and his narrators, but then proceeds to conflate the two nonetheless.

Sōseki must not of course, be identified with the narrators in *Kokoro*. Yet we feel, when reading the novel, that the power which moves the characters to their end manipulates the author himself with equal force and inevitability. And perhaps it is because Sōseki

---

30. Etō, "A Japanese Intellectual," 65.
31. Viglielmo was the translator of Sōseki's last novel *Light and Darkness* and another critic of this bent. Viglielmo, "Kokoro," 170.
32. Quoted in Ishihara, "*Kokoro* no Oidipusu," 183.
33. Miyoshi, "Watoson wa haishinsha ka?" 7.

seems to share this helplessness with his own characters that *Kokoro* is so convincing a novel.[34]

Although McClellan does recognize the importance of *both* narrators—hence of *watakushi*'s sections as well—to the overall impact of the novel, his tendency is to see *watakushi* as both loyal to and similar to his older mentor, thus emphasizing their homosocial communion. However much he may recognize *watakushi*'s importance in the novel, for McClellan the younger man's role is still essentially to help us get a better view of Sensei. "Sensei would lose much of his significance as a human being," he writes, "if we did not see him first, in his full maturity, as he appeared to another man."[35]

This paternalistic homosocial reading of *Kokoro* is thus inextricably tied to an assumption of fidelity and unquestioned hierarchy between Sensei and the younger narrator. Not surprisingly, this leaves very little room for women. McClellan's article says nothing at all about the effect that Sensei's relations with K had on Sensei's wife. His discussion of *The Wayfarer*, in the same article, is also notable for its lack of concern with the female characters in the novel. The feminist critic Komashaku Kimi, for example, has read this novel as a stunning critique of the dehumanizing effects of the marriage system on *both* men and women, but McClellan barely mentions the protagonist Ichiro's wife Onao (to whom Sōseki gives the line about feeling like a "potted plant" that I mentioned earlier) and focuses exclusively on the theme of the isolation of "man."[36]

In an article written in 1986, Miyoshi Yukio also insisted on the absolute fidelity of the bond between Sensei and *watakushi*. When another critic pointed out that this effectively excluded Okusan as an active agent and thus relied on a "capitalist" understanding of women as nothing more than mute commodities passed between men, Miyoshi responded by claiming he was merely channeling Sōseki, asserting that Sōseki's "aesthetic" [*bigaku*] was one in which "men alone were the ones who looked deeply into the nature of love."[37] Miyoshi went on to claim that Sōseki's "basic view of

---

34. McClellan, "The Implications of Sōseki's Kokoro," 362.

35. On the basic *similarity* between Sensei and *watakushi* McClellan writes: "His family will never forgive him for deserting his father's bedside. And Sensei, his only friend, is about to kill himself. We cannot but notice the implied parallel between the fate of the young man and that of Sensei" (ibid., 119).

36. See Komashaku, "Towards an Absolute State'."

37. Miyoshi is quite an unreconstructed chauvinist in this article. He starts out by saying he will just have to accept [*kanju suru*] the criticism that he thinks of women as

women" was encapsulated in the fact that in his novels characters like Okusan and Sōsuke's wife Oyone in *The Gate* are "never told a thing and go heading into a gentle spring."[38] Finally, he mentions rather darkly that "By the way, General Nogi's wife was also named Shizuko."[39] The allusion here was to Sensei's wife Shizu, which leaves one to wonder if Miyoshi's implication was that she ought to have followed her husband in death as well, as did the admirable Nogi Shizuko.[40] Pace Miyoshi, however, the only way that one could actually believe that this exhausts the view of women represented in Sōseki's novels, even in *Kokoro*—perhaps his most homosocial—is by conflating Sensei with Sōseki and ignoring the role of the younger narrator entirely.

One way of reading the insistence of Miyoshi and other critics on elevating Sensei (and/as Sōseki) and subordinating *watakushi* is to compare it to the hierarchical nature of a *nanshoku* relationship. In such a relationship the "bottom" or *wakashu* would offer his older partner, or *nenja*, "obedience, respect, and intimate access to his person" in exchange for the latter's serving as a "role model."[41] The only way in which *watakushi* differs from the *wakashu* in this definition is that in place of access to his "person," he offers his services as the passive addressee of Sensei's testament.[42] If there is a "repressed" homosexuality communicating itself through these readings, moreover, it has a distinctively sadomasochistic feel to it. And yet unlike the more creative and subversive forms of sadomasochism that come to mind—those that appear in the works of Tanizaki Jun'ichirō, for instance—this one is quite resistant to role reversal and performative play. As a mode of reading, moreover, it is literalist and tends to be completely in thrall to the myth of the author.

---

commodities, since he is after all just a normal "liver of life" [*seikatsusha*] in what is, in fact, a capitalist world.

38. Miyoshi, "Sensei wa kokyu ka?" 191.

39. Ibid.

40. In a brilliant piece that outlines the relationship between male homosociality, misogyny, and modernity in modern Japanese novelistic narrative, Sharalyn Orbaugh finds in the linked figures of the bloody deaths of K, Sensei, and General Nogi, "a uniquely male genealogy, giving life to narrative but death to people (including the silent deaths of Shizuko and Shizu)" ("General Nogi's Wife," 17).

41. Pflugfelder, *Cartographies of Desire*, 41.

42. Miyoshi also uses an active/passive distinction to describe Sensei and *watakushi*. The latter is the *kōdō shutai* to *watakushi*'s *mushi no kijutsusha*. ("Watoson wa haishinsha ka?" 7).

In a telling footnote in the same article, Miyoshi offers his definition of literature: "Literature lives only in the time when the author who created it wrote it. It is my firm belief [*shinjō*], therefore, that the job of the literary scholar is to bring the dead back to life in history."⁴³ For paternalistic homosocial readers of *Kokoro* like Miyoshi, Etō, and McClellan, Sōseki himself must be resurrected, just as Sensei wanted somehow to bring K back to life by passing on his burden to the next generation. *Watakushi* is reduced to a passive instrument of Sensei and K's resurrection, communicating their ghostly voices through a morbidly homosocial, sexless *nanshoku*-style community of presumptively male readers. As the critic Koyano Atsushi has put it with regard to the novel and its postwar reception, "In *Kokoro*, ethics, *nanshoku*, and misogyny are inextricably tied together."⁴⁴

By privileging Sensei over *watakushi* as the novel's protagonist, the paternalistic homosocial critics suppressed the possibility of a dynamic interplay between the novel's two narrators and effectively froze *Kokoro* into an atemporal morals textbook. Their critical consensus was reflected and compounded in the popular imagination, moreover, thanks to the fact that *Kokoro* was not only commonly excerpted in high school literature textbooks from the late 1950s on, but that the sections chosen were invariably drawn from Sensei's testament alone (thus extricating it from *watakushi*'s framing narrative).⁴⁵ Just as Sensei, in an attempt to expiate the sin of having betrayed one male friend, unburdens himself to another male friend while insisting that the latter never breathe a word to his wife, *Kokoro* has kept generating new homosocial narratives among communities of men.

One place this happens is in and around Edwin McClellan's 1957 translation of *Kokoro* into English. Just as *watakushi* had to be imagined as a sort of neutral amanuensis who would allow readers to see through him to the towering and heroic figure of Sensei (and Sōseki), the translator, too, for these paternalistic homosocial readers, needed to be as "faithful" as possible. We can see this dynamic very clearly in an encounter between Etō Jun and McClellan described in a recent article by Aida Hirotsugu. Aida quotes Etō describing his first meeting with McClellan in 1964:

---

43. Miyoshi, "Watoson wa haishinsha ka?" 21.
44. Koyano, "*Kokoro* wa dōseiai shōsetsu ka?" 180.
45. *Kokoro* was first excerpted in the high-school textbook *Kōtō kokugo 2*, published by Shimizu shoin in 1956. For an excellent account of the postwar canonization of *Kokoro* via high-school textbooks, see Chapters 1 and 2 of Satō Izumi, *Sōseki*.

In my class on Japanese literature in translation I had used McClellan's translation of Natsume Sōseki's *Kokoro*, and since then the name Edwin McClellan had been carved into my mind—it was a name I could never forget. That same Professor McClellan was now standing on the stage speaking to us. I gazed up at him and became absorbed in his voice. No acceptable translation is possible . . . unless the translator accepts the worldview and values of the author and his characters. McClellan not only achieved that but rendered it in beautiful English. It was for this very reason . . . that I was able to deeply trust the translator of *Kokoro*, Edwin McClellan, before I even set eyes on him.[46]

The article goes on to talk about the "lifelong friendship" between McClellan and Etō, even mentioning how "these feelings of friendship extended to the men's spouses as well." Etō's emphasis on "trust" is fascinating here in the context of his reading of *Kokoro* as being primarily about the *loss* of trust in the modern world. He seems able to trust both McClellan the man and his translation thanks to what he imagines as a complete fidelity on McClellan's part to the "worldview and values" supposedly expressed in Sōseki's novel.

As I will show, however, Etō's enthusiasm had less to do with its literal accuracy and more with its fidelity to the paternalistic homosocial reading that he, McClellan, Miyoshi, and others shared. His remarks on McClellan and his admiration for him, moreover, reflect an idealized communion between men in which narrative is transmitted "faithfully" and values are preserved absolute. If McClellan's accurate translation makes him a faithful *watakushi* to Sōseki's *Kokoro*, Etō's attitude turns him into an awestruck *watakushi* to McClellan's Sensei. A translation is a kind of fossilized act of reading and McClellan's 1957 translation is an excellent, line-by-line example of the paternalistic homosocial reading of *Kokoro* as it was prac-ticed on both sides of the Pacific during the postwar period. Considering it today, especially in comparison with Meredith McKinney's 2010 Penguin version, the reader can see how the reading of the novel has shifted thanks to a corresponding shift in the shape of the homosocial continuum.

Komori the Zombie Slayer:
The Oedipal Homosocial Reading

But before I discuss McClellan's translation in greater detail, I want to introduce a very different reading of *Kokoro* that emerged in response. This ecstatic proliferation of would-be *watakushi*'s in and around the paternalistic homosocial reading would come to a screeching halt in 1985 with the publication in an obscure journal of an article by Komori Yōichi that ef-

---

46. Aida, "Sōseki, Haieku, Etō Jun," 339.

fectively threw a bucket of cold water on this male homosocial "zombie ball." In that article, Komori began with a bracing description of what he called a "sick bias" [*isshu no yamai to mo ieru henshū*] pervading most readings of *Kokoro*.

> Most of the enormous number of essays on *Kokoro* I have before me now are attempts to decode the thought of the "author" Sōseki by focusing on Sensei's discourse in the novel's last section. . . . these readings present a series of dichotomies between "morality and egoism," "love and friendship," "faith and mistrust" as the "correct" framework through which to interpret the work. The sublation [*shiyō*] of these various dichotomies is found in an ascetic taboo on desire and an aestheticization of death backed up by a superior spirituality and ethics, all in the name of "self immolation [*junshi*] for the sake of the spirit of Meiji" to which is accorded a universal value.[47]

A page later, Komori goes on to describe the effect this has had on young readers (including himself): "By making *Kokoro* into a text that functions as a mechanism of nationalist ideology centered around patriarchal values of 'ethics,' 'spirituality,' and 'death,' young readers are forced to kneel before the 'ethical' and 'spiritual' death of 'Sensei' and shrink before the deified author as they contemplate their own ethical and spiritual inadequacies."[48]

In an effort to combat this moralistic, patriarchal, and nationalist reading of *Kokoro*, Komori's article drew attention to *watakushi*'s active role in the framing and narration of Sensei's story. Whereas the paternalistic homosocial reading ignored the novel's narrative complexity to preserve the disinterested objectivity of its young narrator and make Sensei (and Sōseki) into a tragic national hero, Komori argued that the severing of Sensei's letter from the rest of the novel amounted to cutting its "life line" [*seimei no sen*].[49] By shifting the focus back to the first narrator, he read the novel as the story of how the younger man *learned from the mistakes* of his dead mentor. In Komori's reading, the first narrator's account served to relativize Sensei's testament and cast doubt on the morbid homosocial values it put forth. If Komori placed the emphasis on the younger narrator's desire to differentiate [*saika*] himself from Sensei, his collaborator Ishihara Chiaki went even further—reading *watakushi*'s narrative for signs of "Oedipal" ambivalence toward the older man.[50] Both critics disagreed with the paternalistic homosocial reading which foregrounded *watakushi*'s "respect and rever-

---

47. Komori, "*Kokoro* ni okeru hanten suru 'shuki,'" 415–16.
48. Ibid., 416.
49. Ibid., 420.
50. For this argument, see Ishihara, "*Kokoro* no Oidipusu." See also Ishihara, *Kokoro: otona ni narenakatta sensei*, 106.

ence" for Sensei and downplayed or ignored any suggestion of rivalry or ambivalence. For this reason I will refer to Komori and Ishihara's reading as the "Oedipal homosocial" reading.

In his essay, Komori advanced his argument in a provocative, and indeed "Oedipal," fashion, by uncovering through narratological analysis evidence that he claimed proved that *watakushi* went on not only to live with Sensei's wife after the latter's death, but also to have children with her (something Sensei himself was never able to do). With this argument, Komori attacked the consensus among Sōseki scholars that saw *watakushi* as at best a sort of clone of Sensei destined to repeat his fate (McClellan) and at worst a mere "selfless recorder" (Miyoshi) of the older man's story. In place of these views of *watakushi* as a passive and subordinate *wakashu*, Komori offered a reconstructed "afterlife" for the narrative in which "two people [*watakushi* and Sensei's widow] enter freely into an alliance in which there is no separation between mind and body." Unlike his morbidly homosocial mentor, Komori argued, the younger narrator managed to enter into a "living relationship of two free individuals"[51] characterized by openness to the other and the liberation of sexual desire from the constraints of family and nation. In doing so, Komori sought to provide Sōseki's morbid homosocial masterpiece with a reconstructed ending that would point the way toward a brighter modernity associated with heterosexuality. If the paternalistic homosocial readers of *Kokoro* saw it as a story about a past cut off fatefully from the present and thus read it in melancholic and nostalgic terms, the Oedipal homosocial reading understood the narrative's *recursivity* as the sign of its younger narrator's Oedipal victory over his mentor and emphasized the narrative's orientation toward a heterosexual future.

The key sentence from Komori's essay is worth quoting here in all its lyrical enthusiasm:

As Sensei's "blood" (nothing other than the words of his Testament) courses with "new life" [*atarashii inochi*] through his breast, there is only one path for *watakushi* to choose. He must rush to her side, to live a new life together [*arata na sei o tomo ni ikiru*] with "Okusan" who has lost "the only man she can depend on" . . . to "Okusan," who is all alone. His awareness, moreover, of this kind of "isolation" (what he calls the "helplessness of man"[52]) will also give birth to a new logic of life upon the death of the absolute other (the

---

51. Komori, "*Kokoro* ni okeru hanten suru 'shuki,'" 437.

52. The quote is from the last line of Part I. In McClellan's translation it reads in full, "I felt then the helplessness of *man*, and the vanity of *his* life" (Natsume, *Kokoro*, 80 [McClellan]), emphasis mine. Here again, McClellan insists on universalizing the male homosocial. McKinney avoids gendered language, rendering it as "the hopeless frailty of our innately superficial nature." (ibid., 76 [McKinney]).

patriarchal) that guarantees the identity and centrality of the self and the ideology of *junshi* (family logic) that militates a merging with that other.[53]

It is easy to understand Komori's enthusiasm. The swelling tone and progressive fervor speak volumes about the frustration that he and other younger critics in the 1980s and 1990s seem to have felt towards the old guard of Sōseki studies, and the "moralizing" tendency of "national literature" [*kokubungaku*] scholarship in general. In some ways, his argument even resembles a certain strain of queer theory in its insistence on independence from "family logic" and "the patriarchal." In one fascinating moment in the essay, for example, he compares Sensei and K by saying that although both came from the same small town and left their families behind, Sensei does so "passively" as a result of his parent's death and his uncle cheating him out of his inheritance while K actually *chooses* to leave. In his pursuit of "the way," K actively deceives his adopted family and is eventually disowned by them. But he is content with his new life in the big city and covets a kind of creative autonomy. Sensei, on the other hand, by taking up residence with Okusan and Ojōsan and then inviting K to move in as well, works to recreate a sort of "pseudo-family," in the process robbing K of his precious solitude. K comes across in this reading as a sort of radical urban queer, and Sensei as a proponent of rather conservative "family values."

For Komori, *watakushi* may have been infused with Sensei's "blood/writing," but the lesson he learns from it makes him more like this "radical" K—by "liberating" him from all that is patriarchal and familial. But unlike the almost proto-queer K, whose ideal was to remain unswayed by the myth of romantic love, *watakushi*'s liberation for Komori is inextricably tied to his imagined union with Okusan, with whom, Komori waxes lyrical again, "He is able to live as a unit [*kumiawase*] of one free person and another, in a way utterly unrelated to that sort of family concept and as someone who would never become a member of the territory of the family."[54] To keep this relationship from being corrupted or coopted by anything except the "free union" of two autonomous individuals, Komori stops short of arguing that the two *get married*, but argues rather that they simply made a life together and had children, somehow outside of the "territory" of the family system. In the end, Komori claims for *watakushi* and Okusan all of the

---

53. Komori, "*Kokoro* ni okeru hanten suru 'shuki,'" 431.
54. Ibid., 437.

romance of the first flush of love with none of the social entanglements—a kind of heterosexuality without the heteronormativity. This reading is, of course, all the easier to support thanks to the fact that the relationship is reconstructed from the ways in which *watakushi* is *different* from Sensei and is never positively described.

The most important among these differences between *watakushi* and Sensei is that while the older man makes a firm distinction between mind and body—celebrating the former and repressing the latter—the younger man seems more in touch with his physical embodiment. About Okusan, for example, he says at one point that "then my heart, rather than my mind, began to respond to her."[55] The word *watakushi* uses for "heart" here is not the "spiritual" *kokoro* but literally the name of the cardiac organ, the *shinzō*, which he glosses with the English word "heart" in *katakana*. This is one of many instances, according to Komori, where *watakushi* is working to differentiate himself from Sensei. Sensei could only love Okusan in a spiritual way (with his *kokoro*), but *watakushi* does so physically as well. It is *watakushi*'s ability—or willingness—to *desire* Okusan that frees him of the "constraints" of family and nation and that makes him able to "grow up" and leave Sensei behind.

As a description of *watakushi*'s narrative, Komori's analysis is no doubt correct. In its optimism and forward-looking tone, it is also refreshing in comparison to the pessimistic accounts of McClellan and others. I wonder, however, whether he did not go a little too far in his celebration of the younger man's liberated desire. If the "paternalistic homosocial" critics tended to ignore *watakushi* to see only Sensei as the novel's protagonist and to equate his pessimism about the possibility of intimacy between modern individuals with that of a world-weary but wise Sōseki, Komori's championing of *watakushi* depends on the abjection of Sensei. Even *watakushi*'s "progressive" and life-affirming nature comes to light only in implicit comparison with the aloof Sensei, resolved as he is to "go on living as if I were dead."[56] This is very similar to the dynamic between *boku* and the automaton-like Okada in Ōgai's *The Wild Goose*. Komori speaks of *watakushi* and Okusan's reconstructed relationship, moreover, as one that is not only utterly categorically different from, but is *defined in absolute opposition to* [*tettei shite saika suru*] the relationship between Sensei and K.[57] He posits for *watakushi* and Okusan a notion of desire that "has its source in the body," while

---

55. Natsume, *Kokoro*, 39 (McKinney), 39–40 (McClellan), 52 (*SZ*).
56. Ibid., 230 (McKinney), 243 (McClellan), 294 (*SZ*).
57. Komori, "*Kokoro* ni okeru hanten suru 'shuki,'" 437.

describing Sensei and K's desire, as I mentioned earlier, as "a kind of *nanshoku* from which the physical desire has been repressed." Insofar as the relationship between *watakushi* and Okusan is defined in opposition to this "sexless *nanshoku*" between Sensei and K, Komori's reading turns out the be informed by a romantic notion of the liberation of a spontaneous heterosexual desire rooted in the body and productive of identity.

On the other hand, in privileging the younger narrator, Komori attributes to him the same kind of sensitivity toward women that made it possible for the narrator of Ōgai's *The Wild Goose* to narrate Otama's story—and this despite the fact that, unlike *boku*'s detailed account of Otama, *watakushi* has precious little to say about Okusan in the course of his narrative. Even more here than in Ōgai's text, this "sensitivity" serves chiefly as the grist for a competition between men, whether they are Sensei and *watakushi* or Komori and his fellow Sōseki scholars, almost all of whom are men. Komori's critique of *Kokoro*'s homosocial *thematics* (which he identified, as we have seen, with the "patriarchal values of 'ethics,' 'spirituality,' and 'death.'") is thus informed by what is in the end a deeply homosocial and heteronormative narrative in which the younger man's achievement of reproductive heterosexuality—*giving Okusan that baby she wanted*—is held up as a paradigm of successful modernization and maturation. Komori's suturing of *Kokoro*'s "life line," moreover, worked by implicitly "homosexualizing" Sensei and characterizing him as a man stuck in the (homosocial) past. The result is a narrative of development from a homosexual/homosocial past associated with Sensei toward a heterosexual future embodied by *watakushi*.[58]

Translation and the Narratology of Homosociality

Despite these ideological issues, however, Komori and Ishihara's readings of *Kokoro* remain stunning examples of the application of narratological theory to Sōseki's novel. As Atsuko Sakaki has noted, "By applying this 'new' framework, Komori challenged the authority of the *kindai kokubungaku* methodologies that prevailed at the time—that is, Romanticist studies

---

58. Komori's association of Sensei with the past and *watakushi* with the future is one of a series of such narratives of progress in and around what I discuss in the next chapter as *Kokoro*'s "primal scene." The first of these was, of course, Sensei's own characterization of K as " transfixed by the contemplation of his own past." This paragraph ends with the line, "In this respect I was confident that I knew him well." Although this is Sensei's voice, one can hear the voice of the older Sensei and the implied author behind it, questioning his certainty. Why "I *was* confident?" and not "I *am*?" Is Sensei not talking about himself here? Natsume, *Kokoro*, 206 (McKinney), 218 (McClellan), 263 (*SZ*).

of the author-genius and the work-masterpiece."⁵⁹ Sakaki has already provided a useful summary of the debates that ensued,⁶⁰ but it will be useful here to discuss Komori and Ishihara's arguments in more detail for what they reveal about what I would like to call the "narratology of homosociality." Specifically, I want to look at how McClellan's translation of *Kokoro* manages to downplay almost all of the evidence that Komori and Ishihara uncovered for their thesis. A close reading of McClellan's version is a good way both to convey the details of the Oedipal homosocial reading and the surprising consistency with which McClellan's choices reflected not only the paternalistic homosocial consensus but also a unidirectional and teleological understanding of novelistic narrative.

The first piece of evidence Komori offers in his article is a line from the beginning of the novel where *watakushi* explains why he calls his friend "Sensei." I cite it here first in Meredith McKinney's translation: "'Sensei' springs to my lips whenever I summon memories of this man, and I write of him now with the same reverence and respect. It would also feel wrong to use some conventional initial [*yosoyososhii kashiramoji nado*] to substitute for his name and thereby distance him."⁶¹ The first-time reader of this passage will not miss the "reverence and respect" that *watakushi* feels for Sensei. But he or she is less likely to understand the meaning behind his reference to the distancing effect of "some conventional initial." What that reader cannot know, of course, is that Sensei will refer to *his* friend in his testament with just such a "conventional initial" ("K"). *Watakushi*, for his part, *has* read Sensei's letter and *does* know this (as does anyone who is *re*-reading *Kokoro*). Komori argues that this sentence shows the young man trying to differentiate himself from Sensei, by contrasting his own closeness to and *way of writing about* the older man (what Komori calls an "I-you relationship") with Sensei's "impersonal" "third-person" way of writing about his friend K.⁶²

In this passage, then, according to both Komori and Ishihara, *watakushi* is saying that he feels very close to Sensei—so close that he would never use a "conventional initial" to refer to him, but, *in saying this*, he is also distancing and differentiating himself from his friend, saying effectively, "I,

---

59. Sakaki, "The Debates on *Kokoro*," 31–32.
60. According to Ishihara Chiaki, in 1996 there had been about 450 articles written on *Kokoro* since its original publication, but 200 of them were written in the ten years following Komori's article in March 1985. Iida et al., "*Kokoro* ronsō ikō," 156. For Sakaki's summary, see Sakaki, "The Debates on *Kokoro*."
61. Natsume, *Kokoro*, 3 (McKinney), 3 (*SZ*).
62. See Komori, "*Kokoro* ni okeru hanten suru 'shuki,'" 418–19.

unlike Sensei, know how to express my closeness to a male friend." For them, this sentence is crucial, then, as an early indicator of *watakushi*'s complicated feelings toward Sensei and signals that his account may not be entirely objective or "faithful." It is also the first sign of *watakushi*'s implicit claim to have "moved beyond" Sensei and the morbid homosocial past he represents.

For the paternalistic homosocial readers like McClellan, Etō, and Miyoshi, however, for whom *watakushi*'s "reverence and respect" toward Sensei were paramount, the younger narrator's difference and ambivalence were harder to see. McClellan even calls *watakushi*'s feelings for Sensei "love," writing, "It is the young man's love for him that forces Sensei to write his letter."[63] Miyoshi, in his response to Komori and Ishihara, made the argument that *Kokoro* was a serialized novel and that since the original readers could not have known about K yet, Sōseki could not have intended to communicate *watakushi*'s ambivalence to them at this early point in the novel. This is a strikingly "originalist" argument that privileges not only Sōseki's authorial intent but also a relatively small group of initial readers. As Sakaki has noted, it is also singularly unconvincing, considering that this passage is just "a classic example of foreshadowing."[64] It also shows clearly how the paternalistic homosocial reading implies not only an unquestioning belief in authorial intention but a modernizing notion of forward-moving temporality, suggesting that the novel can only be read correctly in "real" or "historical" time and in one, forward direction. It does this, paradoxically, even though it is motivated by a melancholic connection to the past—bringing the dead back to life.

I have cited this passage from McKinney's new translation of *Kokoro* not just because her version is so well done, but because, in McClellan's version, the sentence about the "conventional initial" is, famously, simply not there. This means that in McClellan's version this early indication of differentiation and ambivalence on *watakushi*'s part is missing and all the reader gets is the "reverence and respect" that *watakushi* felt for Sensei: "Whenever the memory of him comes back to me now, I find that I think of him as 'Sensei' still. And with pen in hand, I cannot bring myself to write of him in any other way."[65]

---

63. It is interesting to note here that McClellan's observation is made entirely from Sensei's perspective. Sensei *assumes* that the younger man loves him and neither he nor McClellan bother to ask whether that love is not also shot through with ambivalence ("The Implications of Soseki's *Kokoro*," 364).

64. Sakaki, "The Debates on *Kokoro*," 46.

65. Natsume, *Kokoro*, 1 (McClellan), 3 (*SZ*).

As is often the case with McClellan's translation, the tone is highly elegiac here, especially when juxtaposed to McKinney's crisper version. This may have to do with the postpositive placement of "still" in the first sentence and the sense his version gives of an almost involuntary memory of and reverence toward Sensei on *watakushi*'s part. Whereas McKinney's *watakushi* "summons memories of this man" in a way that makes him an active agent and puts a slight distance between them ("this man"), in McClellan's version the memory "comes back" seemingly of its own accord and *watakushi* passively "finds" that he thinks of him as "'Sensei' still." He has no other choice, moreover, than to use this term of respect. No wonder that Etō was so fond of McClellan's translation; it renders perfectly Etō's and Miyoshi's sense of Sensei's ghostly presence and *watakushi*'s utter passivity.

And yet contrary to what one might expect given Etō's stated impression that he could "deeply trust" the translator of *Kokoro* to communicate Sōseki's values in a faithful and undistorted fashion, McClellan here excises an entire sentence from the text! In pointing this out (and I am not the first to do so), my purpose is not just to expose a mistake, but to ask what McClellan's choice to suppress this sentence has to say about the state of the male homosocial continuum in McClellan's moment. As George Steiner has written, "The failings of the translator . . . localize, they project as on to a screen, the resistant vitalities, the opaque centres of specific genius in the original."[66] My hope is that noticing McClellan's "failing" here will reveal how the specific genius of Sōseki's text is *not* reducible to the paternalistic homosocial reading McClellan's translation helped to impose upon it.

Another piece of evidence that Ishihara cites bears more directly on the possibility that *watakushi* became romantically involved with Okusan after Sensei's death.[67] This is the famous question of "the extra letter." In Chapter 22 of McKinney's translation, upon receiving a short reply to a letter he had written to Sensei asking the latter to help him find a job, *watakushi* notes that this was "the first letter I had ever received from him." Then he goes on to say that "Although one might naturally have thought we corresponded from time to time, in fact we never had. I received only two letters from Sensei before his death. The first was this simple reply. The second was an extremely long letter that he wrote for me shortly before he died."[68]

---

66. Steiner, *After Babel*, 317.
67. See Ishihara, *Kokoro: otona ni narenakatta sensei*, 138–39.
68. Natsume, *Kokoro*, 46 (McKinney), 63 (*SZ*).

This translation is quite "faithful" to Sōseki's Japanese. Its content, however, appears to contradict an earlier statement made by *watakushi* in Chapter 9, where he mentions a postcard and a third letter in addition to the "simple reply" and the "extremely long" one. McKinney's version renders this sentence, again quite faithfully, as "I still have a postcard they sent from the hot springs resort at Hakone, and I received a letter from their visit to Nikkō, with an autumn leaf enclosed."[69]

As Ishihara points out, one could consider that the "postcard" mentioned in this last sentence might not count as a letter. But it is harder to discount the one "received from their visit to Nikkō." Although the Japanese text refers to it not as a *tegami* but uses the term *yūbin* (which means something like "a piece of mail"), given that it encloses an autumn leaf, one might reasonably expect that it contains a proper letter as well, rather than what one might scribble on a postcard. If this "piece of mail" was also from Sensei, why does he claim later that he only received two letters from Sensei during his mentor's life, one short one when he was at home visiting his parents, and one very long one—the "testament" with which the novel ends? One way to explain this discrepancy, Ishihara argues, is to posit that this other letter from Nikkō "with an autumn leaf enclosed" came not from Sensei but from Okusan. Enclosing leaves in letters was a sort of fad among women at this time, which would seem to support this possibility. The sentence in Japanese [*Nikkō e itta toki wa momiji no ha o ichimai hōjikometa yūbin mo moratta*] could also easily be interpreted this way because it doesn't specify who the sender was.

Together with Komori, Ishihara came up with one more fascinating piece of evidence for this theory. When the two critics went back to Sōseki's original manuscript, they found that he had originally written, *but then crossed out*, an additional sentence following this one. The sentence, still legible beneath the lines used to cross it out, read "Of course this was Okusan's taste alone" [*mottomo sore ga okusan dake no shukō de atta ga*].[70]

If Okusan wrote to *watakushi* on her own (a very intimate act when it happened across sexes in Meiji Japan) and even went to the trouble of enclosing an autumn leaf with the letter, might this not imply a level of intimacy between the two that would predict an even greater intimacy after Sensei's death? Of course, one could argue that Sōseki simply forgot about this other letter when he wrote the later sentence in which he has *watakushi* say that he only ever received two letters from Sensei. But as Ishihara has

---

69. Ibid., 19 (McKinney), 25 (*SZ*).
70. Ishihara and Komori, "Sōseki *Kokoro* no genkō o yomu," 9–10.

convincingly argued, this is an excellent example of why it is important to *interpret everything* in a text rather than relying on author-based explanations (such as "Sōseki forgot").[71] While Komori and Ishihara's own interpretation might seem to be relying on a similar notion of the author, especially when they cite the crossed-out text from the manuscript version, it can still stand without that extra piece of evidence. It is primarily a text-based interpretation that in this case happens to be reinforced by the evidence from the manuscript version, which shows Sōseki very carefully modulating how much he wants to give away of what Ishihara has called the "buried Oedipal subplot" of *Kokoro*.

The plot really begins to thicken when considering McClellan's treatment of this "clue" that Sōseki seems so carefully to have left behind: for the first sentence from Chapter 9, he has: "I still have with me a postcard that they sent me from Hakone. And I remember that the time they went to Nikkō, I received from them a letter with a maple leaf enclosed."[72]

For some reason McClellan has inserted the phrase "from them" into Sōseki's sentence. Of course, one does this sort of thing as a translator from Japanese all the time since Japanese sentences often only imply referents that would be clearly indicated by a pronoun in English. Indeed, McClellan has also inserted the "they" in "they went to Nikkō," which doesn't appear in the Japanese either. But Sōseki was actually, relatively speaking, an author who used pronouns in a very conscious and deliberate way, particularly in his later works, including *Kokoro*, such that they sometimes sound almost as if they had been literally translated from English.[73] When Sōseki chooses *not* to make matters perfectly clear by using a pronoun, it tends to mean something. In this case, and when read in light of the fact that he crossed out the sentence about Okusan's taste in letters, it seems clearly to mean that he was planting a clue, but a not too obvious one in order to maintain some mystery as to who exactly sent this letter. McKinney's translation maintains the ambiguity quite effectively, even creating a slightly awkward sentence in English to match the ambiguity in Japanese. One receives letters from people of course, but in McKinney's version *watakushi* "received a letter from *their visit*."[74] McClellan's version, on the other hand, clears up the ambiguity: "I received from them a letter with a maple leaf enclosed." The letter was

---

71. See Ishihara, *Tekusuto wa machigawanai*.

72. Natsume, *Kokoro*, 18 (McClellan), 25 (*SZ*).

73. On this aspect of Sōseki's last novel *Light and Darkness*, see Auestad, "Against the Linguistic Constraints."

74. My emphasis.

from them. In McClellan's sentence, Sensei and his wife are a unit, leaving no space between them into which *watakushi* might intrude.

It is, of course, not possible to know whether McClellan *meant* to do this, nor, ultimately, does it really matter all that much if he did or not. His text, however, is aware of it on some level. In the later passage where *watakushi* explains that he only received two letters from Sensei while he was alive, McClellan makes another strange addition:

> In case I have unwittingly given the impression that there was much correspondence between Sensei and myself, I should like to say here that in all the time I knew Sensei, I received from him only two pieces of correspondence that might strictly be called "letters." One of them was the simple letter that I have just mentioned, and the other was a very long letter which he wrote me shortly before his death.[75]

The added phrase here is of course "that might strictly be called 'letters.'" In Sōseki's Japanese, this sentence reads exactly as McKinney's translation has it: "I received only two letters from Sensei before his death [*watashi wa Sensei no seizen ni tatta nitsū no tegami shika moratte inai*]".[76] McClellan's addition suggests that he picked up on the contradiction with the earlier statement. But rather than trusting that Sōseki knew what he was doing in planting this "clue" about *watakushi* and Okusan's relationship, he seems to have decided that Sōseki must have been mistaken and took it upon himself to "fix" this mistake by inserting this phrase so as to make room for the possibility that the third letter, with an autumn leaf enclosed, was somehow not "strictly" a letter. When combined with his addition of "from them" in the earlier passage the possibility that this other letter might have been from Okusan alone is completely erased. McClellan was clearly an extremely careful reader of Sōseki, but not an absolutely faithful one.

I want to cite one last example to show how remarkably pervasive this tendency is in McClellan's translation while also conveying a little more of the specifics of Komori and Ishihara's reading. The passage in question is the key piece of evidence in Komori's argument that *watakushi* had children with Okusan after Sensei's death. It comes in the form of what he calls a "silent drama" that plays out just beneath the surface of a conversation in Chapter 8 among *watakushi*, Sensei, and Okusan concerning the fact that the couple has no children. Here is the passage in McKinney's translation:

> "It would be nice if we had children, you know," she said, turning to me.
> "Yes, I'm sure," I replied. But I felt no stir of sympathy at her words. I was too young to have children of my own and regarded them as no more than noisy pests.

---

75. Natsume, *Kokoro*, 48 (McClellan), 63 (*SZ*).
76. Ibid., 46 (McKinney), 63 (*SZ*).

"Shall I adopt one for you?" said Sensei.
"Oh, dear me, an adopted child . . . ," she said, turning to me again.
"We'll never have one you know."[77]

After reminding his reader that this conversation is being presented to us by *watakushi*, who therefore has some reason to remember it, Komori notes that Okusan's wistful declaration that it would be "nice if we had children" is said while "turning to me," [*watakushi no hō o muite itta*] as if semiconsciously to ask *watakushi* if he might be able to give her one. At Sensei's mention of the possibility of an adopted child, she turns to *watakushi* yet again [*mata watashi no hō o muita*]. And finally (and this is not quite as clear in McKinney's version), *watakushi* says that he did not have children *at that time* [*kodomo o motta koto no nai* sono toki no *watakushi wa*], which suggests that now, at the moment of narration, after Sensei's death, he *does* have children. Is *watakushi* not hinting here that he had those children ("natural" rather than "adopted" children) with Okusan? Komori argues that he is, and that this scene shows not just a sort of familiar complicity between the two, but the presence between them of precisely the kind of physical desire, which he refers to as both "sexual desire" (*seiyoku* 性欲) and "desire for life" (*seiyoku* 生欲) that was missing from Sensei and Okusan's relationship.[78]

This passage is really the lynchpin in Komori's "scandalous" argument that initiated the *Kokoro* debates and prompted Miyoshi Yukio to write the two articles I cited earlier, the titles of which alone indicate the shock with which the idea was received ("Was Sensei a Cuckold?"; "Was Watson a Traitor?"). If Miyoshi and his like-minded critics had been reading McClellan's text, however, they would have had a slightly easier time defending Sensei from the charge of having been cuckolded by his traitorous "Watson" (the reference is to the Watson in Sherlock Holmes, who is supposed to play a similarly subservient role). Here is McClellan's version:

"It would be so nice if we had children," Sensei's wife said to me.
"Yes, wouldn't it?" I answered. But I could feel no real sympathy for her. At my age, children seemed an unnecessary nuisance.
"Would you like it if we adopted a child?"
"An adopted child? Oh, no," she said, and looked at me.
"But we'll never have one of our own, you know," said Sensei.[79]

The differences here are more subtle but still identifiable. The only blatant omission is the word *mata* (again) in the second to last line. In Sōseki's

---

77. Ibid., 18 (McKinney), 24 (*SZ*).
78. Komori, "*Kokoro* ni okeru hanten suru 'shuki,'" 436.
79. Natsume, *Kokoro*, 17 (McClellan), 24 (*SZ*).

text and in McKinney's this emphasis on repetition serves to underline the urgency of Okusan's desire, and *watakushi*'s awareness of it. Just as importantly, in McKinney's version, as in Sōseki's text, the description of Okusan as "turning to me" emphasizes her body language, in addition to her words. Repeatedly turning her body to *watakushi*, she seems to yearn not just for a baby, but for the physical closeness Sensei does not provide. In McClellan's version Okusan's attention on *watakushi* is still there, but it has been abstracted into speech and a look ("Sensei's wife said to me"; "and looked at me"). If McKinney's translation (and Sōseki's original) suggests a physical yearning expressed in Okusan's *body*, McClellan's demonstrates the effects of the "ascetic taboo on desire" that Komori noted as typical of the paternalistic homosocial reading of *Kokoro*. Also, by rendering Sōseki's phrase "For me, who as yet had no children" [*kodomo o motta koto no nai sono toki no watakushi wa*] as simply "At my age," McClellan downplays the contrast with the present that suggests that he might have children *now*. As was the case with the sentence about the "conventional initial," this flattens the two-timing character of Sōseki's narrative and evokes an absolute past rather than a past imagined through the lens of a different present.

By downplaying in all of these ways the flickers of connection between *watakushi* and Okusan, McClellan's version works to uphold the trust between Sensei and *watakushi*. In each case, McClellan has made the text fit his reading by de-emphasizing the possibility of conflict between Sensei and the young narrator. The irony of this is that in order to maintain his belief in the inviolate and absolute nature of Sensei's account as mediated by a selfless, desireless *watakushi*, a belief that is itself inspired by a worshipful attitude toward Sōseki himself, he has to proceed in his translation as if Sōseki made careless mistakes as a writer.

I want to emphasize again here that in pointing to these various discrepancies between McClellan's and McKinney's translations, my intent is not to call attention to them as mistakes, but rather to read his translation as an index of its historical moment—specifically of the state of the homosocial continuum in 1957. Komori and Ishihara, whose readings may have influenced McKinney's recent translation, were writing in the 1980s and 1990s, during a time when not only narratology, but gender studies, queer theory, and new critiques of nationalism, and other "theories" were in the air. It was also the time both of the critique of modernization and of the emergence of identity politics, all of which are reflected in their readings of the novel. For all these reasons, it is not surprising to find that Komori and Ishihara were not the only ones who reread *Kokoro* along these lines. Beginning in the 1980s many readers seem to have felt frustrated with the paternalistic homosocial reading, with it obsessive focus on the past, and looked for ways to read the novel with an eye to the future. Often this involved cooking up a marriage plot between Okusan and *watakushi*. Sakaki mentions the playwright Hata Kōhei's theatrical adaptation of the novel, *Kokoro: Loneliness and Love* [*Kokoro no kodoku to ai*], written in 1986 and first staged in 1987, which ends with the marriage of Sensei's wife and *watakushi*. Miyakawa Takeo cites a 1980 manga parody of *Kokoro* by Takahashi Rumiko in which a young widow marries and has children with a student teacher whom she met when he taught *Kokoro* to her as a high school student.[80] The motivations of these readings and adaptations differ, but they all point to an anxiety over *Kokoro*'s lack of closure and a tendency to remedy this lack with heterosexual union and children. In 1988 the Canadian critic Patricia Merivale wrote an article in which she speculated on the missing conclusion of the novel to reach the same conclusion as Komori and Ishihara.[81] For Sakaki, the fact that Merivale arrived at the same conclusion as Komori even though she was writing on the basis of McClellan's translation and in complete isolation from Japanese academia suggests "a certain universal plausibility" to Komori's thesis.[82] Given what I have shown of the bias of McClellan's translation, this is remarkable indeed.

The "Gay Homosocial" Reading: Kokoro as "Homo-Novel"

Yet another group of readers have read *Kokoro* in a very different way, picking up on the homoerotic "undercurrents" between both Sensei and K and Sensei and *watakushi*. In 1985, the very same year that Komori's first essay came out, the flamboyant and campy critic and novelist Hashimoto Osamu rather gleefully designated *Kokoro* a "homo-novel" in a long essay in which he took issue with Doi Takeo's use of the term *dōseiai-teki kanjō* or "homosexual-like feelings" to describe *Kokoro*. Whereas Doi made a distinction between such feelings and what he called "homosexuality in the narrow sense" [*kyōgi no dōseiai*], Hashimoto claimed that this was just a way of avoiding having to deal with the homo-eroticism of Sōseki's text and to place a kind of *cordon sanitaire* between those who are "really homosexual" and the rest of the human race. For Hashimoto, pace Doi, there is nothing "homosexual-like" about *Kokoro*. Instead it is a full-fledged gay novel, nothing less than *homo-marudashi*—a phrase that might roughly translate to "queer

---

80. The manga is titled *Mezon ikkoku*. Miyakawa calls its plot "very Komori-like" ("Saiwa sareta *Kokoro*," 191).
81. Merivale, "Silences," 137.
82. Sakaki, "The Debates on *Kokoro*," 35.

as a three-dollar bill," or, as I put it in the Introduction, "full-on homo."[83] In another passage, he quotes, in large, bold-faced type, his own reaction when he first read *Kokoro*, the campiness of which is hard to render in English, but which reads something like: "I thought to myself, Oh. My. *GOD*!!! Sōseki wrote novels about homos! It's true!"[84]

Writing a decade later in 1996, Ōhashi Yōichi called *Kokoro* a "masterpiece of homosexual literature" and celebrated the homoerotic relations among men suggested by the novel for their potential to "rebuild communities ravaged by the relentless advance of capitalism."[85] For Stephen Dodd, writing in 1998, as I mentioned earlier, a reading of *Kokoro* suggested that Sōseki was "open to a wider range of erotic possibilities than has generally been acknowledged."[86]

Dodd, Hashimoto, and Ōhashi were not the first to read Sōseki's works in this way. This "hopeful gay" reading of Sōseki goes back to the earliest days of modern gay identity in Japan. One example, which relates not directly to *Kokoro* but to the biographical Sōseki, can be found in the first issue of what was arguably the first "gay" magazine in Japan. The founding issue of the magazine *Adon* from 1952 includes an article in which one Hara Hiroshi quotes at length from Sōseki's correspondence with his male disciples and finds evidence there (at the risk of shocking "all the gray-haired professors") for a sort of "Greek," or samurai *nanshoku*-style, homoeroticism. The young Suzuki Miekichi in particular seems to have had quite a crush on Sōseki, reportedly writing him a letter that was 5.4 meters (3 *kan*) long and insisting on making a recording of his voice, a desire that Hara describes as a "fetishistic" [*fetishizumu-teki yokubō*]." Hara even compares Miekichi to "one of those lovesick schoolgirls mad for her lady teacher you hear about these days."[87]

---

83. Hashimoto, *Hasu to katana*, 230.
84. Ibid., 225.
85. Ōhashi, "Kuiā fāzāzu no yume, kuiā neishon no yume," 59. Ōhashi's reading is not entirely celebratory. He points out that the novel contains the seeds of fascism as well in its construction of a homosocial community of men centered on the emperor.
86. Dodd, "The Significance of Bodies in Soseki's *Kokoro*," 496.
87. One of the many letters Hara quotes gives a good sense of the light-hearted homoeroticism that seems to have characterized Sōseki's interactions with his "disciples," especially in the early years. In December 1906, Sōseki wrote Morita Sōhei to pass on a letter to him from Suzuki Miekichi. Noting that the young Miekichi was "always using words like '*suitō*' ["how sweet!"] and '*ureshii*' ["I'm so happy!"] he says how happy Morita must be to have a disciple like him. Then he says that passing letters between them makes him feel like a "go-between" or "a version of those female hairdressers from the old novels" [*kō yatte kimi no tegami o Miekichi ni watashite Miekichi no tegami o kimi ni watasu no*

I cite this example even though it has to do with the biographical author rather than the work itself, not as evidence for anything about Sōseki's sexuality per se, but as a record of a powerful gay identification with Sōseki and his milieu that speaks to the severity of the homosocial divide in postwar Japan.[88] If by the 1950s most male critics were turning their melancholic yearning for a lost homosocial continuum into a paternalistic homosocial reading of *Kokoro*, this example shows that others, at the same time, were finding ways to identify with Sōseki across that divide in a way that might be described as homosocial and gay at once.

The most recent chapter in the history of this "gay homosocial" reading of *Kokoro* came in 2008, when the gay, all-male theater group Flying Stage produced a version of the novel that was both explicitly gay and fascinatingly two-timing in conception. In this version, written by Sekine Shin'ichi, the action shifts back and forth from the present, a full century after the action of *Kokoro*, to the Meiji past. In the present, a young, openly gay university student is writing his senior thesis on *Kokoro*, arguing that Sensei's suicide was not a "tribute to the Meiji era" but the result of his unacknowledged love for K. His own Sensei, seemingly a closeted gay man, is skeptical of this reading but encourages him anyway, helped along by a female colleague who describes herself as a fan of *yaoi* fiction and who is therefore more open to the student's reading.[89] In the play's climactic final scene, just as Sensei in the Meiji period is writing to his protégé of his resolve to kill himself, the younger man suddenly appears, having made it back to Tokyo in time to stop him. But as he appears on stage, both men morph into their modern-day counterparts. When Sensei tells his student that his attempt to save the original Sensei's life is implausible because Sō-

---

wa maru de iro no torimochi o shite iru yō na mono da. Mukashi no shōsetsu ni aru onna kamiyui no aryū da to omou]." Hara, "Seishun no akogare." Thanks to Katsuhiko Suganuma for helping me to track down this article. For the full text of Sōseki's letter to Sōhei, see *SZ*, vol. 22, 640.

88. Another recent (2008) example of this sort of identification can be found in Tan'o Yasunori's gossipy book on the "hidden tradition" of *nanshoku* in Japanese culture. Noting that "Even Natsume Sōseki had quite a thing for boys," Tan'o cites, among other things, a letter well known among gay readers that Sōseki wrote to a friend when he was living in Matsuyama in which he complains that there are "hardly any beautiful boys here" (*Nanshoku no keshiki*, 98).

89. *Yaoi* refers to fiction and manga about beautiful boys in love, usually written by and for women, that became popular in Japan beginning in the early 1970s. For a discussion of the origins of the genre in the work of Mori Mari (Mori Ōgai's daughter) and a series of debates about it between gay men and women in the 1990s, see Vincent, "A Japanese Electra and Her Queer Progeny."

seki's novel makes it clear that Sensei is dead from early on in *watakushi*'s narration, the younger man insists on his reading despite this textual evidence. In the following passage, the name "Komiya" refers to the character known as "K" in Sōseki's novel, "Fujiwara" is the student in the present, and Nakajima his "Sensei."

FUJIWARA: I want Sensei to admit his love for Komiya and go on living. I feel incredibly close to Sensei. It's all good. I want to let him know that I understand how much he suffered in those days. And to tell him that now it's normal. I know how you feel. You're not alone. Everybody feels that way. I want to tell him not to die.
NAKAJIMA: Students in the Meiji period didn't speak that way.
FUJIWARA: This is me, speaking in the twenty-first century. To Sensei in the Meiji period.
NAKAJIMA: Your words won't reach him you know.
FUJIWARA: Yes they will. I believe they will.[90]

Like a Japanese version of the "It Gets Better" project that arose in the United States in 2010, this passage calls on the power of futurity to rescue Sensei from a homophobic past. It does so in open and even defiant recognition of its own paradoxical anachronism in a way that eloquently critiques the way in which the "chrononormative" temporal schema of modernity (as described by Elizabeth Freeman) is deeply tied up with the *heteronormative* order.[91] Fujiwara's monologue is also fascinating when read in light of my earlier discussion of the distinction Komori makes between second- and third-person discourse in *watakushi* and Sensei's narratives. As Fujiwara speaks to Sensei in the present *and* the past at once, he seems to waver back and forth between addressing him as "you" and as "he." If *watakushi*'s discourse toward Sensei was, in Komori's reading, more intimate and "second person," in contrast to Sensei's distanced [*yosoyososhii*] way of addressing K, here the two modes are superimposed on top of each other, just as the present seems to merge impossibly with the past. While Fujiwara's hopeful message is, as the later Sensei depressingly points out, unlikely to be transmitted to the Meiji Sensei in any "straight"-forward *historical* sense, it does reach his Sensei Nakajima in the present. There is a palpable sense in Sekine's play that time itself is being reimagined through the sheer force of a two-timing queer desire. At the same time, however, this is all happening in the interest of a recuperative, identity-based politics that makes it both "gay" and "homosocial" at once.

---

90. Sekine, *Shin Kokoro*, 69–70.
91. For a discussion of "chrononormativity," see Freeman, *Time Binds*.

Beyond the Couple

For all their obvious differences, there is an underlying similarity between these "gay homosocial" readings of *Kokoro* by Hara, Sekine, Dodd, Ōhashi, and Hashimoto, and the "Oedipal homosocial" reading of Komori and Ishihara. In their enthusiasm to discover a more satisfying narrative in an otherwise bleak-seeming novel, both tend to attribute to it a more "closural" meaning than it actually possesses—even to the point of exercising considerable ingenuity in doing so. This stands in striking contrast to the paternalistic homosocial critics, who seem to have been happy to let Sōseki have his indeterminate endings. McClellan, for example, writes that "none of [Sōseki's] novels have what might be called a satisfactory ending." He then appends an intriguing footnote in which he concedes that "the Japanese" may have a different sense of what constitutes a satisfactory ending for a novel, but that it is still "worth noting" when an author seems to believe (as, he implies, Sōseki does) that "phases" in a man's life such as marriage or divorce "cannot be treated as entities in realistic fiction."[92]

I have to agree with McClellan here. Even among Japanese novelists, who are hardly well known for closural endings, Sōseki seems to have been singularly unconvinced by the notion that marriage, or its ending in divorce, were meaningful ways to tie up the threads of a novel. Unlike McClellan, however, who saw this as a sign of an almost crippling pessimism about the possibility of *any* kind of connection with other people,[93] I would argue that the lack of "satisfactory endings" in his work came from Sōseki's rich awareness of how our lives are constituted by a whole panoply of different kinds of relationships with others and a healthy skepticism of the idea that the self could ever be fully fleshed out within the terms of *any* single dyadic relationship. Thus, while McClellan quotes the famous line at the end of Sōseki's later novel *Grass by the Wayside* [*Michikusa*] as evidence for the author's bleak pessimism, I see in it an openness to contingency that might even carry the seeds of "happiness."[94] The line reads: *yo no naka ni katazuku nante mono wa hotondo nai*. Here, again, this difference emerges in the translation. McClellan gives the world-weary "Whatever happens will go on

---

92. McClellan, "The Implications of Sōseki's *Kokoro*," 370.

93. "The death of Sensei in *Kokoro* symbolizes Sōseki's final admission, as a novelist, that there is no escape from isolation except through death" (ibid., 358–59).

94. For a fascinating queer theoretical account of the crucial relationship between happiness and contingency that draws on the etymology of the word to argue that rather than being achievable as a goal or an object, happiness is about an openness to "happenstance," see Ahmed, *The Promise of Happiness*.

happening." But I would have it read, "Nothing in the world ever comes to a conclusive end." This openness to contingency, or resistance to closure, is yet another reason why Sōseki's works focus so often on triangular relationships; they make it possible to explode the romantic dyad and show the mediation of desire through any number of third parties.

In both the "gay" and the "straight" readings of *Kokoro* by Komori and Ishihara, however, there is a persistent, romantic tendency to recover a couple—be it Sensei and K, Sensei and *watakushi*, or *watakushi* and Okusan, from out of the thicket of mediated desire. But is there not a way of reading between these options—one that acknowledges the power of the tripartite structure of mediated desire without discounting the emotional force of the dyads that emerge within it?

FIVE

Kokoro *and the Primal Scene of Modern Japanese Homosociality*

"The Saddest of the Genre"

If Sōseki's *Kokoro* is, as I wrote at the beginning of the last chapter, about the transition from a male homosocial to a heterosocial world, it is "about" it both in the figurative sense and in a more literal one as well. It both thematizes this transition and lingers melancholically around and about it, remaining preoccupied with the homosocial past in a way that suggests that it has not been left behind. Hosea Hirata has written that *Kokoro* is "the most masterful instance" of the emergence of historical thinking in modern Japanese literature.[1] By this he means not that *Kokoro* thematizes historical events (indeed, it rather famously ignores them),[2] but that it exemplifies the temporality of modernity in which the past is cut off irrevocably from the present, leaving us with the sense that "something is broken."[3] I want to ask how this sense of disconnection from the past may have been related to the rupture of the male homosocial continuum and the accompanying shift in literary narratives from external to internal mediation of desire.

I begin by reminding the reader of the genre of elegiac romance that I discussed in Chapter 3. Although *Kokoro* differs in important ways from the

---

1. Hirata, "The Emergence of History in Natsume Soseki's *Kokoro*," 186.
2. I refer here to James Fujii's argument that *Kokoro*'s focus on the private sphere has enabled, through its canonization, a collective forgetting of Japan's imperialist expansion ("Death, Empire, and the Search for History in Natsume Sōseki's *Kokoro*").
3. Hirata, "The Emergence of History in Natsume Sōseki's *Kokoro*," 183.

classic examples of this genre (I mentioned *The Great Gatsby* as one of these), a discussion of Sōseki's novel in relation to the elegiac romance is a good place to begin to think about how it narrativizes the homosocial divide. In thinking about *Kokoro* as an elegiac romance, it helps to recall that if Sensei seems "stuck" in a hopelessly homosocial past, as Komori and Ishihara argued, this is at least partly an effect of *watakushi*'s ability to represent himself as having moved on. That is to say that the reader is made aware of Sensei's "pastness" through the contrast he makes with the present and future-oriented *watakushi*. Everything the reader knows about Sensei, including what is written in his testament, comes *through watakushi*. It is he who tells Sensei's story, and he does so for his own purposes. Even more than *boku*'s narrative in *The Wild Goose*, which appeared on the surface to be about Okada but was just as (or even *more*) importantly about *boku*'s having outgrown and progressed beyond Okada, *watakushi*'s account of Sensei can be considered to be all about *watakushi*. In this sense, *watakushi*'s narrative, at least as Komori and Ishihara reconstruct it, is a textbook example of the elegiac romance. Consider the following profile that Kenneth Bruffee offers in his 1983 study of the genre:

> In the fictional past a self-effacing young or middle-aged person, in most elegiac romances to date a male . . . , at one time encountered another person, usually older than himself and also in most cases male . . . and transformed him into a heroic figure by projecting onto him his own private wish-fulfilling fantasies. The friend, apparently gratified by this adulation or (more usually) apparently indifferent to it, accepted the heroic role but did little to return the other's affection. Eventually the "heroic" friend died. Crushed by his loss, the hero worshiper sets out in the dramatized fictional present to memorialize his hero by writing his biography. That biography is the narrator's tale that we read. In the course of ostensibly telling the story of his hero's life, however, the hero worshiper, now the apparently self-effacing narrator, manages to reveal a good deal of himself. His biography of his hero turns out in fact to be an *auto*biography, or sometimes an autobiographical fragment, that explores a crucial phase in the narrator's own emotional development and ends that phase by resolving the problem that gave rise to it. As he tells the tale, the narrator revaluates his hero and himself. By this means, he frees himself from the burden of the obsessive attachment and from its concomitant state of arrested emotional development."[4]

I have cited this passage in its entirety because it describes *watakushi*'s narrative so well—indeed, so perfectly that it is hard to believe that Bruffee gives no indication of ever having read Sōseki's novel. That the parallels are so stunning is a testament to Bruffee's perspicacity in having identified so precisely the parameters of the genre he was describing. He quotes Claudio

---

4. Bruffee, *Elegiac Romance*, 50.

Guillén, who describes genres as "problem solving device[s]" that writers use to disentangle knotty cultural problems.[5] These "devices" are reshaped as authors use them in their own cultural and historical contexts and according to their own tastes and abilities. But even across cultures and contents their basic features can be strikingly consistent, as the uncanny similarity of the above description with *watakushi*'s narrative indicates.

The problem that Bruffee thought the elegiac romance was there to solve had two facets. These were "that heroism and hero worship have ceased to be viable themes in modern literature" and "the experience of catastrophic loss and rapid cultural change—and the need to come to terms with loss and change in order to survive."[6] As for the latter of these, anyone living in Japan's tumultuous Meiji period would have experienced a mind-boggling degree of cultural loss and cultural change. Sōseki's writing was particularly fine-tuned to this issue, so it is not surprising that he would have found the "device" of the elegiac romance a useful one for exploring and dealing with this problem of "catastrophic loss and cultural change." He was also quite articulate about the "loss of the hero" in literature, even writing an essay entitled, "Literature and the Heroic" (1910), in which he noted with some distaste how the Japanese naturalists, with their fixation on humanity's baser instincts, had banished "heroes" from literature. Just because heroic actions seemed more rare in the modern age, Sōseki argued, surely it could not be said that they no longer happened at all.[7]

Kokoro is, of course, a novel about cultural change and loss, and its treatment of Sensei (an appellation which itself implies a sort of hero worship) can certainly be read as an elegy to a lost hero. The paternalistic critics discussed in the previous chapter were especially fond of this reading. McClellan, for example, writes of the "essentially heroic quality of the two men who choose to destroy themselves" in *Kokoro*.[8] But it was Komori and Ishihara's reading that, by showing how *watakushi* managed to get over his hero worship of Sensei and the "arrested development" that it implied, came closest to characterizing *Kokoro* as an elegiac romance. There is, however, one significant reason why *Kokoro* may *not* be an elegiac romance, or, if it is one, is what Patricia Merivale has called "one of the saddest" of the genre.[9] This reason is the lack of an epilogue in which the younger narrator comes back to explain in explicit terms what he has learned from Sensei's death and

---

5. Guillén, *Literature as System*, 72; cited in Bruffee, *Elegiac Romance*, 18.
6. Bruffee, *Elegiac Romance*, 15.
7. "Bungei to hiroikku," in *Sōseki zenshū*, vol. 16, 323–25.
8. McClellan, "The Implications of Soseki's *Kokoro*," 366.
9. Merivale, "Silences," 132.

why he will not repeat the older man's mistakes. Komori and Ishihara went to considerable trouble to imaginatively construct such an epilogue from the "clues" that *watakushi* leaves behind in the novel's first two sections, but the fact remains that *Kokoro* cuts off without making any of this explicit, leaving the reader to think that the novel "lacks precisely that affirmation of life continuing, with fuller awareness, on a firmer footing, which can be found even in the so-called 'saddest story' Ford Maddox Ford's [elegiac romance] *The Good Soldier* (1915)."[10]

What does it mean that Sōseki deprives his younger narrator of the chance to make it perfectly clear that he has in fact gotten past the "state of arrested emotional development" exemplified both by his older mentor and by his own emotional attachment to him? If the elegiac romance, as a genre which is chiefly about the loss of heroes and the impact of massive social and cultural change, could be thought of as the quintessential "modern" genre, moreover, what does it mean that modern Japan's most famous novel "approaches the point where the narrator should be freed without ever actually reaching it"?[11] Could this be related to the fact that, as Komori has written in another article on the novel, "*Kokoro* emerges on the staircase going up to the love for the opposite sex," but never quite gets there either?[12]

External Mediation in "The Heredity of Taste"

In order to understand the ways in which *Kokoro* is and *is not* an elegiac romance, and what this says about the particular shape of the homosocial continuum in Japan at the time it was written, it may be useful here to draw a comparison with a slightly earlier work, Sōseki's 1908 novella "The Heredity of Taste" ["Shumi no iden"]. This work might also be considered an elegiac romance of sorts, but like *Kokoro* it also deviates from the genre, although in different and revealing ways. Like both of the narratives contained within *Kokoro,* "The Heredity of Taste" is a male homosocial narrative—a story about one man told by another. As is the case in Sensei's testament, the narrator has no name (except the more literary and masculine-sounding first-person pronoun *yo*) and the man about whom he writes has a name that starts with a "K." Unlike Sensei, however, the narrator of "Heredity" is quite unabashed in his affection for and "hero worship" of his friend Kō-san, who has recently perished in the bloodbath at Port Arthur during

---

10. Ibid.
11. Ibid.
12. Komori, "*Kokoro* ni okeru dōseiai to iseiai," 165.

the Russo-Japanese War. Kō-san's death is far from heroic—he was used as cannon fodder for General Nogi's infamously Pyrrhic victory there—but the narrator's openly adoring (and definitively elegiac) remembrance of him makes a hero out of him nonetheless. His name, moreover, unlike the abstract, deconstructed triangle that is the Roman letter "K," is written with a Chinese character which means "grand and majestic" (浩). This is a name well suited to a hero (in fact, it can even be pronounced *hiro*). Here is the way the narrator describes his friend:

> When one talks with Kō-san over a brazier one's first impression is of sheer size. He's a big, fine-looking man, dark-complexioned and with a thick beard. When he opens his mouth to tell an exciting story, his listeners' heads have only room for Kō-san. Forgetting the things of today, the things of tomorrow, even about one's own enraptured self [*kikihoreteiru jibun*], nothing remains but Kō-san. Such incidents reveal his inner greatness, and I've always thought that, wherever he goes, he's bound to attract attention.[13]

If this passage suggests that Kō-san himself was able to tell stories that made the listener forget not only about "his own enraptured self" but even about the flow of time itself, so does Soseki's narrator seem genuinely selfless and enraptured as he tells the story of his friend. At these depths within the homosocial fold, the mind goes blank and time stands still. The narrator here is what the paternalistic homosocial critics discussed in the last chapter wanted to believe *watakushi* was—a veritable *wakashu* to Kō-san's *nenja*.[14] The passage is also reminiscent of *boku*'s description of Okada in *The Wild Goose*. But unlike in Ōgai's story, where the narrator's admiration of Okada is soon transformed into a rivalry, in Sōseki's (slightly) earlier text the narrator's admiration of his friend Kō-san has no admixture of competition or ambivalence. This is still very much the world of external mediation. Just as Quixote "worshiped his model" Amadis de Gaul "openly," and "proclaimed aloud the true nature of his desire,"[15] the narrator of "Heredity" quite openly adores his dead friend.

"The Heredity of Taste" does contain a triangle between two men and a woman—but it is not in the least bit rivalrous. After describing Kō-san's death on the battlefield, the narrator tracks down a woman with whom he believes Kō-san may have fallen in love "at first sight," having caught just one glimpse of her before the latter left for Manchuria. The story here has a convoluted, almost slapstick quality about it, but suffice it to say that by

---

13. Natsume, *Ten Nights of Dream, Hearing Things, the Heredity of Taste*, 139; *Sōseki zenshū*, vol. 2, 200.
14. On the *wakashu/nenja* dynamic, see page 98.
15. Girard, *Deceit, Desire, and the Novel*, 10.

playing detective and engaging in some historical "research," our narrator manages to reconstruct an ill-starred love story between Kō-san's grandfather and the woman's grandmother during the waning days of the Tokugawa shogunate. His theory, which he very proudly explains to the reader, is that Kō-san fell in love with this woman at first sight because she has inherited the looks of her grandmother and he the taste of his grandfather. Having proven his theory by confirming that the woman had, in fact, seen and been smitten by Kō-san, he then finds a way to introduce her to Kō-san's mother as a companion and takes satisfaction in the fact that she begins to act almost like a daughter-in-law to the old widow.

Kō-san's death, like K's in *Kokoro*, is described in great detail in "The Heredity of Taste." Along with countless other soldiers, he was made to march into a ditch where they were shot by the Russians until their bodies piled up high enough for the rest of Nogi's army to cross it—a striking image for, among other things, the sacrifices modernity demands in order to cover over the rupture it has introduced with the past. But by resurrecting Kō-san in his text (he speaks of him in the present tense) and so openly expressing his admiration and love for him, the narrator is able to go some way toward repairing the damage.

If *Kokoro* shows how the rift in the homosocial continuum creates an equally serious rift between men and women (like Sensei and his wife), in the world of "The Heredity of Taste," heterosexual romance does not (yet) threaten the homosocial continuum. In the following passage, for example, the narrator describes his feelings for Kō-san in a way that connects it in a continuum with other kinds of culturally valued relationships.

> You consider your wife a woman of quite outstanding beauty so that, if at some notable reception she looks no different from the woman next to her, and fails to draw one single eye, you feel distinctly narked. In your own home, your child lords it, being the uniquely important, patently irreplaceable apple of the family eye. But this young master goes to school, is dressed in a uniform, and becomes indistinguishable from the boy who sits next to him, that commonplace son of the haberdasher across the street. You feel, don't you, just a little bit put out? I feel the same about my Kō-san.[16]

---

16. Natsume, *Ten Nights of Dream, Hearing Things, the Heredity of Taste*, 140; *Sōseki zenshū*, vol. 2, 201. I have quoted this translation verbatim from Wilson and Itō's wonderful version, except the last line, which in their version reads "My feelings about Kō-san are precisely of that sort" [*yo no Kō-san ni okeru mo sono tōri*], which leaves some ambiguity as to whether the genitive *no* attaches to Kō-san or to the implied "feelings." I have chosen the former to emphasize the narrator's closeness to "his" Kō-san.

The passage is nothing other than a short treatise on triangular desire. You want your wife to be noticed by other men, he says, just as you want your child to be different from others. It is not so much their intrinsic qualities but their qualities *in comparison to other*s and *through the eyes of others* that make them so lovable and desirable to "you." That this lesson is being taught so openly to the reader (by a narrator who addresses him/her in the second person) makes the passage itself a prime example of external mediation. This narrator, like the narrators of so much of Edo fiction, is giving us a lesson about desire rather than assuming that it is somehow "natural" and rooted either in the body or in the attractions of the object. He is also, and perhaps not coincidentally, interpellating "us" as men by assuming that we have a "wife." But at the same time, and perhaps because of all of this, he is able to talk about *his* relationship with another man as if it were on the same plane as his reader's relationship with "his" wife. This kind of "premodern" homosociality is also evident thematically in the story itself. The world described in "The Heredity of Taste" is one in which the sexes stick together. For example, the narrator points out the difficulty he had figuring out a way to verify with the woman in question that his "theory" about her and Kō-san is correct. "In Japan, unlike in Europe," he explains,

> relations between men and women remain unenlightened, so that there is virtually no opportunity for a bachelor such as myself to have a private conversation with this unmarried sister. Even if an opportunity presented itself, to pose my questions would probably throw the girl into embarrassed confusion and, even if it didn't, she'd doubtless deny ever having heard of Kō-san.[17]

As I mentioned earlier, the narrator does manage to confirm his theory by more roundabout means. By the end of the tale, through the intercession of the woman's father, he has also managed to bring her together with Kō-san's mother. Before long, the two women have become close and she is acting "more and more like a daughter-in-law." Thus he uses completely "homosocial" or "patriarchal" mechanisms to bring together two people of the same sex as a way of expressing his own love and elegiac affection for another member of his own sex. This could not be more different from *Kokoro*, in which relations between men have become so ambivalent and rivalrous as to threaten the viability of any and all connections with other human beings.

"The Heredity of Taste," then, is an almost exact inversion of *Kokoro*. Whereas *Kokoro* is fixated on the rift between the present and the past and

---

17. Natsume, *Ten Nights of Dream, Hearing Things, the Heredity of Taste*, 201; *Sōseki zenshū*, vol. 2, 245.

between one man and another, "Heredity" is all about repairing those rifts. By reconstructing a "hereditary" love story that extends back into the Edo period, the narrator of "Heredity" forges a connection to the premodern past, just as by introducing the young woman to Kō-san's mother he repairs a tie in the present that has been broken by the horrors of modern warfare. And finally, if *Kokoro* privileges the private and the domestic over the bigger picture of "History," in "The Heredity of Taste," the gruesome description of the battlefield at Port Arthur makes for an explicitly antiwar statement that is unparalleled among Sōseki's works. Although he is not named explicitly in "Heredity," the presence of General Nogi in both texts is also remarkable. In one he appears as an "inept strategist responsible for heavy casualties among the Japanese army on the Asian continent" and in the other as "war hero cum educator and guardian of such virtues as selflessness, military valor, and dedication to the nation."[18] In "Heredity," moreover, the past is still very much alive. If there is a "lesson" to be learned from "Heredity," it is the lesson of the horror of war. With *Kokoro,* by contrast, at least as far as *watakushi* is concerned, the lesson has an inward focus; it is about "growing up" into a heterosexual and leaving the past behind.

Kokoro is, of course, also concerned with hero worship, and with the "experience of catastrophic loss and cultural change." But unlike "The Heredity of Taste," it is a text in which desire is mediated internally and the irrevocable rupture with the past is emphasized. When read alongside "The Heredity of Taste," it becomes possible to see that the rupture with the past in *Kokoro* is also tied to the rupture of the male homosocial continuum. If the narrator of "Heredity" tells his tale in unadulterated admiration of his friend Kō-san, Sensei's narrative tells of a murderous rivalry with K, and *watakushi*'s entire narrative, according to Komori, is about differentiating himself from, and perhaps even cuckolding, Sensei. If "The Heredity of Taste" entails a sort of loving and identificatory connection to the past along with a devastating critique of "progress" in the horrific image of the ditch filling up with bodies,[19] Sensei's narrative lingers suicidally on the homosocial past while *watakushi*'s moves quietly towards a heterosocial future. For all of these reasons, if "The Heredity of Taste" is a last exemplar of a premodern, exter-

---

18. Fujii, "Death, Empire, and the Search for History in Natsume Sōseki's *Kokoro*," 134.

19. Sōseki's critique of progress here reminds me of the bloodbath at the end of Mark Twain's *A Connecticut Yankee in King Arthur's Court*, a novel that up to that point had seemed to be an uncomplicated celebration of Yankee ingenuity and technology but that ends with a devastating critique of that same technology.

nally mediated homosociality, *Kokoro*, like *The Wild Goose*, is among the first instances in Japan of the modern, internally mediated homosocial narrative.

"A New and Utterly Unanticipated Breath of Woman"

With the contrast it makes with "The Heredity of Taste" in mind, I want now to take a closer look at Sensei's narrative in *Kokoro*. The first thing to note about Sensei's story is how both he and K start out in a male homosocial mindset from which women are all but completely excluded. Indeed, it is not hard to see parallels between them and the narrator of "Heredity" and his friend Kō-san. They are also not unlike the younger *boku* and Okada in *The Wild Goose*. The world of Sensei's letter places the reader once again in the past relative to the moment of his narration in 1912, just after the death of the Meiji emperor. The exact date in the past is unclear but probably just around the turn of the twentieth century—some two decades after the setting of Ōgai's novel and not long before "Heredity."[20] Here, too, are two male roommates, both of whom are students accustomed to an environment where the sexes have very little to do with each other. As was the case with Okada, Sensei's male homosocial mindset is associated with a preference for things Chinese. Here is how he describes himself on the day he moves into Okusan's house:

On the day I arrived, I noted the flowers arranged in the alcove, and a *koto* propped beside them. I did not care for either. I had been brought up by a father who appreciated the Chinese style of poetry, calligraphy, and tea making, and since childhood my own tastes had also tended toward the Chinese. Perhaps for this reason I despised this sort of merely charming decorativeness.[21]

The *koto* and the flower arrangement are associated here with an alien femininity that contrasts with Sensei's preferred "masculine" pursuits of "poetry, calligraphy, and tea making."[22] This aloofness from things feminine

---

20. It is not entirely clear when Sensei's story is supposed to have taken place. Ken Ito writes, "The best that we can do in terms of placing the beginning of Sensei's story is to say that his parents died sometime in the mid 1890s." This would put K's suicide sometime just after the turn of the century given that he killed himself just before graduation and it took six years to complete higher school at the time ("Writing Time in Soseki's *Kokoro*," 6).

21. Natsume, *Kokoro*, 147 (McClellan), 141 (McKinney), 179 (*SZ*).

22. The *koto* and the flower arrangement are also associated with a "Japaneseness," such that Sensei's awakening to Ojōsan's charms can also be seen as an awakening to modern national identity. On the central role of the "feminine" in the construction of modern Japanese identity, see Yoda, *Gender and National Literature*.

will not last long, however. In the paragraph immediately following, Sensei describes how, despite his intention to hang some (presumably Chinese) scrolls inherited from his father in his new room, "when I saw the flower arrangement and the *koto*, I lost my courage."[23] His failure to reproduce the male homosocial/Chinese world of his father(s) in his new room is presented as a cowardly capitulation to the "world of females," and implicitly as a betrayal of his father (one of many such betrayals in this text). But soon after this, when he actually meets the young lady of the house, whose presence these objects have already announced, he describes the encounter as nothing short of an epiphanic awakening to a new world. Having assumed that she would somehow resemble her mother who, in her "thoroughly upright, plainspoken" manner as "a typical officer's wife" has struck him as comfortably familiar from his male homosocial perspective,[24] upon first seeing Ojōsan he is confronted instead with his first glimpse of a truly "opposite" sex: "But one look at the girl's face overturned all my preconceptions. In their place a new and utterly unanticipated breath of Woman pervaded me. From that moment the flower arrangement in the alcove ceased to displease me; the *koto* propped beside it was no longer an annoyance."[25]

Sensei is a quick study and soon becomes accustomed to—indeed, he learns to love—Ojōsan's *koto* and flower arrangements. Before long he is going out shopping with Ojōsan and her mother despite the fact that, as he reminds the young man to whom he is writing his letter, "We students were brought up in a different world from today, remember, and it was not the custom in those days to go around in a girl's company."[26]

At this point the reader might reasonably expect Sensei's story to continue in this vein of excited discovery of this new world of women as he leaves behind the world of his father, of other men, and of Chinese things. But Sensei's journey towards heterosexuality will not be a smooth one. First of all, he has yet to experience any sexual desire for Ojōsan. He describes his interest in her as being a spiritual thing "undoubtedly in the grip of Love's higher realm" and specifies that "I felt not the slightest physical urge toward her."[27] Moreover, no sooner does he discover the new world of women she inhabits than he takes it into his head to bring his male friend K into it along with him. K has recently been disowned by his adoptive family, and Sensei, who feels partly responsible for this, wants to help

---

23. Natsume, *Kokoro*, 147 (McClellan), 142 (McKinney), 180 (*SZ*).
24. Ibid., 146 (McClellan), 140 (McKinney), 178–79 (*SZ*).
25. Ibid., 142 (McKinney), 148 (McClellan), 180–81 (*SZ*).
26. Ibid., 155 (McKinney), 161 (McClellan), 196 (*SZ*).
27. Ibid., 149 (McKinney), 155 (McClellan), 189 (*SZ*).

him out by inviting him to live with him. If Sensei was brought up in a male homosocial world and knew nothing of women, this is even more the case for K; indeed, the bookish and boyish K makes Sensei look like Prince Genji himself. K is the son of a priest with "a lot of the samurai in him" but has been adopted by a wealthier family who are paying for him to study medicine.[28] Without telling his adopted family, however, he has switched to studying religion and shows a powerful devotion to "spiritual" matters; at one point Sensei describes him as "more monkish than a monk."[29]

"She Stood Between Us"

The rivalry between Sensei and K is a textbook example of internally mediated desire as described by Girard.[30] It is K's presence as a mediator rather than Ojōsan's inherent charms that spurs Sensei's pursuit of her. K is the perfect mediator for Sensei, who (again, like *boku* in *The Wild Goose* and the narrator of "Heredity") considers his friend "handsomer and more attractive to women than I," and thinks of himself as "no match for him in scholarly ability."[31] Just as importantly, K has "none of that weakness of character that makes most people concerned with what others are thinking."[32] This sort of person, who appears to be completely self-sufficient and "inner-directed," is a good candidate to mediate the desires of others, particularly those of "modern" types like Sensei who feel that they themselves are somehow rudderless and empty inside. But while Sensei recognizes K's superiority, he does not consciously recognize his friend's role as the mediator of his desire. This is one way in which their relationship is typical of internal mediation.

In Sensei's case, moreover, his mediator is *also* his rival in a way that is much more apparent than in *The Wild Goose* and was not the case at all in "Heredity." But however apparent it may be to the reader, the competition between him and K is a one-sided affair and takes place on a subterranean,

---

28. Ibid., 163 (McKinney), 171 (McClellan), 208 (*SZ*).

29. Ibid., 159 (McKinney), 165–66 (McClellan), 201–2 (*SZ*). It is perhaps relevant to note here that Buddhist monasteries and samurai culture were the two primary contexts for idealized representations of *nanshoku* during the Edo and early Meiji periods.

30. Much of the following discussion draws on Sakuta Keiichi's useful application of Girard to Sōseki's novel. See Sakuta, "Nihon no shōsetsu ni arawareta sansha kankei."

31. Natsume, *Kokoro*, 179 (McKinney), 189 (McClellan), 228 (*SZ*).

32. Ibid., 201 (McKinney), 213 (McClellan), 256 (*SZ*).

internalized plane. Instead of openly competing with K-as-rival,[33] Sensei not only keeps his own feelings for Ojōsan a secret, but perversely *encourages* K to open up to Ojōsan and her mother. Rather than allowing K-as-mediator to remain at a distance, then, Sensei actually brings him closer, as I mentioned earlier, by inviting him to come to live with him, Ojōsan, and her mother. As is typical in internal mediation, he does this with very little awareness of either his own motives or its possible consequences. What he tells himself on a conscious level is that by getting K to spend time with Ojōsan and Okusan he hopes to help his monkishly homosocial friend by inducing in him the same awakening to the world of women that he has had. To do so, he goes so far as to make *himself* into the mediator of K's desire. "Aware that under Okusan's kind treatment I myself had grown cheerful, I set about applying the same process to K. . . . I then did my best to use myself as a catalyst to bring them together. At every opportunity I encouraged K to spend time in the company of all three of us."[34] Sensei believes that this female company will "humanize" K and pursues his efforts at conversion with an almost missionary zeal.

> My most important task, I felt, was somehow to make him more human. Filling his own head with the examples of impressive men was pointless, I decided, if it did not make him impressive himself. As a first step in the task of humanizing him, I would introduce him to the company of the opposite sex. Letting the fair winds of that gentle realm blow upon him would cleanse his blood of the rust that had clogged it, I hoped.[35]

If the passage I cited earlier from "Heredity" provided a sort of "lesson" in external mediation, in this passage Sensei explicitly rejects that model. "Filling his own head with the examples of impressive men"—in other words, engaging in unabashed hero worship—is useless, Sensei decides, as long as he himself does not become "impressive." This reveals quite clearly the logic of romantic individualism that will lead to the death of both men when each fails to live up to the ideal it puts forth. Sensei's plan to "humanize" K by devious means—through a process of internal rather than external mediation—turns out to be synonymous with introducing him into the company of "the opposite sex." Representing the homosocial stasis into which K's hero worship has immobilized him as a kind of rusty machine,

---

33. A counterexample in Sōseki's work where the competition between a pair of homosocial rivals *is* on the surface would be Daisuke and Hiraoka in *Sorekara*. Daisuke openly confronts Hiraoka and asks him "Won't you give me Michiyo-san?" (Natsume, *And Then*, 247).
34. Natsume, *Kokoro*, 168, 170 (McKinney); 176, 179 (McClellan); 213, 217 (*SZ*).
35. Ibid., 171 (McKinney), 179–80 (McClellan), 217 (*SZ*).

he imagines it warmed and naturalized by the flow of the fresh blood of heterosexual desire.

The effect on both men of this romantic fantasy is devastating. K comes to believe that his very attraction to the opposite sex signifies the loss of his high-minded principles.[36] And while Sensei is able to have his choice of erotic object validated by K as his mediator, he loses this same mediator when K kills himself out of despair over having lost his ideals. Since K's mediation was integral to Sensei's attraction to Ojōsan, the two are left behind in a marriage without passion presided over by K's ghostly presence.

> When I was with her, K would suddenly loom threateningly in my mind. She stood between us, in effect, and her very presence bound K and me indissolubly together. She was everything I could have wanted, yet because of this unwitting role she played, I found myself withdrawing from her. She, of course, immediately registered this. She felt it but could not understand it.[37]

The power and primacy of the bond between male rivals here is evident in the fact that Sensei actually experiences Okusan's presence as coming between him and K ("She stood between us") rather than what one might expect from an amorous rival—that *he* would stand between Sensei and Okusan.[38] The "us" here is explicitly the male couple.[39] It is hard to imagine a more concise depiction of the tragedy of the internally mediated homosocial triangle for all parties concerned. Haunted by his betrayal of K, Sensei withdraws from his wife into a tortured interiority. Her continued presence, however, both keeps K alive in his mind and reminds him of what he considers his own guilt in his friend's death. But as long as he is unable to tell

---

36. Karatani Kōjin has made a similar observation about K's loss of his ideals (Karatani, "Sōseki's Diversity," 127).

37. Natsume, *Kokoro*, 224 (McKinney), 237 (McClellan), 287 (*SZ*).

38. Sakuta makes an illuminating comparison of *Kokoro* to Sōseki's earlier novel *The Gate*, which also featured a love triangle in the past, among the protagonist Sōsuke, his wife Oyone, and a man named Yasui from whom Sōsuke had "stolen" Oyone years before the novel begins. Although Sōsuke, like Sensei, is haunted by the memory of this, it does not seem to affect his relationship with Oyone, which is one of the most intimate to be found anywhere in Sōseki's work. This is because, according to Sakuta, Yasui remained only an external obstacle and not an internal mediator of their love. In writing *Kokoro*, in which the mediation of desire is both "internal" and primary, Sakuta notes that Sōseki has moved beyond the "romantic and pastoral" notion of love as a dyadic phenomenon seen in *The Gate*. See Sakuta, "Nihon no shōsetsu ni arawareta sansha kankei."

39. I remind the reader here of Sedgwick's observation via Girard (cited in the Introduction) that this bond between male rivals can be "equally powerful and in many senses equivalent" to heterosexual love (*Between Men*, 21).

her why, they both remain trapped. Later he claims that he refuses to tell her the "secret" of K's suicide because "it was agony for me to contemplate this pure creature sullied in any way, you understand."[40] Presumably he is afraid of "sullying" her with the knowledge of his own underhanded behavior in his competition with K. But surely it is also because he is unable to admit to her that his feelings for her are not "pure," but mediated by another man—that they have as much to do with K as with her.

In the terrible zero-sum logic of internally mediated homosocial desire, the inability to admit the role of the mediator yields the romantic fiction that love happens only between two people of the "opposite" sex. Any suggestion of the presence of a mediator (especially one of the same sex) somehow takes away from its romantic "purity." Of course it is Sensei who harbors this romantic fantasy and not the "pure" Ojōsan. As he himself puts it earlier in the novel, "In a word, I had a romantic faith in the nobility of love, while simultaneously practicing a devious form of it."[41] He wants to love a woman "romantically" (for her own sake), but he does so by triangulating his desire through a man.

I want to stress here that in describing the triangle between Sensei, K, and Ojōsan in this way I am not suggesting that Sensei could or should have simply loved Ojōsan "for her own sake." As I discussed in Chapter 1, Sōseki understood very well that desire is *always* the desire of the other, always "mediated" in one way or another. This makes it inevitably "belated" and external to the subject. The problem comes when we try to convince ourselves, by disavowing the role of the mediator, that desire is original and spontaneous to the self or inherent in the attractions of the object. In an increasingly heteronormative Japan, moreover, the fiction of heterosexual romance made it harder and harder openly to admit the mediation of desire, especially when the mediator belonged to the same sex. This is apparent in Sensei's inability first to tell K about his love for Ojōsan and then to tell his wife about his love for K. The "romantic" fiction, which Girard calls the "lie of spontaneous desire" that stops all three parties from recognizing the mediation of their desire, ends up by preventing real connection between any of them.[42]

I have also referred to Sensei's "love for K," but I want to make clear that by saying this I am not claiming that Sensei and "K" were in some sense "really in love" with each other and that if they could only have ad-

---

40. Natsume, *Kokoro*, 225 (McKinney), 237 (McClellan), 288 (*SZ*).
41. Ibid., 189 (McKinney), 200 (McClellan), 241 (*SZ*).
42. Girard, *Deceit, Desire, and the Novel*, 16.

mitted it the tragedy of *Kokoro* could have been avoided. What I *am* saying is that Sensei's commitment to a romantic ideal of "true love" as something that happens between two people of the opposite sex has left him with nowhere to put his feelings for K, *whatever those might have been*. Thus deprived of their own place, these feelings seem to take on a life of their own. The result is that K begins to haunt him: "In short, I had begun to feel an almost magical power in him. Perhaps, I even found myself thinking, he had cast an evil spell that would last the rest of my life."[43] At several points in the text he even compares K to a "devil." [44]

The "love" between Sensei and K, then, is no more "original" or "spontaneous" than Sensei's belated desire for Ojōsan. But there is a way in which its very foreclosure as a result of the rupture of the homosocial continuum lends it a melancholic power that is much greater than any realized connection could have produced. This foreclosed possibility of a love between the two men, in other words, begins to exist as a kind of retrospective fantasy—a supercharged *silence* that serves as a vessel for a collective male nostalgia over a lost homosocial continuum, and even, in the case of the paternalistic homosocial reading I discussed in the last chapter, for the past of Japan itself—what Etō described as "the whole value system of the Meiji era."[45]

The Insurmountable Wall

Sensei provides a striking image for this foreclosed possibility when he explains to K why it was necessary to bring Ojōsan into the picture. "I pointed out [to K]" he says, "that if we two men were to go on talking exclusively to each other forever, we would simply continue in the same straight line."[46] One can hardly picture a better metaphor for the homosocial divide than this. The sentence is even more powerful in McClellan's translation: "'If you

---

43. Natsume, *Kokoro*, 195 (McKinney), 207 (McClellan), 249 (*SZ*).

44. "It was as if I stood there oblivious as the devil brushed by me, unaware that he cast a shadow upon me that would darken my whole life. It was I who brought this man into the house, I must confess" (ibid., 157 [McKinney], 199 [*SZ*]). This begins to anticipate the much more paranoid and perverse relationship between mentor and disciple I discuss in the next chapter on Hamao Shirō's 1929 novella *The Devil's Disciple*.

45. For a related reading of lesbian sexuality "*as* a specific practice of dissimulation produced through the very historical vocabularies that seek to effect its erasure" in Willa Cather's *My Ántonia* (1918), a novel contemporaneous to *Kokoro*, see Butler, "Dangerous Crossings," 145.

46. Natsume, *Kokoro*, 171 (McKinney), 218 (*SZ*).

and I,' I said to him, 'were to spend the rest of our lives as bachelors, forever talking to each other, we would advance merely in straight parallel lines.'"[47]

For Sensei, the only way to get these two parallel lines to intersect was to turn them into a triangle. This is why he invites K—whose very moniker looks like a dent in two parallel lines—to live with him and works so hard to open him up to Ojōsan and the world of women. In the absence of the curves of the homosocial continuum, the two parallel lines are a striking image of an insurmountable homosocial divide. And yet can we not glimpse, in this same image of two "bachelors" walking beside each other, always the same distance apart and into an endless horizon, a vision of a male couple as well? Here is how Sensei himself describes his relationship with K:

> K and I were able to talk about anything. It wasn't as if problems of love [*ai*] or sex [*koi*] never came up, but we always just ended up talking about it in a very abstract way. And we rarely broached it anyway. Mostly we stuck to talking about books or scholarship, our plans for the future, our aspirations, and ideas for bettering ourselves. No matter how close we might have gotten, once things had hardened it wasn't possible to relax the tension. All we could do was stay hard and get closer [*futari wa tada katai nari ni shitashiku naru dake desu*].[48]

I have translated that last line a little provocatively (although quite literally) to make it sound something like a case of "blue balls" in order to emphasize the "enactment" in this passage of a foreclosed, or sublimated homoerotic connection between the two men. Meredith McKinney has the line read (quite beautifully) as: "high minded gravity was integral to our intimacy,"[49] and McClellan, combining it with the previous one, has "the character of our friendship had already been formed, and we could come closer only in a very limited way."[50] Both translations effectively continue the work of sublimation, especially McClellan's, who, unsurprisingly, has a marked tendency to de-eroticize the text and to insert the word "friendship" wherever possible. But when read in the original Japanese the foreclosed desire is a little harder to miss. It is in moments like these that Komori identified "a kind of *nanshoku*-like relation from which the physical desire has been repressed."[51]

As if to immediately redirect the force of this homoeroticism, which I am deliberately describing as foreclosed and sublimated rather than "re-

---

47. Ibid., 180 (McClellan), 218 (*SZ*).
48. Ibid., 227 (*SZ*); my translation.
49. Ibid., 178 (McKinney).
50. Ibid., 188 (McClellan).
51. Komori, "*Kokoro* ni okeru dōseiai to iseiai," 157.

pressed," the very next line finds Sensei talking about his feelings for Ojōsan. Specifically, he describes his inability to tell K about these feelings, which, in classic homosocial fashion, become the justification for yet another fantasy of actually breaking down the barriers between the men, this time in a more violent way. I quote this passage in McClellan's rendition: "Many times, I was on the verge of telling him about Ojōsan, but always I was checked by the insurmountable wall that stood between us. Often, in exasperation, I would feel like hammering a hole somewhere in his head, so that a gentle, warm breeze might blow into it."[52]

How to hammer that hole in K's head? How to cross the parallel lines so that these two men might connect on a more intimate level? What finally accomplishes this is the death of K. After he secures Ojōsan's hand in marriage, having spoken not a word about his feelings to his friend, Sensei resolves to find a way to tell him. K, for his part, has already found out about the engagement from Ojōsan's mother, who had assumed that Sensei had told him already (as one would expect a friend to do). Sensei, meanwhile, decides to tell K "tomorrow." But that very night he is awakened by a cold wind coming into his room, and, noticing that the doors between his room and K's that were "normally closed . . . stood slightly ajar,"[53] he discovers the body of his dead friend.

K had cut open a [sic] carotid artery with a small knife and died instantly. He had no other wound. I learned that blood which I had seen on the wall in the semi-darkness—as though in a dream—had gushed out in one tremendous spurt. I looked at the stains again, this time in the daylight; and I marveled at the power of human blood.[54]

Why has K done this? Later Sensei tells us that he had at first assumed that K had killed himself "because of a broken heart." At the time, he says "the single thought of love had engrossed me, and no doubt this preoccupation influenced my simplistic understanding of the event." Then he wonders whether his friend killed himself out of despair over the "fatal collision between reality and ideals?" This last possibility occurs to Sensei because K had always wanted to think of himself as a "spiritual" person who was unswayed by something as earthly as male-female love. Both of these first possibilities, then, have to do with "the world of women." In the end, however, Sensei concludes that K killed himself because of something that both men shared.

---

52. Natsume, *Kokoro*, 188 (McClellan), 178 (McKinney), 227 (*SZ*).
53. Ibid., 216 (McKinney), 229 (McClellan), 276 (*SZ*).
54. Ibid., 233 (McClellan), 220 (McKinney), 282 (*SZ*).

Finally, I became aware of the possibility that K had experienced a loneliness as terrible as mine [*watashi no yō ni tatta hitori de samishikute shikata ga nakatta kekka*], and wishing to escape quickly from it, had killed himself. Once more, fear gripped my heart. From then on, like a gust of winter wind, the premonition that I was treading the same path as K had done would rush at me from time to time, and chill me to the bone.[55]

As I discussed in the previous chapter, McClellan, in whose translation I have cited this passage, saw Sōseki's work as being about "man's isolation." Both McClellan's translation and his writing about *Kokoro* emphasize this sense of tragic, existential, and even transhistorical isolation. Given that he was writing in the late 1950s, moreover, the "man" here is of course the universal "human"—a category in which women are either included by unthinking default or, more often, unthinkingly *excluded*. But underneath the universalizing terms of his discourse, it seems to me that what McClellan was really describing was the loneliness brought on by the male homosocial divide—a "loneliness" that, despite McClellan's relentlessly androcentric perspective, affected women just as much as men. In a crucial moment in McClellan's essay on *Kokoro*, he suggests that "there will always be an insurmountable wall between two people, no matter how much they may love each other."[56] Who exactly are these "people" to whom he refers? The sentence comes directly in between a mention of Sensei and K and a quote from *Kokoro* in which Sensei describes a conversation with his wife about whether it is ever possible for a man and a woman to truly connect. The "people" in McClellan's sentence could therefore be referring either to Sensei and K or Sensei and Okusan. All of them "may love each other" but all of them are separated by a wall. It is chiefly the wall between the two men, however, that causes the isolation of all three.

Against McClellan's claim that Sōseki himself believed this wall was "insurmountable," however, I want to suggest that Sōseki's novel implies that it didn't have to be. The first evidence I offer for this thesis is the fact that the expression "insurmountable wall," which appears in McClellan's essay *and* his translation, is entirely his invention. In McKinney's translation the line reads, more accurately, "I do not know how often I squirmed with impotent frustration at my inability to speak my heart as I had resolved to do."[57] Sōseki's text, then, does not suggest an absolute impossibility of communication between men, but an inability to do so that causes frustra-

---

55. Ibid., 240–41 (McClellan), 227 (McKinney), 291 (*SZ*).
56. McClellan, "The Implications of Soseki's *Kokoro*," 367.
57. Natsume, *Kokoro*, 178 (McKinney), 227 (*SZ*). The Japanese reads: *watashi wa Ojōsan no koto o K ni uchiakeyō to omoitatte kara, nanben hagayui fukai ni nayamasareta ka shiremasen.*

tion. Sōseki's word for frustration here is *hagayui*, which implies a sort of itching antsy-ness that McKinney renders beautifully as "squirming with impotent frustration." Not a pleasant feeling to be sure. But at least as long as one is feeling *hagayui* one might *try* to do something about the situation. For McClellan, however, the only solution, the only relief, when faced with this "insurmountable wall," is death. "Only death," he writes, "will end the suffering of the protagonists." Although death was indeed the solution that both K and Sensei chose, I cannot agree with McClellan's view that Sōseki's novel implies that this was the only solution.

Komori's answer to the paternalistic homosocial critics like McClellan was to locate another redemptive narrative within the text, associated with the younger narrator's ability to leave Sensei behind. But as I pointed out earlier, Sōseki's novel does not allow *watakushi* to come back at the end with the kind of epilogue that the genre of elegiac romance would demand, in which he tells the reader how he has progressed beyond his hero worship. If the novel itself cannot be said to agree wholeheartedly with the younger narrator's claim to have "outgrown" Sensei, what, then, does it say? What kind of temporality informs the narrative(s) of *Kokoro*, and what does this say about Sōseki's understanding of the state of the homosocial continuum when he was writing? I would like to argue that *Kokoro* is an exemplary two-timing text, a recursive narrative that offers an implicit but powerful critique of *both watakushi*'s modernizing, heteronormative narrative and Sensei's suicidally homosocial one.

The Staircase to Love

In order to see how this works, it will help to go back to the scene with which I opened the previous chapter, in which Sensei and *watakushi* find themselves in a secluded spot in Ueno Park talking about love. As I pointed out, Sensei may "remember" a different historical moment before the "homosocial divide," and it may be this memory that prompts his suggestion that *watakushi* may have come to him out of "love" [*koi*]. But despite the seeming connection with the past that Sensei evinces here, by the time he meets the young narrator, his memories have also been re-scripted to conform to a developmental model of sexuality that is very much up to date. His notion that "you had the impulse to find someone of the same sex as the first step toward embracing someone of the opposite sex"[58] reads like a novelistic rendering of the teleology of sexual development that

---

58. Natsume, *Kokoro*, 27 (McClellan), 27 (McKinney), 36 (*SZ*).

Freud proposed in his "Three Essays on Sexuality."[59] In the first essay of that work, titled "The Sexual Aberrations," the phenomenon of "sexual inversion" provides the initial backward glimpse of the independence of what Freud calls the "sexual aim" from the "sexual object." "Experience of the cases that are considered abnormal [namely, sexual inversion]," Freud writes, "has shown us that in them the sexual instinct and the sexual object are merely soldered together—a fact which we have been in danger of overlooking in consequence of the uniformity of the normal picture, where the object appears to form part and parcel of the instinct."[60]

As someone, like Freud himself, who has "experience" with cases that are (now) considered abnormal, Sensei recognizes that the young man's advances toward him may not be without a sexual component. Whether this experience comes from his own youthful relationship with K or simply from the fact that he belongs to a generation that still remembers that such things as sex between men are possible, Sensei is not fooled by the "uniformity of the normal picture, where the object appears to form part and parcel of the instinct." For Freud and for Sensei, there was no "heterosexual libido" and "homosexual libido" but only one type of "instinct" that could attach itself to various different kinds of objects. He knows, in other words, that there is nothing inevitable or "natural" about a heterosexuality based on the innate attractions of women for men and vice versa.

At the same time, however, and again like Freud, Sensei places this knowledge within the framework of a developmental narrative according to which the homosexual object will eventually be displaced by a heterosexual one. The young narrator, Sensei claims, has been made restless by a love without an object. This is what Freud referred to as the "polymorphous perversion" of the infant. For now, this aimless sexuality has lighted upon another man, but eventually, and inevitably, it will attach itself to a woman. In Sensei's account, *watakushi* will pass from the stage of "polymorphous perversion," where the sexual aim has no object, toward love for a member of his own sex, and finally on to love for a woman. With this attainment of genital heterosexuality, Sensei concludes his uncannily Freudian narrative of sexual development. The young *watakushi*, for his part, finds Sensei's discourse incomprehensible. As I discussed earlier, he claims that his interest

---

59. I have not been able to confirm that Sōseki read Freud, but the developmental model of sexuality was quite widespread at the time. One possible source for Sōseki would have been G. Stanley Hall's *Adolescence*, which had been translated into Japanese in 1910 as *Seinenki no kenkyū* and published by Dōbunkan. On this connection, see the annotated edition in Natsume, *Kokoro, Sōseki bungaku zenchūshaku*, vol. 12, 47.

60. Freud, "Three Essays on the Theory of Sexuality (1905)," 148.

in Sensei has nothing to do with "love." Their mutual incomprehension is made perfectly evident when *watakushi* says, "I think the two things are completely different in nature," to which Sensei responds, "No, they're the same."[61] What *watakushi* sees as a set of categories that are distinct in nature and occupy different *spaces*, Sensei sees as a process in time.

It is crucial here to remember, however, that this scene, like all of *watakushi*'s narrative, has been filtered through *watakushi*'s memory and presented to the reader after the fact. Since *watakushi* is the narrator here, then, the reader cannot discount the possibility that he is telling the story in a way that suits him. The question arises: does *watakushi* still believe that there was a categorical distinction to be made between his friendship with Sensei and love between men and women? If he does believe this, why has he gone to the trouble of relating this particular conversation with Sensei?

As *watakushi* narrates this scene, he already knows about Sensei's "dark secret." He has already read the letter that ends the novel and knows that Sensei never managed to free himself from the guilt of having betrayed K. He knows that for Sensei the passage from loving another man to loving a woman was so burdened with guilt that he found himself shut off from the world, unable to love anyone. Thus despite Sensei's suggestion in this moment that same-sex love is a step on the way toward heterosexual love, the fact remains that Sensei himself was never able to take this step. It was *watakushi*, according to Komori and Ishihara's analysis, who *was* able to take that step.

The point of *watakushi*'s narrative, it seems, is to tell the story of Sensei's inability to get over his past and move on to loving women in order to highlight his own success in both. *Watakushi*'s story (and I would hasten to distinguish this both from the novel *Kokoro* and from Sensei's life) can thus be read not only as a triumphant narrative of heterosexual becoming but also as a kind of cautionary tale that warns of the dangers of an excessive attachment to other men. As Doi Takeo famously, and depressingly, summarized it, "The fates of Sensei and K are the most eloquent testimony to the fact that exclusive concentration on male friendship can frequently drive those concerned to destruction."[62]

Despite what he says in his conversation with Sensei, however, *watakushi*'s connection to his older friend was not entirely categorically distinct from heterosexual love. As critics like Dodd and Hashimoto have pointed out, it is hard to miss its erotic component. Why then would he claim other-

---

61. Natsume, *Kokoro*, 27 (McKinney), 27 (McClellan), 36–37 (*SZ*).
62. Doi, *The Anatomy of Dependence*, 117.

wise? I would argue that by relating this conversation with his older mentor, *watakushi* claims for himself a heterosexual identity not by denying ever having been attracted to Sensei (as his younger self did in this conversation) but by narrating this scene of his former ignorance—and thus simultaneously admitting and disavowing the possibility that he may have attained his current heteronormative adulthood after passing through a "homosexual" stage. At the same time, however, while *watakushi* works hard to tell the story of how he has grown up into a good heterosexual, Sōseki's *Kokoro* (that is to say, the *novel itself*) goes over his head to let us know that this maturation is a product of motivated narrative rather than a natural course of development. It show us, in other words, how *watakushi* asserts or performs his own maturation by projecting "homosexuality" onto his own past and onto Sensei.

This would go a long way towards explaining the homoeroticism evident in the way the narrator describes his relationship with Sensei, beginning with the way he stalks him at the beach when they first meet. And it would make sense of the fact that *watakushi* seems rather proud that his relationship with Sensei was more intimate than the latter's relationship to K. If, during their stroll in Ueno Park, *watakushi* denies outright Sensei's suggestion that there might be an erotic component to their friendship, this could be explained as the result of a split between the younger, "clueless" *watakushi* who is being represented in the novel and the older, "wiser" *watakushi* who is doing the representing. All of this might suggest that the *watakushi* who narrates the first two sections of *Kokoro* has either become aware of or become more accepting of an attraction to Sensei of which his younger self remained ignorant or unconscious. By narrating this scene between Sensei and himself, then, he is able to bring a foreclosed homoeroticism back to life *as a preliminary or preparatory chapter* in his own narrative of development into a heteronormative adult.

This kind of retroactive narrative is typical of what Freud referred to as "deferred action" or *Nachträglichkeit*, according to which, in the summation of Laplanche and Pontalis, "experiences, impressions and memory-traces may be revised at a later date to fit in with fresh experiences or with the attainment of a new stage of development. They may in that event be endowed not only with a new meaning but also with psychical effectiveness."[63]

Of course the possibility of revision at a later date (such as the time of narration) calls into question whether this exchange ever "happened" at all, or at least whether it happened in the way the narrator recounts it. But historical accuracy matters less here than the implied path of development

---

63. Laplanche and Pontalis, *The Language of Psychoanalysis*, 111.

that *watakushi* sets up between the narrated past and present of narration in which he grows not only into his own heterosexuality, but also, and not at all paradoxically, into a position from which his *earlier* homosexuality can be recognized and disavowed at the same time. Sensei's Freudian narrative of sexual development is thus revealed as the narrator's own. And it is by emphasizing his own earlier incomprehension ("I think the two things are totally different") that the narrator demonstrates his retrospective understanding.

But if this is *watakushi*'s narrative, it is not the narrative of *Kokoro*. Sōseki himself was extremely skeptical of the notion of leaving the past behind in this way. As he wrote a decade earlier in his *Theory of Literature* [*Bungakuron*]:

> It would be a terrible mistake simply to look to the past of one's consciousness and assume that because it lies in the past it is necessarily less evolved than it is at present.... To conclude that the tastes of the past are childish in comparison with those of today, particularly when the tastes in question are of a different quality entirely, is never acceptable even if such a judgment is made only with regard to one's own consciousness.[64]

It is also hard to imagine that the same man who wrote this in 1905 and "The Heredity of Taste" just six years before *Kokoro* could have subscribed wholeheartedly to *watakushi*'s program of progress and his Oedipal narrative of internally mediated homosociality. *Kokoro* is not, after all, an elegiac romance. It is a novel that critiques the notions of progress and "maturation" that are inherent in that genre to provide a much more nuanced picture of our relation to the past. For Sōseki, moreover, the narrativization of sexuality-as-development was inseparable from the narratives of the global imperial order of which he remained critical throughout his career.

In many ways, the same could be said of Sigmund Freud, who consistently sought to avoid equating the normal with the normative and knew very well that development is always beset by regressions and repetitions. Despite that knowledge, however, the narrative thrust of Freud's "Three Essays" heads inexorably towards genital heterosexuality. Freud's argument is thus a modernizing argument insofar as it postulates a single trajectory of progress and downplays the role of violence and repudiation that fuels that progress.[65] For Sōseki, however, a Japanese writer who was acutely

---

64. Natsume, *Theory of Literature and Other Critical Writings*, 149; *Sōseki zenshū*, vol. 14, 454.

65. I should note here that Freud was not at all insensitive to the fact of discrimination against homosexuals and other "perverts," at least in his footnotes. But the normalizing thrust of his argument did leave itself open to cooptation by less tolerant readers, as the

aware of his position on the global periphery *and* as a subject of an increasingly rapacious Japanese empire, there was no missing the fact that those who have reached the "next stage" have done so by scrambling over the backs of others, only to kick them in the face to keep from being overtaken. They look back with disdain on where they imagine they came from and see those who are "still there" as qualitatively inferior—even as they disingenuously recite the modernizationist mantra that promises everyone the chance to "catch up."⁶⁶

A final look at McClellan's translation shows how this violent and hierarchical dynamic of modernization remains palpable in Sōseki's words, only to be muted again in McClellan's modernized English. McClellan's rendering is "But it was a step in your life toward love" [*koi ni agaru kaidan nandesu*].⁶⁷ A more literal translation of Sōseki's Japanese would read, "It's a staircase that goes up to erotic love." In McClellan's English, the staircase is transformed into a single "step," a step that, without the mention of a staircase, will be read as a horizontal rather than a vertical one. The verticality of Sōseki's staircase is thus quite literally flattened out as it moves into horizontal English [*yokomoji*]. In the process, the hierarchical character of the ascension to sexual normality that is so evident in the Japanese comes to look like a simple matter of lateral progress [*shinpo*]. The *violence* inherent in this ascent is made clear a few pages later when Sensei explains why he would rather forego *watakushi*'s friendship now than face his contempt in the future. In McClellan's translation the sentence reads, "The memory that you once sat at my feet will begin to haunt you and, in bitterness and shame, you will want to degrade me."⁶⁸ McClellan's "sat at my feet" suggests a child or a dog in complacent subordination to its father or master. But Sōseki's language is one of sexualized submission followed by violent rebellion. Rendered more literally into English, Sōseki's sentence reads "The memory that you once *knelt in front of someone* [*hito no mae ni hizamazuita*] will make you

---

subsequent history of psychoanalysis demonstrated. On Freud's tolerance and its American reception, see Abelove, "Freud, Male Homosexuality, and the Americans."

66. Sōseki makes a wry critique of the fantasy of "catching up" in a world of uneven development in *Botchan*, where Kiyo laments the fact that Botchan, as the second son, will not inherit the house where he grew up: "'If only you were a little older, you could have inherited the house,'" Kiyo sighed. But if I would have been able to inherit it in a few years, I should just as easily have been able to inherit it now. The old lady was so clueless she thought that a few years would give me the right to take my brother's house" (*Botchan*, location 155; *Sōseki zenshū*, vol. 2, 256–57).

67. Natsume, *Kokoro*, 27 (McClellan), 27 (McKinney), 36 (*SZ*).

68. Ibid., 30 (McClellan).

want to stomp on their head [*sono hito no atama no ue ni ashi o nosaseyou to suru*]."⁶⁹ What was a child/dog in McClellan's translation is here a man on his knees in front of another man—as if to render sexual service. The vivid image of "stomping on someone's head" echoes the verticality of the staircase cited earlier to render explicit the violence involved in "moving on." Here "moving on" is "moving up" over someone else's head. Like his earlier insertion of an anodyne "friendship," McClellan's choice to render this violent metaphor with an abstract, psychologizing verb like "degrade" dulls the force of Sōseki's language. Sōseki's text makes no mention of "haunting," or "bitterness and shame," only unremorseful violence.⁷⁰

Sensei's narrative is of course imbued with his own memory of his betrayal of K. If "The Heredity of Taste" showed a world in which men could still express their love and admiration for each other openly, *Kokoro*, written just a few years later, portrays the tragedy of the homosocial divide. But rather than being simply a novel that narrates the transition that *watakushi* believes he has effected towards a heterosocial subjectivity, I propose that it is better thought of as the "primal scene" of modern male homosociality in Japanese literature. I say this for several reasons. Like the primal scene that Freud discussed in his case history of the "Wolf Man," it may be fictional, but, as I showed in the previous chapter, it has continued to exercise profound and very real effects on the imagination of generations of readers.⁷¹ As a story about a man who chooses a woman over a man, it can be read as a dramatization of the transition from a "traditional" male homosocial world of men to a heterosocial modernity. At the same time, like Freud's primal scene, its precise temporal coordinates are vague and its tendency to "haunt" readers installs a recursive temporality that troubles our understanding of linear causality and of the past as "history." As a story imbued with nostalgia, guilt, and regret, and mediated through a succession of different narrators, the transition it narrates is far from over and done with.

---

69. My translation and emphasis.

70. McClellan's translation was not serviceable either for John Bester in his translation of Doi's discussion of homosexuality in *Kokoro*. The sentence discussed above is rendered much more vividly in Bester's translation as "The memory of having kneeled before someone makes one want to trample him underfoot at a later date." Dodd also found it necessary to retranslate the earlier passage about the "staircase to love." See Doi, *The Anatomy of Dependence*, 117; Dodd, "Significance of Bodies in Sōseki's *Kokoro*," 490.

71. For a now classic queer reading of the primal scene in the "Wolf Man," see Edelman, "Seeing Things."

As the discussion of its reception in the last chapter showed, the way a given reader interprets this "primal scene" also says a great deal about his or her identifications, both sexual and political. Readers who are melancholic over a lost male homosocial continuum tend to see it as a tragic story of betrayal and loss of trust in the modern world. Sensei himself could be considered the first of these, whom I have called the "paternalistic homosocial" readers of *Kokoro*. For others, of whom his younger protégé *watakushi* could be said to be the first, Sensei's inability to "get over" this betrayal and, indeed, to see it as anything other than a betrayal, was a sign of a fundamentally misogynous and moribund homosociality. But how do all these readings come together in understanding Sōseki's novel? Is there a way to read the novel's resistance to closure as undermining *watakushi*'s Oedipal narrative? If this is the case (and I believe it is) then the reader is kept suspended in a two-timing, recursive temporality that is both exemplary and critical of modern male homosociality in Japan.

A Shitty Ending

In the last scene before *watakushi*'s departure for Tokyo, he hears his brother's voice calling from their father's sickroom. Preparing himself for the worst, he hurries into the room only to find that the doctor needs help administering a palliative enema. The nurse, exhausted from her labors the night before, has gone to sleep in the room next door and the narrator's older brother stands next to the doctor looking befuddled and unable to help. "My brother," he writes, "who was not used to helping on such occasions, seemed at a loss."[72] As soon as the brother claps eyes on *watakushi* he orders him to assist the doctor and promptly takes a seat. *Watakushi* then places a sheet of oiled paper underneath his father's behind [*chichi no shiri no shita ni aburagami o ategattari shita*]. The use of the verbal auxiliary of enumeration *-tari* here suggests that the narrator did various other things as well to help the doctor administer the enema, but these remain unnamed.[73] The contrast here between the narrator's matter-of-fact competence in the matter of the enema and his older brother's flummoxed paralysis constitutes a powerful claim by *watakushi* that on the eve of his father's death he is well on his way to becoming the mature self who is writing the narrative. In this scene, the father has become an infant, the older brother has become a frightened little boy, and the narrator steps up to take care of them

---

72. Natsume, *Kokoro*, 122 (McClellan), 115 (McKinney), 151 (*SZ*).

73. McClellan seems to have found this scene distasteful enough to clean it up in his translation: "I took his place and helped the doctor" (ibid., 122 [McClellan]).

both. He is more grown up than they are and his maturity is powerfully figured here as the literal ability to *deal with shit*. In a subtle echo of this scene just a page later, the narrator uses the same verb he used to describe placing the sheet of oil paper under his father's buttocks [*ategau*] to describe the way he presses a piece of paper against the station wall to scribble a note to his family before he leaves for Tokyo.[74] Both instances are clearly efforts at closure that foreshadow the way the narrator will eventually put pen to paper in an attempt to put the past to rest.

But *watakushi*'s assertion of independence and maturity is soon undermined. Sensei's letter has arrived just before the scene with the enema. When he manages to steal away from his father's sickbed to flip through it, his eyes come to rest on a line near its end: "By the time this letter reaches you, I shall probably have left this world—I shall in all likelihood be dead."[75] His head swimming with this devastating sentence, *watakushi* begins to "turn the pages over backwards, reading a sentence here and there in the search for some clue as to whether Sensei is still alive.[76] But since neither this letter nor any other can attest to the death of its author, *watakushi* must piece together what he can by reading the whole letter through. And he is only able to do this once he sits down on the train on his way to Tokyo. "Then, with the vigor of decision, I leaped on the Tokyo-bound train. Seated in the thundering third-class carriage, I retrieved Sensei's letter from my sleeve and at last read it from beginning to end."[77]

Between Closure and Dilation

This is the last the reader hears of *watakushi*. Coming on the tail end of the scene of the father's enema, the conjunction of movement with stasis, activity with passivity, that comes of sitting down on a train is a perfect metaphor for the suspended animation into which Sensei's letter plunges him. For as long as he sits on the train, the letter is his only way of knowing whether Sensei is alive or dead. Every word of it thus becomes a possible answer to this pressing question, even as every moment spent reading it is another moment in which *watakushi* is powerless to stop his mentor's

---

74. Ibid., 153 (*SZ*), 123 (McClellan), 116 (McKinney).
75. Ibid., 122 (McClellan), 116 (McKinney), 151 (*SZ*).
76. Ibid., 123 (McClellan), 116 (McKinney), 152 (*SZ*).
77. Ibid., 117 (McKinney), 123 (McClellan), 153 (*SZ*). McClellan has: "In a desperate desire to act [*omoikitta ikioi de*], I boarded the Tokyo-bound train. The noise of the engine filled my ears as I sat down in a third-class carriage. At last I was able to read Sensei's letter from beginning to end."

suicide. When he first receives the letter and glimpses its foreboding end, *watakushi* literally reads the letter backwards as if to reverse the passage of time. But as soon as he begins to read the letter in its proper order, the twists and turns of the story it tells threaten to become what Freud identified as those of life itself: just so many detours on the "circuitous path to death."[78]

Readers of the novel *Kokoro* already know that Sensei is dead when they begin reading his letter. Indeed, it is evident from very early on in *watakushi*'s narrative. But the *watakushi* on the train remains uncertain. This gives rise to a crucial difference between what motivates the reading of *watakushi* on the train and what motivated the older *watakushi* to append Sensei's letter to his own narrative. Trapped on the train and thus deprived of any form of action except, precisely, reading, one can well imagine that *watakushi*-on-the-train would have occupied himself with reading the letter for the duration of his train ride back to Tokyo. In a sense, *watakushi*'s reading becomes a kind of life support for Sensei. This is a mode of reading that actively resists closure. "All I wanted to know at that moment was that Sensei was still alive. Sensei's past, his dark past that he had promised to tell me about, held no interest for me then."[79]

Sensei's "dark past" is, of course, precisely what *watakushi*-on-the-train *has* been interested in up until this point. It is also what the older *watakushi* has been withholding from the reader throughout the novel's first two sections. The story of Sensei's past is also the part of *Kokoro* that gets anthologized in textbooks and upon which the paternalistic critics were so fixated. But all of that has ceased to matter now that Sensei's threatened suicide looms. For *watakushi*-on-the-train ("at that moment"), the possibility of death is held in abeyance as he reads and rereads Sensei's letter. Sensei's dark secrets that once so fascinated him are no longer interesting except to the extent that they offer clues as to whether he is alive or dead. The more powerful the narrative chain of cause and effect from crime to self-punishment, the more likely it is to have eventuated in the ultimate act of expiation. For this reason, one can imagine that *watakushi*-on-the-train would be motivated to discover not narrative continuity and causality but loose ends and unresolved questions that might offer some hope of a derailment. It is with such a hope in mind that he might have read the letter again and again, skipping back and forth to different passages in a desperate search

---

78. Freud, "Beyond the Pleasure Principle," 39.
79. Natsume, *Kokoro*, 123 (McClellan), 116 (McKinney), 152 (*SZ*).

for something that might make it possible to believe that Sensei had not carried through with his threatened suicide.[80]

For the older *watakushi*, on the other hand, the knowledge that Sensei is already dead has made every detail of his letter a testament to his death. This is, of course, why he has given this section the title "Sensei and His Testament" [*Sensei to isho*]. As the ostensible "editor" of the book that is *Kokoro*, the narrator appends Sensei's letter as a kind of extended quotation. Indeed, the entire letter is placed in quotation marks in the Japanese text, although both McClellan and McKinney have removed them in the English translations. For the older narrator the question is not *whether* Sensei is dead but *why* he died. Although the possibility that he *might* be dead suddenly made the story of his life uninteresting for *watakushi*-on-the train, the narrator's knowledge that Sensei *is* dead makes his life into a story.[81] Indeed, it provides the fuel that drives the narrative of *Kokoro* itself. But like the reader of a novel who does not want it to end, *watakushi* on the train passes the time by (re)reading Sensei's letter as he hurtles toward Tokyo and the increasingly inevitable reality of Sensei's death. His "desperate desire to act"[82] by boarding the Tokyo-bound train smacks up against the wish that his journey, and Sensei's life, will be prolonged indefinitely.

The reader of Sōseki's novel, meanwhile, ends up somewhere in between these two extremes of narrative closure and dilation. If *watakushi* came back at the end of the novel to wrap things up and tell of what happened in the intervening years between the events he has just described and the present of his narration, *Kokoro* would be an elegiac romance. But he does not come back. The novel ends with the end of Sensei's letter, and the reader who wants to know more can only go back to *watakushi*'s story

---

80. This way of reading Sensei's letter would seem to suit the letter itself. As Oshino Takeshi argues, Sensei's letter itself is characterized by its "repetitive and recursive language" ("Isho no shohō," 174)." He points out that Sensei begins his letter with a digression concerning his uncertainty as to the validity of his mother's last words. Dying of typhoid, the words she spoke "often left no trace in her memory when the fever subsided. That is why I . . . but never mind" (Natsume, *Kokoro*, 130 [McClellan])." Oshino cites Sensei's uncertainty as an example of his inability to take anyone's words without subjecting them to repeated analysis. The scene sets the tone for the rest of Sensei's testament which, unable to attest to the death of its own author and indeed prolonging his life by its very length, is characterized by prolixity, repetition, and interpretative excess that Oshino contrasts with K's concise suicide note.

81. As Komori writes, "Only because 'Sensei' is dead and because his 'letter' has become his 'testament' has *watakushi* become able to talk of him, pretending to have come to understand 'Sensei'" (quoted in Sakaki, "The Debates on *Kokoro*," 51).

82. Natsume, *Kokoro*, 124 (McClellan), 118 (McKinney), 153 (*SZ*).

to look for the clues left by a narrator who knew, but would not tell, how things would turn out. *Kokoro* is thus a text that not only ends without closure but sends us circling back to its beginning—just as *watakushi* reads Sensei's letter backwards. The scene when *watakushi* runs away from his father's exposed anus and jumps onto a train "in a desperate desire to act" is the closest that *Kokoro* gets to closure. It could be said, then, that the end is buried in the middle of the novel, on the brink of the deaths of two fathers and suspended between passivity and action.

The way *Kokoro* superimposes these two ways of reading—one that hurries to the end and one that keeps looping back to the beginning—is strikingly similar to Freud's description of the life and death instincts in his "Beyond the Pleasure Principle": "One group of instincts rushes forward so as to reach the final aim of life as swiftly as possible," Freud writes, "but when a particular stage in advance has been reached, the other group jerks back to a certain point to make a fresh start and so prolong the journey."[83] Like this later Freud and unlike either of his protagonists, Sōseki was not interested in clean closure. As I have discussed, the novel ends with the end of Sensei's letter and the reader never hears from *watakushi* again. As a result, despite the bildungsroman-like tone of the first two sections of *Kokoro*, the fact that Sensei's letter is left dangling at the end subverts the closure that would otherwise be necessary to lend a decisive meaning to the novel. This would suggest that what Sōseki depicts in *Kokoro* is not so much how one man grew up to become a happily partnered heterosexual, but how he attempts to narrate that maturation into existence.

Watakushi tells us, for example, that he has completed every stage of Freud's narrative of sexual development. First he has moved beyond the oral and separated himself from his mother. This is made clear in his narrative when he expresses his exasperation at his mother for constantly badgering him about asking Sensei to find a job for him. What McClellan and McKinney variously translate as a "position" or a "post" is, in Sōseki's uncannily psychoanalytic Japanese, a *kuchi* (mouth)."[84] He has passed through the anal stage by overcoming his aversion to shit. By metaphorically castrating his own father in the scene of the enema, he will achieve genital heterosexuality. And yet, however hard *watakushi* might be working to prove that he has matured into heteronormative adulthood, the text of *Kokoro* makes it

---

83. Freud, "Beyond the Pleasure Principle," 41. In his insightful application of Freud's work to the understanding of narrative, Peter Brooks sees this back and forth movement as characteristic of the "highly plotted nineteenth-century novel" ("Freud's Masterplot," 90–112).

84. Natsume, *Kokoro*, 107 (McClellan), 100 (McKinney), 134 (*SZ*).

clear that he can only do so at Sensei's expense (not to mention that of his mother and father). In other words, he can only be a (straight) man by keeping very tight control over the narrative and by projecting homosexuality onto his own past and to Sensei.

Sensei, in *watakushi*'s account, has not only failed to "grow up" into a reproductive heterosexual, he has also failed to progress beyond the anal stage. He is shown to be oscillating between destruction (his virtual murder of K and his own suicide) and possessiveness (his unwillingness to share his past with his wife). All of this may be true of Sensei, but it is also true that in *taking the trouble* to portray Sensei in this way, *watakushi* is able both to recognize and disavow his own "anal regressions" along with his youthful "love" [*koi*] for Sensei by placing them in the context of a narrative of sexual development. What might be called *watakushi*'s "anality" is clearly evident in the way he structures his narrative. Like the letter Sensei will eventually write to tell *watakushi* about his past and which forms the last portion of the book, *watakushi*'s narrative is a retrospective one. But, as Ken Ito has noted, the younger man's narrative is different from Sensei's in its tendency to withhold information from the reader. "Knowing precisely how things turn out," Ito writes, "the initial narrator drops hints about events or revelations that lie in the future.... Yet, for all that he intimates, the narrator is surprisingly coy about what he reveals."[85] Like a child in the retention phase who, as Freud put it, "retains his faeces ... for purposes of auto-erotic satisfaction and later as a means of asserting his own will,"[86] *watakushi* doles out information only as it suits him.

The overall effect of this is that the entire text of *Kokoro*, including even Sensei's letter,[87] comes under the tight control of the first narrator. The almost airtight structure of *Kokoro* that results could not be more different, for example, from the digressive and paratactic quality of "The Heredity of Taste" or *I Am a Cat*. And yet despite these "anal" characteristics of *watakushi* himself—characteristics that show up in the tautness of the narrative structure and the almost sadistic scrutiny to which he subjects Sensei—it is Sensei who is portrayed in the novel thematically as being "stuck" in the anal stage. *Watakushi*, meanwhile, seems breezily to have moved on to mature adulthood and wishes only to learn from Sensei's experience. Or at least that is what *watakushi* would like the reader to think.

---

85. Ito, "Writing Time in Soseki's *Kokoro*," 8.
86. Freud, "On Transformations of Instinct as Exemplified in Anal Erotism," 130.
87. It is contained, as I noted earlier, within quotation marks presumably put there by *watakushi*.

Despite what *watakushi* may have intended, however, Sōseki's novel breaks off at the end of Sensei's letter without giving the younger man the opportunity to make an explicit statement of how he has learned from Sensei's mistakes. In this sense, unlike *watakushi*'s narrative, *Kokoro* as a novel does not make a clean break with its own "arrested development" but holds on to a certain nostalgic connection to the past. This recalcitrance is of course what made the novel so appealing to the paternalistic homosocial critics, who saw both Sensei and Sōseki as melancholic heroes with their eyes trained on the past. At the same time, by not actually narrating the eventual union of *watakushi* and Okusan, the novel resists the (heteronormative) closure that Komori and Ishihara's reading imposed (and indeed, that *watakushi* might have intended). One might speculate along with these critics that *watakushi* got together with Okusan, but one will never know for sure.

By depriving the reader of a clear ending, Sōseki makes his novel amenable to a whole spectrum of readings, some of which I have surveyed here. Whether one reads it as "full-on homo," as a national allegory about loneliness and friendship, or about the triumph of a future-oriented heterosexual love over a morbid homosociality, says more about the reader and his or her historical moment than it does about *Kokoro*. In a 1994 book on the *Kokoro* debates, Komori wrote (only half seriously, I imagine), "I hope with all my heart [*kokoro*] that this will be the last book to be written about *Kokoro*. But I know my hope is in vain."[88] Indeed, it seems as if readers will never outgrow *Kokoro*. The attempt to sew the novel's ending back up within *watakushi*'s discourse and thus to move on to other things is bound to fail. It is this lack of closure, this refusal to suture past with present that makes Sōseki's novel such a powerful example of two-timing homosocial narrative.

---

88. Komori, "Nakagaki," 113.

SIX

Gothic Homosociality in The Devil's Disciple

Unanswered Questions

"To order my story properly I should start with the time you and I split up."[1] On its face, this line, written from one man to another in Hamao Shirō's 1929 work *The Devil's Disciple*, is the most concise statement one could hope for of the teleological promise of the homosocial narrative in its normative mode. The text in which it appears takes the form of a long letter written by its narrator Shimaura Eizō to his friend Tsuchida Hachirō, who is identified explicitly as Shimaura's former lover. A properly ordered narrative, Shimaura is saying, would begin with the ending of their affair; the love between the two men that comes before "should" be narrated retrospectively, in light of its (bad) ending and its author's subsequent discovery of "how to love the opposite sex."[2] That would be the "proper" way. And yet this sentence is clearly counterfactual in the context of Hamao's story. It appears on page 13 of the 42-page letter, after Shimaura has already said quite a bit about what came before "the time you and I split up." He has already, for example, reminded Tsuchida with some insistence of the time when they first met at school ten years earlier, when they first became "best friends": "Actually, we were even more than best friends were we not? Was I not always to be seen at your side wherever you were and you at mine, no matter

---

1. Hamao, *The Devil's Disciple*, 13; "Akuma no deshi," 86. Subsequent citations to these titles will be abbreviated as *Devil's* and "Akuma."
2. *Devil's*, 14; "Akuma," 73.

where we went? Were we not known among our dormitory mates as a *Paar*?"³

The sentences here are in the past tense and refer to a relationship that was both intimate and public: the boys were always together and their togetherness was witnessed and validated by others. It even had a name: *Paar*, the German word for "couple" and non-derogatory student slang for a male-male pairing. If all of this was in the past, however, as these sentences appear in the letter, they are addressed very much in the present to the absent Tsuchida. Their tone, both injured and accusatory, has nothing to do with the "proper" way of telling the story that would start out with a clean break from the past. Still stuck on the past in a melancholic present, their two-timing quality is characteristic of the temporality of *The Devil's Disciple* as a whole.

If Shimaura knows what it would take to tell "my story" in its proper order, his letter, which is full of delayed beginnings and recursive loops like this one, is more attuned to the fact that the story it tells does not belong "properly" to him. It is not entirely "my story" because, lacking the communal validation of a world where the homosocial continuum was more intact (the world of their school dormitory), both the letter and the love are left now with a pressing need—the need to have the story of this past relationship validated by Tsuchida as an attentive and loving reader (if not lover), in a very different present. Sensei's letter in *Kokoro* was motivated by a similar need, although at least in that novel the letter made its way into *watakushi*'s hands as a proxy for K. In *The Devil's Disciple*, the text consists of nothing but the letter. There is no way of knowing whether Tsuchida ever read it. This means that the text as a whole is not just resistant to closure (like *Kokoro* was); it is utterly suspended in time. The story it tells lacks a clear beginning and end; if it moves forward at all, it does so not in order to get to that place after "the time you and I split up," but because it aches with the foreclosed possibility of love between men—not as a precious remnant of an idealized and "museumified" past, as was the case in Kawabata's *The Boy*, and not as a stage on the way to heterosexuality, as in both *The Wild Goose* and *Kokoro*, but as something that is still ongoing; even now. Was this not the past we shared? he asks. If, as Dodie Bellamy has written, "Unanswered questions . . . are a form of intimacy,"⁴ this one looks a lot like love. Unfortunately, however, thanks to a number of factors that I explain in this chapter, this love is all too easy to miss.

---

3. *Devil's*, 5; "Akuma," 68–69.
4. Bellamy, *Low Culture*, 228.

Although the two-timing mechanism of homosocial narrative made it possible for love between men to be alluded to in Ōgai's and Sōseki's works as an early chapter in a tale of its transformation into a modernized heterosexuality, by the 1920s even that developmental script started to unravel as the homosocial continuum began to show signs of a more decisive rupture. In the decade and a half that followed *Kokoro*'s publication, a conception of "the homosexual" emerged in Japan not as a point on a universal continuum, but as a different species altogether: a pervert, a predator, and a corruptor of youth. In this new understanding, love between men was neither an outdated custom nor a transitory developmental stage, but a form of "perverse sexual desire" [*hentai seiyoku*] that irrevocably separated those who experienced it from the rest of mankind. Hamao's story gives a detailed depiction of this new and nightmarish vision of the homosexual, although the text never uses the term itself. At the same time, *The Devil's Disciple* is also a two-timing text insofar as the narrator's attitude bears traces of earlier, less stigmatized understandings of male-male sexuality specific to the Japanese tradition and that still shelter in his own not-too-distant past. As Kuroiwa Yūichi has recently written, *The Devil's Disciple* is a text in which "the narrator has reinterpreted a treasured *shudō*-style bond from his student days in terms of the idea of 'homosexuality as perverse sexual desire' that had already become widespread by 1929. But his reinterpretation is not complete; the *nanshoku* concept still lingers as well."[5]

A generation younger than Ōgai and Sōseki, Hamao Shirō (1895–1935) had a strong scholarly and perhaps also a personal interest in male-male love that makes itself known in more or less subtle ways in most of his works. He was well versed in the work of European homophiles and radical sexologists such as Edward Carpenter, Karl-Heinrich Ulrichs, Magnus Hirschfeld, and Havelock Ellis, an expertise which prompted his friend and fellow detective novelist Edogawa Ranpo to refer to him as "my teacher on the subject of homosexuality."[6] He was also among the first generation in Japan to begin to conceive of male same-sex sexuality in terms of an identity with social and psychic ramifications rather than as an aesthetic preference along the lines of premodern *nanshoku* or a developmental stage that would eventually be outgrown.

---

5. Kuroiwa, "'Nanshoku' to 'hentaiseiyoku no aida,'" 379.
6. Edogawa Ranpo, "Futari no shishō," 138. His other teacher, incidentally, was Iwata Jun'ichi, whose correspondence with Minakata Kumagusu I discussed in Chapter 1.

In this chapter, I discuss not so much what Hamao has to teach us "about homosexuality," but what *The Devil's Disciple* tells us about what happened when men in Japan no longer had a place to put their histories of loving other men. By presenting a narrator whose own love for another man in the past has come to seem monstrous and shameful and yet still remains very much a part of him, Hamao's text dramatizes a dilemma no doubt experienced by many men in his day as they felt the homosocial continuum come apart beneath their feet, forever alienating them from themselves and from their own pasts. At the same time, the incompleteness of this shift left their relations with women in the present haunted by unresolved connections to other men in their past. *The Devil's Disciple* brilliantly dramatizes the unfortunate consequences of this dilemma for both its female and male characters.

The plot is as follows: the narrator Shimaura Eizō wants to murder his wife Tsuyuko, whom he despises for her subservice and passivity. With his wife out of the way, Shimaura hopes to marry his mistress, a woman named Sueko, whom he met long before Tsuyuko, but who has recently come back into his life. To this end, Shimaura comes up with what he believes to be a foolproof way of killing Tsuyuko and making it look like an accident. Shimaura himself suffers from insomnia and has an addiction to sleeping powder so extreme that he has to take many times what would be a lethal dose for anyone else in order for it to have any effect on him. When Tsuyuko complains one day of having trouble sleeping herself, he hits on the idea of getting her to take the same oversized dose of sleeping powder as he does, which would be fatal for her drug-naïve system. He plans to do this not by explicitly telling her to take such a large dose, but rather by inducing her to imitate him—by making sure that she sees him taking his. This attempt to use his own addiction to rid himself of his cloying wife takes an unexpected turn, however, when, on the very night that he had hoped that Tsuyuko would die by imitating him, his mistress Sueko, alone in her home, takes the bait instead. Sueko dies of an overdose and Shimaura ends up in jail charged with her murder.

The foregoing plot, which sounds entirely "heterosexual" when presented in this way, is nonetheless framed in its entirety by a relationship between two men. It comes to the reader in the form of a letter that Shimaura writes from jail to his former lover Tsuchida Hachirō, who happens to be a prosecutor in the court where he is being tried for Sueko's murder. It is this letter, as I mentioned earlier, that constitutes the entire text of *The Devil's Disciple*.

Curiously, Shimaura does not ask Tsuchida in the letter to intervene on his behalf legally; rather, he notes that Tsuchida works in the same court where he is being tried, but his case may well have landed on the desk of another prosecutor. Why, then, is he writing this letter? Toward the beginning of the document, Shimaura writes,

> If you had agreed to meet with me I might have been spared the writing of this letter. If I had remembered earlier that my old friend was serving in the court attached to the very prison in which I am being held, I might not have had to suffer as long as I have. I might have been able much earlier to relate the bizarre experiences that I am about to set down here.[7]

If the purpose of writing his letter is not to influence the court's decision about his guilt or innocence, the two conditional sentences here suggest what its purpose actually was. "If you had agreed to meet me" and "If I had remembered earlier": two phrases suggesting physical proximity on the one hand and memory on the other. Togetherness (with Tsuchida) and memory (of Tsuchida) are the two things Shimaura was/is lacking. These are also the two privations for which this letter is meant somehow to make up. The letter itself, in other words, and the relating of the "bizarre experiences" that it accomplishes, serves Shimaura as a partial and belated compensation for his inability to meet directly with Tsuchida. If this substitutive or compensatory effect of the letter applies to the dyad between Shimaura and Tsuchida alone, there is also a historical or social framework operative in which Shimaura writes the letter in the absence of a larger cultural "script" by means of which he might remember and understand (which is to say, *mourn*) his loss of Tsuchida. In this sense the letter might be seen as an attempt to cure himself of a melancholia resulting from his inability to acknowledge that loss for lack of a sanctioned script. In order to understand how this works, it is necessary first to see how Shimaura's personal loss dovetailed with a larger cultural shift.

Between Nanshoku *and* Dōseiai

As I argued in the first chapter, male homosexuality had only recently begun to be pathologized in Japan when Hamao was writing. Thus, in the larger narrative of Japanese cultural history, *The Devil's Disciple* occupies a moment when two very different ways of understanding male-male sexuality were still competing for dominance. This sets up a certain undecidability as to whether the relationship between Shimaura and Tsuchida is to be

---

7. *Devil's*, 3; "Akuma," 68.

understood from the perspective of the premodern tradition of *nanshoku*, or in the psychologized modern model of an interiorized homosexuality.

As previously discussed, the *nanshoku* model in its ideal(ized) form involved a hierarchical relationship of fictive fraternity between two men, where the older brother "offered the youth physical and social protection, a role model, and material aid" and the younger "reciprocated through obedience, respect, and intimate access to his person."[8] The older partner expected loyalty and monogamy from his younger brother, but the practice of *nanshoku* did not preclude marriage to a woman. As such, it retained the possibility of a narrative arc in the form of development toward "responsible," reproductive adulthood and participation for both parties in the homosocial corporate family system (or *ie seido*).

Echoes of the *nanshoku* model abound in *The Devil's Disciple* and may account for the fact that the two men's youthful love story can be narrated in such an uncensored, if not undistorted, form. To the extent that Tsuchida fulfills the role of teacher and benefactor and remains faithful to Shimaura, as indeed he does in the beginning of their relationship, he is an exemplary "older brother." Shimaura refers to the beginning of their relationship as the moment when he became Tsuchida's "one and only little brother" [*muni no ototo*]. Tsuchida, who is a brilliant student, helps Shimaura with his studies, and for two years they are never apart. "You were my older brother" and "my teacher," Shimaura writes. "I respected you and came to believe that you could do no wrong."[9]

If Tsuchida was once an ideal "older brother" in the discourse of *nanshoku*, however, Shimaura thinks very differently about him in the moment of narration. This is partly the result of his having been cruelly abandoned by Tsuchida "because you fell passionately in love with a beautiful boy one year below me in school." Shimaura was clearly devastated by this. "I thought we loved and understood each other," he writes. "I thought our friendship would last forever. But you stopped caring and left me all alone."

This heartbreak alone would be bad enough, but because love between men had become increasingly pathologized in the intervening years, when Shimaura looks back on this youthful love affair, Tsuchida's abandonment of him has begun to appear to him not just as an act of selfishness and insensitivity (as it might for any jilted lover), but also as a symptom of perversion and pathology. Thus, alongside his nostalgic and idealized recollections of Tsuchida who "could do no wrong," he tells a story of seduction

---

8. Pflugfelder, *Cartographies of Desire*, 41.
9. *Devil's*, 5; "Akuma," 69.

and the corruption of innocence. Shimaura describes himself as being "a vulnerable young boy who wouldn't hurt a fly" when he first met Tsuchida. By the time Tsuchida was through with him, however, he had become a person "stimulated by the criminal and the bizarre,"[10] and addicted to alcohol and sleeping medication. He describes himself as a passive victim of Tsuchida's moral suasion, "overawed by the strength of your personality."[11] Not only that, but he claims that Tsuchida went on after he abandoned him to "corrupt" many other "naïve and good-hearted boys" as well. In Shimaura's imagination, Tsuchida's behavior is nothing short of diabolical. "You are a devil," he writes, "Devouring the flesh of humans is not enough for you. You are a hateful devil who won't stop until you have cast their very souls into hell."[12]

In Shimaura's account, then, his description of his relationship with Tsuchida shifts from a language of respect and tutelage in which the bond between the two men, though hierarchically structured, remains un-coerced and mutually beneficial, to a vocabulary of seduction and indoctrination. A benign paternalism of the older for the younger "brother" is now read in terms of quasi-religious enthrallment. In becoming Tsuchida's "disciple," Shimaura writes, "I sold my soul for knowledge. I will have to live with the fact that I sacrificed my body to your strange love, but having sold my soul fills me with regret."[13]

As the agent of seduction and corruption rather than instruction and guidance, Tsuchida leaves the premodern sphere of *nanshoku* altogether and begins to appear in the guise of the modern, pathological homosexual. His transformation from loving pedagogue to perverted predator thus echoes that of the historical discourse of male-male sexuality in Japan more generally. But it is crucial to recognize that this "transitional" narrative is not reducible to a series of discrete stages or events. In other words, although Shimaura may be claiming, like *watakushi* in *Kokoro* and *boku* in *The Wild Goose*, to have "outgrown" the "stage" in which his former lover has remained "stuck," he also represents the "devil" Tsuchida as someone whose perversion is powerful enough to render the very notion of "development" impossible. Progress and development are threatened by an overarching *sameness* that derails the forward movement of narrative. Shimaura's storyline is constantly undermined by his retrospective rancor, its beginning colored

---

10. *Devil's*, 9; "Akuma," 71.
11. *Devil's*, 5; "Akuma," 69.
12. *Devil's*, 6; "Akuma," 69.
13. *Devil's*, 7; "Akuma," 70.

by its end. Vampire-like, Tsuchida has poisoned Shimaura with his "strange love" and they have both stepped outside of time.

"What You Will Never Know"

If *watakushi* in *Kokoro* and *boku* in *The Wild Goose* told their tales in order to distance themselves from a male homosocial past and thereby affirm their modernity as heteronormative subjects, in Hamao's text, written just a decade and a half later, the past has become explicitly homo*sexual*, and the narrator's attempt to distance himself has taken on a new urgency that reflects the ongoing breakdown in the homosocial continuum, even as the idea that love between men is something one "outgrows" continues to linger. Shimaura thus insists simultaneously that he has outgrown and that he has become categorically distinct from his former lover. He tells the story of his own seduction by Tsuchida in order to bind his past homosexual acts into a narrative that begins with his sexual innocence, moves through a homosexual stage, and ends with his achievement of a differentiated (hetero) self. But once he gets there, he also insists that the difference is categorical and complete. This double operation is clearly in evidence in the following passage:

So yes, we were lovers of a sort [*isshu no koibito dōshi datta deshō*] weren't we? And I was dumped by that lover [*sōshite watashi wa sono koibito ni suterareta ni chigai arimasen*]. But once I was abandoned by you and moved away [*hanareta*] from you, I was able to look hard at myself [*watashi wa, jishin o mitsumeru koto ga dekita*], and at the same time to see everything about you, all the way through [*anata jishin o zenbu mitōshite shimatta no desu*].[14]

Shimaura's narrative culminates in a self-knowledge attained through knowingness.[15] He can see himself because he can *see through* Tsuchida. By separating himself from Tsuchida, he is cured of blindness and able to see his former lover for what he now believes he is—a "devil" and a homosexual. This process of what might be called "projective subject formation"

---

14. *Devil's*, 6; "Akuma," 69. I have slightly altered my own translation here to emphasize the peculiarities of Hamao's wording.

15. I use the term "knowingness" here in the sense given it by David Halperin. He writes, "what our culture typically produces, or recognizes, as 'the truth' about gay men and gay sex is not a disengaged, serene, or politically innocuous 'knowledge,' but an array of contradictory and, it would now seem, murderous knowledge-effects: an illusory *knowingness*, that is, which is not only distinct from 'knowledge' but is actually opposed to it, is actually *a form of ignorance*, insofar as it serves to conceal from the supposedly knowledgeable the nature of their own personal and political investments in the systematic misrecognition and abjection of homosexuality" (*Saint=Foucault*, 16); emphasis in original.

is echoed in the verb forms used in the passage, which chart an emergence from a passive state into active subjectivity. Beginning with a conspiratorial copula [*datta deshō*], Shimaura moves on to two iterations of the passive verb "to be dumped" [*suterareta*], then to the intransitive "moved away" [*hanareta*], and finally to two active transitive verbs of seeing: the first ("to look hard" [*mitsumeru*]), responsible and unflinching when the object is himself, and the second ("to see through" [*mitōsu*]), contemptuous and withering when it switches to Tsuchida. The personal pronouns undergo a similar progression—from "we" [*wareware*] to an objectified "that lover" [*sono koibito*] that works to yank the narrator out of the dialogue and into a third-person narrative. Finally, fortified by the distance thus gained, he enters again into dialogue, but this time as a separate subject confronting its abjected object: "I" [*watashi*] versus "you yourself" [*anata jishin*]. The "I" does the seeing now, and it can see itself and "you," too. And yet this assertion of Shimaura's separate (heterosexual) identity is highly unstable. Eventually his story will lead him back to the realization that he is indeed "the devil's disciple": "It was then that I felt the seed that you planted inside me start to grow. I became afraid of myself."[16]

What Shimaura describes here as a fear of "himself" is not unlike what Freud described as the "uncanny": "nothing new or alien, but something which is familiar and old-established in the mind and which has become alienated only through the process of repression."[17] The "uncanny" also, according to Freud, can take the form of the *doppelgänger*—the "other self" who represents "unfulfilled but possible futures." At one point, Shimaura refers to Tsuchida as a "second me," and the two are indeed very much alike.[18] Much like Sensei and K, they start out in the same socioeconomic class and have attended the same schools, and, although Tsuchida has succeeded in his career where Shimaura has not, they both began with the same "brilliant" potential. Shimaura, at least, imagined a happy future for the two of them, together. "I thought we loved and understood each other," he writes to Tsuchida, "I thought our friendship would last forever."[19] In Shimaura's case the "unfulfilled but possible futures" that Freud mentions in connection with the uncanny would have included the foreclosed possibility that Shimaura might not have outgrown his homosexual stage

---

16. *Devil's*, 17; "Akuma," 76.
17. Freud, "The Uncanny," 241.
18. *Devil's*, 22; "Akuma," 78.
19. *Devil's*, 6; "Akuma," 69.

and somehow remained together with Tsuchida. In other words, Tsuchida has come to represent Shimaura's own lost and uncanny "gay future."

Freud's description of the uncanniness of doubles sounds much like a narrative of Shimaura and Tsuchida's relationship. "When all is said and done," he writes, "The quality of uncanniness can only come from the fact of the 'double' being a creation dating back to a very early mental stage, long since surmounted—a stage, incidentally, at which it wore a more friendly aspect. The 'double' has become a thing of terror, just as, after the collapse of their religion, the gods turned into demons."[20]

Tsuchida, although he once wore a more friendly aspect, has indeed become a demon to Shimaura. And this is *both* because he has come to represent "a very early mental stage, long since surmounted" (the stage of "homosexuality") *and* because he represents "unfulfilled but possible futures." The figure of Tsuchida thus encompasses an uncategorizable past and a foreclosed future—*both* of which are generating independent (but highly intertwined) melancholic strains. A third time point is noticeably missing although it is arguably the most important: the present.

In this context, it is significant that Shimaura's name (島浦) is an inversion of "Urashima" (浦島), which in ancient Japanese legend is associated with a character named "Urashima Tarō." One day, Urashima Tarō rescues a turtle who turns out to be the daughter of the God of the Sea. The next day, another turtle comes to take him to the Sea God's underwater palace, where he stays for three days. Upon returning home, however, he finds that three hundred years have passed and everyone he knows is long gone. For Shimaura, literally an inverted Urashima, time has also stopped thanks to his entrancement, not with a beautiful princess from the sea but with a man on solid ground. The name "Shimaura," which means "Island Bay," also contrasts explicitly with the name "Tsuchida" (土田), which is written with the characters for "land" and "rice field," both of which carry connotations of groundedness and stability. Since "da," when written phonetically, is also an informal copula, the name sounds like an emphatic reference to the earth and the land. If Shimaura is an island bobbing in a bay, his repeated apostrophes of—*Tsuchida-san! Tsuchida-san!*—seem to advertise his desire to come back to earth by somehow reconnecting with his former lover.

It is perhaps for this reason that rather than simply decry or deny his former lover's influence, Shimaura proclaims it aloud, sometimes in an accusatory fashion, but other times with an ironic pride. "If I hadn't met you that time when I was a boy," he writes early on in the letter, "I would

---

20. Freud, "The Uncanny," 236.

never have ended up in this place,"[21] while later referring to himself as "the perfect inheritor of your soul." Shimaura's simultaneous insistence in this narrative on *both* his aspirational heterosexuality *and* his history with Tsuchida thus echoes what *watakushi* implied about his relationship with Sensei in *Kokoro* as discussed in the last chapter. If Shimaura's protestations are more overt than *watakushi*'s, this makes *The Devil's Disciple* something like a gothic version of Sōseki's canonical text, a version that exemplifies, in its own uncanny way, the vexed and convoluted, two-timing homosociality of its early twentieth-century moment.

The Gothic Homosocial

I want to stop here for a moment and think a little more about the term "gothic" in its relation to male homosocial desire. In the fifth chapter of Eve Kosofsky Sedgwick's *Between Men*, titled "Toward the Gothic: Terrorism and Homosexual Panic" she locates the origins of both homophobia and homosexual identity in the gothic novel of late eighteenth-century Britain. In earlier moments (in Chapters 2 to 4, she writes of Shakespeare's sonnets, William Wycherley's Restoration drama *The Country Wife*, and Laurence Sterne's *Sentimental Journey*), "the detour of male homosocial desire through the woman is simply assumed as the obligatory norm," but it is in the gothic novel that "the possibility, the attraction, the danger—of simply dropping the female middle term becomes an explicit, indeed an obsessional literary subject. With it comes a much more tightly organized, openly proscriptive approach to sexuality and homosocial bonding."[22]

Of course, the situation in twentieth-century Japan was quite different from late eighteenth-century Britain, thanks to Japan's long (and still quite recent) cultural memory and literary tradition of love between men. Thus while Hamao's *The Devil's Disciple* might strike us as gothic in some ways, it could not be described in the Japanese context as belonging to "the first novelistic form . . . to have close, relatively visible links to male homosexuality."[23] It *could* be said, however, that the fad for what was called "erotic grotesque nonsense" [*ero guro nansensu*] to which Hamao's work, as well as that of his friend Edogawa Ranpo, belonged, had a great deal in common with the gothic. It often happens in modern Japanese literary history that developments that took many decades in Europe seem weirdly compressed into one, just as the order in which they occur is often transposed in un-

---

21. *Devil's*, 10; "Akuma," 71.
22. Sedgwick, *Between Men*, 91.
23. Ibid.

canny ways. So just as the Japanese "romanticism" of the 1890s had already yielded to "naturalism" by the first decade of the twentieth century, both were followed (rather than preceded, as was the case in Britain) by the "gothic" of "erotic grotesque nonsense." Shifts in the structure of male homosocial desire seem to have taken place with similar dispatch. Therefore, in *The Wild Goose* and *Kokoro* "the detour of male homosocial desire through the woman [was] simply assumed as the obligatory norm," but in *The Devil's Disciple* the possibility of "simply dropping the female middle term has become an explicit, indeed an obsessional literary subject." In true gothic style, moreover, the "dropping" of "the female middle term" takes the form of—what else? Murder! *The Devil's Disciple* also conforms to what Sedgwick called, in the title of her dissertation, the striking "coherence of gothic conventions," insofar as the genre is about "one or more males who not only is persecuted by, but considers himself transparent to and often under the compulsion of, another male."[24]

But aside from these provocative parallels, what is most useful about Sedgwick's understanding of the gothic for this book's reading of *The Devil's Disciple* is the way in which she says the gothic offers what she calls "a privileged view of individual and family psychology." It shows, in other words, in highly exaggerated and externalized forms, the mechanisms through which psychological phenomena, such as "misogyny" and "homophobia," are structurally produced and then internalized. Once they are internalized, they tend to be imagined as having been "inside" all along. But in the gothic they are still, as it were, *on their way* inside and the mechanisms of this internalization are also still visible. This may explain the noticeable preoccupation in *The Devil's Disciple* with ingesting various things ranging from sleeping powder to human flesh, as well as the almost cartoonish, melodramatic exaggeration of the language of *The Devil's Disciple*. It is a story about horrible, hateful impulses (namely "misogyny" and "homophobia"), but one that highlights so clearly the structural causation of those impulses that it can be hard to take seriously, by which I mean to actually believe that Shimaura is motivated by some deep-seated hatred for women or for the homosexual that he fears himself to be.

What, then, motivates Shimaura? I think it is quite clearly *not*, at least initially, his hatred for women or for himself but the fact that he has nowhere to put his love for (and grief over) Tsuchida. In their younger days, when the *nanshoku* model (or the updated version of it that prevailed in all-male dormitories at the time) was still in effect, Tsuchida could serve as

---

24. Ibid.

both the mediator and the object of Shimaura's love. Shimaura imitated him openly, just as Don Quixote did with Amadis, but unlike that knight and his hero, the existence in Japan of a sanctioned script for male-male love made it possible for Shimaura to love his mediator as well as imitate him. Once Tsuchida breaks his heart and he leaves school, however, he finds that the only script available to him is the heteronormative one.[25] His response is to compose his own kind of script: a homosocial narrative in which he tells a heterosexual story but recruits Tsuchida as his listener. This, I would argue, just as much or more as his desire to distance himself from homosexuality, is the source of the pressing insistence with which he tells Tsuchida about his newfound appreciation for women. "Tsuchida-*san*," he writes, "I had become your disciple in every way, but your particular brand of sensuality seems not to have penetrated me completely. I felt an intense physical desire for Sueko." It is hard to tell in this sentence which is more important—that he desires Sueko or that he is *telling Tsuchida* that he desires Sueko. These stories he tells about the women in his life, moreover, are barely separable from his own story with Tsuchida. Later he describes his treatment of his wife Tsuyuko in terms that read like an exaggerated, indeed "gothic" version of the way he remembers Tsuchida, that "devil" and devourer of human flesh, as having treated him.

> The pathetic sight of her was nauseating. I hated her so much I wanted to tear her into shreds and eat her. . . . I did everything I could to turn her body and soul into an instrument for my own pleasure, my toy. . . . In the end I tortured her so cruelly that I started to hate myself. I started to feel possessed by her living ghost."[26]

Here the "attraction, the danger—of simply dropping the middle term" is expressed in rather gruesome terms, as the fantasy of *eating* his wife, only to be haunted by her "living ghost." First, active incorporation and then involuntary possession: the narrative here does start to sound suspiciously like his experience with Tsuchida.

In telling the story of his loving relationship with Sueko followed by that of his cruel treatment and attempt to murder his wife Tsuyuko, Shimaura essentially repeats the arc of his ill-fated affair with Tsuchida, which also began with passionate love and ended in callous rejection. The splitting that he effects by viewing one of the women as an ideal lover and the other

---

25. It is important to note here that "leaving school" is both a temporal and a spatial shift.

26. *Devil's*, 18; "Akuma," 76. It is hard not to see this as an echo of the way Sensei in *Kokoro* felt that his wife was standing between him and the ghostly presence of K (see Chapter 4).

as meek, needy, and pathetic, also seems to reflect his inability to reconcile the earlier, loving Tsuchida (who "could do no wrong") with the later devilish one, who has made him feel meek, needy, and pathetic himself. That the two names "Sueko" and "Tsuyuko" are so close phonetically serves as a telling textual trace of this splitting. The story of his love and hatred for each of these women in succession, then, becomes his way of *retelling, to Tsuchida*, his version of his affair with his former lover. If Shimaura himself takes Tsuchida's cruel role in his relations with Tsuyuko, moreover, when he writes of his love for Sueko, it is perfectly clear that it is simply the vessel into which he is pouring his love for Tsuchida: "I won't bore you with the details of how we got together. Let's just say that from that autumn the little forest in Ueno where you and I used to pledge our love to each other became the spot for Sueko and I to do the same."[27] And later, after Sueko dies by accident, he flees to "that village in Kiso where you and I went for summer vacation."[28]

If Shimaura's love for Sueko is a vessel for his earlier love for Tsuchida and the same is true of his hatred for his wife, his plan to kill his Tsuyuko is better read not as a direct emanation of an already internalized misogyny or homophobia—if it were that, he would surely take a more active role in it—but as a kind of *test* for the presence of genuine love and affection amid the belated, compensatory structures he has built to cover over his grief. Finding himself in a relationship with Tsuyuko that has all of the ideology of heteronormative love but none of the affect,[29] he devises an elaborate plan to kill her essentially by inducing her to act as if she loved him by doing precisely what he did in his relationship with Tsuchida—namely by *imitating* the man she supposedly loves by taking the same amount of sleeping powder as he does.

I want to slow down here and return to the idea put forward by Girard that desire is not spontaneous or original to the subject, but fundamentally imitative or "mimetic."[30] Thus, desire does not well up, on its own, nor is it merely a response to the attractions of the object. Instead, people *learn* to desire by imitating the desire of a mediator through the process of "triangular desire." For Girard, this is true of all human desire, but people have historically been more or less willing to recognize the mimetic origins of

---

27. *Devil's*, 13; "Akuma," 73.
28. *Devil's*, 37; "Akuma," 87.
29. "Anyone would have thought this young couple had the world on a string. I even thought so myself. But alas, this was just a daydream" (*Devil's*, 17; "Akuma," 75).
30. For a more in-depth discussion of mediated desire in Girard, see the Introduction to the present study.

their desires. Modern societies, particularly, have been increasingly seduced by the notion of innate or intrinsic desire as the hallmark of individual identity. "I want what I want," a person likes to believe, "because of who I am" *and vice versa*.[31] This essentially Romantic logic, which holds that desire affirms identity, is at the basis of both modern heteronormativity ("My desire for women proves that I am a man") *and* of modern gay identity ("I love men because I am gay / I love women because I am a lesbian.") But if desire is neither an intrinsic "proof" of identity nor an autonomic response to the attractions of the object—if even one's most deeply felt desires are *mimetic* in origin, this introduces a fateful externality to the structure of desire. One is no longer the subject of one's own desire but subject to the influence of the mediator. In contexts where the mediation of desire is openly avowed (which Girard terms external mediation) this does not cause problems. But when the very fact of mediation is disavowed as a result of modern "romantic" ideologies of originality and spontaneity, the results can be tragic.

The Devil's Disciple tells the story of just such a tragedy in exaggerated and overt, which is to say "gothic," fashion. No longer able to acknowledge the fact that his desire is being mediated by Tsuchida, Shimaura is like what Girard called, in a passage cited previously, the "romantic *vaniteux* who does not want to be anyone's disciple. He convinces himself that he is thoroughly *original*."[32] And yet, "the process of mediation creates a very vivid impression of autonomy and spontaneity precisely when we are no longer autonomous and spontaneous."[33] *The Devil's Disciple*, in its gothic wisdom, knows this very well, as when it has Shimaura write to Tsuchida about his undying love for Sueko: "I imagine a woman-hater like you will laugh at the thought of someone who hates his first love but still can't stop thinking of her. But it can't be helped. This is the difference between your personality and mine. I lost her when I was twenty but I always, always remembered her."[34]

The "difference between your personality and mine" is framed here as a difference in sexual orientation, but one has to wonder who cannot stop thinking about whom. Shimaura's effort to distinguish himself from Tsuchida, to claim his own originality and spontaneity, could hardly be more

---

31. It is fascinating to consider how this model, which has been with humankind at least since the dawn of modernity, may be beginning to be dislodged through the ascendancy of "social media" that assume openly and exploit the fact that individual desires are mediated by other people. This may represent a resurgence of "external mediation."
32. Girard, *Deceit, Desire, and the Novel*, 15.
33. Ibid., 38.
34. *Devil's*, 21; "Akuma," 77.

obviously undermined by their clear mediation by his now disavowed, but hardly abandoned, attachment to Tsuchida as mediator. In this way, what Girard calls "internal mediation" could actually be said to produce or necessitate the idea of separate sexualities as a way of disavowing the influence of a same-sex mediator.

Shimaura's carefully laid plans to murder Tsuyuko go nowhere in the end because it turns out that Tsuyuko "knew all about the medicine." He wakes up to find that she has not imitated him after all. When he asks her if she had taken the same amount as he, as he thought she would, she says simply (and probably knowingly) "No, silly. If I took that much it would kill me."[35] If there is anyone in this story who does seem to have "autonomy and spontaneity," it is Tsuyuko in this instant. She is self-contained enough to know how much medicine she needs to take, and is unswayed by Shimaura's influence. At the same time, this would indicate that she does not *love* Shimaura despite his blithe assumption that she does.[36] Thus despite her seeming weakness and dependency—the first character of her name means "dew" (露), long a symbol of evanescence and fragility in classical Japanese poetry—Tsuyuko turns out to be quite a tough customer.[37]

In the end, it is, of course, not Tsuyuko but Sueko who imitates Shimaura. And if imitation is the basis of love, then it is Sueko who loves Shimaura, perhaps even with the same abandon with which Shimaura loved Tsuchida. Thus the extremes of mimetic desire are also "split" between the two women—Tsuyuko is entirely her own woman and free of the suasion of the mediator, whereas Sueko is utterly, indeed *fatally*, at his mercy.

But if Sueko does indeed love Shimaura, this news seems to come out of nowhere in *The Devil's Disciple*. Shimaura has been completely preoccupied with his attempt to induce Tsuyuko to take the medication, and thereby, he hopes, to be together alone with Sueko, thus somehow reliving only the positive parts of his former love for Tsuchida. He is thus completely taken by surprise when Sueko takes the bait instead. When he goes to visit Sueko on the same day when Tsuyuko has failed to die, he discovers the police outside her home and rushes in to find her dead. And yet "strangely enough," he writes,

---

35. *Devil's*, 32; "Akuma," 85.

36. "Tsuyuko loved me," he writes, as always, to Tsuchida. "I wasn't that into her" (*Devil's*, 16; "Akuma," 75).

37. As my colleague Sarah Frederick pointed out to me, Tsuyuko is also quite savvy about using the existing structures or "script" of heteronormativity (her status as Shimaura's "wife") as a kind of external mediator for their relationship—and thus to get what she needs from him while minimizing her emotional investment.

at the time I didn't feel like I was looking at the body of someone I'd lost. It was just a bizarre lump of happy-making flesh. And it was the result of all of my planning.

And then I lost it. A wave of nausea swept over me as I yelled out, "You're wrong! She was murdered. Somebody drugged her. Who would ever take it by mistake?"[38]

In this scene, Shimaura sees Sueko perhaps for the very first time outside of his connection to Tsuchida—she is, suddenly, utterly unmediated. And so he simply does not recognize her at all. But what is "happy-making" about this unrecognizable lump of flesh [*jibun o yorokobasu fushigi na nikukai*]? Perhaps what makes Shimaura happy is that he is seeing Sueko's love for him for the first time as well. In the act of overdosing she has imitated him "mindlessly," just as he once imitated Tsuchida, who got him addicted to sleeping medication.

Insomniac Homosociality

It was their shared insomnia that brought the Shimaura and Tsuchida together in the first place. Unaccustomed to life in the dormitories and overworked with preparations for college entrance exams, Shimaura finds himself unable to sleep for nights on end. Late one night as he wanders the campus he meets Tsuchida, who also has trouble sleeping, and they immediately bond over their common affliction. Shimaura narrates their first meeting in language that evinces a clear connection between sleeplessness and homoeroticism.

Until then you and I had never spoken a word to each other. But there is nothing strange in two dormitory mates having a conversation when they find themselves at two in the morning standing in a schoolyard overgrown with fall grasses. The first thing I said to you was that my nights had been made miserable for the previous month out of an inability to sleep. You were deeply moved by these words. You yourself had suffered from insomnia for two years already. Under the dark skies our conversation drifted towards those sleepless nights and as we spoke a warm intimacy grew between us. By dawn we two were bound in a beautiful friendship [*utsukushiki yūjō*].[39]

In this passage, insomnia serves Shimaura as a metaphor of his love for Tsuchida. Shimaura goes on to explain that he complained of his insomnia on every occasion when he met Tsuchida. He refers to Tsuchida as the one "who showed me the way when it came to insomnia" [*fuminshō ni kakete wa*

---

38. *Devil's*, 36; "Akuma," 87.
39. *Devil's*, 10–11; "Akuma," 72.

senpai de aru anata],⁴⁰ and soon he begins taking sleeping powder under Tsuchida's direction. This "education" in sleeping medication would lead to a terrible addiction and progressively larger doses for both men. The progression here is homologous with that from *nanshoku* to *dōseiai* discussed earlier: education (staying up all night studying) yields to aimless insomnia. *Not sleeping* has been unmoored from its "use value" to become a pathological and solipsistic repetition. As insomnia, it is taken out of the narrative of self-improvement and sent spinning into the circle of drug addiction. And yet it is also, as suggested by the lyrical beauty of the passage I just quoted, the means by which the two of them step outside of time together. It is by *not sleeping together* that the boys are able to ignore the difference between day and night and the progressive temporality of the everyday that would mandate their eventual "graduation" from each other.

So what does it mean that in the end it is Sueko and not either of the men, or Tsuyuko, who dies from an overdose of sleeping powder? One might say that her death was caused, in a sense, by a failed attempt to "catch up" with the intimacy of the two men. It took years for Shimaura and Tsuchida to develop a tolerance for such a huge dose, but the dose was fatal for Sueko. This seems plausible enough, although it perhaps overlooks the extent to which Sueko herself is a construction of Shimaura's homosocial imagination.

Exactly who, or what, killed Sueko, is perhaps the most pressing unanswered question in *The Devil's Disciple*. In my reading, the culprit is the heteronormative context that caused Shimaura to try to contain his love for Tsuchida (an affect now bereft of an ideology) in his relationships with Tsuyuko and Sueko (ideologies without affect). It is this context, and not some internalized homophobia or misogyny locatable within Shimaura or anyone else, that has seen to it that Sueko, whose name means "last child," died for love. In this sense, Hamao's story narrates in no uncertain terms the *structural* violence of Japan's newly emergent heteronormative culture. It is his sudden perception of this violence as he gazes on Sueko's lifeless body that makes Shimaura nauseous and causes him to look elsewhere, desperately, for another *human* culprit in which this seemingly arbitrary systemic violence might be localized and contained. "You're wrong!," he cries after awakening from the momentary trance into which the sight of her "happy-

---

40. I have slightly altered my own translation here to emphasize Hamao's use of the word *senpai*. My published translation reads, "You've been an insomniac longer than I have" (*Devil's*, 26; "Akuma," 81).

making flesh" has put him, "She was murdered. Somebody drugged her. Who would ever take it by mistake?"[41]

In saying now that this is a story about love, I am very aware of how different this description is from the argument I made in an earlier analysis of this work, published in 2009 but actually written in the early 2000s. In that version, I read Hamao's work in a much more "paranoid" mode, as a story more about hate than love and more about identity than desire. I saw it then exclusively as a tale of how Shimaura projected his own earlier and disavowed homosexuality onto Tsuchida in what I called a "desperate attempt" to "differentiate himself from Tsuchida through an insistent narrative of his own achievement of heterosexuality." This, I wrote, was "clearly a means of warding off the 'homo-ness' that threatens to engulf him."[42]

Looking back on it now, I see plenty of moments in the text that would have supported my sense that *The Devil's Disciple* was primarily about the hatred and fear of homosexuality, or "homophobia" and the way its narrator projected his "own" homosexuality onto others. These sentences, for example:

Tsuchida-san. You have no interest in the opposite sex and are no doubt still single.[43]

Tsuchida-san. You are the most dangerous person in this world.

You are a devil. Devouring the flesh of humans is not enough for you. You are a hateful devil who won't stop until you have cast their very souls into hell.[44]

Reading these lines for the first time in the late 1990s, it seemed obvious to me that they were evidence of a new and virulent homophobia that had begun to figure in modern Japanese literature around the time when Hamao was writing. The symptomology, moreover, was classic. In the years since his relationship with Tsuchida ended and thanks to an increasingly heteronormative atmosphere in Japan, Shimaura had come to believe that his capacity to love other men had to be expelled and externalized; the obvious target for this projection was his former lover Tsuchida, who had spurned him for another younger prettier boy years earlier. I quoted the influential work of queer theorist Lee Edelman, who wrote of a phenomenon he called "homographesis" in a 1994 book with that title. In "homographesis," Edel-

---

41. *Devil's*, 36; "Akuma," 87.
42. Vincent, "Hamaosociality," 385.
43. *Devil's*, 17; "Akuma," 76.
44. *Devil's*, 6; "Akuma," 69.

man wrote, "homosexuality is constituted as a category to name a condition that must be represented as determinate, as legibly identifiable, precisely insofar as it threatens to undo the determinacy of identity itself; it must be metaphorized as an essential condition, a sexual orientation, to contain the disturbance it effects as a force of de-orientation."[45]

Finding permission for my own reading in Edelman's theory, I went on to say that

> Shimaura *needs* Tsuchida to be a homosexual. This is an essential part of the story he needs to tell. His is a story of recovery from homosexuality (and criminality, and perhaps even insomnia) that may or may not have been successful. But Tsuchida has no story. He simply *remains* a homosexual with a criminal personality who suffers from insomnia and addiction. Shimaura may be all of these things as well, but he is also addicted to *narrative* in the hope that it will tell him that he is not. And part of that narrative depends on casting Tsuchida as somehow outside narrative, like the death drive itself, circling around in the endless repetition of addiction and seduction, remaining *single* and thus outside of reproduction as well.[46]

I do not think I was entirely wrong when I made this interpretation of Hamao's story. Parts of it, no doubt, look very much like the reading I offered earlier in this chapter. I think it is important, however, to explain how my own reading has shifted since then and what this might have to say about a similar shift both in the homosocial continuum and in queer theory.

The truth is that already at the time I published the earlier version of this chapter I had the nagging sense that I had not done the story justice. By insisting that homosexuality existed in the text only as the result of a phobic projection *outwards* I thought I had rigorously avoided the trap of "essentialism" as my training in queer theory like Edelman's had taught me. I was quite vigilant about this in the article. I asserted, for example, that

> by this I do not mean to say that Shimaura is "really" a closeted homosexual. This is no more demonstrable from this text than the idea that Tsuchida is an exclusive homosexual. . . . [I]ndeed there is no "homosexual" in this text (any more than there are in "reality") except to the extent that such a figure serves to isolate and contain the scourge of sexual perversion in the other.[47]

The problem with this all-too-rigorously anti-essentialist model is that in order for something to be projected out onto someone else, it has to be *inside you* first. Or at least it has to be *somewhere*—tossed around from one

---

45. Edelman, "Homographesis," 14.
46. Vincent, "Hamaosociality," 401.
47. Ibid.

character to another like a hot potato that no one wants to hold. In this way of thinking, precisely because there was no "homosexual" in the text, no one in it could really be free of the fear of having that potato tossed in his direction. And not just in the text, but in "reality" as well. Another way of putting this is to say that in so thoroughly banishing the homosexual from the text, I had only succeeded in saturating it with homophobia. The result was an ominous and paranoid-sounding tone in my own writing (for example, "the death drive," "the scourge of sexual perversion," "the endless repetition of addiction and seduction"). At the same time, it became impossible to even address the question of "love" because I had begun to see everything in terms of fear and phobic projection. If there was "no homosexual in this text," there could be no love either.

So while I remained convinced that my reading was true on some counts, I was not entirely happy with it either. I worried, for one thing, that it might imply that Hamao himself was somehow "homophobic" for having even written a story like this one, even though I felt certain that the story was in fact both aware and critical of the workings of "homophobia." In a footnote to my 2009 article, I reached outside the text to two articles that Hamao wrote in 1930 in which he showed himself to be extremely sympathetic to the plight of men who love men (whom he referred to as *Urninge*, using the term invented by Karl-Heinrich Ulrichs). I described the second of these articles, which took the form of an open letter to all of Japan's *Urninge*, as reading "like a 1970s pamphlet on gay liberation." These articles showed, I wrote, "an extraordinary understanding of the way homophobia functioned in Japanese culture at that time." The fact that he had such an understanding, I went on, "makes it no wonder that he was able to deal so intelligently with the theme in his detective fiction."[48]

In other words, my way around what I now view as a kind of contagion of homophobia that, once I had seen it operating in the text, threatened to infect its author as well, was to argue that Hamao, like Lee Edelman, and like myself, was a *theorist* of homophobia and not a homophobe. In another, earlier but still unpublished version of this chapter, I said this explicitly, and speculated that it might be the reason why the story had recently been rediscovered by scholars with an interest in queer theory (by which, I must

---

48. Vincent, "Hamaosociality," 407–8. In his recent book on boy's love in Japanese literature, Jeffrey Angles has also noted that Hamao's passionate advocacy for Japan's *Urninge* is, at first glance at least, difficult to square with his fiction, and particularly with *The Devil's Disciple*, a story that, as Angles' writes, "does not promote the kind of sympathetic, 'true understanding' of 'same-sex love' he called for in the articles" (*Writing the Love of Boys*, 153).

admit, I was referring mostly to myself). "The way in which the story anticipates work like Edelman's," I wrote,

> may partly explain the renewed interest readers have found in it since the 1990s. "The Devil's Disciple" is in fact an excellent example of a phenomenon that Eve Sedgwick also noted in *The Epistemology of the Closet*, that the very "foundational texts of gay culture"—(she lists Proust's *À la recherche du temps perdu,* Wilde's *The Picture of Dorian Gray* and Melville's *Billy Budd*)—"have often been the identical texts that mobilized and promulgated the most potent images and categories for (what is now visible as) the canon of homophobic mastery."[49] As both an advocate for homosexuals and an analyst of homophobia, then, Hamao was perhaps ahead of his time, although his attitude arguably had as much to do with his access to a cultural memory of a less heteronormative past as it did with an anticipation of a more critically queer future.[50]

I am much less certain as I write this now whether it is in fact possible to be a "theorist of homophobia" without being affected, or *infected*, by homophobia oneself. As Sedgwick wrote more recently, the problem with paranoia (of which homophobia is literally a text-book example),[51] is that it "refuses to be only *either* a way of knowing or a thing known, but is characterized by an insistent tropism toward occupying both positions."[52] If, as she also argued, homophobia and homosexual identity were born together like a pair of monstrous twins in the gothic novel, it may be harder than realized to separate one of them from the other. In other words, it is very hard to theorize about paranoia (or homophobia) without becoming a little paranoid oneself. As long as I was reading in the paranoid mode, I would inevitably end up finding paranoia in what I read.

Looking back, I think I gravitated toward Hamao's story in the first place because of the way it spoke to *my own* experience of homophobia and my own readings in what is now called by some "first-wave" queer theory like Edelman's, which tends toward what Sedgwick has since called "paranoid reading."[53] This mode of reading, which informed so much of queer theory

---

49. Sedgwick, *Epistemology of the Closet*, 49.
50. Unpublished manuscript.
51. Here I am referring to Freud's famous claim that all cases of paranoia can be traced to a repressed "homosexual wish": "it is a remarkable fact that the familiar principle forms of paranoia can all be represented as a contradiction of the single proposition: '*I* (a man) *love him* (a man)', and indeed that they exhaust all the possible ways in which such contradictions could be formulated" ("Psycho-Analytic Notes upon an Autobiographical Account of a Case of Paranoia," 63).
52. Sedgwick, "Paranoid Reading and Reparative Reading," 131.
53. For a fascinating, if at times problematic, look back at the history of queer theory in relation to the AIDS epidemic that uses the term "first-wave queer theory," see Castiglia and Reed, "Queer Theory is Burning."

during the 1990s and early 2000s, was informed not only or even, perhaps, chiefly by what used to be called the "long history of homophobic oppression" going back to the gothic novel or further, but arguably by a much more recent history—namely the immeasurably intensified fear and loathing of homosexuality brought on by the horror of AIDS.

For it was really only at this later date, at least in my own experience as someone who reached puberty as a gay man precisely at the moment in 1981 that AIDS first made its appearance, that the "hot potato" that was "homosexuality" became fatally and wrongly conflated with a virus that everyone was afraid of having tossed in their direction. My choice to write about *The Devil's Disciple* now says more to me about the scariness of that time than the story itself seems scary. In fact it no longer seems scary to me at all—it seems more like a piece of gothic camp.

I hope that the new reading of it I have offered in this chapter, which focuses on Shimaura's broken heart rather than his hateful projections, will help to show that what Shimaura really needed was not the courage to embrace his spoiled gay identity (an idea that would be ludicrously anachronistic and problematically liberationist anyway) but a better narrative with which to mourn his love.

SEVEN

The Still Birth of Gay Identity in Mishima Yukio's Confessions of a Mask

The First Gay Novel?

In an article published in the year 2000, the critic Atogami Shirō described Mishima Yukio's *Confessions of a Mask* as the "dawn of modernity in homosexual literature" [*dōseiai bungaku no kindai kaishi*]. "To be homosexual [*homosekushuaru*] or *dōseai*," Atogami writes, "means nothing more and nothing less than that one's sexual orientation is directed towards the same sex. We can correctly call *Confessions of a Mask* a work of homosexual literature because it objectifies and constructs in language this sort of sexual consciousness that cannot not direct itself towards the same sex."[1]

If there were any doubt that the homosocial continuum had ruptured decisively by the end of the twentieth century, Atogami's bold assertion here would seem to dispel it. His coupling of a singular modernity with an equally singular homosexuality wants to put an end to the "two-timing" tendencies of the homosocial narratives that I have been discussing here. For Atogami, *Confessions*, with its insistence on the unchanging nature of its protagonist's desire, marks the dawn of a new age in which desire is understood not as a developmental trajectory enacted in narrative but a fixed orientation that language objectifies after the fact. If the peculiar double negative with which he describes this positivistic desire suggests a somewhat defensive stance, the insistence behind his words has the unmistakable ring of identitarian affirmation. In this final chapter, I want to address the rea-

---

1. Atogami, "Saisho no dōseiai bungaku," 73.

sons why Atogami may have felt it necessary to make this claim in 2000, and what this suggests about the positioning of Mishima's novel in relation to what Atogami calls "the dawn of modernity in homosexual literature" and the homosocial narratives I have discussed so far.

Of course, on a certain level, to say that *Confessions of a Mask* is a piece of "homosexual literature" is an unremarkable if not stunningly banal claim to make in the year 2000, a half-century after the novel's initial publication in 1949. For generations of gay readers in Japan and elsewhere, Atogami's pronouncement would have been nothing new at all. They had long read *Confessions* as a work of "homosexual literature" and assumed that Mishima himself was of a member of their tribe. *Confessions of a Mask* is included, for example, in Robert Drake's 1998 book, *The Gay Canon: Great Books Every Gay Man Should Read*, along with E. M. Forster's *Maurice*, Jean Cocteau's *Livre blanc*, and Constantine Cavafy's complete poems.[2] In the Japanese context, Fushimi Noriaki notes that the name Mishima Yukio was mentioned with what he calls "annoying frequency" [*unzari suru hodo*] in his interviews with key figures in the gay world of postwar Japan.[3] Many spoke about the impact of Mishima's writing, and *Confessions* in particular, on their understanding of themselves as gay men, and most had a piece of gossip or two about a sighting of Mishima himself at this bar or that, or a friend of a friend who had slept with him. As Fushimi writes, "In the sepia-colored past of the gay world in Japan, Mishima was everywhere."[4] As Fushimi also writes, *Confessions of a Mask* and *Forbidden Colors* [*Kinjiki*], the only other novel that Mishima wrote that dealt explicitly with male homosexuality, helped to cement the image of homosexuality in the popular consciousness of postwar Japan as a form of "abnormal sexuality" [*ijō seiyoku*] in opposition to the older practices associated with the *nanshoku* tradition, while at the same time catalyzing the early development of Japan's emerging gay community in the postwar period. In his 1998 "tell-all" biography of Mishima, for example, Fukushima Jirō describes how he was so thrilled to read of the existence of

---

2. Drake, *The Gay Canon*. The tendency to read *Confessions* autobiographically has resulted in the widespread assumption, especially in the West, that Mishima himself was gay. For example, his name was listed among those of 52 "prominent historical figures from various countries and time periods who are known to have [*sic*] same-sex relationships" inscribed on a mural titled "Into the Light" installed on the ceiling of the James C. Hormel Gay and Lesbian Center of the San Francisco Public Library. For the complete list of names and a photo of the mural, see http://sfpl.org/index.php?pg=2000045301 [accessed April 2, 2012].

3. Fushimi, *Gei to iu keiken*, 355.

4. Ibid., 356.

the gay bar Rudon in Yūrakuchō that features in *Forbidden Colors* (apparently based on one called Braunschweig in Ginza in reality) that, newly arrived in Tokyo from the small town in Kyushu where he grew up, he screwed up the courage to knock on Mishima's door and ask for the bar's address. The depictions in the novel of this bar and other aspects of Tokyo's gay underground, such as the cruising area in Hibiya Park, seem to have served as a first introduction to this world for many men at the time.[5]

The Last Homosocial Narrative?

Despite its importance to later gay readers, however, the critical reception of *Confessions of a Mask*, especially in Japan, has been marked by a striking reluctance to read it as being even primarily about homosexuality, let alone as a text that heralded the "dawn of modernity in homosexual literature." This is surely one reason why Atogami felt it necessary to insist in such stark terms on its status as such as late as 2000. Fukuda Tsuneari's 1950 review essay, for instance, which still appears at the end of the Shinchō paper-back edition of the novel, includes not a single mention of same-sex desire; no small feat, as anyone who has read the novel will recognize.[6] When they have gotten around to addressing the question of love between men in *Confessions*, many critics have preferred to read it not on its own terms—whatever that would be—but as a metaphor for something else. Literary scholar Noguchi Takehiko, for example, argued in 1968 that Mishima had simply "borrowed the figure of the sexually perverted youth to express the alienation towards postwar society which never left him."[7] The feminist scholar Ogura Chikako commented in a 1989 interview that male critics such as Fukuda writing about *Confessions* mostly avoided mentioning the theme of homosexuality, and when they did address it, only did so after making elaborate claims of their ignorance on the subject—in her view because of a fear that any familiarity with the topic on their part might be construed as evidence that they themselves were homosexual.[8] There is

---

5. Fukushima's biography, incidentally, was suppressed immediately after publication by Mishima's heirs, ostensibly because it reproduced some of his letters without permission but clearly also because of its frankness about Mishima's sexuality. The family went on to sue Fukushima successfully for violation of copyright and "personality" right (Fukushima, *Mishima Yukio*, 66–69). For a useful discussion of the suppression of Fukushima's book, see Hiroaki Satō, "Suppressing more than free speech."
6. Fukuda, "*Kamen no kokuhaku* ni tsuite."
7. Noguchi, *Mishima Yukio no sekai*, 108.
8. Ueno, Ogura, and Tomioka, *Danryū bungakuron*, 354.

surely a lot of truth in Ogura's view, and it would have made particular sense in 1989, when homophobic panic about AIDS and male homosexuality was rampant. But the notion of "homophobia," as I argued in the previous chapter, is a blunt and too often distorting critical instrument, and its mere nomination hardly constitutes a useful interpretation of the particular ways in which Mishima's work has been read. Like "homosexuality" itself, homophobia can and has been made to explain a great many things about Mishima and his work, but the results are rarely very enlightening.

I would argue that these critics' relative disinterest in the question of "homosexuality" *per se* in *Confessions of a Mask* is better read as an indicator of the continuing dominance of the ideology of homosocial narrative according to which, as I have argued throughout this book, same-sex sexuality is understood not as an identity but as a developmental stage belonging to adolescence that would eventually and inevitably give way to heterosexuality in adulthood. As Atogami and other more recent critics have argued, Mishima's novel actually struggles mightily against this developmental narrative to assert the unchanging facticity of his narrator's desire. Although this has made it a crucial if perhaps problematically foundational text for those in the gay community who are committed to such an identity, the acceptance of this minoritizing reading of the novel among a wider readership has been seriously hampered by a competing critical and cultural climate in which the homosocial narrative continues to shape understandings of male community and sexuality. While the latter narrative is unambiguously normative and normatizing, moreover, it does not necessarily draw its force from the deep-seated, psychologized antipathy to male-male sexuality that the word "homophobia" implies. This is perhaps why, insofar as their understanding was shaped by this male homosocial narrative, most postwar critics were more than willing to look past Mishima's attempts to insist on his narrator's identity as an "invert" and a "pervert" in order to welcome him back into the homosocial fold, as a man among men. As one critic put it in 1961, in an article that dealt with both *Confessions* and Kawabata's *The Boy*,

What is being portrayed here is a part of the process of sexual maturation that is intertwined with the development of the personality. . . . Human sexuality itself exhibits this sort of diversity, and as long as we understand that literature is the place where these potentials are developed to their utmost expression, there is no point asking about whether it is "normal" or "abnormal."[9]

---

9. Ogikubo, "Kawabata Yasunari / Mishima Yukio," 138.

This reading of sexuality in *Confessions* was at least partly abetted by the fact that much of the novel, especially those parts that recount the narrator's childhood and adolescence, fits comfortably within the constraints of this developmental narrative. The novel treats the young narrator's desire for other boys as one of several forms of sexual fantasy and behavior that constitute his sexual life, together with sadomasochism, masturbation, and cross-dressing. None of these is markedly privileged over any other and the narrator reports on his desires and fantasies in a disarmingly analytic and objective fashion. He talks quite naturally about his same-sex crushes, referring at one point to "the boy with whom I was then in love" with perfect nonchalance.[10] For a "confession," in other words, it is remarkably free of shame and guilt. Although the protagonist here is assuredly a "pervert" in a number of ways, there is little suggestion in the early sections of the novel that this marks him out as irredeemably different from any other boy his age. "Although already in possession of the usual information concerning sex," he writes of this period, "I was not yet troubled with the sense of being different."[11] Later, in Chapter 3, he hears an accusatory voice in his head, but the voice clearly suggests that his problem has to do not with an innate homosexual "orientation" but with his failure to "graduate" from an earlier stage. In fact, the voice sounds like an angry personification of the developmental homosocial narrative itself.

"Think back!—when you were about fourteen you were a boy like other boys. And even at sixteen you were keeping up with them on the whole. But how about now, when you're twenty? . . . Now that you're twenty you're at your wit's end with calf love for an eighteen-year-old girl who knows absolutely nothing! At the age of twenty you're planning to exchange love letters for the first time—haven't you maybe made a mistake in counting your age? And isn't it also true that you've never even yet kissed a girl? What a sad specimen you are!"[12]

The accusation here has nothing to do with identity or orientation. Instead it is all about *time*. If the protagonist is a "sad specimen" it is not because of who he *is*, but because of what he has *not yet done*. This is even more clear in the Japanese text, where the word translated here as "sad specimen" is *rakudai bōzu-me* or "worthless dropout." It is really only in the later sections of the book that the narrator becomes aware of himself as irrevocably *different* from his peers and *Confessions* might be said to approxi-

---

10. Mishima, *Confessions of a Mask*, 98; *Kamen no kokuhaku*, 246. Subsequent citations to these titles will be abbreviated as *Confessions* and *Kamen*.
11. *Confessions*, 80; *Kamen*, 233.
12. *Confessions*, 173; *Kamen*, 301–2.

mate something like "the dawn of modernity in homosexual literature." In those sections, the focus narrows to the protagonist's "abnormal" same-sex object choice, which the novel portrays as a monolithically shameful secret that forces him to live a life of masquerade. Taken together with its first half, however, *Confessions* manages to straddle two very different moments in the history of homosexuality in Japan: one in which male-male sexuality has not yet been cordoned off as a separate and distinct identity, and one in which the homosocial continuum has ruptured for good along the homo-hetero divide.

This has lead to very different interpretations of the novel depending on which moment informs the reader's perspective. The critic and translator Jinzai Kiyoshi was typical of its earliest readers, for whom the homosocial narrative still made the most intuitive sense. For Jinzai, there was something in *Confessions* to which any man could relate. He called it "a world-class example of men's literature [*dansei bungaku*] or even 'male literature' [*osu no bungaku*],"[13] using the term reserved for male animals as if to stress the primal quality of its appeal to the male of the species. But this applied only to the novel's first half. "Reading *Confessions of a Mask*," Jinzai wrote,

left me with an extremely bizarre impression. The first and second halves of the novel were utterly different, as if it had been constructed by forcibly fusing marble and wood together. The first half, that lays out the first-person protagonist's pederastic sexual life [*pederasuto-teki seiseikatsu*] was quite healthy [*kenkō-teki*] and brimming over with perfectly masculine and youthful *erection* and *ejaculation*, while the second half, when the protagonist enters the world of women, has a weakness and lassitude as a work that cannot be explained solely by the curse of impotence that has begun to plague his sex life.[14]

From our perspective on this side of the homosocial divide, Jinzai's reading is striking for the way it treats the narrator's attractions to other boys without judgment as part and parcel of the narrator's youthful masculinity. His attitude toward the younger narrator's sexuality is noticeably similar to the voice in the narrator's head quoted earlier who reminded him, "When you were about fourteen you were a boy like other boys." In another early review with the straightforward title "This is not Abnormal Psychology," the critic Ara Masato wrote,

---

13. Jinzai, "Mishima Yukio," 480. Originally published in *Ningen*, October 1949.
14. Jinzai, "Narushishizumu no unmei," 490. Originally published in *Bungakukai*, March 1952. I have italicized *erection* and *ejaculation* because in Jinzai's text they appear in English. The marble that Jinzai associates with the narrator's "masculine" youth conjures an image of cool hardness (reminiscent of ancient Greece?) in contrast to the softness of wood—not unlike the way Sensei described the stiffness of K in *Kokoro*, so much in need of the "warm breezes" of the world of women.

Everyone has some version of perverse psychology [*tōsaku shinri*] so there is nothing abnormal about it; being nothing more than a physiological phenomenon. But perhaps because he grew up in such a sheltered environment and was never exposed to the elements, he happens to have preserved [this perversion/inversion] even into his early twenties.[15]

One could hardly ask for a clearer expression of the ideology of sexual development that underlies the homosocial narrative. It is perfectly capable of accommodating same-sex sexuality as long as it is understood as a transitional phenomenon on the way towards heterosexuality.[16] As the notion of homosexuality not as a stage but as an immutable identity became more and more available in Japan during the 1980s and 1990s, however, critics came up with increasingly tortured arguments to avoid reading *Confessions* as a piece of "homosexual literature" and, by extension, Mishima himself as a homosexual. Some simply denied it outright, as did Muramatsu Takeshi in his 1990 biography, where he asserted that everything written in *Confessions* was autobiographically accurate "with the exception of those parts involving sexual perversion" [*sei-teki tōsaku ni kakawaru bubun o nozokeba*].[17] In a 2006 article, Satō Hideaki, editor of the journal *Mishima kenkyū* and of the most recent edition of Mishima's collected works, asks rather plaintively whether it is "impossible to imagine that the narrator wants to have sex with Sonoko"—referring to the woman with whom the narrator tries unsuccessfully to awaken his heterosexual desire in the novel's second half. He then goes on to argue that the protagonist's homosexuality is only a "hypothetical identity strategically chosen" to mask a deeper and disavowed *heterosexuality*

---

15. Quoted in Sugimoto, "*Kamen no kokuhaku* ron," 211. Ara here seems to conflate Mishima with his narrator. For the original article, see Ara, "Ijō shinri dewa nai."

16. The coexistence of the minoritizing understanding of sexuality with the universalizing model reflected in Ara Masato's remarks may have been facilitated by the fact that Japanese translators tended to use the same word [*tōsaku*] to translate the psychoanalytic terms for "perversion" and "inversion." Conversely, the fact that the English translation by Meredith Weatherby consistently uses the term "invert" to translate *tōsakusha* may be one reason why *Confessions of a Mask* has been so widely read in English from a minoritarian perspective as a piece of "homosexual literature," while Japanese critics have tended to universalize it. Thus, in English it appears self-evident that Mishima's narrator is referring to "homosexuals" when he notes with satisfaction the "interesting coincidence that Hirschfeld should place 'pictures of St. Sebastian' in the first rank of those kinds of art works in which the invert [*tōsakusha*] takes special delight" (*Confessions*, 41; *Kamen*, 205)." In Japanese, on the other hand, one would be free to interpret *tōsakusha* as "pervert" rather than "invert," as Ara seems to have done.

17. Muramatsu, *Mishima Yukio no sekai*, 141.

waiting to come out.[18] Satō is far from alone in his quixotic desire to read heterosexuality back into *Confessions*. Sugimoto Kazuhiro, for example, argued in 2001 that the focus on the narrator's homosexuality in the first two sections of *Confessions* can be explained *narratologically* not as the "cause" but as the "effect" of the narrator's failed heterosexual relationship with Sonoko in Chapters 3 and 4. It is not, he suggests, because the narrator was homosexual that the relationship with Sonoko did not work out. Rather, he argues that the narrator strategically represents himself as homosexual in the first two sections in order to justify his failure to consummate the relationship with Sonoko in the book's latter half.[19] It is hard to escape the impression, for this reader at least, that the appeal of the narratological argument for Sugimoto has to do with the way it unseats homosexual desire as a primary cause. Needless to say, critics have been much less inclined to explain away heterosexual desire as a narratological construct.

Reading articles like those of Sugimoto and Satō, it is not difficult to understand why Atogami might have felt the need to insist in no uncertain terms on the status of *Confessions* as a piece of "homosexual literature" as late as the year 2000. Although I am very sympathetic to Atogami's argument, or at least to the frustration that no doubt motivated it, I want to take a different approach here. In my reading, Mishima's novel is neither a piece of "homosexual literature" nor a homosocial narrative, but a text that hovers uncomfortably in between. Like other novelists in the tradition of the I-novel, Mishima presents the sexual desire of his protagonist as an undeniable fact in the present. But because this desire is directed towards other men, he must contend with the still dominant homosocial narrative according to which same-sex desire is understood as a transient developmental stage that will eventually yield to a normative, "adult" heterosexuality. Atogami is right to say that *Confessions of a Mask* is orchestrated to contest that assumption and to assert the innate and immutable nature of its protagonist's desire for other men. In doing so, however, it borrows generically from the very homosocial narrative it would oppose: furnishing its narrator's desire with a "history," only to insist on its ahistoricity. This contradictory structure—which boils down to the simultaneous assertions of "This is how I got this way!" and "I was born this way!"—is nothing other than the double bind between "constructivism" and "essentialism" that Sedgwick has identified as characteristic of modern heteronormative cul-

---

18. Satō Hideaki, "Jiko o kataru shisō," 123.
19. Sugimoto, "*Kamen no kokuhaku* ron."

ture.²⁰ It is the paradox born of these twin assertions, moreover, rather than the facticity of the protagonist's desire, that marks Mishima's text precisely *not* as a "homosexual," and still less a "gay" novel, but a novel about the fate of desire itself in the absence of any mediating structures.

An I-Novel in the First Person?

The particular temporality of the desire that *Confessions* constructs for its protagonist can best be understood through an analysis of the text's peculiar status as *an I-novel written in the first person*. In order to better understand what is so peculiar about such a seemingly obvious category, it will be helpful to remind ourselves of the generic parameters of the Japanese I-novel. The canonical I-novel can be defined by its two most salient, and, I would say interrelated characteristics: a focus on male heterosexual desire and a preference for a very particular kind of *third*-person narrative voice. The centrality of male heterosexual desire to the I-novel is well known already so I will not belabor it here.²¹ The particular nature of its third-person voice, however, is perhaps less often remarked upon.²²

The term "I-novel," it turns out, is something of a misnomer. Even though these texts are said to focus on the experiences of their authors, I-novels are not the same as autobiographies and are not necessarily, or even typically, narrated in the first person. Tayama Katai's *The Quilt*, widely recognized as one of the earliest and most influential of the genre, uses third-person narration focalized through its protagonist, as do most of Shiga Naoya's works, as well as postwar exemplars of the genre such as Kojima Nobuo's *Embracing Family* [*Hōyō kazoku*]. As Edward Fowler points out, in most prewar I-novels there is only one character who is referred to as "he"

---

20. For Sedgwick's discussion of this double bind, see *Epistemology of the Closet*, 40–44.
21. For a good discussion of this see Furukawa, "Shizenshugi to dōseiai."
22. I recognize that the definition of the "I-novel," and even the question of whether such a thing exists, has been a matter of much debate. Tomi Suzuki has provided us with a superb account of these debates and reminded us of the ways in which the category itself was a retroactive construction whose supposed characteristics were never entirely separable from those of the Japanese novel *tout court* and, by extension, the (supposedly warped) shape of Japanese modernity itself. While acknowledging these important discussions, however, in this chapter I am using the term in more limited, heuristic sense, as if it actually described a genre with an identifiable set of features. In doing this I take some permission from Jed Esty, who in a recent book on the bildungsroman (another genre that is notoriously hard to define) writes that "genres are almost always empty sets that shape literary history by their negation, deviation, variation, and mutation" (*Unseasonable Youth*, 18). See also Tomi Suzuki, *Narrating the Self*.

[*kare*] throughout and around whom the narrative is focalized.²³ The reader of the I-novel assumes that "he" can be equated with the author and that the novel is a "sincere" account, or confession, of the author's experiences. If this is the case, however, the question arises: if the I-novel is about the author's own experiences, why do so many I-novelists choose to narrate their novels in the third person? As Barbara Mito Reed has argued, the popularity of third-person narration among I-novelists may have to do with the kind of temporal perspective it enables. In most I-novels written in the third-person, Reed writes,

> the temporal focus is oriented whenever possible to the experiencing moment itself. This shows that the narrator's interest does not lie in presenting any change or development between his past and present selves. If anything, it is the opposite; past reality extends into the moment of writing and beyond to the presumed moment of reading. The focus of the accounts is not on the events as formative experiences, so much as on the quality of those experiences.²⁴

The temporality of the so-called I-novel, then, is precisely the opposite of that of the homosocial narratives I have been discussing here, which use first- rather than third-person narration so as to present "change and development between [the narrator's] past and present selves." The young man who narrates the first two sections of *Kokoro*, for example, is motivated by a desire to represent himself as having grown up and progressed beyond his older mentor, just as *boku* in *The Wild Goose* has surpassed his friend Okada by learning to appreciate female difference. The I-novel, by contrast, makes little pretense at developmental or teleological plotting: the past is not the prelude to the present but spills directly into it. The experience of time is immediate, contingent, and fragmentary. This is why I-novels, Reed writes, "commonly concern only limited periods of an author's life, thematizing particular events and issues. Unlike autobiographies, they do not incorporate events spanning an entire lifetime, nor are they ordinarily comprehensive accounts of the major events in the authors' lives."²⁵

Read through the lens of Reed's and Fowler's discussions, Mishima's *Confessions of a Mask* emerges as a strange hybrid of I-novel and homosocial

---

23. "Unlike the English 'he,' which of course refers to any male person previously mentioned, *kare* has a far more circumscribed denotation in Meiji and Taishō literature: specifically, the protagonist through whose eyes the narrator sees and through whose mind the narrator thinks. Indeed, what appears to be a pronoun, a placeholder for any subject of discourse, is in fact more correctly thought of as a proper name, because the use of *kare* is restricted to a single character" (Fowler, *The Rhetoric of Confession*, 36).

24. Reed, "Chikamatsu Shūkō," 75–76.

25. Ibid., 60.

narrative. It appropriates the heterodiegetic I-novel's non-teleological, anti-developmental affirmation of an immediate temporality in order to represent the protagonist's same-sex desire and thereby to combat the normalizing force of the homosocial narrative. But even as it adopts this temporality native to the I-novel, it retains the homodiegetic first-person of the homosocial narrative. Mishima's first person means that, as in other homosocial narratives, there are at least two I's: one in the moment of narration and another in the narrated past. His self is thus always split, while that of the heteronormative "I-novelist" is more able to imagine itself whole. Although this split in the subject is emphasized and exploited in the homosocial narratives of Ōgai and Sōseki, however, in Mishima's text it is *minimized*.

If what he needed was the greater authority and temporal immediacy of the third person to combat the pull of the homosocial narrative in writing *Confessions*, one might of course ask why Mishima did not simply use a third-person narrator to begin with, as did most (confusingly named!) "I-novelists" in the tradition of Japanese naturalism? The answer, I submit, is that as a man who desired other men, Mishima's narrator was unable completely to *de-historicize* and *de-narrativize* his desire after the fashion of a heteronormative "I-novelist." In order to say who he was and what he desired, in other words, he was compelled *also* to say *how he got that way*. Mishima's choice to narrate his novel in the first person rather than the third thus suggests that the cultural dominance of the homosocial narrative meant that male-male sexuality, unlike the heterosexuality of the typical I-novelist, could not simply exist unquestioned in the present. It had to be placed within a narrative. At the same time, however, in order for Mishima to "ground" his narrator's desire with the same ontological authority as that wielded by the I-novelist, he needed to reduce as far as possible the gap between present and past and narrator and narrated. If the "I-novel" in Japan relied on the authority and immediacy of third-person narration to represent male heterosexual desire as an unassailable fact of "nature" and an unchanging force, Mishima's *Confessions* was that bizarre thing: *an I-novel written in the first person* and thus reflecting the still tenuous and *all too narratable* status of male-male desire in 1949.

Kō-chan's Claim

This strategy to reduce the gap between the narrator's present and past begins already on the very first page of *Confessions*, with the following passage in the voice of the novel's narrator, whose name is Kō-chan.

For many years I claimed I could remember things seen at the time of my own birth. Whenever I said so, the grownups would laugh at first, but then, wondering if they were not being tricked, they would look with a slight glint of hatred in their eyes at the pallid face of that unchildlike child. Sometimes I happened to say so in the presence of callers who were not close friends of the family; then my grandmother, fearing I would be taken for an idiot, would interrupt in a sharp voice and tell me to go somewhere else and play.[26]

The claim that little Kō-chan is making here is, obviously, impossible. Even before their laughter subsides the grownups start reeling off "scientific explanations" why: when an infant first emerges from the womb its eyes are not yet open, and even if they were it would not be able to focus. This is not even to speak of whether it would be capable of forming coherent memories. But despite these seemingly unassailable arguments, Kō-chan persists in his belief, and for some reason the grownups are unable just to laugh it off as the product of a childish mind. Their suspicions are aroused by this "unchildlike child" whose preposterous story threatens to upend the hierarchy of before and after. "Even if we think he's a child," he narrates them thinking, "we mustn't let our guard down." The adult narrator guesses that the adults began to worry that he was making this claim as a way of tricking them into telling them "about 'that,' and then what is to keep him from asking, with still more childlike innocence, 'where did I come from? How was I born?'"[27]

If the child in the first paragraph was disturbingly "unchildlike" in his knowing way, here the grownups fear—or the narrator surmises that they fear—that he will come back at them "with still more childlike innocence" [*motto kodomorashiku mujaki ni*] to ask about "that." But why the phrase "still more" if in the previous moment he was already an unchildlike child? Has innocence come *after* knowledge? How is it possible to be *more* innocent? And why is it that the grownups regard Kō-chan with hatred in their eyes for claiming to remember his birth (an understandable if indeed childlike assertion of precocious personhood) only to ascribe to him a childlike innocence when they begin to suspect he is asking about sex in a devious and roundabout way? The latter, at least, is clearly *their* preoccupation and not Kō-chan's. They needn't have worried, Kō-chan tells his reader; he had absolutely no intention of asking about how babies are made. He simply "could not but believe that I remembered my own birth."[28]

---

26. *Confessions*, 1; *Kamen*, 175. I have modified the translation slightly. Weatherby has "they would look distastefully at the pallid face of this unchildlike child," but I thought it important to stay more literally with Mishima's mention of what he terms "light hatred" [*karui nikushimi*].

27. *Confessions*, 2; *Kamen*, 176.

28. *Confessions*, 2; *Kamen*, 176.

If the grownups tell themselves that their suspicions were aroused by the little boy's desire to find out about "that" (an important step in sexual development after all, which Freud called "the sexual researches of children"),[29] one might say that this suspicion is itself a kind of defense mechanism on the part of the adults. It is a way of narrativizing and thereby domesticating the more radical challenge posed by Kō-chan's claim, namely that his conscious self emerged fully formed, like Athena from the head of Zeus. Kō-chan has no interest in ferreting out the grownups' guilty secret of heterosexual sex as a way of understanding where he came from or where he is going. He has no need to hear it from them because he has placed himself outside the very cycle of reproduction and development. If the homosocial narrators I have discussed so far tended to exploit the built-in recursivity of the narrating "I"—its "two-timing" layering of narrating subject and narrated object—both to retrace and to reverse developmental trajectories, Mishima's "I" wants to refuse both development *and* regression right from the start. And what better way to do it than to claim that you remember your own birth?

If this opening chiasmus of past and present signals that *Confessions of a Mask* is a very different kind of narrative from those I have discussed so far, *Confessions* is also different insofar as its narrator speaks in great detail about his sexual desire for his own sex—both at an extremely young age and as an adult.[30] In the context of mid-twentieth-century Japan, where the homosocial narrative still exercised a powerful generic pull, Kō-chan's rejection of developmental narratives cannot be unrelated to his abiding desire for his own sex. Later he writes of his love for his well muscled classmate Ōmi, "If there be such a thing as love that has neither duration nor progress, this was precisely my emotion. The eyes through which I saw Ōmi were always those of a 'first glance' or, if I may say so, of the 'primeval glance.'"[31] One cannot "grow into," or, for that matter, *out of* desire like this. It does not generate teleological or even recursive narratives. His desire as he describes it just *is*, and always has been, like Kō-chan himself,

---

29. See "Infantile Sexuality" in Freud, "Three Essays on the Theory of Sexuality."

30. The closest is Kawabata's *The Boy,* published just in the previous year. But whereas Kawabata's text is unabashed in its evocation of its narrator's love for Kiyono's body and contains depictions of physical, although perhaps not strictly "sexual" intimacy, Mishima's *Confessions* is distinguished by a lack of any actual physical contact. Instead, the focus is on the effect on the narrator's *own* body of the images of the boys that he desires; he is forever getting erections and ejaculating, but always alone.

31. *Confessions*, 72; *Kamen*, 226.

always an "unchildlike child." At another point in the novel he asks, "Why is it wrong for me to stay just the way I am now?"[32]

This brings me to yet another aspect of the extraordinary opening of *Confessions*. The novel's very first words, translated by Weatherby as "for many years" might also be translated, "For a long time." The phrase in Japanese, *nagai aida* sounds a lot like the first words of Marcel Proust's great novel *À la recherche du temps perdu*, which famously opens with the line "For a long time, I went to bed early" [*Longtemps je me suis couché de bonne heure*].[33] Given that Proust's name comes up later in the novel, it seems likely that Mishima was reading Proust and the nod here may be deliberate.[34] But whether intentional or not, the phrase itself and the nature of the opening paragraphs as discussed so far do set up what might be called a "Proustian" question as one of the themes of the novel: that of the knowability of the past in relation to the present, and, by extension, the durability of the self over time. I bring this up here not to emphasize the similarities with Proust, however, but because seeing how *different* Mishima's novel is from his French predecessor might help us to understand better its particular take on identity and desire.

Whereas Proust's novel emphasizes the ability of the novelist to triumph over the past—and the past self—by recreating it in fictional form (thus "recapturing time" as in the title of the final volume), in Mishima's novel the past looms not with the potential for creative recapturing but as an unchanging set of constraints. *À la recherche* begins with the narrator waking up unsure of who and where he is, even wondering whether he is one of the characters in the novel he is reading. Mishima's narrator, on the other hand, paints a picture of himself as an "unchildlike child" who claimed to know exactly who he was from the moment of his birth. The contrast in this regard is indeed so striking that it is easy to imagine it to have been intentional on Mishima's part. In Proust, no major character, least of all the narrator, is ever fully understood or "written off" and it is this founding *uncertainty about the self* that opens up the vast fictional spaces in which Proust will go on to invent, elaborate, and explore the constantly ramifying personalities of his narrator and characters. Sedgwick has written of Proust's project as having in common with that of Henry James an in-

---

32. *Confessions*, 100; *Kamen*, 247.
33. Proust, *The Way by Swann's*, 7; Proust, *Du côté de chez Swann*, 11.
34. In 1947, Mishima might well have been inspired by Proust's massive work when he wrote in his diary that he planned to write an autobiographical novel of 1,450 pages that would take him ten years to complete. For the diary entry, see Tanaka, "Kaidai to kōtei," 682.

exhaustible curiosity about "the multiple, unstable ways in which people may be like or different from each other." Crucially, however, in the case of Proust and James this had nothing to do with "identity" understood as a stable understanding of the self, least of all as defined narrowly in relation to sexual orientation. The desire to classify people according to types for a writer like Proust or James is founded on a profound fascination with "what *kinds* of people there are to be found in one's world" and their exploration of this question leads them to produce what Sedgwick calls, in a wonderful turn of phrase, "nonce taxonomies" or categories that include only one member.[35] This openness of Proust's narrator to that which Leo Bersani has called a "diversified and distinct external world" could not be more different from Mishima's "unchildlike child" cursed with a preternatural self-awareness and locked so cruelly inside his own interiority.[36] Proust's narrator seeks self-understanding in his relations with others and in comparison with his past self, but Mishima's narrator is almost pathologically isolated from others and obsessed with the nature of his own desire, which he considers an essential and unchanging "destiny" with which he has been saddled since birth.

I mention these differences not to say that Mishima comes up short as a novelist vis-à-vis Proust—what writer would not, after all?—but for what they can tell us about Mishimas's view of self and sexuality. Whereas in Proust desire remains an unsolvable enigma productive of an endless chain—and indeed thousands of pages—of baroque analysis and speculation, in *Confessions* the mystery and origins of the protagonist's desire are simply explained and diagnosed in rather flat-footed fashion. It was "because of him," the narrator tells us, for example, of his first love Ōmi, that "I cannot love an intellectual person. Because of him I am not attracted to men who wear glasses. Because of him I began to love strength, an impression of overflowing blood, rough gestures, careless speech, and the savage melancholy inherent in flesh not tainted in any way with intellect."[37]

The emphasis on causality here could hardly be more clear. And yet if what he describes as the "systematic structure of likes and dislikes" that

---

35. "The writing of a Proust or a James," Sedgwick writes, "would be exemplary here: projects precisely of *nonce* taxonomy, of the making and unmaking and *re*making and redissolution of hundreds of old and new categorical imaginings concerning all the kinds it may take to make up a world" (*Epistemology of the Closet*, 23). For more on this aspect of Proust's work, see Litvak, "Taste, Waste, Proust."

36. Bersani, *Marcel Proust*, 18.

37. *Confessions*, 64; *Kamen*, 221. I have modified Weatherby's translation slightly.

Kō-chan has built up is the result of a historical event that occurred at a particular moment in time, namely his meeting with Ōmi, the novel also suggests that the narrator was somehow *born* with an attraction to men like Ōmi. This is suggested by the often-discussed repetition of images of light reflecting in liquids at the beginning and the end of the novel. The first instance, in the novel's opening scene, is the image of a ray of light reflecting off the "brim of the basin in which I received my first bath." The narrator claims to remember this ray of light despite the fact that he had only just emerged from his mother's womb *and* that he was born at eight o'clock in the evening, when it would have been dark outside.[38] As I discussed earlier, his insistence on this memory despite its redoubled impossibility can be read as an example of the way the novel asserts a sort of transcendence of linear temporality.[39]

At the end of the novel, this image of light in water returns in the form of a puddle of spilled beer on a table in a dance hall, "throwing back glittering, threatening reflections."[40] In this final scene, the narrator has been overwhelmed by desire at the sight of the naked muscled torso of a young tough, causing him to completely forget the presence of Sonoko, the woman he had hoped to be able to love. But if this vision of the tattooed youth is a clear repetition of Ōmi as the supposed *primum mobile* of Kō-chan's erotic tastes, the repeated image of light in water brings us back not to Ōmi himself or to the narrator's first vision of him, but to the novel's beginning and the protagonist's birth through a line of association with the ray of light in the basin. On the one hand, the text suggests a history of desire ("It was because of him. . ."), and on the other, an unchanging and, indeed, inborn, "essence"—a linear temporality of cause and effect, and a circular one of predetermination. "Ever since childhood," he writes in Chapter 1,

> my ideas concerning human existence have never once deviated from the Augustinian theory of predetermination. Over and over again I was tormented by vain doubts— even as I continue to be tormented today—but I regarded such doubts as only another sort of temptation to sin, and remained unshaken in my deterministic views. I had been handed what might be called a full menu of all the troubles in my life while still too young to read it. But all I had to do was spread my napkin and face the table. Even the

---

38. *Confessions*, 3; *Kamen*, 176.

39. It is also a kind of declaration by fiat of his intention to write *fiction* even in the guise of an I-novel. At one point he describes the glittering basin as "seeming to be made of gold," which might well remind us of that other famous "basin" associated with the assertion of fiction as fact: Don Quixote's insistence that an ordinary "barber's basin" was in fact the golden "helmet of Mambrino."

40. *Confessions*, 254; *Kamen*, 364.

fact that I would now be writing an odd book like this was precisely noted on the menu, where it must have been before my eyes from the very beginning.[41]

If the writing of the book appears on the "menu" he describes, the reader might imagine that "all the troubles in my life" that are recorded there as well constitute the book's preordained content. If the book was thus somehow already written from the time he was a child, its content cannot have been affected by the life that he has actually led in the interim. And yet that life is its content. This paradoxical collapse of time, and with it the collapse of both causality and agency, will be the temporal logic that determines *Confessions of a Mask* in its entirety. Thus, *Confesssions* reconciles the inevitability of change and development inherent in first person narration with the possibility of permanence held out by the third-person narration that it seems simultaneously to covet. What is the ability to remember one's own birth, after all, if not the ability to see oneself from a third-person perspective?

The Abyss of Unmediated Desire

One has the sense in reading *Confessions* that one is seeing desire in its raw form—not triangulated and belated as it was in *The Wild Goose* and *Kokoro*, and not melancholically displaced as in *The Devil's Disciple*, but *here, now, immediate*. It comes not from outside, moreover, but from a primordial *inside*. If *The Devil's Disciple* showed the process by which something like "sexual orientation" was internalized, in *Confessions* it seems to have been inside all along. And yet despite this (or really rather *because of this*), it has nothing to do with identity; this is not—at all—a "gay novel." Indeed, it is hard to think of a novel that demonstrates more effectively than *Confessions* the corrosion of identity that results from desire imagined as fully inherent and interior to the self.

For Kō-chan, his desire for other men is, paradoxically, both the best and only proof of his individual existence and the greatest threat to the integrity of his self. Here is how he describes his earliest memory—this one, he writes, "unquestionable"—of a night soil man glimpsed while on a walk with a maid:

The four-year-old child that I was regarded the youth with an abnormal scrutiny. Its meaning was not clear to me yet, but this was the first revelation to me of a certain power, a certain dark and strange voice calling out to me.... I had the presentiment that there is in this world a kind of desire like stinging pain. Looking up at that youth,

---

41. *Confessions*, 14–15; *Kamen*, 185.

I was choked by desire, thinking, "I want to change into him," thinking, "I want to *be* him."[42]

As I discussed earlier, Kō-chan claims not to have been aware of an essential difference between himself and his schoolfriends as a child. In this passage, however, the child's desiring scrutiny of the youth is already described as "abnormal" [*ijō*],[43] just as the grown-up Kō-chan's sexuality will be. Already at the age of four he has been ejected from the (homosocial) community of "normal" people. He is alone with his desire and seems always to have been that way. This is perhaps why it is impossible to plot what is being narrated here on a timeline. No sooner does he speak of having felt only a "presentiment" of this "desire like stinging pain" at age four, than he describes himself as actually having felt this desire, seemingly at the same time as the "pre-"sentiment. For a child of four to be "choked by desire" may be as hard to credit as an infant remembering his own birth, but the two memories taken together form an even more extraordinary (if not "abnormal") psychic portrait. On the one hand, Kō-chan claims to have been born with a conscious awareness that precedes any and all inter-subjective interaction with other human beings—an utterly self-contained "self"—and on the other, he describes his "earliest memory" as being dominated by a burning desire to *be someone else*.

In *Confessions of a Mask*, then, desire does not lead to identity; rather, it effaces it. It kicks Kō-chan out of the homosocial continuum and leaves him with no structure through which to mediate or narrativize his desire. This happens quite clearly in the scene where Kō-chan and his (male) classmates watch their classmate Ōmi do a set of pull-ups at the command of their gym teacher to "show them how it's done." All of the boys are entranced by this vision of bulging muscles and shoulders that "swelled like summer clouds." They speak as if in one voice in the following passage:

---

42. *Confessions*, 8–9; *Kamen*, 180. I have modified the first two sentences of Meredith Weatherby's translation. His version reads: "The scrutiny I gave the youth was unusually close for a child of four. Although I did not clearly perceive it at the time he represented my first revelation of a certain power, my first summons by a certain strange and secret voice."

43. Weatherby's translation mutes this to "unusually close" but it is crucial to stick closely to Mishima's language here so as not to lose the pathologizing implications of the term. It may also be significant to note that *ijō* in Japanese has a temporal significance. While the English "abnormal" means "deviating from a norm," *ijō* is composed of two characters meaning "different from [the way it] always [is]."

"Ahhh!" The admiring exclamation of his classmates arose and floated thickly in the air.

Any one of the boys could have looked into his heart and discovered that his admiration was not aroused simply by Ōmi's feat of strength. It was admiration for youth, for life, for supremacy. And it was astonishment at the abundant growth of hair that Ōmi's upraised arms had revealed in his armpits. This was probably the first time we had seen such an opulence of hair; it seemed almost prodigal, like some luxuriant growth of troublesome summer weeds.[44]

The boys' admiration for Ōmi here is clearly sexual, but at least for the other boys (as Kō-chan sees them), the sexuality remains on a continuum with a kind of hero worship. What they seem to feel in this scene is not far from what *boku* felt for Okada in *The Wild Goose* or Sōseki's narrator felt for his "hero" Kō-san in "The Heredity of Taste." As in those texts, sexual attraction mixes relatively unproblematically here with enthusiastic hero worship. The boys' desire also seems externally mediated—even if none of them proclaim their admiration outright, they are openly bound together with the sigh of "Ahhh" as they watch Ōmi's impressive feat. Their admiration, moreover, happens not too far below the surface—in their hearts, yes, but easily discovered there. Kō-chan shares these feelings as well, but for him there is a difference.

As for me, I felt the same as the other boys—with important differences. In my case— it was enough to make me blush with shame—I had had an erection, from the first moment in which I had glimpsed that abundance of his. I was wearing light-weight spring trousers and was afraid the other boys might notice what had happened to me.[45]

The moment that Kō-chan blushes with shame, made painfully aware of the separation between himself and others, might be called the "stillbirth" of "homosexual" identity. It emerges out of Kō-chan's sudden perception of his separateness from the other boys. If *The Wild Goose* featured a man (*boku*) vicariously narrating the shame of a woman (Otama) as a way of narrating himself into a new form of what I called stereoscopic homosociality, here it is a man who bears the full force of the shame. Kō-chan has no one else's story to tell but his own and no less shameful future to expect. Time does not unfold or develop here; it seems to come to a standstill as Kō-chan feels the abyss open between him and his classmates. If his classmates might be imagined as seeing Ōmi as a mediator of their future growth, Kō-chan wants both to be and to *have* Ōmi and he wants it *now*.

---

44. *Confessions*, 77; *Kamen*, 231.
45. *Confessions*, 79; *Kamen*, 232.

Unfortunately, however, there is nothing to mediate Kō-chan's desire in the world of *Confessions of a Mask*. Although the narrator of *The Devil's Disciple* could at least conceive of his relationship with Tsuchida in terms of a *nanshoku* relationship, in *Confessions* the only model for Kō-chan is that of the isolated pervert. Japan's long tradition of love between men is nowhere in sight in Mishima's text. Although the word *nanshoku* does appear in *Confessions*, it has been stripped entirely of its positive associations, recruited as a translation for the English word "sodomite" in a scene towards the novel's end, mentioned earlier, in which the narrator and a classmate are discussing Marcel Proust:

> "You promised to lend me a book by Marcel Proust, remember? Is it interesting?"
> "I'll say it's interesting. Proust was a *sodomite*"—he used the foreign word. "He had affairs with footmen."
> "What's a sodomite?" I asked. I realized that by feigning ignorance I was desperately pawing the air, clutching at this little question for support and trying to find some clue to their thoughts, some indication that they did not suspect my disgrace.
> "A sodomite's a sodomite. Didn't you know? It's a *nanshoku-ka*."[46]

It is ironic, given the earlier discussion of Proust's seemingly limitless curiosity about all of the ways in which people are different from each other, that his name would be invoked here in connection with this bland tautology of sexual identity, now flattened across the globe. A sodomite is a sodomite is a *nanshoku-ka*. End of story.

Unlike the narrators of the homosocial narratives of Sōseki, Ōgai, and Hamao, Kō-chan's desire does not exist on a continuum with the heterosexual. In the paragraph following the conversation about Proust, he finds himself exquisitely alone with his own shame: "It was obvious," he writes, "that my friend had smelled out my secret. Somehow it seemed to me that he was doing all he could to avoid looking at my face."[47] Modern gay identity is born in moments like this, when the circuit of recognition is broken and the other looks away. But if, as Sedgwick writes, "in interrupting identification, shame, too, makes identity," in *Confessions of a Mask* the reparative work of identity formation has not yet begun and for Kō-chan it is impossible to imagine that it ever will.[48] In other words, the isolating force of shame has caused time itself to stop.

---

46. *Confessions*, 227–28; *Kamen*, 342. Meredith uses the variant *danshoku-ka*, which I have changed to *nanshoku-ka* for consistency.
47. *Confessions*, 228; *Kamen*, 342.
48. Sedgwick, *Touching Feeling*, 36.

This is made astonishingly clear in the novel's final scene, to which I now return, in which the sound of Sonoko's voice *reminding him of the time* ("There's only five minutes left") interrupts his fantasizing about the half-naked young man seated across from them and whom only he has noticed. "At this instant," he writes,

> something inside of me was torn in two with brutal force. It was as though a thunderbolt had fallen and cleaved asunder a living tree. I heard the structure, which I had been building piece by piece with all my might up to now, collapse miserably to the ground. I felt as though I had witnessed the instant in which my existence had been turned into some sort of fearful non-being.[49]

If the voice inside his head criticizing him for not having grown up into a good heterosexual was the voice of the homosocial narrative, this passage describes the excruciating ontological horror of the homo/hetero divide. Reminded of "the time" by Sonoko, Mishima's narrator is rudely awakened from his desirous reverie and feels both torn in two and annihilated. It is the pain of this moment that seems retroactively to motivate the writing of the entire novel as an attempt to reconstruct the narrator's life in aesthetic terms and thereby, perhaps, to stitch together the raw wound caused by the ripping apart of the homosocial continuum. If this is the "dawn of modernity in homosexual literature," it is clear what a troubled dawn it was.

In a recent article, Takeuchi Kayo has argued that *Confessions of a Mask* was only understood "retroactively" as a "homosexual novel" in Japan with the subsequent publication of *Forbidden Colors* in 1951.[50] The latter novel included not only scenes of men actually having sex but also extensive descriptions of postwar Tokyo's emerging gay underground—the parks, bars, and other locales where men met. If the narrator of *Confessions* sat alone with his shame-ridden desire, here was a whole gay world. And while it might have been mired in self-hatred and the fear of disclosure, it at least beckoned with the possibility of community. In the 1998 memoir I mentioned at the beginning of this chapter, Fukushima Jirō, one of Mishima's most enthusiastic gay readers, described how he felt when he first heard that *Forbidden Colors* was coming out.

> I was happy to read anything by Mishima, but when I heard that it was a book that treated *nanshoku* in depth I had a presentiment that the Mishima ship that I had awaited

---

49. *Confessions*, 252–53; *Kamen*, 362.
50. See Takeuchi, "Mishima Yukio *Kamen no kokuhaku* to iu hyōshō o megutte."

so impatiently had finally set sail [*machi ni matta hontō no Mishima-bune*]; I felt as if I were hearing the clarion peals of a trumpet announcing the maiden voyage of a fierce and fabulous [*tongatte shareta*] cruise ship in pure, unblemished white.[51]

Fukushima's comment, with its celebratory tone and campy metaphors, is typical of a certain gay embrace of Mishima that, as Fushimi also noted, made him seem ubiquitous in "the sepia-colored past of the gay world." It is crucial to note, however, that it was *Forbidden Colors*, and *not Confessions*, that made this sort of gay-identified appropriation possible. The latter novel includes, for example, angry gay-identified critiques of the oppressively heteronormative atmosphere of postwar Japan from the perspective of its protagonist Yūichi. At one moment, Yūichi is walking in a park hand in hand with another man and a passing student murmurs to the girl he is with, "Look there, they must be homosexuals." The girl replies,

"Oh how awful!"

Yūichi's face reddened in humiliation and anger. He pulled his arm away and put his hands in his pockets. Nobutaka suspected nothing. He was accustomed to treatment like this.

"Them! Them!" Yūichi ground his teeth. "They who pay three hundred and fifty yen for a lunch hour together in a hotel bed, and have their great love affair in the sight of heaven. They who, if all goes well, build their rats-nest love nests. They who, sleepy-eyed, diligently multiply. They who go out on Sundays with all their children to clearance sales at the department stores. They who scheme out one or two stingy infidelities in their lifetimes. They who always show off their healthy homes, their healthy morality, their common sense, their self-satisfaction.

Victory, however, is always on the side of the commonplace. Yūichi knew that all the scorn he could muster could not combat their natural scorn.[52]

Scenes like this in *Forbidden Colors*, full of critical venom against a deadeningly heteronormative postwar society, made readers look back at *Confessions* and read it for the first time as being about "homosexuality." In other words, it could be read in hindsight not as a homosocial narrative but as the traumatic, shame-induced *origin* of the articulate and critical gay voice that seemed to inform the later novel. Thus, Takeuchi argues, in 1954 Nakano Takehiko could write an article in which he claimed that homosexuality was the key to understanding *Confessions of a Mask*.[53] And yet, as I discussed at length in the beginning of this chapter, arguments like Nakano's did not take hold. Critics continued to read *Confessions* through the lens of the homo-

---

51. Fukushima, *Mishima Yukio*, 62.
52. Mishima, *Forbidden Colors*, 238; *Kinjiki*, 330.
53. Cited in Takeuchi, "Mishima Yukio *Kamen no kokuhaku* to iu hyōshō o megutte," 115. For the original article, see Nakano, "*Kamen no kokuhaku* ron."

social narrative for most of the twentieth century, prompting Atogami to come out with his exasperated announcement in 2000 that the novel represented the "dawn of homosexual literature" in Japan.

Ōta Tsubasa has recently argued that *Confessions* is a text that tries to make the narrator's desire, and thereby his *existence*, legible in a heteronormative world. This is why for Kō-chan it is not enough simply to say that he found another man attractive. He must also describe his erections and ejaculations in great detail as an "undeniable physiological sign of his desire" in a context where men's desire for other men is understood as a transitory developmental stage.[54] There is a lot to like in Ōta's argument, especially given the state of *Confessions* criticism in Japan, where many scholars have been nothing less than virtuosic in finding ways to reinterpret, downplay, or even to ignore outright the presence of homosexual desire in the novel. I am even more tempted by Ōta's argument because he is so careful to point out that "gay" as a category had yet to come into existence in Japan in 1949. Although Ōta's reading does not grant Kō-chan identity in his desire, however, he does describe it as a sort of ontological anchor that might implicitly serve as a *precursor* to identity. In other words, it could be the beginning of a *narrative* that might culminate in such an identity, given the right historical conditions. In its wishful, retrospective search for the origins of gay identity, Ōta's argument is a kind of "gay homosocial narrative" not unlike that of Sekine Shin'ichi's recent theatrical adaptation of *Kokoro* as discussed in Chapter 4.

The reason why I cannot agree with Ōta completely is the last piece of this book's argument that desire is best understood not as rooted *in* individual subjects (be they literary characters or real people) but rather as a product of mediation and narrative. Because this book asks not what kind of desire is *in* this text or this character, but what desire *does* in a text, it cannot ascribe any explanatory force to desire in and of itself. Kō-chan's desire in *Confessions* is represented as unbound and unmediated; as such it leads only to the abyss. This is perhaps why, if *Confessions* remains one of the "Great Books Every Gay Man Should Have Read," it is rarely one that gay men *like*. I know when I first read it at the age of twenty I found it terrifying. This brings me to why Fushimi Noriaki used the adverb "annoyingly" when describing how often Mishima's name came up when interviewing denizens of Japan's postwar gay world. Fushimi writes that until the 1980s *Confessions* and *Forbidden Colors* were virtually the only books available on male homosexuality in Japan and that he used to recommend

---

54. Ōta, "Mishima Yukio *Kamen no kokuhaku* ron," 80.

them to friends who were struggling with their sexuality. It was partly the inadequacy of these two books for this purpose, given the dark and depressing picture they painted of gay existence, which motivated him to write his 1990 book *Private Gay Life*, which offered a quirky but optimistic take on gay life in Japan and was the first to be written from an affirmative and gay-identified subject position.[55]

As for *Confessions of a Mask*—it may have put a stop to the homosocial narrative, but it was no gay novel.

---

55. *Private Gay Life* is included in Fushimi, *Gei to iu keiken.*

Epilogue

If Mishima discovered Tokyo's gay underground in the early 1950s, as the detailed accounts of it in *Forbidden Colors* seem to suggest, after *Confessions of a Mask* he also stopped entirely writing in the first person about homosexuality. In the 1950s he became quite an eloquent spokesperson for the notion that love for one's own sex was something to be outgrown and left behind. In an essay written for an advice column in 1955, he described male homosexuality in the Japanese context as "a kind of leftover of the feudal age and not at all a modern phenomenon," and then went on to reassure his readers that even if they had experimented with same-sex desire in their own pasts, "as long as you have pride in yourself as a woman or as a man you will not sink into the distorted and grotesque depths of homosexuality [*yugamerareta gurotesuku na dōseiai no soko*]. The pride you feel for your own sex [*honrai no sei no hokori*] will naturally restore it to you."[1]

In the same article, Mishima goes on to suggest to his readers that they give homosexuality a try. It is no more harmful in and of itself than masturbation, he insists, despite what the sexologists might say. But however much they might enjoy it for a while, he assures them (and perhaps himself since his own marriage was just three years away) they will eventually come to understand that only heterosexuality can provide the social acceptance that everyone craves. If they know what is best for them, they will leave their homosexual days behind and answer the clarion call of their proper gender.

Mishima's comments reveal two things about male homosexuality in the immediate postwar period. If it was still something that any man might

---

1. Mishima, "Shin ren'ai kōza," 396.

experience in his youth, it was also something "distorted and grotesque," a deviation from normative gender identity, and something that was best left behind. By 1955 heteronormativity in Japan had begun to be enforced not just by the normalizing thrust of the homosocial narrative, but by an increasingly irrational fear and abjection of male homosexuality. As the homosocial continuum ruptures more decisively than ever, the story this book has to tell comes to an end.

In this Epilogue, I want to discuss one final canonical novel, by Mishima's contemporary Ōe Kenzaburō (1935–), in which the figure of the homosexual has become relegated to third-person status, and the two-timing quality of the homosocial narrative has been replaced with an unquestioned association between male homosexuality and what is now imagined as an atavistic, antisocial, and irredeemably perverse past.

Ōe's 1964 novel *A Personal Matter* [*Kojin-teki na taiken*] is a third-person retrospective narrative that proceeds chronologically with a minimum of narrative analepses or prolepses. Unlike *The Wild Goose*, *Kokoro*, or *The Devil's Disciple*, or even *Confessions of a Mask*, Ōe's novel does not problematize the relation between story and discourse on a formal level. As a result, its narrative seems to unfold naturally, as chronology links up seamlessly with causality. The reader is never left in doubt as to what has actually happened. Nor does the way the story is told work to create a level of reality that is not reducible to the narrated. If the first-person retrospective narration of those earlier homosocial narratives made it impossible for the reader to forget the subjective nature of the narrative *act*; moreover, Ōe's heterodiegetic narration in *A Personal Matter* works to obscure the artifice of narration by covering over the gap between the present in which the narrative act takes place and the past which is being narrated. Unlike the unsettlingly incomplete narratives of Ōgai, Sōseki, Hamao, and Mishima, *A Personal Matter* is lodged firmly within the linear trajectory of a modernizationist history—it proposes to tell a story of development that is over and done with. And yet however much Ōe's novel works to obscure the subjective structuring force of narrative on a formal level by sticking to the guns of a linear time scheme, it is by no means free of the atemporal realm of perversion. Indeed, it is almost as if the text's careful avoidance of formal, *narrative* perversion had let loose a riot of perversion on the thematic level.

In the postwar historical context of rapid industrial growth of Japan's "economic miracle" combined with a supposed crisis of paternal authority brought on by the recent defeat in World War II and the nation's ongoing subordination to cold-war U.S. hegemony, questions of masculine sexuality and identity were overdetermined and intensified as never before.[2] Ōe's work registers this with great candor, although it is sometimes difficult to tell whether the results are critical or merely symptomatic, especially when it comes to his treatment of male homosexuality.[3] As Iwamoto Yoshio wrote in 2004 with regard to another novel written in 1959, "Indeed, it is difficult to fathom Ōe's attitude towards homosexuality. In his frequent assertions of serving as voice for the underdog, for those relegated to the margins, does he include homosexuals? At best, his stance seems ambiguous."[4]

A Personal Matter recounts a sex and alcohol drenched week spent by its protagonist "Bird" that begins with the birth of his brain-damaged son. Horrified by the thought of being tied down by a handicapped child for the rest of his life, Bird first solicits the help of a doctor to have the baby's milk substituted with sugar water in the hope that it will die before an operation can be performed. When the baby refuses to die, he removes it from the hospital and takes it to a "shady abortionist."[5] In the last few pages of the novel, however, Bird decides to spare the baby's life and take on the responsibilities of fatherhood. Having done so, his father-in-law praises him for having finally grown up. "You've changed," his father-in-law says approvingly, "A childish nickname like Bird doesn't suit you anymore."[6]

A Personal Matter thus ends with its narrator morphing from an irresponsible, even potentially *murderous* child-father into a responsible adult, and doing so with a speed so dramatic it is hard to credit. What makes this transformation possible within the symbolic economy of the novel is the presence of two figures: one female and one male homosexual through whose abjection Bird purchases his newfound maturity. Thus despite the redemptive promise of the novel's ending, *A Personal Matter* is at the same time a stunning example of the hypostatization and abjection of both female sexuality and male homosexuality that marked the postwar period. As such it is an excellent text through which to understand the afterlife of the homosocial narrative.

---

2. On the so-called crisis of paternalism in the postwar period, and the despairing critiques of Japan as a "maternal society" by critics, including Etō Jun, that resulted, see Yoda, "The Rise and Fall of Maternal Society."

3. For a critique of the misogyny evidenced in Ōe's work as a symptom of masculine anxiety resulting from the U.S. Occupation, see Hillenbrand, "Doppelgängers."

4. Iwamoto, "Ōe Kenzaburō's *Warera no jidai*," 50.

5. Ōe, *A Personal Matter*, 143; *Kojin-teki na taiken*, 219. Subsequent citations will use the abbreviated titles *Personal* and *Kojin-teki*.

6. *Personal*, 165; *Kojin-teki*, 252.

The narrative of *A Personal Matter* begins and ends with the haunting figures of male homosexuals. As the novel opens, "Bird" is passing the time in the back alleys of Tokyo waiting for his wife to give birth when he stops to contemplate his own somewhat pathetic figure as it is reflected in a shop window. After two paragraphs in which he ruminates on the fact that at 27 he is still as scrawny and birdlike as he was at the age of 15 (when he was given the nickname "Bird") he catches sight of a "woman with a definitively peculiar quality" in the shop window. When he turns around, "feeling as though a monster were stalking him from behind," he realizes that the "woman" in question is a man in drag who has momentarily mistaken him for a potential sex partner.

> That queen saw me watching his reflection in the window as if I were waiting for someone, and he mistook me for a pervert, thought Bird. A humiliating mistake, but inasmuch as the queen had recognized her error the minute Bird had turned around, Bird's honor had been redeemed. Now he was enjoying the humor of the confrontation.[7]

As the "queen" walks away in "consternation at her own rash mistake," Bird permits himself to indulge in the fantasy of what might have happened had he agreed to go home with "her." He imagines the conversation they might have had about his fear of getting "locked up in the cage of a family" for good once the baby arrives, and of his dream to travel to Africa. The queen, he imagines,

> would take pains to pick up the seeds of everything that's threatening me, one by one he'd gather them in, and certainly he would understand. Because a youth who tries so hard to be faithful to the warp in himself that he ends up searching the street in drag for perverts, a young man like that must have eyes and ears and a heart exquisitely sensitive to the fear that roots in the backlands of the subconscious.[8]

Bird even goes so far as to picture to himself a scene of homosexual domestic bliss the next morning as he and the "queen" shave together while listening to the news on the radio, "sharing a soap dish." But soon he cuts himself off to return the fantasy to the safer realm of male camaraderie. "Spending a night together might be going too far, but at least he should have invited the young man for a drink."[9] In the end, he does neither, and the "queen" fades back into the alleys from which s/he emerged as Bird moves on to confront the news that his baby has been born with a horrific

---

7. *Personal*, 3–4; *Kojin-teki*, 10. I have slightly modified Nathan's translation here.
8. *Personal*, 5; *Kojin-teki*, 11.
9. *Personal*, 5; *Kojin-teki*, 12.

brain hernia. From this moment on, time seems to stand still as Bird tries to figure out the best way to rid himself of the "monster" baby.

The maternal understanding and benevolence that he imagined the "queen" capable of providing is soon provided in reality by the character Himiko, an ex-girlfriend from Bird's college days. Himiko is extremely well educated but unable, like all of their other female classmates, to put her education to any use as a result of the virulent misogyny of 1960s Japanese society. She is also still reeling from the suicide of her young husband, another friend of Bird's from college. Himiko never leaves her apartment except at night, when she ventures out in her red MG convertible in search of fleeting sexual adventures. Her outsider status and experience of suffering lend her a sort of saint-like quality and it is to her perpetually darkened apartment that Bird retreats to wait for news of his newborn son. The reader soon learns that Bird raped Himiko when the two of them were still in college, but Himiko is serenely matter of fact about this experience, even when she tells Bird that the rape was also the first time she had ever had sex. In the intervening years, Himiko has become something of a "sexual expert" and it is through sex that she proposes to heal Bird of his horror of the "dark recesses where that grotesque baby was created."[10] "Is your fear limited to the vagina and the womb?" she asks Bird, "Or are you afraid of everything female, of my existence as a woman for example?"[11] When it turns out that Bird is afraid of her breasts as well, Himiko suggests that it might be easier if Bird were to "approach me from behind." She has always thought of Bird as someone to whom younger men looked up and asks him "Haven't you ever been to bed with one of those younger brothers?"[12]

This question goes unanswered by Bird, but soon he finds himself terrifically aroused by Himiko's proposal. Bird timidly asks Himiko whether she would not be humiliated by being fucked from behind. Would she derive any pleasure from it? "At the moment," Himiko says with "unbounded gentleness," "I am only interested in doing something for you, Bird."[13] The scene that follows is a depiction of anal sex, described as "the most malefic sex, a fuck rife with ignominy" in which Bird loses himself entirely to the pleasure of dominating Himiko.[14] Each burst of pleasure for Bird is met with a cry of agony from Himiko. But with beatific forbearance Himiko allows Bird his enjoyment. After it is over, he wonders if "the humanity

---

10. *Personal*, 82; *Kojin-teki*, 126.
11. *Personal*, 83; *Kojin-teki*, 129.
12. *Personal*, 84; *Kojin-teki*, 130.
13. *Personal*, 84; *Kojin-teki*, 131.
14. *Personal*, 85; *Kojin-teki*, 131.

could be restored to their relationship after coition this inhuman."[15] But it seems that such inhumanity is just what the doctor ordered. Within two pages Bird is fucking Himiko the other way around, no longer afraid of her femininity and eager to fulfill his duty to her as a man, "Like a soldier accompanying a comrade in arms to private battle, Bird stood by in stoic self-restraint while Himiko wrested from their coition the *genuine* something that was all her own."[16]

Coming almost exactly at the midpoint of the novel, this scene is the crucial moment when Bird begins to transform himself with Himiko's help into the responsible adult he will be at the end of the novel. It is a painfully overdetermined narrative of sexual development from an inherently misogynous homosexuality towards a fully heteronormative maturity. Himiko's selfless efforts are crucial to help Bird overcome his fear of the "dark, infinite," "grotesque universe" "teeming with everything anti-human" that he glimpses in the vagina and the womb. But Himiko herself must be left behind when it is time for Bird to return to his own family.

The next chapter shows that Bird has a history of abandoning people. When his long-suffering and nameless wife accuses him from her hospital bed of being "the type of person who abandons someone weak when that person needs you most"[17] she reminds him of a young friend that he abandoned in his youth. This friend, named Kikuhiko, is the second male homosexual to appear in the text. Bird's first abandonment of Kikuhiko occurred when the two of them were hired to track down a mentally ill patient who had escaped from an asylum. When the younger Kikuhiko became afraid and exhausted and wanted to give up the hunt and return home, Bird shamed the boy by revealing his knowledge of the latter's affair with a homosexual American working for the Occupation.[18] Kikuhiko subsequently moved to Tokyo and opened a gay bar, which he named after himself.

Along with Himiko and the drag queen from the opening scene of the novel, Kikuhiko joins the crowd of perverts who will shepherd Bird along on his journey to maturity. The name Kikuhiko, written with the character

---

15. *Personal*, 86; *Kojin-teki*, 133.
16. *Personal*, 90; *Kojin-teki*, 139.
17. *Personal*, 99; *Kojin-teki*, 153.
18. Like most homosexuals in Ōe's early works, Kikuhiko sleeps exclusively with foreigners, and Americans in particular. Nathan describes this one as "an American homosexual in the CIA," but Ōe's Japanese text has *CIE no dōseiai no Amerika-jin*. CIE (the Civil Information and Education Section) was a cultural agency under the U.S. Occupation. Later in the text this person is referred to by Himiko as an "American cultural officer" (*Personal*, 99, 147; *Kojin-teki*, 153, 225).

for "chrysanthemum" (菊) followed by two characters read phonetically that carry the meaning of "comparison with the past" (比古), encapsulates in itself the normalizing homosocial narrative structure of *A Personal Matter*. The chrysanthemum has long been associated in Japan with the practice of male-male sex.[19] And it is through the figure of Kiku*hiko* that a homosexual past is conjured with which Bird can "compare" his present and move on towards a healthy and heteronormative future.

In what is perhaps the only instance in *A Personal Matter* to depart from the conventions of plausible realism, Himiko coincidentally turns out to be a patron of the gay bar "Kikuhiko," thus placing her clearly within the same symbolic orbit of perversion as its homosexual owner. "What a coincidence," she exclaims when it turns out they have this acquaintance in common. "Bird, why don't we go there after!" *After*, that is, they take the baby to the doctor (also one of Himiko's lovers) whom Himiko recommends to murder it. "*After*, Bird thought, *after* abandoning the baby with a shady abortionist."[20] The emphasis on the sequence of before and after begins a process whereby Bird is awakened to the *consequences* of what he is about to do. It marks a dawning awareness of the passage of linear time that has somehow been arrested since Bird heard the news about his baby. Soon after this moment, as Bird and Himiko speed in Himiko's MG toward the clinic of the "shady abortionist," Himiko asks Bird what time it is and he discovers that his watch has stopped, its hands frozen "at a nonsensical hour."[21] As they listen to a radio announcement that the Japan Anti-Nuclear Warfare League has come out in support of the resumption of nuclear weapons testing by the Soviets, Bird finds himself unable to care. Like his broken watch, Bird begins to sense that he is out of step with the rest of the world, in which "mankind's one and only time" was passing.[22] Locked in the nightmare of his own personal hell in which time has stopped, Bird has given up on all hope of futurity for himself or anyone else as he and Himiko rush to the clinic to kill his deformed baby.

In these last pages of the novel there is a struggle between precisely the two temporalities that have I have discussed throughout this book. The

---

19. One famous example of this association is in Ueda Akinari's tale "The Chrysanthemum Vow" ["Kikka no chigiri"] collected in his *Tales of Moonlight and Rain* [*Ugetsu monogatari*] (1776). It is the story of a samurai who, finding himself far away on the battlefield at the time when he had promised to rendezvous with his lover, commits suicide so that he can arrive on time as a ghost.

20. *Personal*, 147; *Kojin-teki*, 225.

21. *Personal*, 149; *Kojin-teki*, 228.

22. *Personal*, 150; *Kojin-teki*, 229.

arrested time of perversion is here explicitly linked to an apolitical and infanticidal privacy, a "personal matter" that is contrasted with the forward moving public time of politics and responsibility to others. Bird's dawning awareness of his responsibilities as a parent comes as a result of his comparison of himself with the homosexual Kikuhiko, and it is in the bar by that name that he finally realizes he must stop running away from his own destiny and "grow up." Kikuhiko comes across as a frightening and uncanny figure who occupies his own perverse temporality. When Bird and Himiko first discover their common acquaintance with Kikuhiko, it is by his age that they determine his identity. It is not, however, in its exactitude but in its ambiguousness that Kikuhiko's age reveals who he is. "How old a guy is he?" asks Bird when Himiko mentions that she knows someone by the name of Kikuhiko. "It's hard to tell with faggots like that, four, maybe five years younger than you."[23] Later, when the two of them settle down in Kikuhiko's bar for the "wake" of Bird's baby, Kikuhiko makes Bird uneasy because of his indeterminate age.

> Bird reached for the glass of whisky that had been poured for him and, feeling something tighten in his chest, hesitated. Kikuhiko—he can't be more than twenty-two yet he looks like a more formidable adult than I; on the other hand, he seems to have retained a lot of what he was at fifteen—like an amphibian at home in two ages, Kikuhiko.[24]

As Bird is literally arrested in mid-reach for the glass of whisky by the sight of Kikuhiko, the reader follows on to a sentence bounded on both ends by the repetition of Kikuhiko's name. The proper noun Kikuhiko is there in this sentence where the verb should be so that the sentence has no main verb at all and remains suspended in tenseless time like Kikuhiko himself, an "amphibian at home in two ages." Given that Kikuhiko's name itself might be translated as something like "comparison with one's homosexual past," the text could hardly be more obviously suggesting that Bird is engaging here in the kind of projection that we have identified as characteristic of homosocial narrative in its normative mode. Bird sees the homosexual Kikuhiko as a lost part of himself, like the "queen" who emerged from behind his own reflection in the shop front window at the beginning

---

23. *Personal*, 147; *Kojin-teki*, 224–25. Nathan's translation makes Himiko sound slightly more homophobic than she is in Japanese, where she says "those people" [*aaiu hitotachi*] rather than "faggots."

24. *Personal*, 159; *Kojin-teki*, 242. I have slightly altered Nathan's translation here to retain the structure in Japanese, where "Kikuhiko" comes at the beginning and the end of the sentence.

of the novel.²⁵ If he is a part of himself, however, it is a part of him from which he has since become utterly and decisively estranged. "Strange," he reflects, "he was more conscious of talking to the proprietor of a gay bar (it was his first time) than to a sometime friend whom he hadn't seen in years."²⁶

In the conversation that follows, the comparison with Kikuhiko becomes the catalyst for Bird's decision to save his baby. "You stopped mixing with me and my kind and went to a college in Tokyo didn't you?" Kikuhiko comments. "But I've been like falling steadily ever since that night and look at me now—tucked away nice and comfy in this nelly little bar. Bird, if you hadn't . . . gone on alone that night, I might be in a very different groove now."²⁷ When Himiko "audaciously" suggests that Kikuhiko might not have "become a homosexual" if Bird had not abandoned him, Kikuhiko calmly insists, "A homosexual is someone who has chosen to practice homosexuality isn't he? I made that decision myself. So the responsibility is all my own."²⁸ While Kikuhiko claims "responsibility" for having "become a homosexual," he also contrasts his own fallen state with what he perceives to be Bird's subsequent development. "I'm sure you've been on the rise all the time I've been falling."²⁹

This comment hits Bird where it hurts because it could not be further from the truth. He has hardly been on the rise. He has just been fired from

---

25. Right before he sees the "queen," Bird is thinking of himself as a creature somehow outside of time. "This was a fair description of Bird at fifteen: nothing had changed at twenty. How long would he continue to look like a bird? No choice but living with the same posture from fifteen to sixty-five, was he that kind of person?" (*Personal*, 3; *Kojin-teki*, 10).

26. *Personal*, 159; *Kojin-teki*, 242.

27. *Personal*, 160; *Kojin-teki*, 244.

28. Here also I have slightly altered Nathan's translation. Whereas Ōe's Japanese literally says "a homosexual" [*homosekushuaru*] is someone who has chosen "to practice homosexualty" [*dōseiai o jikkō suru*]," Nathan's translation reads, "A homosexual is someone who has chosen to let himself love a person of the same sex." By inserting the words "love," "person," and "let himself" Nathan makes Kikuhiko's comment sound much more romantic and "queer affirmative" than it is in Japanese. It is perhaps for this reason that this very sentence made its way onto an Internet site devoted to quotes affirming the idea of queerness as a choice. Given the way Kikuhiko and other homosexuals are depicted in Ōe's early novels, it would be difficult to make the case that the quote's inclusion on this site is the result of anything other than a generous mistranslation on Nathan's part. See http://www.queerbychoice.com/experiquotes.html [accessed April 2, 2012].

29. *Personal*, 160; *Kojin-teki*, 244.

his job, he has fallen back into a cycle of alcoholism and despair, and now he has decided to murder his own child. But the site of Kikuhiko tucked away in his "nelly little bar" seems to steel Bird's resolve to get back on track. "I'm not twenty anymore," he tells Kikuhiko, at which point the latter's face "froze over with icy indifference. 'The old gray mare just ain't what she used to be,' he said, and moved abruptly to Himiko's side."[30] It is at this moment that Bird parts ways with both Kikuhiko and Himiko. He becomes disgusted with Kikuhiko and his "icy indifference": "After a blank of *seven years* it had taken him just *seven minutes* of conversation to eliminate everything worthy of their mutual curiosity."[31] Just a few lines later Bird "effortlessly" vomits the whisky Kikuhiko served him onto the bar counter and declares, "I've decided to take the baby back to the university hospital and let them operate."[32] Himiko becomes "hysterical" and tries to convince him to carry through with their plan and to accompany her on that trip to Africa. But Bird is firm in his resolve. When Kikuhiko tells Himiko to get ahold of herself and give up on the "selfish" Bird, the male homosexual and the heterosexual woman split into two equally powerful forces impelling Bird back to his wife and family, the former through "hatred" and the latter through "love." Kikuhiko, whom the narrator now refers to as his "former friend" looks at Bird with "something akin to raw hatred in his eyes," and Himiko suddenly reverts to the "infinitely generous, tender, placid Himiko."[33] Not only has the past he shared with Kikuhiko and Himiko now lost all its meaning except as a prelude to this moment, but the same is true for his entire life up until the point of his sudden awakening to futurity. "If I die in an accident now before I save the baby, my whole 27 years of life will have meant exactly nothing. Bird was stricken with a sense of fear more profound than any he had ever known."[34]

In the scene that follows, Bird is shown being welcomed back into the fold of the family. As he moves away from his wife and her mother who had "stopped to cluck and coo over the baby," he joins his father-in-law for a man-to-man chat in which the latter tells him, in a line quoted earlier

---

30. *Personal*, 161; *Kojin-teki*, 245.
31. *Personal*, 161; *Kojin-teki*, 245.
32. *Personal*, 161; *Kojin-teki*, 246.
33. *Personal*, 163; *Kojin-teki*, 248. As D. A. Miller has written, "straight men unabashedly *need* gay men, whom they forcibly recruit to enter into a polarization that exorcises the 'woman' in man through assigning it to a class of man who may be considered no 'man' at all. Only between the woman and the homosexual together may the normal male subject imagine himself covered front and back" ("Anal Rope," 135).
34. *Personal*, 163; *Kojin-teki*, 249.

and with a voice "warm with a relative's affection" "You've changed. . . . A childish nickname like Bird doesn't suit you anymore."[35] So Bird has finally "grown up." He has entered a new temporality in which *the future* will triumph over the past. "I'm going to have to put away as much as I can for his future as well as our own,"[36] Bird tells his father-in-law as the two of them cement a now unalloyed homosocial bond. Bird has never been very fond of his wife and here it is the father-in-law who not only places his imprimatur on Bird's newfound maturity, but also overshadows in his quiet authority the conjugal bond itself. Bird's resolution to "put away as much [money] as I can" for the future of that family is a perfect economic metaphor for the shift from waste to (re)productivity that was figured in the scene where Bird was "cured" of his fear of women as Himiko gently shepherded him from anal to vaginal sex. His journey to normality is now complete.

In *A Personal Matter*, the homosocial narrative has congealed into a one-way trajectory toward heteronormative adulthood powered by the abjection of gay men like Kikuhiko and women like Himiko. If Shimaura in *The Devil's Disciple* remained melancholically stuck on Tsuchida, Bird leaves Kikuhiko behind without looking back. Himiko, for her part, manages to be a sexual temptress and a beatific mother substitute all at once, as if Sōseki's Kiyo and Madonna from *Botchan* had been recombined into their original gestalt. That such extreme gendered visions appear here, in the work of one of the leading figures of the Japanese left, and in a novel as canonical as this one, suggests how widespread and unquestioned they had become by 1964. It also suggests the crucial importance of theorizing the connections between misogyny and homophobia directed at men in the postwar period. Although this is a project for another book, I hope that this one, in its focus on the prehistory of this moment, will help to make visible those connections and contribute to the process of rethinking the overly simplistic "division of labor" between feminist and queer approaches that I described in the introduction.

In rethinking it myself, it has been extremely useful to go back to the original emergence of queer theory from its feminist sources—that moment in the early 1980s when Sedgwick first formulated the notion of the homosocial continuum in order to begin to dislodge and complicate two wide-

---

35. *Personal*, 165; *Kojin-teki*, 252.
36. *Personal*, 165; *Kojin-teki*, 251.

spread but equally inadequate assumptions that she described as characterizing most work that had been done until that point on the relationship between gay men and feminism. These were, namely, "either that gay men and all women share a 'natural,' transhistorical alliance and an essential identity of interests (for example, in breaking down gender stereotypes); or else that male homosexuality is an epitome, a personification, an effect, or perhaps a primary cause of woman-hating."[37] The former assumption of alliance is, of course, an appealing idea and perhaps a good strategy in some cases, but in Japan in particular, where the very word "woman-hater" [*onna-girai*] once referred to a man who loved men, it is simply impossible to assume. If the rise of homophobia in twentieth-century Japan was inseparable from the rise of a newly interiorized gender hierarchy that affected both gay men and women (as *A Personal Matter* makes painfully clear), this makes their coalition both intellectually and politically crucial. At the same time, it must be said that gay men's nostalgic (if perhaps understandable) attraction to a premodern tradition of misogynist male-male eroticism has constantly threatened to pull this fragile coalition apart.

The figure of Mishima Yukio is perhaps the best example of both the potential and the limits of a possible coalition between gay men and feminists in Japan. In a fascinating roundtable about Mishima in 1989, Japan's leading academic feminist Ueno Chizuko noted approvingly that Mishima might have been "the Japanese Foucault" if he had not been "killed by homophobia" in 1970. For Ueno's interlocutor Tomioka Taeko, however, it was not homophobia but *marriage* that killed Mishima, by which she meant Mishima's own implacable misogyny that made his own marriage miserable for him. This debate set the stage for a major shift in the relations between feminists and gay men in Japan during the decade that followed. For feminists like Tomioka, male homosexuality, understood as "woman-hating," was indeed the very logic of patriarchy, whereas, for others like Ueno, male homosexuals were its victims along with women. Even Ueno, however, who comes across as more sympathetic to Mishima in this roundtable, would later write explicitly that her own understanding of Mishima and male homosexuality in general was hobbled by the lack of the conceptual apparatus provided by Sedgwick's work on homosociality, which made it possible for the first time to theorize homophobia and misogyny as interlinked but not synonymous phenomena.[38]

---

37. Sedgwick, *Between Men*, 19–20.

38. For the discussion of Mishima as the "Japanese Foucault," see Ueno, Ogura, and Tomioka, *Danryū bungakuron*, 346. For her later "conversion" to a more queer-

Surely both Ueno and Tomioka were right in a sense: Mishima *was* a victim of homophobia *and* he held shockingly misogynist views. That such a situation was not at all paradoxical or exceptional for much of the twentieth century in Japan is a testament to a homosocial continuum with a very particular shape and dynamic, the outlines of which this book has tried to trace.

As I hope this book has also shown, however, homophobia and misogyny as they appear around the figure of Mishima or in a work like Ōe's *A Personal Matter*, are less the stubborn remnants of a traditional culture than the affective precipitates of a modern homosocial narrative frozen into immobility. If sexuality became a matter for narration rather than nomination in the first half of Japan's twentieth century, it congealed into identity over the course of its second. In this book, I have turned neither to narrative nor to identity, but to the *narratology* of sexuality, both to understand why it matters whose voice is speaking, and to practice the vital art of looking forward and backward at once.

---

friendly perspective (partly as a result of a discussion with Japanese gay activists), see Ueno, "Gei to feminizumu wa kyōtō dekiru ka."

Reference Matter

Works Cited

Abelove, Henry. "Freud, Male Homosexuality, and the Americans." In *Deep Gossip*, 1–20. Minneapolis, MN: University of Minnesota Press, 2003.
Ahmed, Sara. *The Promise of Happiness*. Durham, NC: Duke University Press, 2010.
Aida Hirotsugu. "Sōseki, Haieku, Etō Jun: *Kokoro* no kizuna." *Bungei shunju* 86, no. 11 (October 2008): 334–41.
Angles, Jeffrey. "Haunted by the Sexy Samurai: Ranpo's Mobilization of the Queer Past in 'Shudō mokuzuzuka.'" *PAJLS: Proceedings of the Association for Japanese Literary Studies* 9 (2008): 101–9.
———. "Seeking the Strange: *Ryōki* and the Navigation of Normality in Interwar Japan." *Monumenta Nipponica* 63, no. 1 (2008): 101–41.
———. *Writing the Love of Boys: Origins of Bishōnen Culture in Modernist Japanese Literature*. Minneapolis, MN: University of Minnesota Press, 2011.
Ara Masato. "Ijō shinri dewa nai." *Tosho shinbun*, July 23, 1949.
Armstrong, Nancy. *Desire and Domestic Fiction: A Political History of the Novel*. New York: Oxford University Press, 1987.
Atogami Shirō. "Saisho no dōseiai bungaku: *Kamen no kokuhaku* ni okeru kindai no kokuin." *Bungei kenkyū* 150, no. 9 (2000): 69–80.
Auestad, Reiko Abe. "Against the Linguistic Constraints: Narratological Structure and Writing Style in Natsume Sōseki's *Meian*." *Japan Forum* 5, no. 2 (1993): 231–43.
———. *Rereading Sōseki: Three Early Twentieth-Century Japanese Novels*. Iaponia insula, Bd. 7. Wiesbaden: Harrassowitz, 1998.
Bellamy, Dodie. "Low Culture." In *Biting the Error: Writers Explore Narrative*, 226–37. Toronto, ON: Coach House Books, 2004.
Bersani, Leo. *Marcel Proust: The Fictions of Life and of Art*. New York: Oxford University Press, 1965.
———. *The Freudian Body: Psychoanalysis and Art*. New York: Columbia University Press, 1986.
Blowers, Geoffrey H., and Serena Hsueh-Chi Yang. "Freud's Deshi: The Coming of Psychoanalysis to Japan." *Journal of the History of the Behavioral Sciences* 32, no. 2 (1997): 115–26.

Bowring, Richard. *Mori Ōgai and the Modernization of Japanese Culture*. Cambridge, UK: Cambridge University Press, 1979.

Brooks, Peter. "Freud's Masterplot: A Model for Narrative." In *Reading for the Plot: Design and Intention in Narrative*, 90–112. Cambridge, MA: Harvard University Press, 1984.

Bruffee, Kenneth A. *Elegiac Romance: Cultural Change and Loss of the Hero in Modern Fiction*. Ithaca, NY: Cornell University Press, 1983.

Butler, Judith. "Dangerous Crossings: Willa Cather's Masculine Names." In *Bodies That Matter: On the Discursive Limits of "Sex,"* 143–66. New York: Routledge, 1993.

———. "Against Proper Objects." *Differences* 6, nos. 2–3 (1994): 1–26.

Case, Alison. "Gender and History in Narrative Theory: The Problem of Retrospective Distance in *David Copperfield* and *Bleak House*." In *A Companion to Narrative Theory*, ed. James Phelan and Peter J. Rabinowitz, 312–21. Oxford, UK: Blackwell, 2005.

Castiglia, Christopher, and Christopher Reed. "Queer Theory Is Burning: Sexual Revolution and Traumatic Unremembering." In *If Memory Serves: Gay Men, AIDS, and the Promise of the Queer Past*, 145–74. Minneapolis, MN: University of Minnesota Press, 2012.

Chow, Rey. "Modernity and Narration: In Feminine Detail." In *Woman and Chinese Modernity: The Politics of Reading between West and East*, 84–120. Minneapolis, MN: University of Minnesota Press, 1991.

Davis, Darrell William. "Historical Uses and Misuses: The Janus Face(s) of 'The Abe Clan.'" *Film History* 7, no. 1 (Spring 1995): 49–68.

Dodd, Stephen. "The Significance of Bodies in Soseki's *Kokoro*." *Monumenta Nipponica* 53, no. 4 (1998): 473–98.

Doi, Takeo. *The Anatomy of Dependence*. Tokyo: Kodansha International, 1973.

Drake, Robert. *The Gay Canon: Great Books Every Gay Man Should Read*. 1st ed. New York: Anchor Books, 1998.

Driscoll, Mark. "Seeds and (Nest) Eggs of Empire: Sexology Manuals/Manual Sexology." In *Gendering Modern Japanese History*, ed. Barbara Molony and Kathleen Uno, 191–224. Harvard East Asian Monographs 251. Cambridge, MA: Harvard University Asia Center, 2005.

Edelman, Lee. "Homographesis." In *Homographesis: Essays in Gay Literary and Cultural Theory*, 3–23. New York: Routledge, 1994.

———. "Seeing Things: Representation, the Scene of Surveillance, and the Spectacle of Gay Male Sex." In *Inside/out: Lesbian Theories, Gay Theories*. Ed. Diana Fuss, 93–118. New York: Routledge, 1991.

———. *No Future: Queer Theory and the Death Drive*. Series Q. Durham, NC: Duke University Press, 2004.

Edogawa Ranpo. "Futari no shishō." In *Gunshū no naka no Robinson*, vol. 5 of *Edogawa Ranpo korekushon*, by Edogawa Ranpo, Hirohisa Shinpo, and Yuzuru Yamamae, 137–39. Tokyo: Kawade shobō shinsha, 1995.

Esty, Jed. *Unseasonable Youth: Modernism, Colonialism, and the Fiction of Development*. Oxford, UK: Oxford University Press, 2011.

Etō Jun. "A Japanese Meiji Intellectual: An Essay on *Kokoro*." In *Essays on Natsume Sōseki's Works*, by Nihon Yunesuko kokunai iinkai, 49–65. Tokyo: Japan Society for the Promotion of Science, 1972.

Foucault, Michel. *The History of Sexuality: An Introduction*. Vol. 1. New York: Vintage Books, 1978.
Fowler, Edward. *The Rhetoric of Confession: Shishōsetsu in Early Twentieth-Century Japanese Fiction*. Berkeley, CA: University of California Press, 1988.
Freeman, Elizabeth. *Time Binds: Queer Temporalities, Queer Histories*. Durham, NC: Duke University Press, 2010.
Freud, Sigmund. "Beyond the Pleasure Principle." In *The Standard Edition of the Complete Psychological Works of Sigmund Freud*, ed. James Strachey, vol. 18, 1–64. London: Hogarth Press, 1995.
———. "Psycho-Analytic Notes upon an Autobiographical Account of a Case of Paranoia." In *The Standard Edition of the Complete Psychological Works of Sigmund Freud*, ed. James Strachey, vol. 12, 33–82. London: Hogarth Press, 1995.
———. "Three Essays on the Theory of Sexuality (1905)." In *The Standard Edition of the Complete Psychological Works of Sigmund Freud*, ed. James Strachey, vol. 7, 123–245. London: Hogarth Press, 1995.
———. "On Transformations of Instinct as Exemplified in Anal Erotism." In *The Standard Edition of the Complete Psychological Works of Sigmund Freud*, ed. James Strachey, vol. 17, 127–33. London: Hogarth Press, 1995.
———. "The Uncanny." In *The Standard Edition of the Complete Psychological Works of Sigmund Freud*, ed. James Strachey, vol. 17, 217–53. London: Hogarth Press, 1955.
Fujii, James. "Death, Empire, and the Search for History in Natsume Sōseki's *Kokoro*." In *Complicit Fictions: The Subject in the Modern Japanese Prose Narrative*, 126–50. Berkeley, CA: University of California Press, 1993.
Fujimori Kiyoshi. "Kyōsei-teki iseiai taisei-ka no seishun: *Sanshirō*, *Seinen*." *Bungaku* 3, no. 1 (2002): 120–33.
Fukuda Kōson. "*Kamen no kokuhaku* ni tsuite." In *Kamen no kokuhaku*, by Mishima Yukio. Tokyo: Shinchō bunko, 1997.
Fukushima Jirō. *Mishima Yukio: tsurugi to kankō*. Tokyo: Bungei shunjū, 1998.
Furukawa Makoto. "Shizen shugi to dōseiai: Meiji-matsu seiyoku no jidai." *Sōbun* 380 (September 1996): 10–13.
———, ed. *Ansoroji bungei sakuhin ni egakareta dōseiai*. Kindai Nihon no sekushuariti 35. Tokyo: Yumani shobō, 2009.
Fushimi Noriaki. *Gei to iu keiken zōhoban*. Tokyo: Potto shuppan, 2004.
Fushimi Noriaki, Kakinuma Eiko, and Nishino Kōji. "Zadankai: Mishima Yukio kara gei bungaku e." *Queer Japan*, vol. 2. Tokyo: Keisō shobō, 2000.
Gan Bao. *In Search of the Supernatural: The Written Record*. Trans. Kenneth J. DeWoskin and James Irving Crump. Stanford, CA: Stanford University Press, 1996.
Genette, Gérard. *Narrative Discourse: An Essay in Method*. Ithaca, NY: Cornell University Press, 1980.
Gilbert, Sandra M., and Susan Gubar. *The Madwoman in the Attic: The Woman Writer and the Nineteenth-Century Literary Imagination*. New Haven, CT: Yale University Press, 1979.
Girard, René. *Deceit, Desire, and the Novel; Self and Other in Literary Structure*. Baltimore, MD: Johns Hopkins University Press, 1965.
Grimes, William. "Eve Kosofsky Sedgwick, a Pioneer of Gay Studies and a Literary Theorist, Dies at 58." *New York Times*, April 15, 2009, sec. Arts. http://www.nytimes.com/2009/04/15/arts/15sedgwick.html.

Guillén, Claudio. *Literature as System; Essays Toward the Theory of Literary History.* Princeton, NJ: Princeton University Press, 1971.
Halperin, David M. *Saint=Foucault: Towards a Gay Hagiography.* Oxford, UK: Oxford University Press, 1995.
Hamao Shirō. "Akuma no deshi." In *Satsujin shōsetsu shū*, 68–91. *Hamao Shirō zenshū*, vol. 1. Tokyo: Chūsekisha, 2004.
———. "Did He Kill Them?" In *The Devil's Disciple*, trans. J. Keith Vincent. London: Hesperus Press, 2011.
———. "Dōseiai kō." *Fujin saron*, vol. 2, no. 9 (September 1930): 136–42.
———. "Futatabi dōseiai ni tsuite." *Fujin saron*, vol. 2, no. 11 (November 1930): 58–65.
———. *The Devil's Disciple.* Trans. J. Keith Vincent. London: Hesperus Press, 2011.
Hara Hiroshi. "Seishun no akogare: bungō Sōseki to Komiya Toyotaka." *Adonis* 1 (1952): 7–11.
Hartley, Barbara. "The Ambivalent Object of Desire: Contesting Gender Hegemonies in Kawabata Yasunari's *Shonen* [novel]." *Asian Studies Review* 30, no. 2 (2007): 123–40.
Hasegawa Kōzō and Tsukikawa Kazuo, eds. *Minakata Kumagusu nanshoku dangi.* Tokyo: Yasaka shobō, 1991.
Hashimoto Osamu. *Hasu to katana.* Tokyo: Kawade bunko, 1986.
Hattori, Masa. "*Gan* seiritsu no shakai-teki sokumen ni kansuru ichi kōsatsu: Mori Ōgai ni okeru Meiji 13-nen no imi." *Shakai mondai kenkyū* 18, no. 3 (1968): 1–17.
Herman, David. "Re-Minding Modernism." In *The Emergence of Mind: Representations of Consciousness in Narrative Discourse in English*, 243–72. Lincoln, NE: University of Nebraska Press, 2011.
Herrero-Brasas, Juan A. "The Love of Comrades." In *Walt Whitman's Mystical Ethics of Comradeship: Homosexuality and the Marginality of Friendship at the Crossroads of Modernity*, 83–116. Albany, NY: State University of New York Press, 2010.
Hill, Christopher. "Mori Ōgai's Resentful Narrator: Trauma and the National Subject." *positions: east asia cultures critique* 10:2 (2012): 366–97.
Hillenbrand, Margaret. "Doppelgängers, Misogyny, and the San Francisco System: The Occupation Narratives of Ōe Kenzaburō." *Journal of Japanese Studies*, vol. 33, no. 2 (2007): 383–414.
Hirata, Hosea. "The Emergence of History in Natsume Soseki's *Kokoro*." In *Discourses of Seduction: History, Evil, Desire, and Modern Japanese Literature*, 183–206. Harvard East Asian Monographs 242. Cambridge, MA: Harvard University Asia Center, 2005.
Hori Tatsuo. "Les joues en feu." In *The Shōwa Anthology: Modern Japanese Short Stories*, ed. Van C. Gessel and Tomone Matsumoto, 28–37. 1st ed. Tokyo: Kodansha International, 1985.
———. "Moyuru hoo." In *Hori Tatsuo zenshū*, vol. 1. Ed. Nakamura Shin'ichirō et al, 207–21. Tokyo: Chikuma shobō, 1977.
Hong Bian, ed. Qingpingshan tang huaben (Story telling promptbooks from Qingpingshan studio). Ming edition Reprint. Beijing: Wenxue guji kanxing she, 1987.
Hosoya Hiroshi. "*Gan* no 'modokashisa.'" *Mori Ōgai kenkyū* 8 (1999): 165–83.
Hwang, Jong-yon. "The Emergence of Aesthetic Ideology in Modern Korean Literary Criticism: An Essay on Yi Kwang-su." *Korea Journal*, 39:4 (Winter 1999): 5–35.
Iida Yūko. *Karera no monogatari: Nihon kindai bungaku to jendā.* 1st ed. Nagoya: Nagoya daigaku shuppankai, 1998.

---. "*Kokoro*-teki sankakkei no saiseisan." *Kōbe jogakuin daigaku kenkyujo yakuin/Kobe College Studies* 42, no. 2 (1995): 1–15.
Iida Yūko, Ishihara Chiaki, Komori Yōichi, Seki Reiko, and Hiraoka Toshio. "*Kokoro* ronsō ikō." *Sōseki kenkyū*, no. 6 (1996): 156–91.
Ishihara Chiaki. "*Kokoro* no Oidipusu." In *Hanten suru Sōseki*, 182–203. Tokyo: Seidosha, 1997.
---. *Kokoro: otona ni narenakatta sensei*. Risō no kyoshitsu. Tokyo: Misuzu shobō, 2005.
---. *Tekusuto wa machigawanai: shōsetsu to dokusha no shigoto*. Tokyo: Chikuma shobō, 2004.
Ishihara Chiaki and Komori Yōichi. "Sōseki *Kokoro* no genkō o yomu." *Bungaku* 3, no. 4 (October 1992): 2–12.
Ito, Ken K. "Writing Time in Sōseki's *Kokoro*." In *Studies in Modern Japanese Literature: Essays and Translations in Honor of Edwin McClellan*, ed. Dennis Washburn and Alan Tansman, 3–29. Michigan Monograph Series in Japanese Studies 20. Ann Arbor, MI: Center for Japanese Studies, University of Michigan, 1997.
Iwamoto Yoshio. "Ōe Kenzaburō's *Warera no jidai*." *World Literature Today*, vol. 76, no. 1 (Winter, 2002): 43–51.
Jacobowitz, Seth. "Translator's Introduction." In *The Edogawa Rampo Reader*, by Edogawa Ranpo, trans. Seth Jacobowitz, xv–xlvii. Fukuoka: Kurodahan Press, 2008.
Jameson, Fredric. "Magical Narratives: On the Dialectical Use of Genre Criticism." In *The Political Unconscious: Narrative as a Socially Symbolic Act*, 89–136. London: Routledge, 2002.
---. "Third-World Literature in the Era of Multinational Capitalism." *Pretexts: Studies in Writing and Culture* 3, no. 1–2 (1991): 82–104.
Jinzai Kiyoshi. "Mishima Yukio: Kamen to kokuhaku to." In *Jinzai Kiyoshi zenshū*, vol. 6, 479–82. Tokyo: Bunjidō shoten, 1976.
---. "Narushishizumu no unmei." In *Jinzai Kiyoshi zenshū*, vol. 6, 482–93. Tokyo: Bunjidō shoten, 1976.
Kakinuma Eiko. *Tanbi shōsetsu, gei bungaku bukku gaido*. 1st ed. Tokyo: Byakuya shobō, 1993.
Kamei Hideo. "'An Oddball Rich in Dreams': Mori Ōgai and His Critics." In *Transformations of Sensibility: The Phenomenology of Meiji Literature*, ed. Michael K. Bourdaghs, 67–85. Ann Arbor, MI: Center for Japanese Studies, University of Michigan, 2002.
---. "The Disappearance of the Non-Person Narrator: Changing Sensibilities in Futabatei Shimei." In *Transformations of Sensibility: The Phenomenology of Meiji Literature*, ed. Michael K. Bourdaghs, 1–22. Ann Arbor, MI: Center for Japanese Studies, University of Michigan, 2002.
Karatani Kōjin. *Origins of Modern Japanese Literature*. Post-Contemporary Interventions. Durham, NC: Duke University Press, 1993.
---. "Sōseki's Diversity: On *Kokoro*." In *Contemporary Japanese Thought*, ed. Richard Calichman, 119–29. Weatherhead Books on Asia. New York, NY: Columbia University Press, 2005.
Kawabata Yasunari. *Shōnen*. In *Kawabata Yasunari zenshū*, vol. 10, 141–256. Tokyo: Shinchōsha, 1980.
---. "*Shōnen*-shō." In *Kawabata Yasunari*, ed. Saeki Shōichi and Matsumoto Ken'ichi, 57–76. Sakka no jiden 15. Tokyo: Nihon tosho sentā, 1994.

———. *The Dancing Girl of Izu and Other Stories*. Trans. J. Martin Holman. Washington, DC: Counterpoint, 1998.

———. *The House of the Sleeping Beauties and Other Stories*. Tokyo: Kodansha International, 2004.

Kern, Adam L. *Manga from the Floating World: Comicbook Culture and the Kibyōshi of Edo Japan*. Harvard East Asian Monographs 279. Cambridge, MA: Harvard University Asia Center, 2006.

Kimura Naoe. *"Seinen" no tanjō: Meiji Nihon ni okeru seijiteki jissen no tenkan*. 1st ed. Tokyo: Shin'yōsha, 1998.

Kōda Rohan. *Pagoda, Skull, and Samurai: 3 Stories by Kōda Rohan*. Trans. Chieko Irie Mulhern. Rutland, VT: Charles E. Tuttle Company, 1985.

———. *Hige otoko*. In *Rohan zenshū*, vol. 5. Tokyo: Iwanami shoten, 1978.

Komashaku, Kimi. "Towards an Absolute State: Marriage in Sōseki's *Kōjin*." *U.S.-Japan Women's Journal*, no. 3 (1992): 54–83.

Komori Yōichi. "Hyōshō to shite no nanshoku." In *Ōgai no sakuhin*, vol. 2, 235–58. Kōza Mori Ōgai. Tokyo: Shin'yōsha, 1997.

———. "*Kokoro* ni okeru dōseiai to iseiai." In *Sōryoku tōron: Sōseki no* Kokoro, ed. Komori Yōichi et al, 141–65. Tokyo: Kanrin shobō, 1993.

———. "*Kokoro* ni okeru hanten suru 'shuki.'" In *Kōzō toshite no katari*, 415–40. Tokyo: Shin'yōsha, 1988.

———. "Nakagaki." In *Sōryoku tōron: Sōseki no* Kokoro, ed. Komori Yōichi et al, 113. Tokyo: Kanrin shobō, 1993.

Koyano Atsushi. "*Kokoro* wa dōseiai shōsetsu ka?" In *Natsume Sōseki o Edo kara yomu*, 173–210. Tokyo: Chūō kōronsha, 1995.

Kuroiwa Yūichi. "'Nanshoku' to 'hentai seiyoku no aida': 'Akuma no deshi' to 'Kotō no oni' ni okeru dansei dōseiai no hyōshō." *Hitotsubashi ronsō* 134, no. 3 (2005): 374–93.

———. "'Homosexuel' no dōnyū to sono hen'yō." *Ronshō kuia* 1 (2008): 57–76.

———. "Hori Tatsuo 'Moyuru hoo' no dansei dōseiai hyōshō: Maruseru Purūsuto 'Sodomu to gomora' 1 to no hikaku kara." In *Bunka hyōshō o yomu: jendā kenkyū no genzai*, ed. Ochanomizu daigaku 21-seiki COE program jendā kenkyū no furontia Project D "Nihon bungaku ryōiki," 33–41. Tokyo: Ochanomizu daigaku 21-seiki COE program jendā kenkyū no furontia, 2008.

Laplanche, Jean, and Jean-Bertrand Pontalis. *The Language of Psychoanalysis*. Trans. Donald Nicholson-Smith. New York: W. W. Norton, 1973.

Letourneau, Charles Jean Marie. *The Evolution of Marriage and of the Family*. London: W. Scott, 1891.

Litvak, Joseph. "Taste, Waste, Proust." In *Strange Gourmets: Sophistication, Theory, and the Novel*, 77–111. Durham, NC: Duke University Press, 1997.

Maeda Ai. "Berlin 1888: Mori Ōgai's 'Dancing Girl.'" In *Text and the City: Essays on Japanese Modernity*, ed. James A. Fujii, 295–328. Durham, NC: Duke University Press, 2004.

Marcus, Marvin. *Paragons of the Ordinary: The Biographical Literature of Mori Ōgai*. SHAPS Library of Asian Studies. Honolulu, HI: University of Hawai'i Press, 1993.

Martin, Biddy. "Extraordinary Homosexuals and the Fear of Being Ordinary." *Differences: A Journal of Feminist Cultural Studies* 6, no. 2–3 (1994): 100–125.

Matz, Jesse. "Maurice in Time." *Style* 34, no. 2 (2000): 188–211.

———. "'You Must Join My Dead': E. M. Forster and the Death of the Novel." *Modernism/Modernity* 9, no. 2 (April 2002): 303–17.
McClellan, Edwin. "The Implications of Soseki's *Kokoro*." *Monumenta Nipponica* 14, no. 3/4 (October 1, 1958): 356–70.
McDonald, Keiko. "The Wild Geese Revisited: Mori Ōgai's Mix of Old and New." In *Inexorable Modernity: Japan's Grappling with Modernity in the Arts*, ed. Hiroshi Nara, 201–15. Lanham, MD: Lexington Books, 2007.
McLelland, Mark J. *Queer Japan from the Pacific War to the Internet Age*. Lanham, MD: Rowman and Littlefield, 2005.
Merivale, Patricia. "Silences: Soseki Natsume's *Kokoro* and Canadian Elegiac Romance." In *Nature and Identity in Canadian and Japanese Literature*, ed. Kinya Tsuruta and Theodore Goosen, 127–41. Toronto, ON: University of Toronto and York University Joint Center for Asia Pacific Studies, 1988.
Miller, D. A. "Anal Rope." In *Inside/out: Lesbian Theories, Gay Theories*, ed. Diana Fuss, 119–41. New York: Routledge, 1991.
———. *Narrative and Its Discontents: Problems of Closure in the Traditional Novel*. Princeton, NJ: Princeton University Press, 1981.
Minakata Kumagusu and Iwata Jun'ichi. "Morning Fog (Correspondence on Gay Lifestyles)." In *Partings at Dawn*, trans. William Sibley, 134–71. San Francisco, CA: Gay Sunshine Press, 1996.
Mishima Yukio. *Confessions of a Mask*. Trans. Meredith Weatherby. New York: New Directions, 1958.
———. "Shin ren'ai kōza." In *Mishima Yukio hyōron zenshū*, vol. 4, 361–435. Tokyo: Shinchōsha, 1989.
———. *Forbidden Colors*. Trans. Alfred H. Marks. New York: Vintage International, 1999.
———. *Kamen no kokuhaku*. In *Ketteiban: Mishima Yukio zenshū*, vol. 1, 167–364. Tokyo: Shinchōsha, 2000.
———. *Kinjiki*. In *Ketteiban: Mishima Yukio zenshū*, vol. 3. Tokyo: Shinchōsha, 2000.
Miyakawa Takeo. "Saiwa sareta *Kokoro*." In *Sōryoku tōron: Sōseki no Kokoro*, ed. Komori Yōichi et al, 179–201. Tokyo: Kanrin shobō, 1994.
Miyazaki Kasumi. "Erosu no tsumi to norowareta kako: *Mon* ni yomu erosu no kindaiteki hensei to otokotachi no yokubō no yukue." *Bungaku* 5, no. 1 (2004): 183–210.
Miyoshi, Masao. *Accomplices of Silence: The Modern Japanese Novel*. Berkeley, CA: University of California Press, 1974.
———. *Off Center: Power and Culture Relations between Japan and the United States*. Cambridge, MA: Harvard University Press, 1991.
Miyoshi Yukio. "'Sensei' wa kokyu ka?" *Kaien* 5, no. 11 (1986): 190–91.
———. "Watoson wa haishinsha ka?: *Kokoro* saisetsu." *Bungaku* 56, no. 5 (1988): 7–21.
Mizumura, Minae. "Resisting Woman: Reading Sōseki's *Gubijinsō*." In *Studies in Modern Japanese Literature: Essays and Translations in Honor of Edwin McClellan*, ed. Dennis Washburn and Alan Tansman, 23–37. Michigan Monograph Series in Japanese Studies 20. Ann Arbor, MI: University of Michigan Press, 1997.
Moffat, Wendy. *A Great Unrecorded History: A New Life of E.M. Forster*. 1st ed. New York: Farrar, Straus and Giroux, 2010.
Mori Ōgai. *Vita Sexualis*. Trans. Kazuji Ninomiya and Sanford Goldstein. Tokyo: Charles Tuttle Company, 1972.
———. *Ōgai zenshū*. 38 vols. Tokyo: Iwanami shoten, 1981.

———. *Youth and Other Stories*. Trans. J. Thomas Rimer. Honolulu, HI: University of Hawai'i Press, 1994.

———. *The Wild Goose*. Trans. Burton Watson. Michigan Monograph Series in Japanese Studies 14. Ann Arbor, MI: Center for Japanese Studies, University of Michigan, 1995.

Mori Ōgai and Kawamura Keikichi. *Seiyoku zassetsu*. In *Ōgai igaku zuihitsu hyōron zenshū*. Vol. 1. Tokyo: Nihon iji shinpō shuppanbu, 1949.

Morimoto Takako. "*Kōjin*-ron: Romanchikku rabu no haitai to homosōshiariti no kihi." *Sōseki kenkyū*, no. 15 (2002): 59–75.

Muramatsu Takeshi. *Mishima Yukio no sekai*. Tokyo: Shinchōsha, 1990.

Mushanokōji Saneatsu. *Friendship*. Trans. Ryūzō Matsumoto. Tokyo: Hokuseidō Press, 1958.

———. *Yūjō, Ai to Shi: (hoka) Chiisaki sekai*. 1st ed. Tokyo: Ōbunsha, 1965.

Nakano Takehiko. "*Kamen no kokuhaku* ron." *Kindai bungaku* (January 1954): 69–71.

Nakayama Kazuko. "*Sorekara*: Natsume Sōseki 'shizen no mukashi' to wa nani ka." *Kokubungaku kaishaku to kyōzai no kenkyū* 36, no. 1 (1991): 64–66.

———. "*Sorekara*: 'shizen no mukashi' to homosōsharu na yokubō." In *Sōseki, josei, jendā*, 80–91. Nakayama Kazuko korekushon 1. Tokyo: Kanrin shobō, 2003.

Narushima Ryūhoku. *New Chronicles of Yanagibashi and Diary of a Journey to the West: Narushima Ryūhoku Reports from Home and Abroad*. Trans. Matthew Fraleigh. Cornell East Asia Series 151. Ithaca, NY: East Asia Program, Cornell University, 2010.

Natsume Sōseki. *And Then: Natsume Sōseki's Novel Sorekara*. Trans. Norma Moore Field. Michigan Classics in Japanese Studies 17. Ann Arbor, MI: Center for Japanese Studies, University of Michigan, 1997.

———. *Botchan*. Trans. Matt Trevaud. Richmond, IN: Ray Ontko & Co., 2009. Kindle edition.

———. *Inside My Glass Doors*. 1st ed. Boston, MA: Tuttle, 2002.

———. *Kokoro*. Trans. Edwin McClellan. Chicago: Henry Regnery, 1957.

———. *Kokoro*. Vol. 9 of *Sōseki zenshū*. Tokyo: Iwanami shoten, 1993.

———. *Kokoro*. Vol. 12 of *Sōseki bungaku zenchūshaku*, ed. Ishihara Chiaki, Nakajima Kunihiko, and Fujii Hidetada. Tokyo: Wakakusa shobō, 2000.

———. *Kokoro*. Trans. Meredith McKinney. New York: Penguin, 2010.

———. *Sōseki zenshū*. 29 vols. Tokyo: Iwanami shoten, 1993–96.

———. *Ten Nights of Dream, Hearing Things, the Heredity of Taste*. Trans. Aiko Itō and Graeme Wilson. Rutland, VT: Tuttle, 1974.

———. *Theory of Literature and Other Critical Writings*. Ed. Michael K Bourdaghs, Atsuko Ueda, and Joseph A Murphy. New York: Columbia University Press, 2009.

———. *To the Spring Equinox and Beyond*. Trans. Kingo Ochiai and Sanford Goldstein. Tuttle Classics. Boston, MA: Tuttle, 2004.

———. *The Wayfarer (Kōjin)*. Trans. Beongcheon Yu. Detroit, MI: Wayne State University Press, 1967.

Nishimura Suimu. "Shō rekishi-ka." In *Ansoroji bungei sakuhin ni egakareta dōseiai*, ed. Furukawa Makoto, 2–45. Kindai Nihon no sekushuariti 35. Tokyo: Yumani shobō, 2009.

Noguchi Takehiko. *Mishima Yukio no sekai*. Tokyo: Kōdansha, 1968.

Ōe Kenzaburō. *Kojin-teki na taiken*. Tokyo: Shinchō bunko, 1981.

———. *A Personal Matter*. Trans. John Nathan. New York: Grove Press, 1969.

Ogikubo Yasuyuki. "Kawabata Yasunari/Mishima Yukio: *Shōnen* to *Kamen no kokuhaku*." *Kokubungaku kaishaku to kanshō* 31:8 (1966): 138–40.

Ōhashi Yōichi. "Kuiā fāzāzu no yume, kuiā neishon no yume: *Kokoro* to homosōsharu." *Sōseki kenkyū*, no. 6 (1996): 46–59.

Oishi Naoki. "Mori Ōgai *Gan* shiron: katarite 'boku' no isō to 'monogatari' no sosei." *Kokugo to kokubungaku* 73, no. 2 (1996): 42–55.

Orbaugh, Sharalyn. "General Nogi's Wife: Representations of Women in Narratives of Japanese Modernization." In *In Pursuit of Contemporary East Asian Culture*, ed. Stephen Snyder and Xiaobing Tang, 7–31. Boulder, CO: Westview Press, 1996.

Oshino Takeshi. "Isho no shohō: pen to noizu." In *Sōryoku tōron: Sōseki no Kokoro*, ed. Komori Yōichi et al, 166–78. Tokyo: Kanrin shobō, 1994.

Ōta Tsubasa. "*Kaijin* ni okeru nanshoku-teki yōso." *Bungaku kenkyū ronshū* 21 (2004): 163–76.

———. "Mishima Yukio *Kamen no kokuhaku* ron: kakō sareta kokuhaku." *Bunka keishōgaku ronshū* 2 (2005): 88–78.

———. "Mori Ōgai *Seinen* ron: 'seinen' to 'bishōnen.'" *Bungaku kenkyū ronshū* 23 (2005): 251–63.

———. "Origuchi Shinobu 'Kuchibue' shiron: shintai ishiki no henka to ikyō e no dōkei." *Bungaku kenkyū ronshū* 26 (n.d.): 225–34.

Pak Yuha. *Nashonaru aidentiti to jendā: Sōseki, bungaku, kindai*. Tokyo: Tosho shuppan Kurein, 2007.

Pflugfelder, Gregory M. *Cartographies of Desire: Male-Male Sexuality in Japanese Discourse*. Berkeley, CA: University of California Press, 1999.

Phelan, James. *Living to Tell about It: A Rhetoric and Ethics of Character Narration*. Ithaca, NY: Cornell University Press, 2005.

Proust, Marcel. *The Way by Swann's*. Trans. Lydia Davis. London: Penguin Books, 2003.

———. *Du côté de chez Swann*. Paris: Éditions Gallimard, 1954.

Reed, Barbara Mito. "Chikamatsu Shūkō: An Inquiry into Narrative Modes in Modern Japanese Fiction." *Journal of Japanese Studies*, no. 14 (Winter 1988): 59–76.

Reichert, Jim. *In the Company of Men: Representations of Male-Male Sexuality in Meiji Literature*. Stanford, CA: Stanford University Press, 2006.

Robertson, Jennifer. "Dying to Tell: Sexuality and Suicide in Imperial Japan." In *Queer Diasporas*, ed. Cindy Patton, 38–70. Durham, NC: Duke University Press, 2000.

Routledge Encyclopedia of Narrative Theory. Ed. David Herman, Manfred Jahn, and Marie-Laure Ryan. London: Routledge, 2005.

Sakaki, Atsuko. "The Debates on *Kokoro*: A Cornerstone." In *Recontextualizing Texts: Narrative Performance in Modern Japanese Fiction*, 29–54. Harvard East Asian Monographs 180. Cambridge, MA: Harvard University Asia Center, 1999.

———. "Thinking Beauty, Unseeing Scholar: Displaced Narrative Authority in Mori Ōgai's *Gan*." In *Recontextualizing Texts: Narrative Performance in Modern Japanese Literature*, 137–81. Harvard East Asian Monographs 180. Cambridge, MA: Harvard University Asia Center, 1999.

Sakuta Keiichi. "Nihon no shōsetsu ni arawareta sansha kankei." In *Kojin shugi no unmei: kindai shakai to shakaigaku*, 131–86. Iwanami shinsho. Tokyo: Iwanami shoten, 1981.

Sasaki Hideaki. "Otoko no kizuna: *Kōjin* no dōseishakai-teki na shakai." In *"Atarashii Onna" no tōrai: Hiratsuka Raichō to Sōseki*, 305–23. 1st ed. Nagoya: Nagoya daigaku shuppankai, 1994.

Satō Hideaki. "Jiko o kataru shisō: *Kamen no kokuhaku* no hōhō." *Kokugo to kokubungaku* 83, no. 11 (2006): 119–31.

Satō, Hiroaki. "Suppressing more than free speech." *Japan Times Online*, December 29, 2008. http://search.japantimes.co.jp/cgi-bin/eo20081229hs.html.

Satō Izumi. *Kokugo kyōkasho no sengoshi.* 1st ed. Shirīzu kotoba to shakai 4. Tokyo: Keisō shobō, 2006.

———. *Sōseki: katazukanai "kindai."* NHK raiburari 145. Tokyo: NHK shuppan, 2002.

Schalow, Paul Gordon. "The Invention of a Literary Tradition of Male Love: Kitamura Kigin's *Iwatsutsuji.*" *Monumenta Nipponica* 48, no. 1 (1993): 1–31.

Schor, Naomi. *Reading in Detail: Aesthetics and the Feminine.* New York: Methuen, 1987.

Sedgwick, Eve Kosofsky. *Between Men: English Literature and Male Homosocial Desire.* New York: Columbia University Press, 1985.

———. *Epistemology of the Closet.* Berkeley, CA: University of California Press, 1990.

———. "Willa Cather and Others." In *Tendencies*, 167–76. Durham, NC: Duke University Press, 1993.

———. *Kurozetto no ninshikiron: sekushuariti no 20-seiki.* Trans. Tonoka Naomi. Tokyo: Seidosha, 1999.

———. *Otokodōshi no kizuna: Igirisu bungaku to homosōsharu na yokubō.* Trans. Uehara Sanae and Kanazawa Miyuki. Nagoya: Nagoya daigaku shuppankai, 2001.

———. "Shame, Theatricality, Queer Performativity: Henry James's *The Art of the Novel.*" In *Touching Feeling: Affect, Pedagogy, Performativity*, 35–65. Durham, NC: Duke University Press, 2003.

———. "Paranoid Reading and Reparative Reading; or, You're So Paranoid You Probably Think This Essay Is About You." In *Touching Feeling: Affect, Pedagogy, Performativity*, 123–52. Durham, NC: Duke University Press, 2003.

Sedgwick, Eve Kosofsky, Adam Frank, and Irving E. Alexander. *Shame and Its Sisters: A Silvan Tomkins Reader.* Durham, NC: Duke University Press, 1995.

Sekine Shin'ichi. *Shin Kokoro.* Unpublished playscript, 2008.

Sezaki Keiji. "Umibe no homososhiariti: aruiwa sono karetsu ni tsuite." *Kindai bungaku shiron*, no. 47 (2009): 15–49.

Shirane, Haruo, ed. *Early Modern Japanese Literature: An Anthology, 1600–1900*, Translations from the Asian classics. New York: Columbia University Press, 2002.

Sibley, William F. Review of Reichert, *In the Company of Men: Representations of Male-Male Sexuality in Meiji Literature*. *Modern Philology* 106, no. 2 (November 1, 2008): 327–32.

Snyder, Stephen. *Fictions of Desire: Narrative Form in the Novels of Nagai Kafū.* Honolulu, HI: University of Hawai'i Press, 2000.

Steiner, George. *After Babel: Aspects of Language and Translation.* 3rd ed. New York: Oxford University Press, 1998.

Stockton, Kathryn. *The Queer Child, or Growing Sideways in the Twentieth Century.* Durham, NC: Duke University Press, 2009.

Sugimoto Kazuhiro. "Kamen no kokuhaku ron: Sonoko to no monogatari o megutte." In *Mishima Yukio no hyōgen*, ed. Matsumoto Tōru, Satō Hideaki, and Inoue Takashi, vol. 2, 204–20. Mishima Yukio ronshū. Tokyo: Bensei shuppan, 2001.

Suzuki, Michiko. *Becoming Modern Women: Love and Female Identity in Prewar Japanese Literature and Culture.* Stanford, CA: Stanford University Press, 2010.

———. "Writing Same-Sex Love: Sexology and Literary Representation in Yoshiya Nobuko's Early Fiction." *Journal of Asian Studies* 65, no. 3 (2006): 575–99.

Suzuki, Tomi. *Narrating the Self: Fictions of Japanese Modernity*. Stanford, CA: Stanford University Press, 1996.
Takahara Eiri. *Muku no chikara: "shōnen" hyōshō bungakuron*. Tokyo: Kōdansha, 2003.
Takeuchi Kayo. "Mishima Yukio *Kamen no kokuhaku* to iu hyōshō o megutte: 1950-nen zengo no dansei dōseiai hyōshō ni kansuru kōsatsu." *F-GENS jānaru* 9 (September 2007): 111–17.
Tanaka Michiko. "Kaidai to kōtei." In *Kettei-ban: Mishima Yukio zenshū*, vol. 1, 659–706. Tokyo: Shinchōsha, 2000.
Tanizaki Jun'ichirō. "The Children." In *The Gourmet Club: A Sextet*, trans. Anthony Chambers, 15–46. New York: Kodansha International, 2003.
———. *Quicksand*. Trans. Howard Hibbett. 1st ed. New York: Knopf, 1994.
Tan'o Yasunori. *Nanshoku no keshiki: iwaneba koso are*. Tokyo: Shinchōsha, 2008.
Tayama Katai. *The Quilt and Other Stories by Tayama Katai*. Trans. by Kenneth G. Henshall. Tokyo: University of Tokyo Press, 1981.
The Plum in the Golden Vase, or, Chin P'ing Mei. Vol. 1, *The Gathering*. Trans. David Tod Roy. Princeton library of Asian translations. Princeton, NJ: Princeton University Press, 1997.
Ubukata Tomoko. "*Wita Sekusuaris* nanshoku no mondai-kei." In *Seishin bunseki izen: muishiki no Nihon kindai bungaku*, 143–58. Tokyo: Kanrin shobō, 2009.
Ueda, Atsuko. "Colonial Ambivalence and the Modern *Shōsetsu*: *Shōsetsu shinzui* and De-Asianization." In *Impacts of Modernities*, ed. Thomas Lamarre and Kang Nae-hui, 179–206. Traces: a multilingual series of cultural theory and translation 3. Hong Kong: Hong Kong University Press, 2004.
———. "The Production of Literature and the Effaced Realm of the Political." *Journal of Japanese Studies* 31, no. 1 (2005): 61–88.
Ueno Chizuko. "Gei to feminizumu wa kyōtō dekiru ka." In *Hatsujō sōchi: erosu no shinario*, 241–58. Tokyo: Chikuma shobō, 1998.
Ueno Chizuko, Ogura Chikako, and Tomioka Taeko. *Danryū bungakuron*. Tokyo: Chikuma shobō, 1992.
Uno Kōji. "Futari no Aoki Aizaburō." In *Uno Kōji zenshū*, vol. 3, ed. Hirotsu Kazuo et al, 196–241. Tokyo: Chūō kōronsha, 1968.
Van Compernolle, Timothy J. *The Uses of Memory: The Critique of Modernity in the Fiction of Higuchi Ichiyō*. Cambridge, MA: Harvard University Asia Center, 2006.
Varela, Francisco J., Evan Thompson, and Eleanor Rosch. *The Embodied Mind: Cognitive Science and Human Experience*. Cambridge, MA: MIT Press, 1991.
Viglielmo, Valdo. "*Kokoro*: A Descent into the Heart of Man." In *Approaches to the Modern Japanese Novel*, ed. Kinya Tsuruta and Thomas E. Swann. Tokyo: Sophia University Press, 1976.
Vincent, J. Keith. "Hamaosociality: Narrative and Fascism in Hamao Shirō's 'The Devil's Disciple.'" In *The Culture of Japanese Fascism*, ed. Alan Tansman, 381–408. Durham, NC: Duke University Press, 2009.
———. "The Novel and the End of Homosocial Literature." *PAJLS: Proceedings of the Association for Japanese Literary Studies*, no. 9 (2008): 230–39.
———. "A Japanese Electra and Her Queer Progeny." *Mechademia* 2 (December 2007): 64–79.
Washburn, Dennis C. *The Dilemma of the Modern in Japanese Fiction*. New Haven, CT: Yale University Press, 1995.

Yasuda Tokutarō. "Dōseiai no rekishikan." In *Senzenki dōseiai kanren bunken shūsei*, vol. 3, 320–23. Tokyo: Fuji shuppan, 2006.

Yoda, Tomiko. "First-Person Narration and Citizen-Subject: The Modernity of Ōgai's 'The Dancing Girl.'" *Journal of Asian Studies* 65, no. 2 (2006): 277–306.

———. "The Rise and Fall of Maternal Society: Gender, Labor, and Capital in Contemporary Japan." *South Atlantic Quarterly* 99, no. 4 (Fall 2000): 865–902.

———. *Gender and National Literature: Heian Texts in the Constructions of Japanese Modernity*. Durham, NC: Duke University Press, 2004.

Index

Abe Auestad, Reiko, 87–88n, 110n
"The Abe Family" ["Abe Ichizoku"], 84–85
Abelove, Henry, 143n
absentmindedness. *See* mindlessness
adolescence, 25–31, 88, 139n, 178–79
Adon (magazine), 115
Ahmed, Sarah, 118n
Aida Hirotsugu, 99–100
AIDS, 173n, 174, 178
The Anatomy of Dependence [*Amae no kōzō*], 89, 140, 144n
And Then [*Sorekara*], 13, 131n
Angles, Jeffrey, 8, 26n, 32n, 172n
Ara Masato, 180–81
Ariwara no Narihira, 17
Armstrong, Nancy, 74n
Atogami Shirō, 175, 182, 197
authorial audience, 59

"The Bearded Samurai" ["Hige otoko"], 60
Bellamy, Dodie, 153
Bersani, Leo, 5, 189
Bester, John, 144n
"Beyond the Pleasure Principle," 147, 149, 149n
bisexuality (in Freud's *Three Essays on Sexuality*), 33

bishōnen, 8, 47n
The Blue Stockings [*Seitō*], 53
Botchan, 90, 143n, 209
The Boy [*Shōnen*], 1–2, 10–11, 15, 25–31, 153, 178, 187n
Brooks, Peter, 5, 149n
Browning, Robert, 59
Bruffee, Kenneth, 63–65, 72, 121–22
Butler, Judith, 9n, 134n

Carpenter, Edward, 154
Case, Alison, 78n
Cather, Willa, 134n
Cavafy, Constantine, 176
Chambers, Anthony, 1n
character narration, 59
Chinese literature, rejection of, 71–72, 129
Chow, Rey, 68n
chrononormativity, 117
"The Chrysanthemum Vow" ["Kikka no chigiri"], 205n
closure (in Soseki's novels), 118–19
Confessions of a Mask [*Kamen no kokuhaku*], 22; as homosexual literature, 175–77; as men's literature, 180; as heterosexual love story, 181–82; as hybrid of I-novel and homosocial narrative, 184–85; comparison to Proust, 188–91; and unmediated desire, 191–95

"Confessions of Ranpo" ["Ranpo uchi-akebanashi"], 30
A Connecticut Yankee in King Arthur's Court (Twain), 127n

"The Dancing Girl" ["Maihime"], 56, 57n, 58, 73–74
The Dancing Girl of Izu [*Izu no odoriko*], 10, 10n, 27–28
Davis, Darrell William, 85
deferred action (*Nachträglichkeit*), 141
The Devil's Disciple ["Akuma no deshi"], 21–22, 152–54; plot summary, 155, 191, 194, 200, 209
Don Quixote (Cervantes), 16–17, 18, 66, 124, 164, 190n
disclosure functions, 59, 60, 61
Dodd, Stephen, 88, 89, 115, 118, 140, 144n
Doi Takeo, 89, 114, 140
A Doll's House (Ibsen), 53
Drake, Robert, 176
Driscoll, Mark, 33n, 48n

Edelman, Lee, 144n, 170–73
Edogawa Ranpo, 6, 8n, 30–31, 32n, 154, 162
elegiac romance, 63–65, 68, 72, 75, 78, 120–23, 138, 142, 148
Ellis, Havelock, 89, 154
Embracing Family [*Hōyō kazoku*], 183
enactment (in cognitive psychology), 44n
Epistemology of the Closet (Sedgwick), 3n, 11, 85n, 173, 189n
Etō Jun, 95–96, 99, 201n
Esty, Jed, 183n
The Evolution of Marriage and the Family (Letourneau), 89
external mediation, 16–17, 38–39, 48n, 65n, 123–26, 131, 166n, 193

feminism, 53n, 55, 97, 209–11
Fitzgerald, F. Scott, 62, 64
"Five-Storied Pagoda," ["Gojū no tō"], 59–60
Flying Stage Theater Company, 116

focalization, 54, 77n, 183, 184
Forbidden Colors [*Kinjiki*], 177, 195–96
Ford, Maddox Ford, 123
Forster, E. M., 6n, 14n, 176
Foucault, Michel, 11, 46
Fowler, Edward, 183–84, 184n
Fraleigh, Matthew, 16n
Frederick, Sarah, 167n
Freeman, Elizabeth, 117
Freud, Sigmund, 33–34, 48–50 *passim*, 139–40, 142–43n, 144, 147–50 *passim*, 160–61, 173n, 187
free indirect discourse, 52
Friendship [*Yūjō*], 7
From Within My Glass Doors [*Garasudo no naka*], 88
Fujii, James, 120n, 127
Fujimori Kiyoshi, 4n
Fukuda Kōson, 177
Fukushima Jirō, 176–77, 195–96
Furukawa Makoto, 4n, 183n
Fushimi Noriaki, 176, 196, 197–98
Futabatei Shimei, 7, 18n

The Gate [*Mon*], 91, 98
gay child, 15n
gay homosociality, 114–19, 197
gay past. *See* queer past
gay readers/reading, 61, 62, 176–77
gay underground, 177, 195, 198
Genette, Gérard, 77, 77n
Genji, 17, 28, 130
genre, 122, 183n
Girard, René, 15–20
The Good Soldier (Ford), *123*
gothic homosociality, 162–68
Grass by the Wayside [*Michikusa*], 118
The Great Gatsby (Fitzgerald), 62, 64, 75, 121
Grilled and Basted Edo-Born Playboy [*Edo umare uwaki no kabayaki*], 16n, 17
Guillén, Claudio, 121–23

Hall, G. Stanley, 25n, 139n
Halperin, David, 159n
Hamao Shirō, 8n, 21–22, 154, 172–73
Hara Hiroshi, 115

Hartley, Barbara, 1n, 8, 10, 27
Hashimoto Osamu, 11n, 114–15, 188, 140
Heike, Tales of the [*Heike monogatari*], 60n
"The Heredity of Taste" ["Shumi no iden"], 123–28, 142, 144, 150, 193
hero worship, 5, 16–17, 64–65, 72, 75, 99, 121–31 *passim*, 138, 193
Herrero-Brasas, Juan A., 88n
heterodiegetic narration, 19, 52, 56, 61, 66, 77, 200
heteronormative narrative/reading, 6n, 14n, 49, 58–61, 61n, 164,
heterosociality, 40, 63, 83, 90–91, 120, 144
Higuchi Ichiyō, 53
Hill, Christopher, 74n
Hirata, Hosea, 120
Hiratsuka Raichō, 53
Hirschfeld, Magnus, 32, 32n, 154, 181n
homodiegetic narration, 19–20, 61, 65, 81, 185
homophobia, 58, 88n, 91n, 162–65 *passim*, 169–74 *passim*, 178, 209–11
homosexuality: Japanese translations of, 48–49; as perverse desire, 154; as sexual orientation, 175; as abnormal sexuality, 176;
homosexual literature, 22, 115, 175–77, 180, 181n, 195
homosocial continuum: definition of, 3n; tension between two ends, 10–14 *passim*; charting the shape of, 24; rupture in Europe and U.S., 33; state of, circa 1911, 45, 51, 61, 62; in sixteenth-century Japan, 60; in *Kokoro*, 87–90 *passim*, 135, 138, 145; translation as index of, 100, 108, 113; yearning for, 116, 134; and disconnection from the past, 120; in "The Heredity of Taste," 123, 125, 127; in Meiji Japan, 91n; in *The Devil's Disciple*, 153–55 *passim*, 159; shift as a result of AIDS, 171, 174; rupture in *Confessions of a Mask*, 175, 200, 209, 211
homosocial desire: in Sedgwick, 3n, 11, 13; centrality to modern Japanese literature, 9; narratology of, 14; in *Vita Sexualis*, 39–42; and narrative enactment, 44; pleasures and perils of, 45; in *The Wild Goose*, 51, 82; and internal mediation, 133; relation to the gothic, 162–63
homosocial fold, 40, 124, 178
homosocial narrative: two-timing and, 2, 4, 24, 31, 34, 154, 176, 187, 200; definition of, 4, 19–20, 24–42; as national allegory, 34–35; *The Wild Goose* as, 50–51, 58, 62, 80–83; *Kokoro* as, 90–92, 151; reception of *Kokoro* as, 99; "The Heredity of Taste" as, 123; in normative mode, 153, 205, 206; *The Devil's Disciple* as, 164; *Confessions of a Mask* and, 178, 182, 185, 198; personification of, 179; and ideology of sexual development, 181; temporality of, 184; afterlife of, 201, 209
homosocial triangle, 5, 7, 12, 16, 37–38, 40n, 81, 132
homosociality (male): varieties of, 4–5; stereoscopic, 5, 58, 80; patriarchal, 5, 93–100; Oedipal, 5, 100–105; gothic, 5, 162–68; gay, 5, 114–17, 197; in *The Wayfarer*, 8–9n; distinction from homosexuality, 12–14, 210; and the seashore, 50n; formal, 58; internally mediated, 58, 128, 132–33, 142; pre-modern, 74, 126; externally mediated, 127–28; romantic/novelistic, 65–73, 85; primal scene of, 90, 144–45; Sharalyn Orbaugh on, 98n; narratology of, 105–6; insomniac, 168–a70
Hori Tatsuo, 4n, 6, 8n
Hosoya, Hiroshi, 77n
"The House of Sleeping Beauties" ["Nemureru bijo"], 10
Hwang, Jon-yong, 70n

I Am a Cat [*Wagahai wa neko de aru*], 90
I-novel, 20n, 182–85, 183n, 190n,
Ibsen, Henrik, 53
Ihara Saikaku, 16n, 17
Iida Yūko, 8–9, 11n
Inagaki Taruho, 8n

insomniac homosociality, 168–70
interiority, 37, 40, 53, 60, 73, 74, 81, 132, 189
internalization, 163
internal mediation, 17–19, 130–34, 166–67
inversion, 181n
Ishihara Chiaki, 101–2, 105–14 *passim*, 118
"It Gets Better" campaign, 117
Ito, Ken, 128n, 150
Iwamoto Yoshio, 201
Iwata Jun'ichi, 25, 30, 154n

Jacobowitz, Seth, 30–31
James, Henry, 11, 188–89
Jameson, Fredric, 34n
Jinzai Kiyoshi, 180

Kamei Hideo, 83n
Karatani Kōjin, 83n, 84, 132n
Kawabata Yasunari, 1–2, 6, 10, 15, 25–31, 153, 178, 187n
Kawakami Bizan, 43, 45
Ken'yūsha, 45n
Kern, Adam, 17n
kibyōshi, 15
Kimura Naoe, 80n
Kitamura Kigin, 28
knowingness, 159n
Kōda Rohan, 47n, 59–60
kōha/nanpa typology, 46–47, 52, 54
Kojima Nobuo, 183
Kokoro: plot summary, 92–93; paternalistic homosocial reading of, 93–100, canonization in textbooks, 95n, 147; Oedipal homosocial reading of, 100–114; translations of, 105–14; debates on, 106n; manuscript of, 109–10; gay homosocial reading of, 114–18; as elegiac romance, 121–23; comparison to "The Heredity of Taste," 123–28; internal mediation in, 130–34; resistance to closure, 146–51
kokubungaku, 105–6
Komashaku Kimi, 8, 97

Komori Yōichi, 46n, 100–114, 135, 138, 140, 148n, 151
Koyano Atsushi, 99
Krafft-Ebing, Richard von, 47, 49
Kuroiwa Yūichi, 4n, 8n, 48, 49n, 154,

Laplanche and Pontalis, 141
"Les joues en feu" ["Moyuru hoo"], 4n, 6n
Letourneau, Charles, 89
Life of a Sensuous Man [*Kōshoku ichidai otoko*], 16n, 17
Light and Darkness [*Meian*], 90, 96n, 110n
"Literature and the Heroic" ["Bungei to hiroikku"], 122
The Little Historian [*Shō rekishi-ka*], 35–37
Maeda Ai, 83n
Marcus, Marvin, 85n
Martin, Biddy, 9n
Masaoka Shiki, 70, 72, 88
Matz, Jesse, 6n, 14n
Maurice (Forster), 6n, 14n, 176
McClellan, Edwin, 96–100 *passim*, 104, 106–14, 118–19, 122, 134–38 *passim*, 143–44, 145n, 148, 149
McDonald, Keiko, 49n
McKinney, Meredith, 100, 103n, 106–13 *passim*, 135, 137, 138, 148, 149
McLelland, Mark, 4n, 27
Meiji Emperor, 84, 93, 128
Meiji period, 15, 17, 35n, 44, 51, 70, 73, 91n, 117, 122
Memories of Yugashima [*Yugashima no omoide*], 10n, 27, 29
Merivale, Patricia, 114, 122
Miller, D. A., 208n
mimetic desire, 165–66, 167
Minakata Kumagusu, 25, 30
mindlessness, 40–42 *passim*, 82, 124, 168
minoritization/universalization (of male-male sexuality), 8, 21n, 22, 33, 62, 89, 178, 181n,
misogyny: critique of in Sōseki, 91, 97; link with homosociality and modernity, 98n; and *nanshoku*, 99; in *The Devil's Disciple*, 163, 165, 169; in Ōe's work, 201; in 1960s Japan, 203;

connection with homophobia, 209;
 in Mishima, 210–a11
Miyatake Gaikotsu, 33
Miyazaki Kasumi, 4n, 91n
Miyoshi, Masao, 20, 51n, 56, 73
Miyoshi Yukio, 96, 97–99, 102, 107, 108, 112
Mizumura, Minae, 90n
modernization, 34, 56, 70, 91n, 95n, 143, 200
Moon on the Lake Commentary [*Kogetsu-shō*], 28
Mori Kainan, 70
Morimoto Takako, 8, 13n
Mori Ōgai: as scholar of sexology, 47; reading of Freud, 48; translation of *A Doll's House*, 53; experiments with narrative, 56–57; attitude towards women, 73; anachronism in, 84–85; debate with Tsubouchi Shōyō, 85; historical fiction of, 84–85
Muenzaka, 82n
Muramatsu Takeshi, 181
Murayama Kaita, 8n
Mushanokōji Saneatsu, 6, 7
My Ántonia (Cather), 134n
"My Last Duchess" (Browning), 59

Nakano Takehiko, 196
Nakayama Kazuko, 8, 12–14
nanpa. See *kōha/nanpa* typology
narrators: in the Edo period, 15–16, 126; gender and sexuality of, 43–45
narratology: application to Sōseki's work, 105–6; of homosociality, 105–14
narrator functions, 59
nanshoku: prevalence in Satsuma, 36, 37; in *Vita Sexualis*, 46–47; in *The Youth*, 48; as latent, 46n; hierarchical nature, 98; and misogyny, 99; sexless form in *Kokoro*, 105, 135; in idealized form, 130, 157; lingering into modernity, 154; progression toward *dōseiai*, 156–59, 169; contrast with *ijō seiyoku*, 176; conflation with sodomy in *Confessions*, 194
Narushima Ryūhoku, 16n

Nathan, John, 204n, 206n, 207n
naturalism, 19, 45n, 47n, 122, 163, 185
naturalization (of narrative techniques), 58, 59, 59n, 65
nenja. See *wakashu/nenja* pairing
Niou, Prince, 17
Nishimura Suimu, 35
Nogi Maresuke, 84, 87n, 93, 95, 124, 125, 127
Nogi Shizuko, 93, 98, 98n
Noguchi Takehiko, 177
nonce taxonomies, 189

Oda Nobunaga, 32
Oedipal homosocial reading (of *Kokoro*), 100–114
Ōe Kenzaburō, 200–209
Ogikubo Yasuyuki, 178
Ogura Chikako, 177, 210
Ōhashi Yōichi, 115, 118
Ōishi Naoki, 77
Orbaugh, Sharalyn, 98n
Origuchi Shinobu, 6
Oshino Takeshi, 148n
Ōta Tsubasa, 4n, 8n, 87n, 197

paranoid reading, 173–74
paternalistic homosocial reading (of *Kokoro*), 93–100, 145
paternalism, crisis of, 201n
A Personal Matter [*Kojin-teki na taiken*], 200–209
perverse sexual desire [*hentai seiyoku*], 32, 154
perversion, 4n, 5, 33, 47n, 158, 171, 181n; temporality of, 206
Pflugfelder, Gregory, 4n, 24, 35n, 47n, 88
Phelan, James, 59, 61–62, 64–65
The Plum in the Golden Vase [*Jin Ping Mei*], 70
polymorphous perversion, 139
The Poppy [*Gubijinsō*], 90, 95n
Port Arthur, 123–24, 127
progress, critiques of, 2–4, 19, 23, 72–73, 105n, 127, 142–44, 169, 187
primal scene, 90, 144–45

Private Gay Life [*Puraibēto gei raifu*], 198
Proust, Marcel, 173, 188–89, 194
Psychopathia Sexualis (Krafft-Ebing), 47

queer past, 4, 14, 25, 30, 32n, 37
queer theory, 8–15, 103, 171–74
The Quilt [*Futon*], 18–19, 183
Quixote. *See Don Quixote*

À la recherche du temps perdu (Proust), 188–89
redundant telling, 59–61
Reed, Barbara Mito, 184
Reichert, Jim, 4n, 24, 47n, 60, 88
represssive hypothesis, 11
risshin shusse, 51
romance vs. novel, 65–73
romanticism, 18, 23, 39, 51, 64–73 *passim*, 105–6, 131–33, 163, 166
Rubin, Gayle, 8n

Saikaku. *See* Ihara Saikaku
Sakaki, Atsuko, 56–57, 71n, 79n, 81n, 105–7 *passim*, 144
Sakuta Keiichi, 130n, 132n
Santō Kyōden, 16, 17
Sasaki Hideaki, 8
Satō Hideaki, 181
Satō, Hiroaki, 177n
Satō Izumi, 95n, 99n
Satomi Ton, 6
Satsuma domain, 36, 37
Schor, Naomi, 68n
scripts, 21, 156, 164, 167n
In Search of the Supernatural [*Soushenji*], 67n
Sedgwick, Eve Kosofsky: on the homosocial continuum, 3; codified version of, 11–14; use of and critique of Girard, 15; later work on shame, 75, 194; "Axiom 5," 85; on homosocial triangles, 7, 132n; on the gothic, 162–63; on "canon of homophobic mastery," 173; on paranoid reading, 173–74; on the double bind, 182–83; on

Proust, James, and nonce taxonomies, 188–89; on gay men and feminism, 209–10
Seinan War, 93
Sekine Shin'ichi, 116–17, 197
sexology, 24, 25, 26, 32, 33n, 49, 88
sexual orientation, 12, 46, 166–67, 171, 175, 179, 189, 191
shame, 7, 22; and elegiac romance, 64–65; and identity, 75–77; *boku*'s shame, 79–80; in *The Devil's Disciple*, 155; in *Confessions of a Mask*, 179, 180, 193–94, 196
sharebon, 15
Shiga Naoya, 183
Shimazaki Tōson, 28
shudō, 15, 24, 32, 33, 34n, 37, 154
Sibley, William, 11, 25n, 52, 89n
Snyder, Stephen, 57, 73n
Steiner, George, 108
Sugimoto Kazuhiro, 182
Suzuki Miekichi, 115, 115n
Suzuki, Tomi, 95n, 183n

Takahara Eiri, 8
Takeuchi Kayo, 195
Tanaka Kōgai, 33
Tanizaki Jun'ichirō, 1n, 6, 98
Tan'o Yasunori, 116n
Tayama Katai, 18, 183
Theory of Literature [*Bungakuron*], 142
Three Essays on Sexuality (Freud), 33, 48, 50, 139, 142, 187n
To the Spring Equinox and Beyond [*Higan-sugi made*], 37–39, 49
Tokugawa Ieyasu, 32
Tomkins, Silvan, 75–76
Toyotomi Hideyoshi, 32
translation: of *The Dancing Girl of Izu*, 10n; of "homosexuality," 32, 48n, 49n; Ōgai's of Ibsen, 53; Etō Jun on, 99–100; as fossilized act of reading, 100; McClellan vs. McKinney's of *Kokoro*, 105–14, 188–19, 135, 137, 143–45, 148; George Steiner on, 108; of "invert," 181n; of *nanshoku-ka* as "sodomite," 194; queer affirmative

mistranslations in *A Personal Matter*, 206n, 207n
triangular desire, 15–16, 38, 58, 119, 125–26, 165–67
Tsubouchi Shōyō, 71, 84
Twain, Mark, 127n
"two-timing": definitions of, 2, 4, 24, 33, 34; in *The Boy*, 27, 31; and "latent" *nanshoku* in *Vita Sexualis*, 46n; in *The Wild Goose*, 66, 72, 80n; in *Kokoro*, 91, 113, 116, 117, 138n, 145, 151; in *The Devil's Disciple*, 153, 154, 162; in *Confessions of a Mask*, 175, 176, 187; absence of in *A Personal Matter*, 200

Ubukata Tomoko, 4n
Ue Mukō, 70
Ueda Akinari, 205n
Ueda, Atsuko, 66n, 70n, 71n
Ueno Chizuko, 210–11
ukiyozōshi, 15
Ulrichs, Karl-Heinrich, 154, 172
Urashima Tarō, 161

uncanny, 160–62
Uno Kōji, 6
Urninge, 172

Viglielmo, Valdo, 96
Vita Sexualis [*Wita sekusuarisu*], 30

wakashu/nenja pairing, 98, 124
Washburn, Dennis, 57
The Wayfarer [*Kōjin*], 8–9n, 38, 50, 90, 97
Weatherby, Meredith, 181n, 186n, 188, 192n
"The Whistle" ["Kuchibue"], 6n, 8
Whitman, Walt, 88, 88n
The Wild Goose [*Gan*], 20, 43–85, 104, 105, 121, 124, 128, 130, 153, 158, 159, 163, 184, 191, 193, 200

yaoi, 54n, 116n
Yasuda Tokutarō, 31–32
Yoda, Tomiko, 57n, 78, 128n, 201n
Yosano Tekkan, 70, 72
The Youth [*Seinen*], 87n, 47–49

Harvard East Asian Monographs
(*out-of-print)

 *1. Liang Fang-chung, *The Single-Whip Method of Taxation in China*
 *2. Harold C. Hinton, *The Grain Tribute System of China, 1845–1911*
  3. Ellsworth C. Carlson, *The Kaiping Mines, 1877–1912*
 *4. Chao Kuo-chün, *Agrarian Policies of Mainland China: A Documentary Study, 1949–1956*
 *5. Edgar Snow, *Random Notes on Red China, 1936–1945*
 *6. Edwin George Beal, Jr., *The Origin of Likin, 1835–1864*
  7. Chao Kuo-chün, *Economic Planning and Organization in Mainland China: A Documentary Study, 1949–1957*
 *8. John K. Fairbank, *Ching Documents: An Introductory Syllabus*
 *9. Helen Yin and Yi-chang Yin, *Economic Statistics of Mainland China, 1949–1957*
 10. Wolfgang Franke, *The Reform and Abolition of the Traditional Chinese Examination System*
 11. Albert Feuerwerker and S. Cheng, *Chinese Communist Studies of Modern Chinese History*
 12. C. John Stanley, *Late Ching Finance: Hu Kuang-yung as an Innovator*
 13. S. M. Meng, *The Tsungli Yamen: Its Organization and Functions*
 *14. Ssu-yü Teng, *Historiography of the Taiping Rebellion*
 15. Chun-Jo Liu, *Controversies in Modern Chinese Intellectual History: An Analytic Bibliography of Periodical Articles, Mainly of the May Fourth and Post-May Fourth Era*
 *16. Edward J. M. Rhoads, *The Chinese Red Army, 1927–1963: An Annotated Bibliography*
 *17. Andrew J. Nathan, *A History of the China International Famine Relief Commission*
 *18. Frank H. H. King (ed.) and Prescott Clarke, *A Research Guide to China-Coast Newspapers, 1822–1911*
 *19. Ellis Joffe, *Party and Army: Professionalism and Political Control in the Chinese Officer Corps, 1949–1964*
 *20. Toshio G. Tsukahira, *Feudal Control in Tokugawa Japan: The Sankin Kōtai System*
 *21. Kwang-Ching Liu, ed., *American Missionaries in China: Papers from Harvard Seminars*
 *22. George Moseley, *A Sino-Soviet Cultural Frontier: The Ili Kazakh Autonomous Chou*

Harvard East Asian Monographs

23. Carl F. Nathan, *Plague Prevention and Politics in Manchuria, 1910–1931*
*24. Adrian Arthur Bennett, *John Fryer: The Introduction of Western Science and Technology into Nineteenth-Century China*
*25. Donald J. Friedman, *The Road from Isolation: The Campaign of the American Committee for Non-Participation in Japanese Aggression, 1938–1941*
*26. Edward LeFevour, *Western Enterprise in Late Ching China: A Selective Survey of Jardine, Matheson and Company's Operations, 1842–1895*
27. Charles Neuhauser, *Third World Politics: China and the Afro-Asian People's Solidarity Organization, 1957–1967*
*28. Kungtu C. Sun, assisted by Ralph W. Huenemann, *The Economic Development of Manchuria in the First Half of the Twentieth Century*
*29. Shahid Javed Burki, *A Study of Chinese Communes, 1965*
30. John Carter Vincent, *The Extraterritorial System in China: Final Phase*
31. Madeleine Chi, *China Diplomacy, 1914–1918*
*32. Clifton Jackson Phillips, *Protestant America and the Pagan World: The First Half Century of the American Board of Commissioners for Foreign Missions, 1810–1860*
*33. James Pusey, *Wu Han: Attacking the Present Through the Past*
*34. Ying-wan Cheng, *Postal Communication in China and Its Modernization, 1860–1896*
35. Tuvia Blumenthal, *Saving in Postwar Japan*
36. Peter Frost, *The Bakumatsu Currency Crisis*
37. Stephen C. Lockwood, *Augustine Heard and Company, 1858–1862*
38. Robert R. Campbell, *James Duncan Campbell: A Memoir by His Son*
39. Jerome Alan Cohen, ed., *The Dynamics of China's Foreign Relations*
40. V. V. Vishnyakova-Akimova, *Two Years in Revolutionary China, 1925–1927*, trans. Steven L. Levine
41. Meron Medzini, *French Policy in Japan During the Closing Years of the Tokugawa Regime*
42. Ezra Vogel, Margie Sargent, Vivienne B. Shue, Thomas Jay Mathews, and Deborah S. Davis, *The Cultural Revolution in the Provinces*
43. Sidney A. Forsythe, *An American Missionary Community in China, 1895–1905*
*44. Benjamin I. Schwartz, ed., *Reflections on the May Fourth Movement.: A Symposium*
*45. Ching Young Choe, *The Rule of the Taewŏngun, 1864–1873: Restoration in Yi Korea*
46. W. P. J. Hall, *A Bibliographical Guide to Japanese Research on the Chinese Economy, 1958–1970*
47. Jack J. Gerson, *Horatio Nelson Lay and Sino-British Relations, 1854–1864*
48. Paul Richard Bohr, *Famine and the Missionary: Timothy Richard as Relief Administrator and Advocate of National Reform*
49. Endymion Wilkinson, *The History of Imperial China: A Research Guide*
50. Britten Dean, *China and Great Britain: The Diplomacy of Commercial Relations, 1860–1864*
51. Ellsworth C. Carlson, *The Foochow Missionaries, 1847–1880*
52. Yeh-chien Wang, *An Estimate of the Land-Tax Collection in China, 1753 and 1908*
53. Richard M. Pfeffer, *Understanding Business Contracts in China, 1949–1963*

Harvard East Asian Monographs

*54. Han-sheng Chuan and Richard Kraus, *Mid-Ching Rice Markets and Trade: An Essay in Price History*
 55. Ranbir Vohra, *Lao She and the Chinese Revolution*
 56. Liang-lin Hsiao, *China's Foreign Trade Statistics, 1864–1949*
*57. Lee-hsia Hsu Ting, *Government Control of the Press in Modern China, 1900–1949*
*58. Edward W. Wagner, *The Literati Purges: Political Conflict in Early Yi Korea*
*59. Joungwon A. Kim, *Divided Korea: The Politics of Development, 1945–1972*
 60. Noriko Kamachi, John K. Fairbank, and Chūzō Ichiko, *Japanese Studies of Modern China Since 1953: A Bibliographical Guide to Historical and Social-Science Research on the Nineteenth and Twentieth Centuries, Supplementary Volume for 1953–1969*
 61. Donald A. Gibbs and Yun-chen Li, *A Bibliography of Studies and Translations of Modern Chinese Literature, 1918–1942*
 62. Robert H. Silin, *Leadership and Values: The Organization of Large-Scale Taiwanese Enterprises*
 63. David Pong, *A Critical Guide to the Kwangtung Provincial Archives Deposited at the Public Record Office of London*
*64. Fred W. Drake, *China Charts the World: Hsu Chi-yü and His Geography of 1848*
*65. William A. Brown and Urgrunge Onon, translators and annotators, *History of the Mongolian People's Republic*
 66. Edward L. Farmer, *Early Ming Government: The Evolution of Dual Capitals*
*67. Ralph C. Croizier, *Koxinga and Chinese Nationalism: History, Myth, and the Hero*
*68. William J. Tyler, tr., *The Psychological World of Natsume Sōseki*, by Doi Takeo
 69. Eric Widmer, *The Russian Ecclesiastical Mission in Peking During the Eighteenth Century*
*70. Charlton M. Lewis, *Prologue to the Chinese Revolution: The Transformation of Ideas and Institutions in Hunan Province, 1891–1907*
 71. Preston Torbert, *The Ching Imperial Household Department: A Study of Its Organization and Principal Functions, 1662–1796*
 72. Paul A. Cohen and John E. Schrecker, eds., *Reform in Nineteenth-Century China*
 73. Jon Sigurdson, *Rural Industrialism in China*
 74. Kang Chao, *The Development of Cotton Textile Production in China*
 75. Valentin Rabe, *The Home Base of American China Missions, 1880–1920*
*76. Sarasin Viraphol, *Tribute and Profit: Sino-Siamese Trade, 1652–1853*
 77. Ch'i-ch'ing Hsiao, *The Military Establishment of the Yuan Dynasty*
 78. Meishi Tsai, *Contemporary Chinese Novels and Short Stories, 1949–1974: An Annotated Bibliography*
*79. Wellington K. K. Chan, *Merchants, Mandarins and Modern Enterprise in Late Ching China*
 80. Endymion Wilkinson, *Landlord and Labor in Late Imperial China: Case Studies from Shandong by Jing Su and Luo Lun*
*81. Barry Keenan, *The Dewey Experiment in China: Educational Reform and Political Power in the Early Republic*
*82. George A. Hayden, *Crime and Punishment in Medieval Chinese Drama: Three Judge Pao Plays*

Harvard East Asian Monographs

 *83. Sang-Chul Suh, *Growth and Structural Changes in the Korean Economy, 1910–1940*
  84. J. W. Dower, *Empire and Aftermath: Yoshida Shigeru and the Japanese Experience, 1878–1954*
  85. Martin Collcutt, *Five Mountains: The Rinzai Zen Monastic Institution in Medieval Japan*
  86. Kwang Suk Kim and Michael Roemer, *Growth and Structural Transformation*
  87. Anne O. Krueger, *The Developmental Role of the Foreign Sector and Aid*
 *88. Edwin S. Mills and Byung-Nak Song, *Urbanization and Urban Problems*
  89. Sung Hwan Ban, Pal Yong Moon, and Dwight H. Perkins, *Rural Development*
 *90. Noel F. McGinn, Donald R. Snodgrass, Yung Bong Kim, Shin-Bok Kim, and Quee-Young Kim, *Education and Development in Korea*
 *91. Leroy P. Jones and Il SaKong, *Government, Business, and Entrepreneurship in Economic Development: The Korean Case*
  92. Edward S. Mason, Dwight H. Perkins, Kwang Suk Kim, David C. Cole, Mahn Je Kim et al., *The Economic and Social Modernization of the Republic of Korea*
  93. Robert Repetto, Tai Hwan Kwon, Son-Ung Kim, Dae Young Kim, John E. Sloboda, and Peter J. Donaldson, *Economic Development, Population Policy, and Demographic Transition in the Republic of Korea*
  94. Parks M. Coble, Jr., *The Shanghai Capitalists and the Nationalist Government, 1927–1937*
  95. Noriko Kamachi, *Reform in China: Huang Tsun-hsien and the Japanese Model*
  96. Richard Wich, *Sino-Soviet Crisis Politics: A Study of Political Change and Communication*
  97. Lillian M. Li, *China's Silk Trade: Traditional Industry in the Modern World, 1842–1937*
  98. R. David Arkush, *Fei Xiaotong and Sociology in Revolutionary China*
 *99. Kenneth Alan Grossberg, *Japan's Renaissance: The Politics of the Muromachi Bakufu*
 100. James Reeve Pusey, *China and Charles Darwin*
 101. Hoyt Cleveland Tillman, *Utilitarian Confucianism: Chen Liang's Challenge to Chu Hsi*
 102. Thomas A. Stanley, *Ōsugi Sakae, Anarchist in Taishō Japan: The Creativity of the Ego*
 103. Jonathan K. Ocko, *Bureaucratic Reform in Provincial China: Ting Jih-ch'ang in Restoration Kiangsu, 1867–1870*
 104. James Reed, *The Missionary Mind and American East Asia Policy, 1911–1915*
 105. Neil L. Waters, *Japan's Local Pragmatists: The Transition from Bakumatsu to Meiji in the Kawasaki Region*
 106. David C. Cole and Yung Chul Park, *Financial Development in Korea, 1945–1978*
 107. Roy Bahl, Chuk Kyo Kim, and Chong Kee Park, *Public Finances During the Korean Modernization Process*
 108. William D. Wray, *Mitsubishi and the N.Y.K, 1870–1914: Business Strategy in the Japanese Shipping Industry*
 109. Ralph William Huenemann, *The Dragon and the Iron Horse: The Economics of Railroads in China, 1876–1937*
*110. Benjamin A. Elman, *From Philosophy to Philology: Intellectual and Social Aspects of Change in Late Imperial China*
 111. Jane Kate Leonard, *Wei Yüan and China's Rediscovery of the Maritime World*

Harvard East Asian Monographs

112. Luke S. K. Kwong, *A Mosaic of the Hundred Days: Personalities, Politics, and Ideas of 1898*
*113. John E. Wills, Jr., *Embassies and Illusions: Dutch and Portuguese Envoys to K'ang-hsi, 1666–1687*
114. Joshua A. Fogel, *Politics and Sinology: The Case of Naitō Konan (1866–1934)*
*115. Jeffrey C. Kinkley, ed., *After Mao: Chinese Literature and Society, 1978–1981*
116. C. Andrew Gerstle, *Circles of Fantasy: Convention in the Plays of Chikamatsu*
117. Andrew Gordon, *The Evolution of Labor Relations in Japan: Heavy Industry, 1853–1955*
*118. Daniel K. Gardner, *Chu Hsi and the "Ta Hsueh": Neo-Confucian Reflection on the Confucian Canon*
119. Christine Guth Kanda, *Shinzō: Hachiman Imagery and Its Development*
*120. Robert Borgen, *Sugawara no Michizane and the Early Heian Court*
121. Chang-tai Hung, *Going to the People: Chinese Intellectual and Folk Literature, 1918–1937*
*122. Michael A. Cusumano, *The Japanese Automobile Industry: Technology and Management at Nissan and Toyota*
123. Richard von Glahn, *The Country of Streams and Grottoes: Expansion, Settlement, and the Civilizing of the Sichuan Frontier in Song Times*
124. Steven D. Carter, *The Road to Komatsubara: A Classical Reading of the Renga Hyakuin*
125. Katherine F. Bruner, John K. Fairbank, and Richard T. Smith, *Entering China's Service: Robert Hart's Journals, 1854–1863*
126. Bob Tadashi Wakabayashi, *Anti-Foreignism and Western Learning in Early-Modern Japan: The "New Theses" of 1825*
127. Atsuko Hirai, *Individualism and Socialism: The Life and Thought of Kawai Eijirō (1891–1944)*
128. Ellen Widmer, *The Margins of Utopia: "Shui-hu hou-chuan" and the Literature of Ming Loyalism*
129. R. Kent Guy, *The Emperor's Four Treasuries: Scholars and the State in the Late Chien-lung Era*
130. Peter C. Perdue, *Exhausting the Earth: State and Peasant in Hunan, 1500–1850*
131. Susan Chan Egan, *A Latterday Confucian: Reminiscences of William Hung (1893–1980)*
132. James T. C. Liu, *China Turning Inward: Intellectual-Political Changes in the Early Twelfth Century*
*133. Paul A. Cohen, *Between Tradition and Modernity: Wang T'ao and Reform in Late Ching China*
134. Kate Wildman Nakai, *Shogunal Politics: Arai Hakuseki and the Premises of Tokugawa Rule*
*135. Parks M. Coble, *Facing Japan: Chinese Politics and Japanese Imperialism, 1931–1937*
*136. Jon L. Saari, *Legacies of Childhood: Growing Up Chinese in a Time of Crisis, 1890–1920*
137. Susan Downing Videen, *Tales of Heichū*
138. Heinz Morioka and Miyoko Sasaki, *Rakugo: The Popular Narrative Art of Japan*
139. Joshua A. Fogel, *Nakae Ushikichi in China: The Mourning of Spirit*

Harvard East Asian Monographs

140. Alexander Barton Woodside, *Vietnam and the Chinese Model: A Comparative Study of Vietnamese and Chinese Government in the First Half of the Nineteenth Century*
*141. George Elison, *Deus Destroyed: The Image of Christianity in Early Modern Japan*
142. William D. Wray, ed., *Managing Industrial Enterprise: Cases from Japan's Prewar Experience*
*143. T'ung-tsu Ch'ü, *Local Government in China Under the Ching*
144. Marie Anchordoguy, *Computers, Inc.: Japan's Challenge to IBM*
145. Barbara Molony, *Technology and Investment: The Prewar Japanese Chemical Industry*
146. Mary Elizabeth Berry, *Hideyoshi*
147. Laura E. Hein, *Fueling Growth: The Energy Revolution and Economic Policy in Postwar Japan*
148. Wen-hsin Yeh, *The Alienated Academy: Culture and Politics in Republican China, 1919–1937*
149. Dru C. Gladney, *Muslim Chinese: Ethnic Nationalism in the People's Republic*
150. Merle Goldman and Paul A. Cohen, eds., *Ideas Across Cultures: Essays on Chinese Thought in Honor of Benjamin I. Schwartz*
151. James M. Polachek, *The Inner Opium War*
152. Gail Lee Bernstein, *Japanese Marxist: A Portrait of Kawakami Hajime, 1879–1946*
*153. Lloyd E. Eastman, *The Abortive Revolution: China Under Nationalist Rule, 1927–1937*
154. Mark Mason, *American Multinationals and Japan: The Political Economy of Japanese Capital Controls, 1899–1980*
155. Richard J. Smith, John K. Fairbank, and Katherine F. Bruner, *Robert Hart and China's Early Modernization: His Journals, 1863–1866*
156. George J. Tanabe, Jr., *Myōe the Dreamkeeper: Fantasy and Knowledge in Kamakura Buddhism*
157. William Wayne Farris, *Heavenly Warriors: The Evolution of Japan's Military, 500–1300*
158. Yu-ming Shaw, *An American Missionary in China: John Leighton Stuart and Chinese-American Relations*
159. James B. Palais, *Politics and Policy in Traditional Korea*
*160. Douglas Reynolds, *China, 1898–1912: The Xinzheng Revolution and Japan*
161. Roger R. Thompson, *China's Local Councils in the Age of Constitutional Reform, 1898–1911*
162. William Johnston, *The Modern Epidemic: History of Tuberculosis in Japan*
163. Constantine Nomikos Vaporis, *Breaking Barriers: Travel and the State in Early Modern Japan*
164. Irmela Hijiya-Kirschnereit, *Rituals of Self-Revelation: Shishōsetsu as Literary Genre and Socio-Cultural Phenomenon*
165. James C. Baxter, *The Meiji Unification Through the Lens of Ishikawa Prefecture*
166. Thomas R. H. Havens, *Architects of Affluence: The Tsutsumi Family and the Seibu-Saison Enterprises in Twentieth-Century Japan*
167. Anthony Hood Chambers, *The Secret Window: Ideal Worlds in Tanizaki's Fiction*
168. Steven J. Ericson, *The Sound of the Whistle: Railroads and the State in Meiji Japan*
169. Andrew Edmund Goble, *Kenmu: Go-Daigo's Revolution*

Harvard East Asian Monographs

170. Denise Potrzeba Lett, *In Pursuit of Status: The Making of South Korea's "New" Urban Middle Class*
171. Mimi Hall Yiengpruksawan, *Hiraizumi: Buddhist Art and Regional Politics in Twelfth-Century Japan*
172. Charles Shirō Inouye, *The Similitude of Blossoms: A Critical Biography of Izumi Kyōka (1873–1939), Japanese Novelist and Playwright*
173. Aviad E. Raz, *Riding the Black Ship: Japan and Tokyo Disneyland*
174. Deborah J. Milly, *Poverty, Equality, and Growth: The Politics of Economic Need in Postwar Japan*
175. See Heng Teow, *Japan's Cultural Policy Toward China, 1918–1931: A Comparative Perspective*
176. Michael A. Fuller, *An Introduction to Literary Chinese*
177. Frederick R. Dickinson, *War and National Reinvention: Japan in the Great War, 1914–1919*
178. John Solt, *Shredding the Tapestry of Meaning: The Poetry and Poetics of Kitasono Katue (1902–1978)*
179. Edward Pratt, *Japan's Protoindustrial Elite: The Economic Foundations of the Gōnō*
180. Atsuko Sakaki, *Recontextualizing Texts: Narrative Performance in Modern Japanese Fiction*
181. Soon-Won Park, *Colonial Industrialization and Labor in Korea: The Onoda Cement Factory*
182. JaHyun Kim Haboush and Martina Deuchler, *Culture and the State in Late Chosŏn Korea*
183. John W. Chaffee, *Branches of Heaven: A History of the Imperial Clan of Sung China*
184. Gi-Wook Shin and Michael Robinson, eds., *Colonial Modernity in Korea*
185. Nam-lin Hur, *Prayer and Play in Late Tokugawa Japan: Asakusa Sensōji and Edo Society*
186. Kristin Stapleton, *Civilizing Chengdu: Chinese Urban Reform, 1895–1937*
187. Hyung Il Pai, *Constructing "Korean" Origins: A Critical Review of Archaeology, Historiography, and Racial Myth in Korean State-Formation Theories*
188. Brian D. Ruppert, *Jewel in the Ashes: Buddha Relics and Power in Early Medieval Japan*
189. Susan Daruvala, *Zhou Zuoren and an Alternative Chinese Response to Modernity*
*190. James Z. Lee, *The Political Economy of a Frontier: Southwest China, 1250–1850*
191. Kerry Smith, *A Time of Crisis: Japan, the Great Depression, and Rural Revitalization*
192. Michael Lewis, *Becoming Apart: National Power and Local Politics in Toyama, 1868–1945*
193. William C. Kirby, Man-houng Lin, James Chin Shih, and David A. Pietz, eds., *State and Economy in Republican China: A Handbook for Scholars*
194. Timothy S. George, *Minamata: Pollution and the Struggle for Democracy in Postwar Japan*
195. Billy K. L. So, *Prosperity, Region, and Institutions in Maritime China: The South Fukien Pattern, 946–1368*
196. Yoshihisa Tak Matsusaka, *The Making of Japanese Manchuria, 1904–1932*

Harvard East Asian Monographs

197. Maram Epstein, *Competing Discourses: Orthodoxy, Authenticity, and Engendered Meanings in Late Imperial Chinese Fiction*
198. Curtis J. Milhaupt, J. Mark Ramseyer, and Michael K. Young, eds. and comps., *Japanese Law in Context: Readings in Society, the Economy, and Politics*
199. Haruo Iguchi, *Unfinished Business: Ayukawa Yoshisuke and U.S.-Japan Relations, 1937–1952*
200. Scott Pearce, Audrey Spiro, and Patricia Ebrey, *Culture and Power in the Reconstitution of the Chinese Realm, 200–600*
201. Terry Kawashima, *Writing Margins: The Textual Construction of Gender in Heian and Kamakura Japan*
202. Martin W. Huang, *Desire and Fictional Narrative in Late Imperial China*
203. Robert S. Ross and Jiang Changbin, eds., *Re-examining the Cold War: U.S.-China Diplomacy, 1954–1973*
204. Guanhua Wang, *In Search of Justice: The 1905–1906 Chinese Anti-American Boycott*
205. David Schaberg, *A Patterned Past: Form and Thought in Early Chinese Historiography*
206. Christine Yano, *Tears of Longing: Nostalgia and the Nation in Japanese Popular Song*
207. Milena Doleželová-Velingerová and Oldřich Král, with Graham Sanders, eds., *The Appropriation of Cultural Capital: China's May Fourth Project*
208. Robert N. Huey, *The Making of 'Shinkokinshū'*
209. Lee Butler, *Emperor and Aristocracy in Japan, 1467–1680: Resilience and Renewal*
210. Suzanne Ogden, *Inklings of Democracy in China*
211. Kenneth J. Ruoff, *The People's Emperor: Democracy and the Japanese Monarchy, 1945–1995*
212. Haun Saussy, *Great Walls of Discourse and Other Adventures in Cultural China*
213. Aviad E. Raz, *Emotions at Work: Normative Control, Organizations, and Culture in Japan and America*
214. Rebecca E. Karl and Peter Zarrow, eds., *Rethinking the 1898 Reform Period: Political and Cultural Change in Late Qing China*
215. Kevin O'Rourke, *The Book of Korean Shijo*
216. Ezra F. Vogel, ed., *The Golden Age of the U.S.-China-Japan Triangle, 1972–1989*
217. Thomas A. Wilson, ed., *On Sacred Grounds: Culture, Society, Politics, and the Formation of the Cult of Confucius*
218. Donald S. Sutton, *Steps of Perfection: Exorcistic Performers and Chinese Religion in Twentieth-Century Taiwan*
219. Daqing Yang, *Technology of Empire: Telecommunications and Japanese Expansionism in Asia, 1883–1945*
220. Qianshen Bai, *Fu Shan's World: The Transformation of Chinese Calligraphy in the Seventeenth Century*
221. Paul Jakov Smith and Richard von Glahn, eds., *The Song-Yuan-Ming Transition in Chinese History*
222. Rania Huntington, *Alien Kind: Foxes and Late Imperial Chinese Narrative*
223. Jordan Sand, *House and Home in Modern Japan: Architecture, Domestic Space, and Bourgeois Culture, 1880–1930*

Harvard East Asian Monographs

224. Karl Gerth, *China Made: Consumer Culture and the Creation of the Nation*
225. Xiaoshan Yang, *Metamorphosis of the Private Sphere: Gardens and Objects in Tang-Song Poetry*
226. Barbara Mittler, *A Newspaper for China? Power, Identity, and Change in Shanghai's News Media, 1872–1912*
227. Joyce A. Madancy, *The Troublesome Legacy of Commissioner Lin: The Opium Trade and Opium Suppression in Fujian Province, 1820s to 1920s*
228. John Makeham, *Transmitters and Creators: Chinese Commentators and Commentaries on the Analects*
229. Elisabeth Köll, *From Cotton Mill to Business Empire: The Emergence of Regional Enterprises in Modern China*
230. Emma Teng, *Taiwan's Imagined Geography: Chinese Colonial Travel Writing and Pictures, 1683–1895*
231. Wilt Idema and Beata Grant, *The Red Brush: Writing Women of Imperial China*
232. Eric C. Rath, *The Ethos of Noh: Actors and Their Art*
233. Elizabeth Remick, *Building Local States: China During the Republican and Post-Mao Eras*
234. Lynn Struve, ed., *The Qing Formation in World-Historical Time*
235. D. Max Moerman, *Localizing Paradise: Kumano Pilgrimage and the Religious Landscape of Premodern Japan*
236. Antonia Finnane, *Speaking of Yangzhou: A Chinese City, 1550–1850*
237. Brian Platt, *Burning and Building: Schooling and State Formation in Japan, 1750–1890*
238. Gail Bernstein, Andrew Gordon, and Kate Wildman Nakai, eds., *Public Spheres, Private Lives in Modern Japan, 1600–1950: Essays in Honor of Albert Craig*
239. Wu Hung and Katherine R. Tsiang, *Body and Face in Chinese Visual Culture*
240. Stephen Dodd, *Writing Home: Representations of the Native Place in Modern Japanese Literature*
241. David Anthony Bello, *Opium and the Limits of Empire: Drug Prohibition in the Chinese Interior, 1729–1850*
242. Hosea Hirata, *Discourses of Seduction: History, Evil, Desire, and Modern Japanese Literature*
243. Kyung Moon Hwang, *Beyond Birth: Social Status in the Emergence of Modern Korea*
244. Brian R. Dott, *Identity Reflections: Pilgrimages to Mount Tai in Late Imperial China*
245. Mark McNally, *Proving the Way: Conflict and Practice in the History of Japanese Nativism*
246. Yongping Wu, *A Political Explanation of Economic Growth: State Survival, Bureaucratic Politics, and Private Enterprises in the Making of Taiwan's Economy, 1950–1985*
247. Kyu Hyun Kim, *The Age of Visions and Arguments: Parliamentarianism and the National Public Sphere in Early Meiji Japan*
248. Zvi Ben-Dor Benite, *The Dao of Muhammad: A Cultural History of Muslims in Late Imperial China*
249. David Der-wei Wang and Shang Wei, eds., *Dynastic Crisis and Cultural Innovation: From the Late Ming to the Late Qing and Beyond*

Harvard East Asian Monographs

250. Wilt L. Idema, Wai-yee Li, and Ellen Widmer, eds., *Trauma and Transcendence in Early Qing Literature*
251. Barbara Molony and Kathleen Uno, eds., *Gendering Modern Japanese History*
252. Hiroshi Aoyagi, *Islands of Eight Million Smiles: Idol Performance and Symbolic Production in Contemporary Japan*
253. Wai-yee Li, *The Readability of the Past in Early Chinese Historiography*
254. William C. Kirby, Robert S. Ross, and Gong Li, eds., *Normalization of U.S.-China Relations: An International History*
255. Ellen Gardner Nakamura, *Practical Pursuits: Takano Chōei, Takahashi Keisaku, and Western Medicine in Nineteenth-Century Japan*
256. Jonathan W. Best, *A History of the Early Korean Kingdom of Paekche, together with an annotated translation of* The Paekche Annals *of the* Samguk sagi
257. Liang Pan, *The United Nations in Japan's Foreign and Security Policymaking, 1945–1992: National Security, Party Politics, and International Status*
258. Richard Belsky, *Localities at the Center: Native Place, Space, and Power in Late Imperial Beijing*
259. Zwia Lipkin, *"Useless to the State": "Social Problems" and Social Engineering in Nationalist Nanjing, 1927–1937*
260. William O. Gardner, *Advertising Tower: Japanese Modernism and Modernity in the 1920s*
261. Stephen Owen, *The Making of Early Chinese Classical Poetry*
262. Martin J. Powers, *Pattern and Person: Ornament, Society, and Self in Classical China*
263. Anna M. Shields, *Crafting a Collection: The Cultural Contexts and Poetic Practice of the* Huajian ji 花間集 *(Collection from Among the Flowers)*
264. Stephen Owen, *The Late Tang: Chinese Poetry of the Mid-Ninth Century (827–860)*
265. Sara L. Friedman, *Intimate Politics: Marriage, the Market, and State Power in Southeastern China*
266. Patricia Buckley Ebrey and Maggie Bickford, *Emperor Huizong and Late Northern Song China: The Politics of Culture and the Culture of Politics*
267. Sophie Volpp, *Worldly Stage: Theatricality in Seventeenth-Century China*
268. Ellen Widmer, *The Beauty and the Book: Women and Fiction in Nineteenth-Century China*
269. Steven B. Miles, *The Sea of Learning: Mobility and Identity in Nineteenth-Century Guangzhou*
270. Lin Man-houng, *China Upside Down: Currency, Society, and Ideologies, 1808–1856*
271. Ronald Egan, *The Problem of Beauty: Aesthetic Thought and Pursuits in Northern Song Dynasty China*
272. Mark Halperin, *Out of the Cloister: Literati Perspectives on Buddhism in Sung China, 960–1279*
273. Helen Dunstan, *State or Merchant? Political Economy and Political Process in 1740s China*
274. Sabina Knight, *The Heart of Time: Moral Agency in Twentieth-Century Chinese Fiction*
275. Timothy J. Van Compernolle, *The Uses of Memory: The Critique of Modernity in the Fiction of Higuchi Ichiyō*

Harvard East Asian Monographs

276. Paul Rouzer, *A New Practical Primer of Literary Chinese*
277. Jonathan Zwicker, *Practices of the Sentimental Imagination: Melodrama, the Novel, and the Social Imaginary in Nineteenth-Century Japan*
278. Franziska Seraphim, *War Memory and Social Politics in Japan, 1945–2005*
279. Adam L. Kern, *Manga from the Floating World: Comicbook Culture and the* Kibyōshi *of Edo Japan*
280. Cynthia J. Brokaw, *Commerce in Culture: The Sibao Book Trade in the Qing and Republican Periods*
281. Eugene Y. Park, *Between Dreams and Reality: The Military Examination in Late Chosŏn Korea, 1600–1894*
282. Nam-lin Hur, *Death and Social Order in Tokugawa Japan: Buddhism, Anti-Christianity, and the* Danka *System*
283. Patricia M. Thornton, *Disciplining the State: Virtue, Violence, and State-Making in Modern China*
284. Vincent Goossaert, *The Taoists of Peking, 1800–1949: A Social History of Urban Clerics*
285. Peter Nickerson, *Taoism, Bureaucracy, and Popular Religion in Early Medieval China*
286. Charo B. D'Etcheverry, *Love After* The Tale of Genji: *Rewriting the World of the Shining Prince*
287. Michael G. Chang, *A Court on Horseback: Imperial Touring & the Construction of Qing Rule, 1680–1785*
288. Carol Richmond Tsang, *War and Faith:* Ikkō Ikki *in Late Muromachi Japan*
289. Hilde De Weerdt, *Competition over Content: Negotiating Standards for the Civil Service Examinations in Imperial China (1127–1279)*
290. Eve Zimmerman, *Out of the Alleyway: Nakagami Kenji and the Poetics of Outcaste Fiction*
291. Robert Culp, *Articulating Citizenship: Civic Education and Student Politics in Southeastern China, 1912–1940*
292. Richard J. Smethurst, *From Foot Soldier to Finance Minister: Takahashi Korekiyo, Japan's Keynes*
293. John E. Herman, *Amid the Clouds and Mist: China's Colonization of Guizhou, 1200–1700*
294. Tomoko Shiroyama, *China During the Great Depression: Market, State, and the World Economy, 1929–1937*
295. Kirk W. Larsen, *Tradition, Treaties and Trade: Qing Imperialism and Chosŏn Korea, 1850–1910*
296. Gregory Golley, *When Our Eyes No Longer See: Realism, Science, and Ecology in Japanese Literary Modernism*
297. Barbara Ambros, *Emplacing a Pilgrimage: The Ōyama Cult and Regional Religion in Early Modern Japan*
298. Rebecca Suter, *The Japanization of Modernity: Murakami Haruki between Japan and the United States*
299. Yuma Totani, *The Tokyo War Crimes Trial: The Pursuit of Justice in the Wake of World War II*

Harvard East Asian Monographs

300. Linda Isako Angst, *In a Dark Time: Memory, Community, and Gendered Nationalism in Postwar Okinawa*
301. David M. Robinson, ed., *Culture, Courtiers, and Competition: The Ming Court (1368–1644)*
302. Calvin Chen, *Some Assembly Required: Work, Community, and Politics in China's Rural Enterprises*
303. Sem Vermeersch, *The Power of the Buddhas: The Politics of Buddhism During the Koryŏ Dynasty (918–1392)*
304. Tina Lu, *Accidental Incest, Filial Cannibalism, and Other Peculiar Encounters in Late Imperial Chinese Literature*
305. Chang Woei Ong, *Men of Letters Within the Passes: Guanzhong Literati in Chinese History, 907–1911*
306. Wendy Swartz, *Reading Tao Yuanming: Shifting Paradigms of Historical Reception (427–1900)*
307. Peter K. Bol, *Neo-Confucianism in History*
308. Carlos Rojas, *The Naked Gaze: Reflections on Chinese Modernity*
309. Kelly H. Chong, *Deliverance and Submission: Evangelical Women and the Negotiation of Patriarchy in South Korea*
310. Rachel DiNitto, *Uchida Hyakken: A Critique of Modernity and Militarism in Prewar Japan*
311. Jeffrey Snyder-Reinke, *Dry Spells: State Rainmaking and Local Governance in Late Imperial China*
312. Jay Dautcher, *Down a Narrow Road: Identity and Masculinity in a Uyghur Community in Xinjiang China*
313. Xun Liu, *Daoist Modern: Innovation, Lay Practice, and the Community of Inner Alchemy in Republican Shanghai*
314. Jacob Eyferth, *Eating Rice from Bamboo Roots: The Social History of a Community of Handicraft Papermakers in Rural Sichuan, 1920–2000*
315. David Johnson, *Spectacle and Sacrifice: The Ritual Foundations of Village Life in North China*
316. James Robson, *Power of Place: The Religious Landscape of the Southern Sacred Peak (Nanyue 南嶽) in Medieval China*
317. Lori Watt, *When Empire Comes Home: Repatriation and Reintegration in Postwar Japan*
318. James Dorsey, *Critical Aesthetics: Kobayashi Hideo, Modernity, and Wartime Japan*
319. Christopher Bolton, *Sublime Voices: The Fictional Science and Scientific Fiction of Abe Kōbō*
320. Si-yen Fei, *Negotiating Urban Space: Urbanization and Late Ming Nanjing*
321. Christopher Gerteis, *Gender Struggles: Wage-Earning Women and Male-Dominated Unions in Postwar Japan*
322. Rebecca Nedostup, *Superstitious Regimes: Religion and the Politics of Chinese Modernity*
323. Lucien Bianco, *Wretched Rebels: Rural Disturbances on the Eve of the Chinese Revolution*
324. Cathryn H. Clayton, *Sovereignty at the Edge: Macau and the Question of Chineseness*
325. Micah S. Muscolino, *Fishing Wars and Environmental Change in Late Imperial and Modern China*

Harvard East Asian Monographs

326. Robert I. Hellyer, *Defining Engagement: Japan and Global Contexts, 1750–1868*
327. Robert Ashmore, *The Transport of Reading: Text and Understanding in the World of Tao Qian (365–427)*
328. Mark A. Jones, *Children as Treasures: Childhood and the Middle Class in Early Twentieth Century Japan*
329. Miryam Sas, *Experimental Arts in Postwar Japan: Moments of Encounter, Engagement, and Imagined Return*
330. H. Mack Horton, *Traversing the Frontier: The Man'yōshū Account of a Japanese Mission to Silla in 736–737*
331. Dennis J. Frost, *Seeing Stars: Sports Celebrity, Identity, and Body Culture in Modern Japan*
332. Marnie S. Anderson, *A Place in Public: Women's Rights in Meiji Japan*
333. Peter Mauch, *Sailor Diplomat: Nomura Kichisaburō and the Japanese-American War*
334. Ethan Isaac Segal, *Coins, Trade, and the State: Economic Growth in Early Medieval Japan*
335. David B. Lurie, *Realms of Literacy: Early Japan and the History of Writing*
336. Lillian Lan-ying Tseng, *Picturing Heaven in Early China*
337. Jun Uchida, *Brokers of Empire: Japanese Settler Colonialism in Korea, 1876–1945*
338. Patricia L. Maclachlan, *The People's Post Office: The History and Politics of the Japanese Postal System, 1871–2010*
339. Michael Schiltz, *The Money Doctors from Japan: Finance, Imperialism, and the Building of the Yen Bloc, 1895–1937*
340. Daqing Yang, Jie Liu, Hiroshi Mitani, and Andrew Gordon, eds., *Toward a History Beyond Borders: Contentious Issues in Sino-Japanese Relations*
341. Sonia Ryang, *Reading North Korea: An Ethnological Inquiry*
342. Susan Huang, *Picturing the True Form: Daoist Visual Culture in Traditional China*
343. Barbara Mittler, *A Continuous Revolution: Making Sense of Cultural Revolution Culture*
344. Hwansoo Ilmee Kim, *Empire of the Dharma: Korean and Japanese Buddhism, 1877–1912*
345. Satoru Saito, *Detective Fiction and the Rise of the Japanese Novel, 1880–1930*
346. Jung-Sun N. Han, *An Imperial Path to Modernity: Yoshino Sakuzō and a New Liberal Order in East Asia, 1905–1937*
347. Atsuko Hirai, *Government by Mourning: Death and Political Integration in Japan, 1603–1912*
348. Darryl E. Flaherty, *Public Law, Private Practice: Politics, Profit, and the Legal Profession in Nineteenth-Century Japan*
349. Jeffrey Paul Bayliss, *On the Margins of Empire: Buraku and Korean Identity in Prewar and Wartime Japan*
350. Barry Eichengreen, Dwight H. Perkins, and Kwanho Shin, *From Miracle to Maturity: The Growth of the Korean Economy*
351. Michel Mohr, *Buddhism, Unitarianism, and the Meiji Competition for Universality*
352. J. Keith Vincent, *Two-Timing Modernity: Homosocial Narrative in Modern Japanese Fiction*